Qualitative Research in Nursing

Advancing the Humanistic Imperative

SECOND EDITION

Helen J. Streubert, EdD, RN
Associate Professor and Chairperson
Department of Nursing
College Misericordia
Dallas, Pennsylvania

Dona R. Carpenter, EdD, RN, CS
Associate Professor
Department of Nursing
University of Scranton
Scranton, Pennsylvania

Lippincott
Philadelphia • New York • Baltimore

Acquisitions Editor: Margaret Zuccarini
Assistant Editor: Sara Lauber
Project Editor: Nicole Walz
Senior Production Manager: Helen Ewan

Production Coordinator: Michael Carcel
Design Coordinator: Doug Smock
Indexer: M. L. Coughlin

2nd Edition

9   8   7   6   5   4   3   2   1

Library of Congress Cataloging in Publications Data

Streubert, Helen J.
    Qualitative research in nursing : advancing the humanistic imperative / Helen J. Streubert, Dona Rinaldi Carpenter.—2nd ed.
        p.   cm.
    Includes bibliographical references and index.
    ISBN 0-7817-1628-4 (alk. paper)
        1. Nursing—Research—Methodology.   2. Sociology—Research—Methodology.   I. Carpenter, Dona Rinaldi.   II. Title.
    [DNLM: 1. Nursing Research—methods.   2. Research Design.
3. Quality Assurance, Health Care.   4. Ethics, Nursing.   WY
20.5S915q   1999]
RT81.5.S78   1999
610.73′07′2—dc21
DNLM/DLC
for Library of Congress   98-41414
                                                                              CIP

Care has been taken to confirm the accuracy of the information presented and to describe generally accepted practices. However, the authors, editors, and publisher are not responsible for errors or omissions or for any consequences from application of the information in this book and make no warranty, express or implied, with respect to the contents of the publication.

The authors, editors and publisher have exerted every effort to ensure that drug selection and dosage set forth in this text are in accordance with current recommendations and practice at the time of publication. However, in view of ongoing research, changes in government regulations, and the constant flow of information relating to drug therapy and drug reactions, the reader is urged to check the package insert for each drug for any change in indications and dosage and for added warnings and precautions. This is particularly important when the recommended agent is a new or infrequently employed drug.

Some drugs and medical devices presented in this publication have Food and Drug Administration (FDA) clearance for limited use in restricted research settings. It is the responsibility of the health care provider to ascertain the FDA status of each drug or device planned for use in their clinical practice.

This book is dedicated to four individuals who constantly challenge my thinking. To my partner, Michael, who constantly challenges me to believe that castles really do exist. To my son, Michael, who challenges me to remain authentic in all things. To my son, Matthew, who challenges me to find new ways to be in relationships. And to my beloved mother, Libby, who challenges me always to be more than who I think I am.

HJS

This book is dedicated to my children Emily Joy and Brian Wells Jr., who surround me with love and happiness always.

DRC

ABOUT THE AUTHORS

Helen J. Streubert, EdD, RN, is Professor and Chairperson of the Nursing Department at College Misericordia, Dallas, Pennsylvania, where she teaches qualitative research to undergraduate nursing and interdisciplinary graduate students. Her research interests continue to be in the areas of phenomenology as method, clinical education, and patients' experiences of illness. Dr. Streubert has authored and co-authored articles and book chapters on qualitative research and also presents her work at professional conferences.

Dona Rinaldi Carpenter, EdD, RN, CS, is Associate Professor of Nursing and Director of the RN-BS Track at the University of Scranton, Scranton, Pennsylvania where she teaches medical-surgical nursing and nursing research to undergraduate and graduate students. Her research interests focus on doctoral education in nursing, professional commitment, and quality of life. She has authored and co-authored several articles and book chapters and has presented her work at national and international meetings.

CONTRIBUTORS

Sandra Beth Lewenson, EdD, RN, is Associate Dean of the College of Nursing at Pace University, Pleasantville, New York. Her research focus is nursing's historical relationship with the women's suffrage movement at the beginning of the 20th century. She has published several books and articles on the topic.

Joan M. Jenks, PhD, RN, is Associate Professor and Director of the Baccalaureate Division in the Department of Nursing, College of Allied Health Sciences, Thomas Jefferson University, Philadelphia, Pennsylvania. She teaches qualitative research methods to undergraduate and graduate students in nursing and occupational therapy. Her research focuses on decision making using naturalistic approaches. She has researched and published valuable insights about nurse clinical decision making, contributing to the understanding of this complex process.

PREFACE

The second edition of *Qualitative Research in Nursing: Advancing the Humanistic Imperative* presents the same essentials of qualitative inquiry as applied to nursing that the first edition offered, but now expands the discussion considerably to include ethical issues, grant writing, and clinical application of qualitative methods. The same sound philosophic and methodologic framework that guided the development of the first edition remains, with substantial addition of content referent to the conduct of a qualitative investigation.

This book is intended to begin the dialogue for individuals interested in using qualitative inquiry approaches and offers the reader an orderly and systematic approach to learning the discipline of qualitative methods. To become competent as a qualitative researcher, one needs to read, study, observe, participate in, and discuss the realities of the art and practice of the method. However, it is only through engagement of ideas that one can participate in and contribute to advancing the humanistic imperative.

Since the publication of the first edition of the textbook, the body of qualitative research has expanded considerably. Most notably, the review of published manuscripts addressing clinical practice issues has substantially increased, while those related to educational and administrative issues have decreased. This change in the pattern of published qualitative research reflects the importance of the method to the investigation of phenomenon important to nursing and follows the direction of nursing research in general as it grounds the discipline in practice.

The original text arose from a fundamental need to bring to the reader a sense of direction in the implementation of inquiry methods that value new ways of knowing and celebrate the human experience. The second edition builds on these needs and expands the discussion of ethical issues and qualitative inquiry to show the application to practice.

Our understanding of nursing evolves from a fundamental belief that nursing is and always has been a holistic process whose foundation is grounded in the life experiences of human beings as they experience all aspects of the health continuum. We firmly believe that research conducted out of the context of human experience has the potential to create knowledge that is disconnected to the realities of practice. Further, we believe that pursuing the mastery of any new skill requires fundamental understanding of its history, basic parts, context, and outcomes. Therefore, the second edition of this text continues the dialogue related to the acquisition of qualitative research skills while building on fundamental issues relevant to the methods discussed.

As in first edition, this text introduces the reader to the historical background of the approaches discussed. It shares the "parts" of the approaches, the "appropriate contexts" in which to use them and the intended "outcomes" that one who uses the approaches should expect. Knowing these parts allows for integration and synthesis, ultimately providing greater understanding of the whole and authentication of the findings of human inquiry.

Organization

The text is organized to facilitate the reader's comprehension of each approach and to provide examples of how the approaches have been used in nursing practice, education, and administration.

In Chapter 1, Philosophy and Theory: Foundations of Qualitative Research, the reader is introduced to the traditions of science, the interpretations of what constitutes science, perceptions of reality, and the influences of critical theory and feminism on the discipline of qualitative research.

In Chapter 2, The Conduct of Qualitative Research: Common Essential Elements, characteristics that are common to all qualitative research approaches are addressed. Essential areas include identifying the phenomenon of interest, explication of beliefs, settings for data collection, participant selection, methods for data generation, and management. Detailed discussion of rigor in qualitative research concludes this chapter.

Chapter 3, Ethical Requirements of Qualitative Research, is an in-depth discussion of issues that may present ethical dilemmas for the qualitative researcher. The chapter includes ethical concerns such as confidentiality and anonymity, informed consent, the interpretation and reporting of qualitative results, participant–investigator relationships, and working with vulnerable populations.

In Chapter 4, Phenomenology as Method, an in-depth description of philosophic and methodologic comceptualization is offered. An overview of specific phenomenological perspectives including descriptive and interpretive provides the framework for choosing and implementing the approach. A table listing the procedural steps for implementing a phenomenological study from the perspective of six phenomenologists is included, and is an excellent resource for the would-be phenomenological researcher.

Chapter 5, Phenomenology in Practice, Education, and Administration, is an outstanding complement to Chapter 4, detailing for the reader application of the approach in the perspective practice, education, and administration. Published works are reviewed for their contributions made to the qualitative phenomenological literature. A particular strength in all the companion chapters is the use of evaluation guidelines specific to the approach being discussed. In addition, a table at the end of all companion chapters provides the reader with a resource for examining published works using the various approaches discussed throughout the book.

Chapter 6, Grounded Theory as Method, Chapter 8, Ethnography as Method, Chapter 10, Historical Research Method, Chapter 12, The Action Research Method, follow the format found in Chapter 4. This includes an in-depth discussion of the philosophic and methodologic issues specific to the approach. Data generation and treatment as well as ethical issues specific to the particular approach are discussed in detail.

Chapters 7, 9, 11, and 13 repeat the format found in Chapter 6, incorporating a detailed examination of published studies that illustrate a particular approach followed by guidelines for critiquing the approach used. All of these chapters include tables that offer a substantial resource list of studies completed in the areas of education, administration, and practice. Finally, each of these chapters includes a reprint of a selected study that illustrates the qualitative method discussed in that chapter.

Chapter 14, Triangulation as a Qualitative Research Strategy, brings a new and important dimension to the second edition. This chapter examines the issues of data, investigator, theory, and methodologic triangulation. It is intended to enhance the reader's understanding of the different ways triangulation can be useful to the researcher.

Chapter 15, A Practical Guide for Sharing Qualitative Research Results, provides a full description of issues related to funding qualitative research projects and dissemination of qualitative research findings. It details for the reader the potential triumphs and the pitfalls in moving qualitative research into a public forum. An example of a funded grant is included following the chapter. The published research article that resulted from the funded study is reprinted in Chapter 5.

Key Features and Benefits

The following features are included in the philosophic and methodologic framework.

- Description of the philosophic underpinnings of each approach. This description provides more than the "how" of the approach; it presents the underlying assumptions of the approaches.
- Detailed description of procedural steps used in each of the approaches. This offers the reader the opportunity to learn step by step how the approach is implemented.

- Tables profiling studies conducted using each of the approaches. These tables offer the reader an excellent resource for further exploring the existing body of knowledge specific to the approach being discussed.
- In-depth discussion of published research studies that have used the approaches under discussion. This examination shares with the reader not only what has been published but also the strengths and weaknesses of the studies reviewed.
- Specific critiquing guidelines available in all companion chapters for each of the approaches. These guidelines help the reader understand the specific questions that should be asked of research studies that have used or will be using the approach.
- Inclusion of chapters on action research. This methodology used in other disciplines is gaining increasing acceptance in nursing. Readers will benefit from having this cutting-edge information available to them.
- Inclusion of companion chapters. Comparison chapters describing application of each of the approaches included in this text provide strong evidence of the impact these qualitative research methods are having on the discipline of nursing and the potential benefits they will continue to have. These chapters all provide the neophyte qualitative researchers with clear descriptions of what is expected from the researchers who will evaluate their work.
- Inclusion of a sample of a funded qualitative research grant, as well as the published manuscript from the study.
- New chapters on Ethical Considerations In Qualitative Research and Triangulation.
- Tables highlighting the methods described as they have been used to study nursing practice issues.

We hope that this book will serve as both a starting point for the new researcher and a reference for more experienced nurses. It is expected that each method detailed will offer the reader a sound understanding of qualitative research methods.

Helen J. Streubert
Dona Rinaldi Carpenter
July 16, 1998

ACKNOWLEDGMENTS

The authors wish to acknowledge the process of feminist thinking that has influenced the writing of both the first and second editions of this textbook. When the chapter authors came together during the first writing there was a clear commitment to another voice, another way of creating meaning. This commitment has grown and become even stronger in the preparation of the second edition. We wish to acknowledge those who have shaped our thinking and our way of being—our colleagues, teachers, students, friends, and family.

Specifically, we wish to acknowledge those who have been most closely involved in the production of the second edition of this text. The authors are grateful for the editorial direction and assistance of Margaret Zuccarini, Sara Lauber, and Nicole Walz; the technical support of Michelle Zick; and the research assistance of Shannon A. Murray, Erin K. Carr, Carol J. Hilferty, Rose Sadowski, and Mary Ellen Dziedzic.

CONTENTS

Philosophy and Theory: Foundations of Qualitative Research

The tradition of science is uniquely quantitative. The quantitative approach to research has been justified by its success in measuring, analyzing, replicating, and applying knowledge gained from this paradigm. In more recent years, scientists have been challenged to explain phenomena that defy measurement. The inability to quantitatively measure some phenomena and the dissatisfaction with the results of measurement of other phenomena have led to an intense interest in using other approaches to study particularly human phenomena. This interest has led to an acceptance of qualitative research approaches as another way to discover knowledge. One cannot help but be struck by the "success of qualitative research methods in the marketplace of academic ideas" (Atkinson, 1995, p. 117). The use of qualitative methods to discover knowledge is far more commonplace today than 10 years ago.

The tradition of using qualitative methods to study human phenomena is grounded in the social sciences. The tradition arose because aspects of human values, culture, and relationships were unable to be described fully using quantitative research methods. More recently, the practice of qualitative research has expanded to clinical settings because "empirical approaches have proven to be of limited service in answering some of the challenging and pressing clinical questions, especially where human subjectivity and interpretation are involved" (Thorne, 1997, p. 28).

Nurses and other health care professionals clearly want to grasp and sense the lived experience of their clients, to enter into the world their clients inhabit, and to understand the basic social processes that illuminate human health and illness events (Thorne, 1997, p. 288).

This chapter shares with the reader the foundations of qualitative research. It is hoped that presentation of the qualitative knowledge structure will generate excitement for the qualitative research paradigm as an alternative to quantitative inquiry.

Philosophic Underpinnings of Qualitative Research

From a philosophic viewpoint, the study of humans is deeply rooted in descriptive modes of science. Human scientists have been concerned with describing the fundamental patterns of human thought and behavior since early times. Descartes's view of science was long held as the only approach to new knowledge. His ideas were grounded in an objective reality, a position that supported the idea that cause and effect could explain all things. Kant is attributed with questioning the fundamental nature of reality as seen through a Cartesian lens. He opened discussion about human rationality. Kant proposed that perception was more than the act of observation. For him, all reality was not explainable by cause and effect. He raised issues supporting the notion that nature was not independent of thought or reason (Hamilton, 1994). What was observed, therefore, was not the only reality.

The concept of scientific versus practical reason was born of Kant's ideas about nature, specifically as the concept relates to perception (Ermath, 1978; Hamilton, 1994). Later existentialists advanced Kant's ideas to explore reality as it is perceived rather than as an observed phenomenon only. Kant's ideas about freedom and practical reasoning emancipated science. Scientists questioned whether empiricism was the only way to gain knowledge. Later philosophers such as Husserl furthered Kant's propositions, and, eventually, the German school of philosophy developed and expanded the ideas about self, self-consciousness, reality, and freedom.

The early debates about science and reality established the foundations of the qualitative paradigm that many social scientists use today. Qualitative research offers the opportunity to focus on finding answers to questions centered on social experience, how it is created, and how it gives meaning to human life (Denzin & Lincoln, 1994). Knowing how social experiences construct an individual's reality is an important assumption. Based on this assumption, an exploration of ways of knowing is appropriate.

If one takes the ontologic position that reality is apprehensible, then the positivist or empiricist framework becomes one's reference point. However, it seems inconceivable that individuals can believe they are able to fully apprehend reality. According to Denzin and Lincoln (1994), post-positivists believe there is *a* reality to be known but have conceded that this reality only will be "imperfectly or probabilistically apprehendable [sic]" (p. 109). Critical theorists and constructivists see reality from a dynamic standpoint. The critical theorist perspective is that reality is "shaped by social, political, cultural, economic, ethnic, and gender values" (Denzin & Lincoln, 1994, p. 109). The constructivist, however, sees reality as "relativism-local and specific" (Denzin & Lincoln, 1994, p. 109). Therefore, "reality is actually realities" (Lincoln, 1992, p. 379). Clearly, it is a post-positivist viewpoint that supports the notion of a dynamic reality.

According to Cheek (1996), "The qualitative research enterprise is about allowing multiple readings of the same reality to surface" (p. 503). In a human enterprise such as nursing, it is imperative that nurses embrace a research tradition that provides for the most meaningful way to describe and understand human experiences. Recognizing that reality is dynamic is the first step in establishing a truly humanistic perspective of research.

Ways of Knowing

Belenky, Clinchy, Goldberger, and Tarule's (1986) viewpoint on knowing has provided a lens to question why objective science has been accepted as the predominant route to truth. Their exploration of the way women come to know supports a feminist ideology. However, holders of this viewpoint sometimes view feminist ideas as subjective and, therefore, less valuable than traditional positivist science. This way of thinking is changing as scientists become increasingly comfortable with the diversity in society and the richness of exploring and using multiple methods of inquiry to discover particular phenomena.

The idea of *received knowledge* is an important premise set forth by Belenky et al. (1986). Individuals learn usually by being told—by receiving knowledge. All too frequently, though, the act of being told limits the opportunity to engage the self in a dialogue about what is real. When presented with received knowledge, the receiver of the knowledge should ask, "What are my perceptions about this knowledge as it is presented to me?"

From the time individuals are young, they are told by people who "know"—usually adults they view as authority figures—the beliefs or knowledge they should retain. These authority figures present most of the knowledge they share as truths. These truths are usually facts that, in some way, have been passed on or proven to be correct. The proof of correctness often occurs as a direct result of an objective manipulation of factors or variables.

Empirical scientists who support a Cartesian framework believe that if objective measurement cannot be assigned to a phenomenon, then the importance and thus the existence of the phenomenon may be in question. Many contemporary scientists and philosophers question the value of this system, particularly in situations that include humans and their interactions with other humans. Little available objectively derived measurement exists that is meaningful when one studies human phenomena within a social context. The concepts of objectivity, reduction, and manipulation, which are fundamental to empirical science, defy the authentic fiber of humans and their social interactions.

With the belief that science should inform the lives of people who interact and function in society, researchers need to examine all parts of reality—subjective reality as well as its objective counterpart. Researchers should acknowledge knowing in the subjective sense and value it equally so that scientific knowledge will represent the views of people who experience life. The early phenomenologists believed that the only reality was the one that is perceived. Thus, the measurement of perception challenges the empirical scientist. Perception is not objective; rather, perception is a way of observing and processing those things that are present to the self. For example, two individuals may observe the same lecture and leave the classroom with different interpretations of what the lecturer said. Each individual's interpretation is based on what that person perceived to be reality—a reality that is developed and constructed over a lifetime of receiving, processing, and interpreting information, as well as engaging in human interaction. The internalization of what becomes known as belief systems comes from perception and construction of what is real for the individual.

Ways of Knowing in Nursing

In her seminal work on ways of knowing in nursing, Carper (1978) identified four fundamental patterns that emerge as the way nurses come to know: empirical knowing, aesthetic knowing, personal knowing, and moral knowing. *Empirical knowing* represents the traditional, objective, logical, and positivist tradition of science. Empirical knowing and thus empirical science is committed to providing explanations for phenomena and then controlling them. An example of empirical knowing is the knowledge derived from the biologic sciences that describes and explains human function. Through this description and explanation, biologic scientists have been able to predict and control certain aspects of human structure and function. Treatment of diabetes mellitus is an example of empirical research being applied in the health care field. From their empirical studies, biologic scientists know that providing insulin to individuals with diabetes mellitus controls the symptoms created by the nonfunctioning pancreas. The nursing profession's alignment with empirical knowing and its subsequent pursuit of this mode of inquiry follows the positivist paradigm, which believes that objective data, measurement, and generalizability are essential to the generation and dissemination of knowledge.

Aesthetic knowing is the art of nursing. The understanding and interpretation of subjective experience and the creative development of nursing care are based on an appreciation of subjective expression. Aesthetic knowing is abstract and defies a formal description and measurement. According to Carper (1978),

> The aesthetic pattern of knowing in nursing involves the perception of abstract particulars as distinguished from the recognition of abstracted

universals. It is the knowing of the unique particular rather than an exemplary class. (p. 16)

Aesthetic knowing in nursing provides the framework for the exploration of qualitative research methodologies. Qualitative research calls for a recognition of patterns in phenomena rather than the explication of facts that will be controllable and generalizable. An example of aesthetic knowing is the way a nurse would provide care differently for two elderly women who are preparing for cataract surgery, based on the nurse's knowledge of each woman's particular life patterns.

Personal knowing requires that the individual—in this case, the nurse—know the self. The degree to which an individual knows oneself is determined by his or her abilities to self-actualize. Movement toward knowledge of the self and self-actualization requires comfort with ambiguity and a commitment to patience in understanding. Personal knowing is a commitment to authentication of relationships and a *presencing* with others, that is, the enlightenment and sensitization humans bring to genuine human interactions. Personal knowing deals with the fundamental *existentialism* of humans, that is, the capacity for change and the value placed on becoming.

Personal knowing also supports the qualitative research paradigm. In the conduct of qualitative inquiry, researchers are obligated by the philosophic underpinnings of the methodologies they use to accept the self as part of the research enterprise and to approach research participants in a genuine and authentic manner. An awareness of one's beliefs and understandings is essential to fully discover the phenomena studied in a qualitative research inquiry. Furthermore, qualitative researchers believe there is always subjectivity in their pursuit of the truth. The very nature of human interactions is based on subjective knowledge. In the most objective research endeavor, subjective realities will affect what is studied. "Scientific research, as a human endeavor to advance knowledge, is influenced by the sociocultural and historical context in which it takes place and is considered neither value free, objective, nor neutral" (Henderson, 1995, p. 59).

Moral knowing reflects our ethical obligations in a situation or our ideas about what should be done in a given situation. Through the moral way of knowing, individuals come to a realization of what is right and just. As with personal knowing and aesthetic knowing, moral knowing is another abstract dimension of how it is that individuals come to know a situation. Moral knowing is based on traditional principles and codes of ethics or conduct. This type of knowing becomes most important when humans face situations in which decisions of right and wrong are blurred by differences in values or beliefs. Moral knowing requires an openness to differences in philosophic positions. Ethics and logic are required to examine the intricacies of human situations that do not fit standard formulas for conduct.

The importance of sharing ways of knowing is to offer the reader a context in which to judge the appropriateness of nursing knowledge and the way that nurses develop that knowledge. It is only through examinations of current belief structures that people are able to achieve their own standards of what will be best in a given situation.

More recently, May (1994) and Sandelowski (1994) have expanded on the idea of knowing as it relates to nursing knowledge. May (1994) used the term *abstract knowing* (p. 10) to describe the analytic experience of knowing:

> The rigorous implementation and explication of method alone never explains the process of abstract knowing, regardless of which paradigm the scientist espouses and which method is chosen. Method does not produce insight or understanding or the creative leap that the agile mind makes in the struggle to comprehend observation and to link them together. Regardless of the paradigmatic perspective held by the scientist, the process of knowing itself cannot be observed and measured directly, but only by its product. (p. 13)

May (1994) further suggested that knowledge is "shaped *but not completely defined* by the process through which it is created" (p. 14). Based on her ideas about knowing, she gave credibility to what she called "magic" (p. 16), which is similar to the intuitive connections discussed in Benner's (1984) work on expert clinical judgment. Based on her conversations with and observations of qualitative researchers, May (1994) determined that, at a certain point, pattern recognition creates the insight into the phenomenon under study. She believed that the ability to see knowledge is a result of intellectual rigor and readiness (magic). Her ideas support the concept of intuition or, as she labeled it, "abstract knowing" in nursing research.

Sandelowski (1994) took a position on knowing similar to the aesthetic knowing described by Carper (1978): We must accept the art as well as the science of research. Sandelowski believed that the two are not mutually exclusive.

> What differentiates the arts from the sciences is not the search for truth per se, but rather the kinds of truths that are sought. Science typically is concerned with propositional truths, or truth about something. Art is concerned with universal truths, with being true to: even with being more true to life than life itself. (Hospers as cited in Sandelowski, 1994, p. 52)

Both May (1994) and Sandelowski (1994) provide us with an expansion of the original positions on truth offered by Carper (1978). These authors provide a validation for knowing other than in the empirical sense. Most important, they offer nurse–researchers a way to discover knowledge that complements the positivist paradigm and gives voice to other ways of knowing. In the case of qualitative research and nursing practice, it is only through examination of the prevailing ideologies that nurses will be able to decide which ideology most reflects their personal patterns of discovery and creation of meaning.

Meaning of Science

Science is defined in a number of ways. Kerlinger (1986) described the static view of science as a "way of explaining observed phenomena" (p. 7). Namenwirth (1986) defined it as "a system of gathering, verifying, and systematizing information about reality" (p. 19). Guba (1990), in sharing a view of empirical science, articulated the meaning of science as it is practiced within the premise of value-neutral, logical empirical methods that promise "the growth of rational control over ourselves and our worlds" (p. 317). Each of these three definitions gives a different perception of the truth.

Much of what individuals know about science in the nursing profession is based on the empirical view of science, which places significant value on rationality, objectivity, prediction, and control. The question arises: Is this view of science consistent with the phenomena of interest to nurses? The empirical view of science permeates many aspects of human activity. In adopting this view, one adopts a value system. Many empiricists believe that if a phenomenon is not observable, the question that should be asked is, Is it real? If a particular phenomenon does not conform to reality as is currently known, empiricists could judge it to be irrational and therefore unimportant. If a phenomenon is studied without controls protecting the objectivity of the study, then it is said to lack rigor or is soft science and therefore results in unusable data. If the findings from an inquiry do not lead to generalization that contributes to the prediction and control of the phenomena under study, some empiricists would argue that this is not science.

An empiricist view of science has permeated society and has structured what is valued. Feminist scholars have suggested that the scientific paradigm that focuses on prediction and control has gained wide acceptance because of its roots in a male paradigm. Historically, women have played only a small role in the creation of knowledge. Therefore, the definitions and values of science have been largely created by male scientists who have valued prediction and control over description and understanding.

An empirical, objective, rational science has significant value when the phenomenon of interest is other than human behavior. However, the goals of this type of science—prediction and control—are less valuable when the subject of the inquiry is unable to be made objective.

As a result of the limitations that result from a positivist view of science, philosophers and social scientists have offered an alternative path to discovery that places value on the study of human experiences. In this model, researchers acknowledge and value subjectivity as part of any scientific inquiry. Human values contribute to scientific knowledge; therefore, neutrality is impossible. Prediction is thought to be limiting and capable of creating a false sense of reality. In a human science framework, the best scientists can hope for in creating new knowledge is to provide understanding and interpretation of phenomena within context. Human science and the methods of inquiry that accompany it offer an opportunity to study and create meaning that will enrich and inform human life.

INDUCTION VERSUS DEDUCTION

Knowledge is generated from either an inductive or deductive posture. *Inductive reasoning* moves "from the particular to the general" (Feldman, 1998, p. 137). For example, a nurse interested in studying the experiences of women in labor would interview women who have undergone labor to discover their experiences of labor. Within context, the nurse could make statements about the labor experience that might be applicable to understanding the labor experience for women not in the study. Hence, qualitative research methods are inductive.

Deductive reasoning "moves from the general to the particular" (Feldman, 1998, p. 137). A researcher interested in conducting research within a deductive framework would develop a hypothesis about a phenomenon and then would seek to prove it. For example, a nurse wanting to know about the labor experience might hypothesize that women in labor experience more pain when they do not use visualization techniques during transition. The researcher's responsibility in such a study would be to identify a pain measure and then collect data on women in the transition phase of labor to determine whether they experience more or less pain based on the use of visualization techniques. Within a deductive framework, the researcher could use the study findings to predict and ultimately control the pain experience of laboring women. Deductive reasoning is the framework for quantitative research studies.

Both frameworks are important in the development of knowledge. Based on the question being asked, the researcher will select either an inductive or deductive stance.

Relationship of Theory to Research

In addition to understanding the framework from which the researcher enters the research enterprise, it is significant to be aware of the relationship of theory to research, specifically, qualitative research. Mitchell and Cody (1992) proposed that "all knowledge is theory-laden" (p. 170). What exactly is theory? According to Morse and Field (1995), "Theory is a systematic explanation of an event in which constructs and concepts are identified and relationships are proposed and predictions made" (p. 4). If we think about qualitative research, which advocates the necessity of being atheoretical, the idea of theory appears in opposition to the basic tenets of the qualitative research process. However, this idea may not be true. From a philosophic standpoint, Mitchell and Cody (1992) have suggested that all knowledge is theory laden. The intersection of these two apparently divergent positions occurs in light of the definition of theory and its position in the qualitative research process.

Morse and Field's (1995) definition of theory *is* contradictory to the basic tenets of qualitative research as a discovery process. However, the discovered information may lead to the development of yet unknown theories. Not all qualitative research studies lead to theory development, but certainly specific studies and approaches used in qualitative research will lead to theory development. Grounded theory is an example of such an approach. In grounded theory, the researcher's goal is to develop theory to describe a particular social process.

As an example of how a study or group of studies may lead to theory development, Estabrooks, Field, and Morse (1994) proposed that through an analysis and synthesis of completed qualitative research studies, the aggregation of qualitative research studies can lead to the development of midrange theory. This example clearly demonstrates the potential use of qualitative research for theory development.

If we review the position of Mitchell and Cody (1992) stated earlier, it is necessary to reexamine the definition of theory. According to these authors, qualitative research approaches represent a theoretical position and thus a way in which qualitative research is theory driven. To accept the position of Mitchell and Cody (1992), and many philosophers before them, one must accept the notion that the concepts and constructs represented in qualitative research methodologies represent a form of theory. Morse (1992) also has supported this position: She stated that conceptual frameworks and theories may be used as the theoretical basis for research to fit the research within the paradigmatic perspective of a discipline. As an example, she offered anthropologic use of culture as the underlying theory in ethnography.

The point of offering these descriptions of theory is to place the role of theory development within the context of qualitative research. It is generally accepted that qualitative research findings have the potential to create theory. In the instance of grounded theory, the method is dedicated to the discovery of theory. With regard to theoretical positions attributed to method, the term theory represents a particular epistemologic position that many qualitative researchers accept.

OBJECTIVE VERSUS SUBJECTIVE DATA WITHIN A NURSING CONTEXT

Empirical scientists believe that the study of any phenomena must be devoid of subjectivity (Namenwirth, 1986). Furthermore, they have contended that objectivity is essential in guiding the way to the truth. The problem with this position is that no human activity can be performed without subjectivity. Because it is a human quest for knowledge, it is logical to presume that human activity will be necessary to seek knowledge.

Based on his reading and interpretation of Hanson (1958), Phillips (1987) has suggested that objectivity is impossible: "The theory, hypothesis, framework, or background knowledge held by an investigator can strongly influence what he sees" (p. 9). Kerlinger (1979) also proposed that "the procedures of science are objective and not the scientists. Scientists, like all men and women, are opinionated, dogmatic, and ideological" (p. 264). Therefore, the idea of objectivity loses its meaning. On some level, all research endeavors have the subjective influence of the scientist. Procedural objectivity is the goal; however, even it is biased because the scientist will interpret the findings. Even if the findings of a study are statistical (thought to be an objective measure), the scientist interprets the statistical data through a lens of opinions and bias about what the numbers say (MacKenzie, 1981; Taylor, 1985).

Humanistic scientists value the subjective component of the quest for knowledge. They embrace the idea of subjectivity, recognizing that humans are incapable of total objectivity because they have been situated in a reality constructed by subjective experiences. Meaning, and therefore the search for the truth, is possible only through social interaction. The degree to which the scientist is part of the development of scientific knowledge is debated even by the humanistic scientists. Post-empiricists accept the subjective nature of inquiry but still support rigor and objective study through method. The objectivity post-empiricists speak of is one of context. For example, post-empiricist scientists would acknowledge their subjective realities and then, always being aware of them, seek to keep them apart from data collection, but to include them in the analysis and the final report.

Constructivist humanistic scientists believe that "knowledge is the result of a dialogical process between the self-understanding person and that which is encountered—whether a text, a work of art, or the meaningful expression of another person" (Smith, 1990, p. 177). Clearly, subjectivity is acknowledged, but the degree to which it is embraced is based on philosophic beliefs.

Humanistic scientists see objectivity in its empirical definition to be impossible. The degree to which a researcher can be objective, and therefore, unbiased, is determined by the philosophic tradition to which the human scientist ascribes. That subjectivity is included in the discussion of human science conveys an understanding that participation in the world prohibits humans from ever being fully objective.

Nurse–researchers engaged in qualitative research recognize the subjective reality inherent in the research process and embrace it. They are bound by method to acknowledge their subjectivity and to place it in a context that permits full examination of the effect of subjectivity on the research endeavor and description of the phenomenon under study.

Grounding Research in the Realities of Nursing

Nurse–scientists have the responsibility of developing new knowledge. The practice question that needs answering will drive the research paradigm selected. If a nurse–scientist is interested in discovering the most effective way to suction a tracheostomy tube, then a quantitative approach will be the appropriate way to study the problem. But, if the nurse–scientist is interested in discovering what the experience of suctioning is for people who are suctioned, qualitative research methods are more appropriate. What the nurse–scientist must do is clearly define the problem and then identify whether it requires an inductive or deductive approach. Only the researcher can determine what the explicit question is and how best to answer it. As Lincoln (1992) pointed out, the area of health research is open to inquiry and the qualitative model is a superior choice over conventional methods.

EMANCIPATION

In recent years, much has been written about "emancipatory research" (Henderson, 1995). Two predominant paradigms permeate what is published: critical theory and feminist theory. *Critical theory,* as described by Habermas (1971), is a way to develop knowledge that is free, undistorted, and unconstrained. According to Habermas, the predominant paradigm in science was not reflective of people's reality. He found that empiricism created cognitive dissonance. The goal of critical theory is to "unfreeze lawlike structures and to encourage self reflections for those whom the laws are about" (Wilson-Thomas, 1995, p. 573). "Critical [theorists] . . . sought to expose oppressive relationships among groups and to enlighten those who are oppressed" (Bent, 1993, p. 296).

Similarly, *feminist theory* takes the idea of emancipation further and speaks specifically to women's lives. Feminist theorists value women and women's experiences (Hall & Stevens, 1991). Feminist scholars believe that the traditional laws of science limit and preclude the discovery of what is uniquely feminist.

In both paradigms, the predominant themes are liberating the study participants and making their voices heard. Sigsworth (1995) identified seven fundamental conditions that are necessary for feminist research that, when editorialized, are appropriate for critical theorist ideas about research as well. These conditions are (1) the research should be focused on the experiences of the population studied, their perceptions, and their truths; (2) "artificial dichotomies and sharp boundaries are suspect in research involving human beings" (Sigsworth, 1995, p. 897); (3) history and concurrent events are always considered when planning, conducting, analyzing, and interpreting findings; (4) the questions asked are as important as the answers discovered; (5) research should not be hierarchical;

(6) researchers' assumptions, biases, and presuppositions are part of the research enterprise; and (7) researchers and research participants are partners whose discoveries lead to understanding.

According to Hall and Stevens (1991), qualitative methods are more in line with the feminist perspective as well as with critical theorist ideas. The tenets offered earlier are primary in conducting a study regardless of the methodology used. However, by their stated purposes, the methods of qualitative research are far more accommodating to the ideas supported by critical and feminist theorists. Researchers should consider and can apply the methods of qualitative research to any of the methods described in this text.

Summary

This chapter has offered the fundamental ideas supporting qualitative research as a specific research paradigm. In addition, the chapter has shared the relationship of historical, practical, and theoretical ideas. It is hoped that these ideas have piqued the reader's interest and will lead to exploration of the specifics of qualitative research as they are developed in this text.

REFERENCES

Atkinson, P. (1995). Some perils of paradigms. *Qualitative Health Research, 5*(1), 117–124.
Belenky, M. F., Clinchy, B. M., Goldberger, N. R., & Tarule, J. M. (1986). *Women's ways of knowing.* New York: Basic Books.
Benner, P. (1984). *From novice to expert.* Menlo Park, CA: Addison-Wesley.
Bent, K. N. (1993). Perspectives on critical and feminist theory in developing nursing praxis. *Journal of Professional Nursing, 9*(5), 296–303.
Carper, B. (1978). Fundamental patterns of knowing in nursing. *Advances in Nursing Science, 1*(1), 13–23.
Cheek, J. (1996). Taking a view: Qualitative research as representation. *Qualitative Health Research, 6*(4), 492–505.
Denzin, N. K., & Lincoln, Y. S. (Eds.). (1994). *Handbook of qualitative research.* Thousand Oaks, CA: Sage.
Ermath, M. (1978). *Wilhelm Dilthey: The critique of historical reason.* Chicago: University of Chicago Press.
Estabrooks, C. A., Field, P. A., & Morse, J. M. (1994). Aggregating qualitative findings: An approach to theory development. *Qualitative Health Research, 4*(4), 503–511.
Feldman, H. (1998). Theoretical framework. In G. LoBiondo-Wood & J. Haber (Eds.), *Nursing research: Methods, critical appraisal, and utilization* (4th ed., pp. 133–154). St. Louis, MO: Mosby.
Guba, E. G. (1990). *The paradigm dialogue.* Newbury Park, CA: Sage.
Habermas, J. (1971). *Knowledge and human interests* (J. J. Strapiro, trans.). Boston: Beacon Press.
Hall, J. M., & Stevens, P. E. (1991). Rigour in feminist research. *Advances in Nursing Science, 22*(3), 16–29.
Hamilton, D. (1994). Traditions, preferences, and postures in applied qualitative research. In N. K. Denzin & Y. S. Lincoln (Eds.), *Handbook of qualitative research* (pp. 60–69). Thousand Oaks, CA: Sage.
Hanson, N. R. (1958). *Patterns of Discovery.* Cambridge: Cambridge University Press.
Henderson, D. J. (1995). Consciousness raising in participatory research: Method and methodology for emancipatory inquiry. *Advances in Nursing Science, 17* (3), 58–69.

Kerlinger, F. N. (1979). *Behavioral research: A conceptual approach.* New York: Holt, Rinehart & Winston.

Kerlinger, F. N. (1986). *Foundations of behavioral research* (3rd ed.). New York: Holt, Rinehart & Winston.

Lincoln, Y. S. (1992). Sympathetic connections between qualitative methods and health research. *Qualitative Health Research, 2*(4), 375–391.

MacKenzie, D. (1981). *Statistics in Great Britain: 1885–1930.* Edinburgh, Scotland: Edinburgh University Press.

May, K. A. (1994). Abstract knowing: The case for magic in method. In J. Morse (Ed.), *Critical issues in qualitative research methods* (pp. 10–21). Thousand Oaks, CA: Sage.

Mitchell, G. J., & Cody, W. K. (1992). The role of theory in qualitative research. *Nursing Science Quarterly, 6*(4), 170–178.

Morse, J. M. (1992). The power of induction. *Qualitative Health Research, 2*(1), 3–6.

Morse, J. M., & Field, P. A. (1995). *Qualitative research methods for health professionals.* Thousand Oaks, CA: Sage.

Namenwirth, M. (1986). Science seen through a feminist prism. In R. Bleier (Ed.), *Feminist approaches to science* (pp. 18–41). New York: Pergamon Press.

Phillips, D. C. (1987). *Philosophy, science, and social inquiry.* New York: Pergamon Press.

Sandelowski, M. (1994). The proof is in the pottery: Toward a poetic for qualitative inquiry. In J. Morse (Ed.), *Critical issues in qualitative research methods* (pp. 44–62). Thousand Oaks, CA: Sage.

Sigsworth, J. (1995). Feminist research: Its relevance to nursing. *Journal of Advanced Nursing, 22,* 896–899.

Smith, J. K. (1990). Alternative research paradigms and the problem of criteria. In E. G. Guba (Ed.), *The paradigm dialogue* (pp. 167–187). Newbury Park, CA: Sage.

Taylor, C. (1985). *Human agency and language.* Cambridge, England: Cambridge University Press.

Thorne, S. (1997). Phenomenological positivism and other problematic trends in health science research. *Qualitative Health Research, 7*(2), 287–293.

Wilson-Thomas, L. (1995). Applying critical social theory in nursing education to bridge the gap between theory, research and practice. *Journal of Advanced Nursing, 21,* 568–575.

The Conduct of Qualitative Research: Common Essential Elements

In an age of rapidly changing information, professionals need to make significant decisions based on solid rationale. This chapter shares the reasons for choosing a qualitative approach to inquiry and describes the common elements of the qualitative research process. Based on this overview of the important aspects of qualitative research, the reader will be able to decide whether qualitative inquiry offers an opportunity to explore the questions that arise from his or her practice.

Obviously, to fully engage in one of the methods discussed in this book, the reader will need a solid understanding of the method and its assumptions. In addition, it is essential to engage a research mentor (Morse, 1997). As Morse (1997) has offered, one cannot learn to drive a car by reading the manual, hence, the researcher should not assume that one can conduct a qualitative study by reading this or any other qualitative research text. A mentor will make "shifting gears" a more effective process.

Initiating the Study: Choosing a Qualitative Approach

EXPLORING THE COMMON CHARACTERISTICS OF QUALITATIVE RESEARCH

In the conduct of research, certain attributes are common to the discovery enterprise. This is true of both qualitative and quantitative designs. This section explores those common characteristics of qualitative research.

Qualitative researchers have emphasized six significant characteristics in their research: (1) a belief in multiple realities, (2) a commitment to identifying an approach to understanding that supports the phenomenon studied, (3) a commitment to the participant's viewpoint, (4) the conduct of inquiry in a way that limits disruption of the natural context of the phenomena of interest, (5) acknowledged participation of the researcher in the research, and (6) the conveyance of an understanding of phenomena by reporting in a literary style rich with participant commentaries.

The idea that multiple realities exist and create meaning for the individuals studied is a fundamental belief of qualitative researchers. Instead of

15

searching for one reality—one truth—researchers committed to qualitative research believe that individuals actively participate in social actions, and through these interactions come to know and understand phenomena in different ways. Because people do understand and live experiences differently, qualitative researchers do not subscribe to one truth but, rather, to many truths.

Qualitative researchers are committed to discovery through the use of multiple ways of understanding. These researchers address questions about particular phenomena by finding an appropriate method or approach to answering the question. The discovery leads the choice of method rather than the method leading the discovery.

In some cases, more than one qualitative approach or more than one data collection strategy may be necessary to fully understand a phenomenon. For example, in her work on clinical decision making, Jenks (1993) found that, based on information discovered during focus group meetings, there was a need to observe nurses in practice that then led to individual interviews about practices observed. In this instance and in other qualitative research studies, researchers are committed to discovering information. Method and data collection strategies may change as needed, rather than being prescribed before the inquiry begins. This process differs from the way positivist science is developed.

Commitment to participants' viewpoints is another characteristic of qualitative research. Use of unstructured interview, observation, and artifacts grounds researchers in the real life of study participants. Researchers are co-participants in the discovery and understanding of the realities of the phenomena studied. Qualitative researchers will conduct extensive interviews and observations, searching documents and articles of importance to fully understand the context of what is researched. The purpose of the extensive investigation is to provide a view of reality that is important to the study participants, rather than to the researchers. For example, in work on students' perceptions of caring for dying clients, Beck (1997) clearly provided the students with the framework for telling their story by using a phenomenological inquiry approach. Instead of using an instrument to look at students' perceptions, which would include preestablished ideas about what the experience is like for care-givers of dying clients, Beck (1997) used an open-ended question to collect their experiences. An open-ended question allowed the participants to share *their* stories, in *their own* words, rather than being forced into preestablished lines of thinking developed by researchers.

Another characteristic of qualitative research is conduct of the inquiry in a way that does not disturb the natural context of the phenomena studied. Researchers are obligated to conduct a study so that it alters the context of the phenomena as little as possible. Using ethnographic research to illustrate this characteristic, the ethnographer would study a particular culture with as little intrusion as possible. Living among study participants is one way to minimize the intrusion and maintain the natural context of the setting. It is unrealistic to believe that the introduction of an unknown individual would not change the context of the relationships and activities observed; however, the researcher's prolonged presence should have the effect of minimizing the intrusion.

All research affects the study participants in some way. The addition of any new experience changes the way people think or act. The important factor in qualitative research that makes the difference is the serious attention to discovering the *emic view,* that is, the insider's perspective. What is it like for the participant? Qualitative researchers explore the insider's view with utmost respect for the individual's perspective and his or her space.

Researcher as instrument is another characteristic of qualitative research. The use of the researcher as instrument requires an acceptance that the researcher is part of the study. Because the researcher is the observer, interviewer, or the interpreter of various aspects of the inquiry, objectivity serves no purpose. Qualitative investigators accept that all research is conducted with a subjective bias. They further believe that researcher participation in the inquiry has the potential to add to the richness of data collection and analysis. Objectivity is a principle in quantitative research that documents the rigor of the science. In qualitative research, rigor is most often determined by the study participants. Do they recognize what the researcher has reported to be their culture or experience? The acknowledgment of the subjective nature of qualitative research and the understanding that researchers affect what is studied is fundamental to the conduct of qualitative inquiry.

Whether the approach is phenomenological, ethnographic, action research, grounded theory, or historical, qualitative researchers will report the study findings in a rich literary style. Participants' experiences are the findings of qualitative research. Therefore, it is essential these experiences be reported from the perspective of the people who have lived them. Inclusion of quotations, commentaries, and stories adds to the richness of the report and to the understanding of the social interactions experienced by the study participants. Table 2-1 describes the contrasts between quantitative and qualitative research.

All six characteristics guide qualitative researchers on a journey of discovery and participation. Doing qualitative research is similar to reading a good novel. When conducted in the spirit of the philosophy that supports it, qualitative research is rich and rewarding, leaving researchers with a desire to understand more about the phenomena of interest.

SELECTING THE METHOD BASED ON PHENOMENON OF INTEREST

An acceptance of the basic tenets of qualitative research is the first step in initiating a study. Once researchers understand that principles will guide all that is done, they can begin to explore various methods. The choice

TABLE 2-1   **Comparison of Quantitative and Qualitative Research Methods**

Quantitative	Qualitative
Objective	Subjectivity valued
One reality	Multiple realities
Reduction, control, prediction	Discovery, description, understanding
Measurable	Interpretative
Mechanistic	Organismic
Parts equal the whole	Whole is greater than the parts
Report statistical analyses	Report rich narrative
Researcher separate	Researcher part of research process
Subjects	Participants
Context free	Context dependent

of method depends on the question being asked. Because each method is explained in depth in the following chapters, the comments that follow serve only as a guide to method selection based on the phenomena of interest.

Say that a nurse is interested in studying the experiences of women who have had lumpectomies as breast cancer treatment. To fully understand the experiences of these women, the nurse would use a phenomenological approach. The purpose of phenomenology is to explore the lived experience of individuals. Phenomenology provides researchers with the framework for discovering what is like to live the experience.

If the nurse–researcher is interested in the progression of surgical intervention in the treatment of breast cancer and its political antecedents, a historical inquiry is the research approach of choice. Clearly, review of personal documents, diaries, research papers and proceedings, newspaper articles, and commentaries would provide the information for this type of study.

Another question that might be important to answer is, What is it like to be a cancer survivor? Based on the preceding comments, phenomenology may be the method of choice; however, assume that it is not the experience of being a survivor that the researcher is interested in but, rather, the process that the individual goes through in accepting survival as the outcome of a cancer diagnosis. In this case, the research method selected would be grounded theory. The researcher is more interested in understanding the process of surviving rather than the actual experience of being a cancer survivor. The outcome is what determines the method. More specifically, the researcher interested in the process of survivorship is committed to developing a theory about the process an individual goes through to claim survivorship as the outcome.

In a related situation, a nurse might be interested in studying the culture of cancer clients' self-help groups. In this case, the nurse–researcher would want to observe and collect information about group members, their activities, values, and life ways, as well as participate in a group session. In doing so, a full understanding of the culture of the group studied would become available.

If a nurse–researcher is interested in social change as it relates to women and cancer, an action research study might be the appropriate choice. By studying the women who have been active in reforming cancer care, the researcher has the potential to learn from the experiences of the women involved, how they participated in reforming cancer care, and how they ultimately participated in effecting a change. In this case, the action researcher would be serving two masters: theory and practice (Jenks, 1995).

Clearly, this limited description suggests researchers may use a number of research methods to address specific practice questions. Researchers need to clearly identify the focus of the inquiry and then choose the method that will most effectively answer the question.

UNDERSTANDING THE PHILOSOPHIC POSITION

After researchers have identified the question to be answered and have made explicit the approach to studying the question, a thorough under-standing of the philosophic assumptions that are the foundation of the method is essential. Too frequently, novice qualitative researchers develop and implement research studies without having a solid understanding of the philosophic underpinnings of the method. This lack of understanding has the potential of leading to sloppy science, resulting in misunderstood findings. For instance, phenomenology is an approach that can be used to study lived experience. But based on the philosophic position supported by the researcher, different interpretations might occur. To further illustrate this point, phenomenologists who support Edmund Husserl—a prominent leader of the phenomenological movement—and his followers believe that the purpose of phenomenology is to provide pure understanding. Supporters of the philosophic positions of Martin Heidegger and his col-leagues believe that phenomenology is interpretive. Neither group is incor-rect; rather, each just approaches the study of lived experience with differ-ent sets of goals and expectations.

The comments offered here should develop an appreciation for the importance of understanding the method chosen and its philosophic underpinnings. Making explicit the school of thought that guides an inquiry will help researchers to conduct a credible study and help those people who use the findings apply the results within the appro-priate context.

USING THE LITERATURE REVIEW

In the development of a quantitative research study, an interested researcher would begin with an extensive literature search on the topic of interest. This review documents the necessity for the study and provides for a discussion of the area of interest and related topics. It helps the researcher decide whether the planned study has been conducted and whether significant results were discovered. Furthermore, it helps the researcher refine the research question and build a case for why the topic of interest should be studied and how the researcher will approach the topic.

Qualitative researchers do not generally begin with an *extensive* literature review. Purists would argue that no literature review should be conducted before the inquiry begins. Some qualitative researchers accept that a cursory review of the literature may help focus the study. The reason for not conducting the literature review initially is to protect investigators from leading the participants in the direction of what the researchers have previously discovered. For instance, a researcher is interested in developing a theory about the processes a client goes through in accepting the necessity of an amputation. If the researcher reviews all of the literature on amputees, he or she might develop preconceived notions about amputees. The researcher may not have held the beliefs before the review, but, following the literature review, now has information that could affect how he or she collects and analyzes data. Pinch (1993) has suggested that researchers learn more about phenomena when conducting qualitative studies if they are "strangers." One way to remain a stranger is to limit intake of information about the focus of the study before conducting the study.

It is important to conduct the literature review after analyzing the data. The purpose of reviewing the literature in a qualitative study is to place the findings in the context of what is already known. Unlike a quantitative study, researchers do not use the literature search to establish grounds for the study or to suggest a theoretical or conceptual framework. Its purpose is to tell the intended readership how the findings fit into what is already known about the topic. Furthermore, it is not meant to confirm or argue existing findings.

EXPLICATING THE RESEARCHER'S BELIEFS

Before starting a qualitative study, it is in the researcher's best interest to reveal his or her thoughts about the topic as well as personal perceptions and biases. The purpose of this activity is to bring to consciousness and explicate what is believed about a topic. By revealing what the researcher believes, the researcher should be in a better position to approach the topic honestly and openly. Explication of personal beliefs makes the investigator more aware of the potential judgments that may occur during data collection and analysis based on the researcher's belief system rather than on the actual data revealed by participants.

For example, say that the topic of interest to the researcher is quality of life in individuals diagnosed with multiple sclerosis. The researcher has an interest in the topic based on a long history of working with individuals with end stage disease. The researcher's perception is that people with multiple sclerosis live sad, limited existences. If the researcher does not explicate these perceptions, he or she may lead informants to describe their experiences in the direction of the researcher's own beliefs, for example, through the questions the researcher might ask. In asking questions to validate the investigator's ideas, the participants may not be heard. The act of expressing one's ideas should help remind the researcher to listen and see what is real for the informants rather than what is real for the researcher. Schutz (1970) has recommended that researchers follow this process of describing personal beliefs about their assumptions to help them refrain from making judgments about phenomena based on personal experiences.

Once they have revealed their thoughts, feelings, and perceptions about phenomena, it is recommended that researchers bracket those thoughts, feelings, and perceptions. *Bracketing* is the cognitive process of putting aside one's own beliefs, not making judgments about what one has observed or heard, and remaining open to data as they are revealed. Specifically, in descriptive phenomenology, this activity is carried out before the beginning of the study and is repeated throughout data collection and analysis. In ethnographic work, keeping a diary of personal thoughts and feelings is an excellent way to explicate the researcher's ideas. Once revealed, the researcher can set them aside. By conducting this disclosure, researchers are able to keep their eyes open and to remain cognizant of when data collection and analysis reflect their own personal beliefs rather than informants' beliefs.

CHOOSING THE SETTING FOR DATA COLLECTION

The setting for qualitative research is the field. The *field* is the place where individuals of interest live—where they experience life. The inquiry will be conducted in the homes, neighborhoods, classrooms, or sites selected by the study participants. The purpose of conducting research in the field is to alter as little as possible the natural settings where phenomena occur. For instance, if an investigator were interested in studying the culture of an intensive care unit (ICU), he or she would visit an ICU. If the researcher were interested in studying the clinical decision-making skills of nurses, he or she would go to nurses who carry out this skill and ask them where they want to be interviewed or observed.

Being in the field requires a reciprocity in terms of decision making. Participants will decide what access to information they will permit the researcher. For instance, if interested in studying the experiences of people who have received a cancer diagnosis, a researcher would need access to people who have had this life situation. Participants may not wish to share their thoughts or feelings in one sitting or at all. In this situation, the duality of investigator and informants in qualitative research is clear. Negotiation may be possible to obtain information that the participants are reluctant to share. However, the conduct of qualitative research with its requirement of close social interaction may create a situation that can either limit or enhance access to information. It also has the potential to create ethical dilemmas that need careful attention. Only by being in the field will the researcher be truly aware of the strengths and potential weaknesses in this common feature of qualitative research.

SELECTING PARTICIPANTS

Qualitative researchers generally do not label the individuals who inform their inquiry as *subjects*. The use of the terms *participants* or *informants* illustrates the position to which qualitative researchers subscribe. Their position is that individuals who take part in the research are not acted on but, rather, are active participants in the study (Morse, 1991). The participants' active involvement in the inquiry helps others to better understand their lives and social interactions.

Individuals are selected to participate in qualitative research based on their firsthand experience with a culture, social interaction, or phenomenon of interest. For instance, if an ethnographer is interested in studying the culture of a first-year nursing class, then the informants for the study must be those students who have experienced and participated in the culture. Unlike quantitative research, there is no need to randomly select individuals, because manipulation, control, and generalization of findings are not the intent of the inquiry. The researcher interested in a first-year nursing class culture should interview as many first-year nursing students as possible to obtain a clear understanding of the culture. Lincoln and Guba (1985) and Patton (1990) have labeled this type of sampling *purposeful sampling;* it has also been called *theoretical sampling* (Glaser & Strauss, 1967; Patton, 1980). Theoretical sampling, used primarily in grounded theory, is one particular type of purposeful sampling (Coyne, 1997). Theoretical sampling is a complex form of sampling based on concepts that have proven theoretical relevance to the evolving theory (Coyne, 1997; Strauss & Corbin, 1990). What both of these terms denote is a commitment to observing and interviewing people who have had experience with the culture or phenomena of interest. The concern of researchers is to develop a rich or dense description of the culture or phenomenon, rather than using sampling techniques that support generalizability of the findings.

ACHIEVING SATURATION

A feature that is closely related to the topic of sampling is saturation. *Saturation* refers to the repetition of discovered information and confirmation of previously collected data (Morse, 1994). This means that, rather than sampling a specific number of individuals to gain significance based on some statistical manipulation, the qualitative researcher is looking for repetition and confirmation of previously collected data. For example, Beck (1992) was interested in studying the experience of postpartum depression. Her sample consisted of women who had experienced this phenomenon. Beck continued interviewing this group until she achieved repetition of the salient points (themes). She was able to recognize the repetition and determined that the addition of new informants confirmed her findings rather than added new information.

Morse (1989) has warned that saturation may be a myth. She believed that if another group of individuals were observed or interviewed at another time, new data might be revealed. The best that a qualitative researcher can hope for in terms of saturation is to saturate the specific culture or phenomenon at a particular time.

GENERATING DATA

A variety of strategies can be used to generate qualitative research data. The strategies offered are not meant to be exhaustive but rather descriptive of the more common data collection techniques.

CONDUCTING INTERVIEWS

One of the most frequently used data collection strategies is the open-ended interview. Open-ended interviews provide participants with the opportunity to fully explain their experience of the phenomena of interest. Interviews generally are conducted face to face. To facilitate sharing by the research participants, it is good practice to conduct the interview in space and time that is most comfortable for the participants. The more comfortable each participant is, the more likely he or she will reveal the information sought.

Interviews can be brief and with specific intent, such as verifying previously reported information. Or interviewing can cover a longer period, either in one sitting or over a prolonged time. A life history would be an example of data collection that may continue for a long time at each sitting and also over weeks, months, or years.

"The *structured interview* [italics added] refers to a situation in which an interviewer asks each respondent a series of preestablished questions with a limited set of response categories" (Fontana & Frey, 1994, p. 363). Structured interviews are more likely to occur in quantitative rather than qualitative research studies. An *unstructured interview* provides the opportunity for greater latitude in the answers provided. In the unstructured interview, the researcher asks open-ended questions, for example, "Tell me, what is the experience of nursing an abusive client?" In this example, there is no set response; the respondent is able to move about freely in his or her description of caring for an abusive client. The unstructured interview is a more common technique in a qualitative study.

Another interview technique gaining support across disciplines is narrative picturing. The definition of this technique has been debated, according to Stuhlmiller and Thorsen (1997). Generally speaking, *narrative picturing* is a strategy that grew out of therapeutic work with survivors of trauma called Traumatic Incident Reduction (Stuhlmiller & Thorsen, 1997, p. 142). In this technique, interviewers ask participants to imagine or picture an event or sequence of events as a method of describing an experience. It is a medium for conveying understanding and creating meaning of experiences (Brody, 1987; Stuhlmiller & Thorsen, 1997).

Regardless of the data collection strategies used (although they are important in interviewing), researchers need to gain access to participants. Access is an extremely important consideration when designing data collection strategies. When interviewing is the major way the researcher will collect data, it is important to determine how he or she will accomplish access. The way in which researchers present themselves to prospective study participants will affect the level and type of participation provided.

After the researcher gains access, it is important to establish rapport by conveying a sense of interest and concern for the research informant. The research participant must trust the researcher before he or she will feel comfortable revealing information.

USING FOCUS GROUPS

Focus groups are another strategy for collecting qualitative research data. A *focus group* is "a semi-structured group session, moderated by a group leader, held in an informal setting, with the purpose of collecting information on a designated topic" (Carey, 1994, p. 226). Focus groups are particularly suited to the collection of qualitative data because they have the advantages of being inexpensive, flexible, stimulating, cumulative, elaborative, assistive in information recall, and capable of producing rich data (Fontana & Frey, 1994; MacDougall & Baum, 1997). The major disadvantage of focus groups is *group think,* a process that occurs when stronger members of a group or segments of the group have major control or influence over the verbalizations of other group members (Carey & Smith, 1994). Generally, a good group leader can overcome the tendency of group think if he or she is mindful of its potential throughout data collection. The advantages of focus groups as a data collection strategy outweigh the disadvantage.

Focus groups have been used to collect information on a variety of topics. They are thought to be most useful when the topic of inquiry is considered sensitive. In situations in which the topic may be extremely sensitive, White and Thomson (1995) have recommended using telephone focus groups. Through these groups, participants are able to maintain their anonymity as they participate in group conversations about an issue. Murray (1997) has suggested using virtual focus groups, which use computer-mediated communications such as e-mail. Murray (1997) has pointed out that asynchronous computer communication requires the least amount

of specialized software, therefore permitting more individuals to participate. Researchers should exercise caution when using e-mail as an information exchange media because anonymity can be compromised.

USING A WRITTEN NARRATIVE

Written responses by qualitative research participants are not new as a
data collection strategy. Many researchers prefer written narratives to the
spoken word because such narratives permit participants to think about
what they wish to share. In addition, written narratives reduce costs by
eliminating transcription requirements for audiotape interviews. The disadvantage of written narratives is the lack of spontaneity in responses
that may occur. The popularity of the written narrative suggests it has
proven itself to be an effective means of collecting qualitative research
data.

In using written narratives, it becomes extremely important to be clear
about what it is researchers wish the participant to write about. Because
the researcher often is not present during the actual writing, it is essential
that directions be focused to get the desired information. Researchers may
need to establish mechanisms to request clarification in the event that the
written document provided is unclear.

USING CHAT ROOMS

With the increasing use of computer-mediated communications, the opportunities to collect data on-line grows daily. Chat rooms on the World
Wide Web allow interested parties to log on and communicate synchro-
nously. The transmissions and responses occur in real time as opposed
to being delayed. A number of chat rooms are available on the Internet.
Although their use as a data collection strategy has not been fully developed or completely explored, the opportunities abound. As Waskul and
Douglas (1996) have pointed out, computer-mediated communications
present "conceptual, theoretical and methodological challenges—the resolution of which represents the seeds of academic advancement" (p. 130).

USING PARTICIPANT OBSERVATION

Participant observation is a method of data collection that comes from
the anthropologic tradition. Therefore, it is the method of choice in ethnography. Generally, four types of participant observation are discussed in
the literature. The first is *complete observer,* in which the researcher is a
full observer of participants' activities. There is no interaction between
the researcher and participants.

Observer as participant is the second type of participant observation.
In this situation, the predominant activity of the researcher is to observe
and potentially to interview. The majority of the researcher's time is spent
in observation, however. To "fit" into the setting, the researcher may
engage in some activities with the participants.

Participant as observer is the third type of participant observation. In this situation, the researcher acknowledges interest in studying the group; however, the researcher is most interested in doing so by becoming part of the group. A great deal has been written about "going native." This phrase was coined to demonstrate the inherent problem in getting too involved. That is, the researcher becomes so engrossed in group activities, he or she loses sight of the real reason for being with the group.

The fourth type of participant observation is called *complete participant*. Complete participation requires that the researcher conceal his or her purpose. The ethical standards accepted by all disciplines makes concealment unacceptable. Unfortunately, it is difficult to justify this method. Because of a real concern for the ethics involved in data collection, individuals should not become complete participants.

Researchers should explore fully the reasons for selecting the various approaches to participant observation before initiating a study, realizing that, based on the circumstances, they may move among the approaches. There is no requirement to use only one approach; however, it is important for researchers to know which one to select in a given situation and for what reason.

USING FIELD NOTES

Field notes are the notations ethnographers generally make to document observations. These notes become part of data analysis. When recording field notes, it is important that researchers document what they have heard, seen, thought, or experienced. Chapter 8 offers examples of types of field notes, with detailed descriptions of how to write them.

MANAGING DATA

How researchers manage data will greatly affect the ease with which they collect the data. As addressed earlier, researchers may collect data in a number of ways. Storage and retrieval are other important considerations. A great deal of qualitative data has the capacity to be stored on computers using a variety of available computer applications. It is beyond the scope of this book to fully share the vast programs available and their use. It is essential for qualitative researchers interested in using computer software to acquire and preview qualitative data analysis software and work with various software packages to determine which will be the most useful.

Richards and Richards (1994) have offered that if data are in text format and are part of a word processing document, computer analysis offers several features. Seven of these features are as follows:

1. the ability to handle multiple documents on-screen in separate windows, which will facilitate viewing text that is similar throughout the document and will allow "cut and paste" editing
2. the ability to format files
3. the ability to include pictures, graphs, or charts to illustrate ideas

TABLE 2-2   Computerized Qualitative Data Management Programs

Computer Programs	Source
Atlas/ti	SCOLARI, Sage Publications, Inc. 24555 Teller Road Thousand Oaks, CA 91320 (805) 499-1325 scolari@sagepub.com www: http://www.scolari.com
Ethnograph (version 4)	Qualitative Research Management 73-425 Hilltop Desert Hot Springs, CA 92241-7821 (760) 329-7026 Hallock_Hoffman@MCIMail.com
Hyper Research for Windows	Research Ware, Inc. P.O. Box 1258 Randolph, MA 02368-1258 (781) 961-3909 researchwr@aol.com
Martin	Martin School of Nursing University of Wisconsin–Madison 600 Highland Avenue Madison, WI 53792 pwipperf@macc.wisc.edu (608) 263-5336
Nudist 4	SCOLARI, Sage Publications, Inc. 24555 Teller Road Thousand Oaks, CA 91320 (805) 499-1325 scolari@sagepub.com www: http://www.scolari.com

4. the ability to add video or audio data
5. good text-searching abilities
6. publish and subscribe facility, which allows for text to be changed in one document and automatically updated in a linked document
7. the ability to link documents using hypertext, which permits readers to easily move from document to document and creates a unique ability to annotate text using hypertext links; these links facilitate memo writing about identified information. (p. 450)

These features are available in computer applications that would not be available in the more traditional storage formats such as handwritten files.

Table 2-2 offers an overview of commonly used computer packages. "The CAQDAS World Wide Web Page (http://www.soc.surrey.ac.uk/caqdas/) makes available to the research community a selection of demonstration versions of qualitative data analysis packages for download" (Lewins, 1996, p. 300) and preview.

Qualitative researchers will need to practice working with these packages and, in some cases, use computer consultants to navigate all the various program features. However, ultimately, the rewards of using a qualitative data analysis package will outweigh the time spent in learning about the various packages.

PERFORMING DATA ANALYSIS

When researchers have collected all data, it is then necessary to begin analysis. The amount of data collected and the style in which researchers have stored the data will either facilitate or impede data analysis. Analysis of qualitative research is a hands-on process. Researchers must become deeply immersed in the data (sometimes referred to as "dwelling" with the data). This process requires inquirers to commit fully to understanding what the data say. It requires a significant degree of dedication to reading, intuiting, analyzing, synthesizing, and reporting the discoveries.

Data analysis in qualitative research actually begins when data collection begins. As researchers conduct interviews or observations, they maintain and constantly review records to discover additional questions they need to ask or to offer descriptions of their findings. Usually these questions or descriptions are embedded in the observations and interviews. Qualitative researchers must "listen" carefully to what they have seen, heard, and experienced to discover the meanings. The cyclic nature of questioning and verifying is an important aspect of data collection and analysis. In addition to the analysis that occurs throughout the study, a protracted period of immersion occurs at the conclusion of data collection. During this period of dwelling, investigators question all prior conclusions in light of what they have discovered in the context of the whole. Generally, this period of data analysis consumes a considerable amount of time. Researchers will spend weeks or months with data based on the amount of data available for analysis.

The actual process of data analysis usually takes the form of clustering similar data. In many qualitative approaches, these clustered ideas are referred to as *themes,* which are structural meaning units of data. They help researchers cluster information and discover the meanings intended in what the researchers have observed and heard.

Once researchers have explicated all themes relevant to a study, they write them up in a way that is meaningful to the intended audience. Developing a research report based on qualitative study findings is discussed in detail in Chapter 15.

DEMONSTRATING TRUSTWORTHINESS

Rigor in qualitative research is demonstrated through researchers' attention to and confirmation of information discovery. The goal of rigor in qualitative research is to accurately represent study participants' experiences.

There are different terms to describe the processes that contribute to rigor in qualitative research. Guba (1981) and Guba and Lincoln (1994) have identified the following terms that describe operational techniques supporting the rigor of the work: credibility, dependability, confirmability, and transferability.

Credibility includes activities that increase the probability that credible findings will be produced (Lincoln & Guba, 1985). One of the best ways to establish credibility is through prolonged engagement with the subject matter. Another way to confirm the credibility of findings is to see whether the participants recognize the findings to be true to their experiences (Yonge & Stewin, 1988). Lincoln and Guba have called this activity "member checks" (p. 314). The purpose of this exercise is to have those people who have lived the described experiences validate that the reported findings represent their experiences.

Dependability is a criterion met once researchers have determined the credibility of the findings. The question to ask is, How dependable are these results? Similar to validity in quantitative research, in which there can be no validity without reliability, the same holds true for dependability: There can be no dependability without credibility (Lincoln & Guba, 1985).

Confirmability is a process criterion. The way researchers document the confirmability of the findings is to leave an *audit trail,* which is a recording of activities over time that another individual can follow. This process can be compared to a fiscal audit (Lincoln & Guba, 1985). The objective is to illustrate as clearly as possible the evidence and thought processes that led to the conclusions. This particular criterion can be problematic, however, if you subscribe to Morse's (1989) ideas regarding the related matter of saturation. It is the position of this author that another researcher may not agree with the conclusions developed by the original researcher.

Transferability refers to the probability that the study findings have meaning to others in similar situations. Transferability has also been labeled "fittingness." The expectation for determining whether the findings fit or are transferable rests with potential users of the findings and not with the researchers (Greene, 1990; Lincoln & Guba, 1985; Sandelowski, 1986). As Lincoln and Guba (1985) have stated,

> It is . . . not the naturalist's task to provide an *index of transferability;* it is his or her responsibility to provide the *data base* that makes transferability judgement possible on the part of potential appliers. (p. 316)
>
> These four criteria for judging the rigor of qualitative research are important. They define for external audiences the attention qualitative researchers render to their work.

Summary

This chapter has described the elements common to qualitative research as well as prevalent terms and their use. Chapter 3 presents a detailed description of the ethical requirements of qualitative research. The introductory chapters have offered neophyte researchers an overview of the common concerns related to and the theoretical foundations of this unique way of conducting research.

REFERENCES

Beck, C. T. (1992). The lived experience of postpartum depression: A phenomenologicalal study. *Nursing Research, 42*(3), 166–170.

Beck, C. T. (1997). Nursing students' experiences caring for dying patients. *Journal of Nursing Education, 36*(9), 408–415.

Brody, H. (1987). *Stories of sickness.* New Haven, CT: Yale University Press.

Carey, M. A. (1994). The group effect in focus groups: Planning, implementing, and interpreting focus group research. In J. M. Morse (Ed.), *Critical issues in qualitative research methods* (pp. 225–241). Thousand Oaks, CA: Sage.

Carey, M. A., & Smith, M. W. (1994). Capturing the group effect in focus groups: A special concern for analysis. *Qualitative Health Research, 4*(1), 123–127.

Coyne, I. T. (1997). Sampling in qualitative research. Purposeful and theoretical sampling: Merging or clear boundaries? *Journal of Advanced Nursing, 26,* 623–630.

Fontana, A., & Frey, J. H. (1994). Interviewing: The art and science. In N. K. Denzin & Y. S. Lincoln (Eds.), *Handbook of qualitative research* (pp. 361–376). Thousand Oaks, CA: Sage.

Glaser, B. G., & Strauss, A. (1967). *The discovery of grounded theory.* Chicago: Aldine.

Greene, J. C. (1990). Three views on nature and role of knowledge in social science. In E. Guba (Ed.), *The paradigm dialogue* (pp. 227–245). Newbury Park, CA: Sage.

Guba, E. G. (1981). Criteria for assessing the trustworthiness of naturalistic inquiries. *Educational Communication and Technology Journal, 29, 75–92.*

Guba, E. G., & Lincoln Y. S. (1994). Competing paradigms in qualitative research. In N. K. Denzin & Y. S. Lincoln (Eds.), *Handbook of qualitative research* (pp. 105–117). Thousand Oaks, CA: Sage.

Jenks, J. M. (1993). The pattern of personal knowing in nurse clinical decision making. *Journal of Nursing Education, 32*(9), 399–405.

Jenks, J. M. (1995). New generation research approaches. In H. J. Streubert & D. R. Carpenter (Eds.), *Qualitative research in nursing* (pp. 242–268). Philadelphia: Lippincott.

Lewins, A. (1996). The CAQDAS Networking Project: Multilevel support for the qualitative research community. *Qualitative Health Research, 6*(2), 298–303.

Lincoln, Y. S., & Guba, E. G. (1985). *Naturalistic inquiry.* Beverly Hills, CA: Sage.

MacDougall, C., & Baum, F. (1997). The devil's advocate: A strategy to avoid group think and stimulate discussion in focus groups. *Qualitative Health Research, 7*(4), 532–541.

Morse, J. M. (1989). Strategies for sampling. In J. M. Morse (Ed.), *Qualitative nursing research: A contemporary dialogue* (pp. 117–131). Rockville, MD: Aspen.

Morse, J. M. (1991). Subjects, respondents, informants and participants? *Qualitative Health Research, 1*(4), 403–406.

Morse, J. M. (1994). Designing funded qualitative research. In N. K. Denzin & Y. S. Lincoln (Eds.), *Handbook of qualitative research* (pp. 220–235). Thousand Oaks, CA: Sage.

Morse, J. M. (1997). Learning to drive from a manual? *Qualitative Health Research, 7*(2), 181–183.

Murray, P. J. (1997). Using virtual focus groups in qualitative research. *Qualitative Health Research, 7*(4), 542–549.

Patton, M. Q. (1980). *Qualitative evaluation methods.* Beverly Hills, CA: Sage.

Patton, M. Q. (1990). *Qualitative evaluation and research methods.* Newbury Park, CA: Sage.

Pinch, W. J. (1993). Investigator as stranger. *Qualitative Health Research, 3*(4), 493–498.

Richards, T. J., & Richards, L. (1994). Using computers in qualitative research. In N. K. Denzin & Y. S. Lincoln (Eds.), *Handbook of qualitative research* (pp. 445–462). Thousand Oaks, CA: Sage.

Sandelowski, M. (1986). The problem of rigor in qualitative research. *Advances in Nursing Science, 8*(3), 27–37.

Schutz, A. (1970). *On phenomenology and social relations.* Chicago: University of Chicago Press.

Strauss, A., & Corbin, J. (1990). *Basics of qualitative research: Grounded theory procedures and techniques.* Newbury Park, CA: Sage.

Stuhlmiller, C. M., & Thorsen, R. (1997). Narrative picturing: A new strategy for qualitative data collection. *Qualitative Health Research, 7*(1), 140–149.

Waskul, D., & Douglas, M. (1996). Considering the electronic participant: Some polemical observations on the ethics of on-line research. *Information Society, 12,* 129–139.

White, G. E., & Thomson, A. N. (1995). Anonymized focus groups as a research tool for health professionals. *Qualitative Health Research, 5*(2), 256–261.

Yonge, O., & Stewin, L. (1988). Reliability and validity: Misnomers for qualitative research. *The Canadian Journal of Nursing, 20*(2), 61–67.

CHAPTER 3

Ethical Requirements in Qualitative Research

Professional nursing practice and health-related disciplines such as medicine face issues that require sound ethical and moral decision making on a daily basis. The ethical dilemmas in our practice are becoming increasing complex as science and technology provide the ability to intervene in ways we never thought possible. Do not resuscitate orders, the withholding of nutrition, and informed consent issues are part of the daily responsibilities associated with a health care career that involves direct relationships with humans.

With regard to research, ethical considerations have and always will be a critical consideration. Engaging in a research study brings with it a personal and professional responsibility to ensure the design of both quantitative and qualitative studies that are morally and ethically sound. Human rights must always be protected; therefore, guidelines have been established, such as the professional guidelines *Human Rights Guidelines for Nurses in Clinical and Other Research* (American Nurses Association 1975) and the *Code for Nurses* (American Nurses Association 1985). However, these guidelines are "inadequate in scope when applied to a qualitative research endeavor" (Robley, 1995, p. 46).

Qualitative research brings with it a new set of ethical considerations. "Although ethical consideration and issues impact quantitative research, they do so in unique and more fragile ways in qualitative research" (Robley, 1995, p. 45). Issues surrounding informed consent, anonymity and confidentiality, data generation, treatment, and participant–researcher relationships take on new and sometimes unanticipated ethical considerations in qualitative investigations.

With the emergence of qualitative research in nursing and related disciplines such as philosophy, sociology, and anthropology, the research agenda is encumbered by new and evolving ethical requirements. At times, the ethical issues in a qualitative investigation are unclear. Despite efforts to inform the participants and to anticipate outcomes, there is little control over what might surface in a qualitative interview. Researchers ultimately must be responsible for ethical decision making in the conduct of any investigation. That responsibility, however, becomes difficult—if not impossible—in a qualitative research design, in which the ethical implications may be unclear or unanticipated.

Researchers must observe certain basic principles when conducting an investigation. First, participants must not be harmed, thereby supporting the principle of *nonmaleficence*. In any qualitative investigation, if researchers sense that the interview is causing issues to surface that may result in serious consequences, they must protect the welfare of the participants, perhaps by ending the interview or providing follow-up counseling and referrals. Researchers must obtain informed consent, and informant participation must be voluntary, thereby supporting the principle of *autonomy*. Furthermore, researchers must assure participants that confidentiality and anonymity will be upheld and that participants will be treated with dignity and respect. The principles of *beneficence* and *justice* are upheld in this regard (Beauchamp & Childress, 1994).

This chapter explores the ethical requirements associated with a qualitative research study. It addresses issues related to informed consent, participant–researcher relationships, confidentiality, anonymity, sample size, and data analysis. The topics in this chapter are related to each of the methods presented in the text; therefore, whether readers are engaged in phenomenological, grounded theory, ethnographic, or action research, they should give full consideration to these topics. Ultimately, qualitative researchers must remain sensitive to and aware of the possibilities of ethical issues arising that they may not have anticipated. This stance leaves researchers in the best position to address any issues that present during the conduct of an investigation. Table 3-1 provides qualitative researchers with an "ethics checklist" they can use to evaluate qualitative research from an ethical perspective.

Informed Consent Process and Qualitative Research

Informed consent is the subject of discussion on a regular basis in health care settings. Consent forms for necessary procedures for diagnosis and treatment of health-related problems are a familiar component of the hospital setting. There is an expectation that, when clients sign a consent form, they are fully aware of both the health benefits and the actual or potential risks to their health (hence, the term *informed consent*). Informed consent in research holds a similar meaning, with additional essential dimensions.

The emergent design of a qualitative investigation presents qualitative researchers with ethical considerations related to informed consent. Polit and Hungler (1997) defined informed consent as follows: "Informed consent means that participants have adequate information regarding the research; are capable of comprehending the information; and have the power of free choice, enabling them to consent voluntarily to participate in the research or decline participation" (Polit & Hungler, 1997, p. 134). This definition fits well with quantitative designs; however, the very nature

TABLE 3-1   The "Ethics Checklist": A Guide for Critiquing the Ethical Aspects of a Qualitative Research Study

Topic	Guiding Questions
Phenomenon of interest	1. Is the research study relevant, important, and most appropriately investigated through a qualitative design? 2. Are any aspects of the research or phenomenon of interest that appear to be misleading either in terms of the true purpose or misleading to participants? 3. Is the research primarily being conducted for personal gain on the part of the researcher or is there evidence that the research will somehow contribute to the greater good?
Review of the literature	1. Has the literature review been obviously biased? 2. Has the researcher concentrated only on the articles he or she thought to be relevant or has all the available literature been reviewed? 3. Has the researcher referenced only those articles which support his or her ideas? 4. Is there evidence of plagiarism or quoting out of context? 5. Is the basis for inclusion of the articles referred to clear?
Research design	1. Is the physical and psychological well-being of the subjects protected? 2. Is consent freely given? 3. How were vulnerable populations recruited?
Sampling	1. Is the confidentiality of participants protected?
Data Generation	1. If more than one researcher collected data, were they adequately prepared? 2. Is there evidence or falsified or fabricated data? 3. Is there intentional use of data collection methods to obtain biased data? 4. Was data collection covert? Why? 5. Have the participants been mislead with regard to the nature of the research? 3. Is there evidence of deception?
Data analysis	1. Was data analysis conducted by more that one person? 2. Is there evidence of data manipulation to achieve intended findings? 3. Is there evidence of missing data that may have been lost or destroyed?
Conclusions and Recommendations	1. Is there evidence of intentional false or misleading conclusions and recommendations? 2. Is confidentiality broken given the presentation of the findings?

(Adapted from: Firby, P. (1995). Critiquing the ethical aspects of a study. *Nurse Researcher, 3*(1), 35–41.

of a qualitative investigation can result in immediate concerns. Of particular concern is the notion that participants will have information regarding the research. Although a participant may consent to a study on the life experience of open heart surgery, new issues may emerge within the context of the interview for which the participant and, perhaps, even the researcher were unprepared.

"As a minimum, it [informed consent] requires that prospective human subjects are given true and sufficient information to help them decide whether they wish to be research participants" (Behi & Nolan, 1995, p. 713). The open, emerging nature of qualitative research methods in most cases makes informed consent impossible, because neither researchers nor participants can predict exactly how data will present themselves either through interview or participant observation (Holloway & Wheeler, 1995; Ramos, 1989; Robley, 1995). As Robley (1995) pointed out, "Questions of ethics arise within the context of the shifting focus of the study, the unpredictable nature of the research and the trust relationship between the researcher and the participant" (p. 45).

"The inherent unpredictability of the research process undermines the spirit of informed consent and endangers the assurance of confidentiality, two basic ethical safety nets in more quantitative research" (Ramos, 1989, p. 58). For example, in a study on the meaning of quality of life for individuals with type I [insulin-dependent] diabetes mellitus, data collection might begin with one open-ended question: "Tell me in as much detail as possible: What does it mean to have quality of life with type I insulin-dependent diabetes mellitus?" The researcher's probing questions to elicit a more detailed understanding can literally open a Pandora's box. Issues surrounding compliance or noncompliance may arise that endanger the client's health, or perhaps the client is depressed and concerned about issues related to loss, death, and dying. What may emerge is impossible to predict, but both researchers and participants must be informed and prepared to address issues of informed consent throughout the investigation.

The emergent design of qualitative research demands a different approach to informed consent. *Consensual decision making,* also called *process informed consent,* is more appropriate for the conduct of a qualitative investigation. This approach requires that researchers, at varying points in the research process, reevaluate participants' consent to participate in the study. According to Munhall (1988), a process consent encourages mutual participation: "Because qualitative research is conducted in an ever-changing field, informed consent should be an ongoing process. Over time, consent needs to be renegotiated as unexpected events or consequences occur" (p. 156). Information about how the researcher enters the field, participants' time commitment, and what will become of the findings are all important components to process consent (Munhall, 1988). Participants must know from the beginning of and be reminded throughout the investigation that they have the right to withdraw from the research study at any time. A process consent offers the opportunity to change the original consent as the study emerges and change becomes necessary. "Common sense plays a large part in renegotiating informed consent. If our focus should change, we need to ask participants for permission to change the first agreement. Continually informing and asking permission establishes the needed trust to go on further in an ethical manner" (Munhall, 1988, p. 157).

It is essential that researchers and participants discuss and clarify their understanding of the investigation (Alty & Rodham, 1998; Raudonis, 1992). As Alty and Rodham (1998) have emphasized, "At the best of times, it is difficult to know if the person you are talking to really has the same understanding of the topic as you do, indeed, if the researcher has an accurate understanding of what the subject is expressing" (p. 277).

For children, people with certain mental illnesses or learning disabilities, or unconscious or acutely ill people, researchers may obtain informed consent by proxy. Issues related to dealing with vulnerable populations are covered later in this chapter.

Covert participant observation, which results when participants are unaware they are being observed, presents another ethical concern for qualitative researchers. Covert participant observation is sometimes a necessary component to the data generation in some qualitative investigations. The rationale from the researcher's perspective would be to ensure that collected data are true and accurate. This type of data generation is grounded in the idea that, when the participants are aware they are being observed, their behavior will change. For example, Clarke (1996) discussed the use of covert participant observation in a secure forensic unit and the ethical issues that emerged from this method of data generation. Clarke emphasized the need to obtain an "uncontaminated picture of the unit" (p. 37).

A researcher's integrity can become damaged if the researcher uses deception to generate data. Some researchers claim that deception in the form of covert observations—or not completely describing the aims of the study or its procedures—is sometime necessary to get reliable and valid data (Douglas, 1979; Gans, 1962). Punch (1994) agreed that field-related deception may be necessary, provided the interests of the subjects are protected. Others have argued that the need for covert research is exaggerated (Bulmer, 1982). Johnson (1992) further examined

> the moral problems inherent in complete participant observation and [argued] against secretly invading the privacy of others despite the apparent lack of tangible harm. He [explored] the issue from both the positive and negative and [suggested] that if the researcher does not plan to obtain informed consent, one must show how the data can only be gained in this manner. Stringent justification is necessary if participant observation is proposed. (cited in Robley 1995, p. 47)

The use of covert participant observation must be given serious consideration in the conduct of a qualitative investigation. Researchers must consider available alternative solutions for data generation provided those solutions will maintain the integrity of the study.

CONFIDENTIALITY AND ANONYMITY

The principles of beneficence and justice apply with regard to providing confidentiality and anonymity for research study participants. According to Polit and Hungler (1997), "A promise of confidentiality to participants is a guarantee that any information the participant provides will not be publicly reported or made accessible to parties other than those involved in the research" (p. 138) and "anonymity occurs when even the researcher cannot link a participant with the data for that person" (p. 137).

The very nature of data collection in a qualitative investigation makes anonymity impossible. The personal, one-to-one interaction during the interview process allows researchers to know the participants in ways that are impossible and unnecessary in quantitative designs. Qualitative research methods such as participant observation and one-to-one interviews make it "impossible to maintain anonymity at all stages; in other words, when using these methods, becoming cognizant of the source of data is unavoidable" (Behi & Nolan, 1995, p. 713).

Small sample size and thick descriptions provided in the presentation of the findings can present problems in maintaining confidentiality (Behi & Nolan, 1995; Holloway & Wheeler, 1995; Lincoln & Guba, 1987; Ramos, 1989; Robley, 1995). Dena Davis (1992) discussed thick descriptions as follows: "We learn from our experiences and we need to present the fruits of that learning in a full-bodied way that invites our audience to share that experience with us, and also to judge the legitimacy of our results" (p. 13). Robley (1995) emphasized that thick descriptions are extremely important to the meaning of the research and offered a solution supported by the works of Cowles (1988), Davis (1991), and Lincoln and Guba (1987): "If the narrative requires it, retain it and return to the respondent for permission, verification, and justification" (p. 48).

Often, if the research has been conducted close to home and the sample is familiar to others, the details given in the thick slices of data used to support and verify themes may reveal research participants' identities. The researcher must make every effort to ensure that confidentiality is a promise kept. "Guaranteeing confidentiality implies that the research subject's data will be used in such a way that no-one else but the researcher knows the source" (Behi & Nolan, 1995, p. 713). As Robley (1995) has pointed out, "Guarding against disclosure that may create unacceptable risks for the respondents is accomplished in part by respecting the need for withdrawal of revealing material during the interview process, and in part through the process of member checking and negotiated outcomes" (p. 46).

ETHICAL CONSIDERATIONS RELATED TO THE
RESEARCHER–PARTICIPANT RELATIONSHIP

The data generation strategies associated with a qualitative investigation include such approaches as one-to-one interviews, focus groups, and participant observation. These particular data generation strategies necessitate a close, personal relationship with participants. The researcher is the tool for data collection and, as such, comes to know participants in a personal way. The boundaries of the relationship may become blurred as the research progresses, and role confusion may lead to ethical concerns for the investigation. As Ramos (1989) explained, "The respondent and the investigator interact verbally, and their relationship can range from one of civil cooperation to camaraderie in problem-solving to the abiding trust and dependency of the therapeutic alliance" (p. 59).

"Nurses are legally, culturally, and historically bound to nurture and protect the health and welfare of their patients" (Ramos, 1989, p. 57). So, when participants confuse the researcher's role with that of a counselor or therapist, and unrelated issues of concern emerge, the protection of the participants' welfare must always take precedence over the research. Researchers must not move from the role of instrument in the investigation to that of counselor or therapist. "Research in nursing constitutes a delicate balance between the principles of rigorous investigation and a nurturing concern for patient welfare" (Ramos, 1989, p. 57). Investigators can attempt to guide the interview and maintain focus on the topic under investigation. Following the closure of the interview, researchers should recap for the participants issues of concern that emerged during the interview and should also provide follow-up.

Researchers must also consider the selection of participants for a qualitative research study from an ethical standpoint. "An ethical basis for selection would also involve attention to the inclusion of those whose voices need to be heard: women, minorities, children, the illiterate, and those with less personal or professional status. Social responsibility calls for attention to diversity" (Robley, 1995, p. 46).

Sensitive Issues Arising in the Conduct of Qualitative Research

The interview may be one of the few opportunities participants have to discuss the issue at hand, and the topic may well be a sensitive one. Alty and Rodham (1998) have given perspective to sensitive issues:

> The ouch! factor is a term that describes certain experiences encountered in the process of conducting qualitative research. These experiences include those ranging from a short sharp shock to the researcher to those situations and experiences that can develop into a chronic ache if not addressed early. (p. 275)

Sensitive issues also may arise in research conducted with vulnerable populations such as dying people (Raudonis, 1992), children and adolescents (Faux, Walsh, & Deatrick, 1988), families (Demi & Warren, 1995), lesbians and gay men (Platzer & James, 1997), and individuals with intellectual disabilities (Llewellyn, 1995). Certain topics such as the "sudden violent death of a loved one, controversial involvement in political activity, a crumbling relationship, legal incarceration, and a life-threatening illness" (Cowles, 1988, p. 163) are extremely sensitive topics and place participants in a vulnerable situation as the researcher asks the necessary probing questions to elicit the necessary data. Given the intensity of the interaction between researcher and participant, the researcher also may be in a vulnerable position. As Robley (1995) has observed,

> Subjectivity and collaboration makes the researcher vulnerable. Emotionally immersed in the lived experience of others, continually sensitive to the potentially injurious nature of language, and experiencing the rights of passage as an interviewer/observer—all require an inner strength that can be enhanced by self care. The researcher can use the ethics committee as a guide and support throughout the process. [He or she] can use debriefing to explore personal responses and weigh risk/benefits. Personal education in ethics and consultation with experts when it is believed that the nurse researcher is being hurt is advocated. (p. 48)

Do not stray from the focus of the investigation. Recognize that participants may need to talk but make clear that the researcher will address the issue after the interview. "All research (particularly that which focuses on sensitive issues) may stir up emotions of such intensity that failure to provide an opportunity for the respondent to talk may be perceived as irresponsible" (Alty & Rodham, 1998, p. 279). Allowing time for feedback and discussion of participants' feelings brings with it the possibility that the researcher will hear too much, but it must be done. After each interview, ask participants if they need follow-up. Provide a contact for additional help (Alty & Rodham, 1998; Holloway & Wheeler, 1995).

Interpretation of Data and the Reporting of Subjective Interpretations

The interpretation of data and the reporting of findings require that researchers spend time reading and rereading verbatim transcriptions of interviews and field notes. Procedures such as bracketing (defined in Chapter 2) are required if researchers are to have any confidence in the final data analysis. Researchers must keep any presuppositions or personal biases separate or set aside throughout the entire investigation. Having a second researcher review the data and verify categories can also serve as a validity check. According to Ramos (1989),

The investigator, even with the validation of inferences afforded by the relationship with the respondent, imposes his or her logic and values onto the communicated reality of the respondent. He or she imposes his or her subjective reality upon the interpretation of meaning-data from the respondent. The researcher cannot extract correct meanings unilaterally. Without the validation afforded by member checking, a leap in logic could occur, and a serious misinterpretation of sensitive information could ensue. (p. 60)

Returning final descriptions to participants so that they may validate that the interpretation of the interview or observation is authentic and true further adds to the final data analysis. This procedure can assist researchers in verifying that there were no serious misinterpretations or omissions of critical information.

Summary

The process of conducting a qualitative investigation is complex, personal, and intense. Data collection methods prevent anonymity and may result in the development of close, intimate relationships between participants and the researcher. In addition, presentation of the findings with thick descriptions and slices of raw data may complicate issues of confidentiality. Researchers must consider and address the vulnerability of certain populations. These issues are important in the ongoing development and use of qualitative research methods.

Although established ethical guidelines may give some direction, the ethical and moral picture of qualitative research is much more complicated. Even though an ethical review board may have reviewed a research study, problems may still arise. "We should not simply assume that because research has been accepted by a committee it is morally justifiable in its methods" (Firby, 1995, p. 36). Ethical guidelines for qualitative research will continue to emerge, and researchers must consider those guidelines from a different perspective than those associated with quantitative designs.

REFERENCES

Alty, A., & Rodham, K. (1998). The ouch! factor: Problems in conducting sensitive research. *Qualitative Health Research, 8*(2), 275–282.

American Nurses Association. (1975). *Human rights guidelines for nurses in clinical and other research*. Kansas City, MO: Author.

American Nurses Association. (1985). *Code for nurses with interpretive statements*. Kansas City, MO: Author.

Beauchamp, T. L., & Childress, J. F. (1994). *Principles of biomedical ethics* (3rd ed.). Oxford, England: Oxford University Press.

Behi, R., & Nolan, M. (1995). Ethical issues in research. *British Journal of Nursing, 4*(12), 712–716.

Bulmer, M. (Ed.). (1982). *Social research ethics*. New York: Macmillan.

Clarke, L. (1996). Covert participant observation in a secure forensic unit. *Nursing Times, 92*(48), 37–40.

Cowles, K. V. (1988). Issues in qualitative research on sensitive topics. *Western Journal of Nursing Research, 10*(2), 163–179.

Davis, D. S. (1991). Rich cases: The ethics of thick description. *Hastings Center Report, 21*(4), 12–16.

Demi, A. S., & Warren, N. A. (1995). Issues in conducting research with vulnerable families. *Western Journal of Nursing Research, 17*(2), 188–202.

Douglas, J. D. (1979). Living morality versus bureaucratic fiat. In C. B. Klockers & F.W.O. Connor (Eds.), *Deviance and decency: The ethics of research with human subjects* (pp. 13–33). Beverly Hills, CA: Sage.

Faux, S. A., Walsh, M., & Deatrick, J. A. (1988). Intensive interviewing with adolescents. *Western Journal of Nursing Research, 10*(2), 180–194.

Firby, P. (1995). Critiquing the ethical aspects of a study. *Nurse Researcher, 3*(1), 35–41.

Gans, H. J. (1962). *The urban villagers: Group and class in the life of Italian-Americans.* New York: Free Press.

Holloway, I., & Wheeler, S. (1995). Ethical issues in qualitative nursing research. *Nursing Ethics, 2*(3), 223–232.

Lincoln, Y. S., & Guba, E. (1987). Ethics: The failure of positivist science. *Review of Higher Education, 12,* 221–240.

Llewellyn, G. (1995). Qualitative research with people with intellectual disability. *Occupational Therapy International, 2,* 108–127.

Munhall, P. (1988). Ethical considerations in qualitative research. *Western Journal of Nursing Research, 10*(2), 150–162.

Platzer, H., & James, T. (1997). Methodological issues conducting sensitive research on lesbian and gay men's experience of nursing care. *Journal of Advanced Nursing, 25,* 626–633.

Polit, D. F., & Hungler, B. P. (1997). *Nursing research: Methods, appraisal, and utilization* (4th ed.). Philadelphia: Lippincott.

Punch, M. (1994). Politics and ethics in qualitative research. In N. K. Denzin & Y. S. Lincoln (Eds.), *Handbook of qualitative research* (pp. 86–97). Thousand Oaks, CA: Sage.

Ramos, M. C. (1989). Some ethical implications of qualitative research. *Research in Nursing and Health, 12,* 57–63.

Raudonis, B. A. (1992). Ethical considerations in qualitative research with hospice patients. *Qualitative Health Research, 2*(2), 238–249.

Robley, L. R. (1995). The ethics of qualitative nursing research. *Journal of Professional Nursing, 11*(1), 45–48.

Phenomenology as Method

Phenomenology has been and continues to be an integral field of inquiry that cuts across philosophic, sociologic, and psychologic disciplines. This rigorous, critical, systematic method of investigation is a recognized qualitative research approach applicable to the study of phenomenon important to the discipline of nursing. Phenomenological inquiry brings to language perceptions of human experience with all types of phenomena. Because professional nursing practice is enmeshed in people's life experiences, phenomenology as a research method is well suited to the investigation of phenomena important to nursing. As noted by Beck (1994), "Phenomenology affords nursing new ways to interpret the nature of consciousness in the world" (p. 499).

Phenomenological inquiry continues to be a developing science in terms of its application to nursing as a research method. This chapter addresses a variety of methodological interpretations related to the discipline of phenomenological inquiry. It incorporates a discussion of the fundamental differences between descriptive and interpretive phenomenology. Highlights of specific elements and interpretations of this research method provide readers with a beginning understanding of common phenomenological language and themes. This chapter also addresses methodological concerns specific to conducting a phenomenological investigation. It provides introductory concepts for researchers interested in phenomenological investigation and should ideally move researchers to seek out additional related readings that are necessary to acquire an in-depth understanding of the approach.

Phenomenology Defined

Phenomenology is a science whose purpose is to describe particular phenomena, or the appearance of things, as lived experience. Cohen (1987) has pointed out that phenomenology was first described as the study of phenomena or things by Immanual Kant in 1764. Merleau-Ponty (1962) answered the question, What is phenomenology?, in the preface to his text *Phenomenology of Perception*. His description reflects the flow of phenomenological thinking and makes clear that, to this day, this question has not been answered. Merleau-Ponty offered the following description:

Phenomenology is the study of essences; and according to it, all problems amount to finding definitions of essences: the essence of perception, or the essence of consciousness, for example. But phenomenology is also a philosophy which puts essences back into existence, and does not expect to arrive at an understanding of man and the world from any starting point other than that of their "facticity." It is a transcendental philosophy which places in abeyance the assertions arising out of the natural attitude, the better to understand them: but it is also a philosophy for which the world is always "already there" before reflection begins—as an inalienable presence; and all its efforts are concentrated upon re-achieving a direct and primitive contact with the world, and endowing that contact with a philosophical status. It is the search for a philosophy which shall be a "rigorous science," but it also offers an account of space, time and the world as we "live" them. It tries to give a direct description of our experience as it is, without taking account of its psychological origin and the causal explanations which the scientist, the historian or the sociologist may be able to provide. (p. vii)

Herbert Spiegelberg (1975) is perhaps best known as the historian of the phenomenological movement. He defined phenomenology as "the name for a philosophical movement whose primary objective is the direct investigation and description of phenomena as consciously experienced, without theories about their causal explanation and as free as possible from unexamined preconceptions and presuppositions" (p. 3).

Spiegelberg (1975) and Merleau-Ponty (1962) described phenomenology as both a philosophy and a method. Phenomenology was further explained by Wagner (1983) as a way of viewing ourselves, others, and everything else whom or with which we come in contact in life. "Phenomenology is a system of interpretation that helps us perceive and conceive ourselves, our contacts and interchanges with others, and everything else in the realm of our experiences in a variety of ways, including to describe a method as well as a philosophy or way of thinking" (Wagner, 1983, p. 8).

Omery (1983) addressed the question, What is the phenomenological method? Although researchers have interpreted this question in a variety of ways, the approach is inductive and descriptive in its design. Phenomenological method is "the trick of making things whose meanings seem clear, meaningless, and then, discovering what they mean" (Blumensteil, 1973, p. 189).

Lived experience of the world of everyday life is the central focus of phenomenological inquiry. Schutz (1970) described the world of everyday life as the "total sphere of experiences of an individual which is circumscribed by the objects, persons, and events encountered in the pursuit of the pragmatic objectives of living" (p. 320). In other words, it is the lived experience that presents to the individual what is true or real in his or her life. Furthermore, it is this lived experience that gives meaning to each individual's perception of a particular phenomenon and is influenced by everything internal and external to the individual. Perception is important in phenomenological philosophy and method, as explained by Merleau-Ponty (1956):

> Perception is not a science of the world, nor even an act, a deliberate taking up of a position. It is the basis from which every act issues and it is presupposed by them. The world is not an object the law of whose constitution I possess. It is the natural milieu and the field of all my thoughts and of all my explicit perceptions. Truth does not "dwell" only in the "interior man" for there is no interior man. Man is before himself in the world and it is in the world that he knows himself. When I turn upon myself from the dogmatism of common sense or the dogmatism of science, I find, not the dwelling place of intrinsic truth, but a subject committed to the world. (p. 62)

Phenomenology is as much a way of thinking or perceiving as it is a method. The goal of phenomenology is to describe lived experience. To further clarify both the philosophy and method of phenomenology, it is helpful to gain a sense of how the movement developed historically. An overview of the roots of phenomenology as a philosophy and science follows.

Phenomenological Roots

The phenomenological movement began around the first decade of the 20th century. This philosophic movement consisted of three phases: (1) Preparatory, (2) German, and (3) French. The following describes common themes of phenomenology within the context of these three phases.

PREPARATORY PHASE

The Preparatory phase was dominated by Franz Brentano (1838–1917) and Carl Stumpf (1848–1936). Stumpf was Brentano's first prominent student, and through his work demonstrated the scientific rigor of phenomenology. Clarification of the concept of intentionality was the primary focus during this time (Spiegelberg, 1965). *Intentionality* means that consciousness is always consciousness of something. Merleau-Ponty (1956) explained that "interior perception is impossible without exterior perception, that the world as the connection of phenomena is anticipated in the consciousness of my unity and is the way for me to realize myself in consciousness" (p. 67). Therefore, one does not hear without hearing something or believe without believing something (Cohen, 1987).

GERMAN PHASE

Edmund Husserl (1857–1938) and Martin Heidegger (1889–1976) were the prominent leaders during the German or second phase of the phenomenological movement. Husserl (1931, 1965) believed that philosophy should become a rigorous science that would restore contact with deeper human concerns and that phenomenology should become the foundation for all philosophy and science. According to Spiegelberg (1965), Heidegger followed so closely in the steps of Husserl that his work is probably a direct outcome of Husserl's. The concepts of essences, intuiting, and phenomenological reduction were developed during the German phase (Spiegelberg, 1965).

Essences are elements related to the ideal or true meaning of something, that is, those concepts that give common understanding to the phenomenon under investigation. Essences emerge in both isolation and in relationship to one other. According to Natanson (1973), "Essences are unities of meaning intended by different individuals in the same acts or by the same individuals in different acts" (p. 14). Essences, therefore, represent the basic units of common understanding of any phenomenon. For example, in a study on the meaning of commitment to nursing (Rinaldi, 1989), the essences (or basic units of common understanding of the phenomenon of commitment) related to commitment to nursing included altruism, devotion, dedication, caring, being there, trust, loyalty, and nurturance. In another study by Zalon (1997) entitled, "Pain in Frail, Elderly Women After Surgery," the three major themes or essences described were the immediate reality of pain, security, and dealing with pain. "The immediate reality of pain consisted of the feeling, awareness, and past imposing on the present. Security consisted of comfort and trust. Dealing with pain consisted of endurance, control, and self-discovery of strategies, the most predominant of which was being still to relieve pain" (Zalon, 1997, p. 21).

Intuiting is an eidetic comprehension or accurate interpretation of what is meant in the description of the phenomenon under investigation. The intuitive process in phenomenological research results in a common understanding about the phenomenon under investigation. Intuiting in the phenomenological sense requires that researchers imaginatively vary the data until a common understanding about the phenomenon emerges. Through imaginative variation, researchers begin to wonder about the phenomenon under investigation in relationship to the various descriptions generated. To further illustrate, in the study on commitment to nursing (Rinaldi, 1989), the essences of commitment gleaned from the data were varied in as many ways as possible and compared with participants' descriptions. From this imaginative variation, a relationship between the essences of commitment and to whom or what the nurse was committed emerged. For example, the nurse may be committed to clients, colleagues, the employing institution, the profession, or self. To whom or what the nurse is committed is then examined in relationship to the essences of commitment. Researchers might vary the essences of commitment with each example of the person to whom or thing to which the nurse is committed. Some essences may apply when the issue is commitment to clients and other essences if the issue is commitment to the institution.

Phenomenological reduction is a return to original awareness regarding the phenomenon under investigation. Husserl specified how to describe, with scientific exactness, the life of consciousness in its original encounter with the world through phenomenological reduction. Husserl (1931, 1965) challenged individuals to go "back to the things themselves" to recover this original awareness. Husserl's reference "to the things" meant "a fresh approach to concretely experienced phenomena, as free as possible from conceptual presuppositions and an attempt to describe them as faithfully as possible" (Spiegelberg, 1975, p. 10).

Phenomenological reduction begins with a suspension of beliefs, assumptions, and biases about the phenomenon under investigation. Isolation of pure phenomenon, versus what is already known about a particular phenomena, is the goal of the reductive procedure. The only way to really see the world clearly is to remain as free as possible from preconceived ideas or notions. Complete reduction may never be possible because of the intimate relationship individuals have with the world (Merleau-Ponty, 1956).

As part of the reductive process, phenomenological researchers must first identify any preconceived notions or ideas about the phenomenon under investigation. Having identified these ideas, the researchers must bracket or separate out of consciousness what they know or believe about the topic under investigation. *Bracketing* requires researchers to remain neutral with respect to belief or disbelief in the existence of the phenomenon. Bracketing begins the reductive process and, like that process, must continue throughout the investigation. Essentially, researchers set aside previous knowledge or personal beliefs about the phenomenon under investigation to prevent this information from interfering with the recovery of a pure description of the phenomenon. Bracketing must be constant and ongoing if descriptions are to achieve their purest form.

FRENCH PHASE

Gabriel Marcel (1889–1973), Jean Paul Sartre (1905–1980), and Maurice Merleau-Ponty (1905–1980) were the predominant leaders of the French or third phase of the phenomenological movement. The primary concepts developed during this phase were embodiment and being-in-the-world. These concepts refer to the belief that all acts are constructed on foundations of perception or original awareness of some phenomenon. Lived experience, given in the perceived world, must be described (Merleau-Ponty, 1956). Munhall (1989) explained these key concepts, originally described by Merleau-Ponty, as follows:

> Embodiment explains that through consciousness one is aware of being-in-the-world and it is through the body that one gains access to this world. One feels, thinks, tastes, touches, hears, and is conscious through the opportunities the body offers. There is talk sometimes about ex-

panding the mind or expanding waistlines. The expansion is within the body, within the consciousness. It is important to understand that at any point in time and for each individual a particular perspective and/or consciousness exists. It is based on the individual's history, knowledge of the world, and perhaps openness to the world. Nursing's focus on the individual and the "meaning" events may have for an individual, is this recognition that experience is individually interpreted. (p. 24)

Phenomenology is a dynamic philosophy that evolved and changed throughout the movement. Different philosophers may have different interpretations of phenomenology as both a philosophy and method. The dynamic nature and evolving interpretations provide phenomenological researchers with a variety of options from which to choose when embarking on an investigation of this nature. The following presents these options, along with other issues related to actually conducting a phenomenological investigation.

At this juncture are words of caution: Imperative to gaining an in-depth understanding of the method and philosophy of phenomenology is a return to the original works. Readers should take the time to read the works of Husserl, Heidegger, Merleau-Ponty, Spiegelberg, and others to ensure a solid foundation and understanding of the philosophy behind the method. It is also advised that beginning researchers connect with a mentor who can guide their development in the area of phenomenology. Paley (1997) suggested that "a problematic feature of the way in which phenomenology has been imported into nursing is that sources tend to be second–hand and several 'tiers' in the literature are apparent" (p. 187). Paley's work offers an excellent discursive addressing how original concepts can become distorted when interpreted secondhand. It provides an important lesson and reminder to researchers who are embarking on a phenomenological investigation to return to the original works.

Fundamental Characteristics of the Phenomenological Method

Phenomenology as a research method is a rigorous, critical, systematic investigation of phenomena. "The purpose of phenomenological inquiry is to explicate the structure or essence of the lived experience of a phenomenon in the search for the unity of meaning which is the identification of the essence of a phenomenon, and its accurate description through the everyday lived experience" (Rose, Beeby, & Parker, 1995, p. 1124).

Several procedural interpretations of phenomenological method are available as guidelines to this research approach (Colaizzi, 1978; Giorgi, 1985; Munhall & Boyd, 1993; Paterson & Zderad, 1976; Spiegelberg, 1965, 1975; Streubert, 1991; van Kaam, 1959; van Manen, 1984). Because there is more than one legitimate way to proceed with a phenomenological investigation, the appropriateness of the method to the phenomenon of interest should guide the method choice. Table 4-1 provides an overview of the various procedural interpretations documented. See Chapter 5 for samples of research that apply the approaches described in Table 4-1.

SIX CORE STEPS

Spiegelberg (1965, 1975) identified a core of steps or elements central to phenomenological investigations. These six steps are (1) descriptive phenomenology, (2) phenomenology of essences, (3) phenomenology of appearances, (4) constitutive phenomenology, (5) reductive phenomenology, and (6) hermeneutic phenomenology (Spiegelberg, 1975). A discussion of each of the six elements follows. Researchers do not need to adopt all the steps to consider them method. Most commonly, phenomenological researchers will use descriptive phenomenology, phenomenology of essences, and reductive phenomenology. Hermeneutic or interpretive phenomenology is discussed as an interpretation that really is separate in itself. As Spiegelberg (1965) has explained, the purpose of this discussion is to "present this method as a series of steps, of which the later will usually presuppose the earlier ones, yet not be necessarily entailed by them" (p. 655).

DESCRIPTIVE PHENOMENOLOGY
Descriptive phenomenology involves "direct exploration, analysis, and description of particular phenomena, as free as possible from unexamined presuppositions, aiming at maximum intuitive presentation" (Spiegelberg, 1975, p. 57). Descriptive phenomenology stimulates our perception of lived experience while emphasizing the richness, breadth, and depth of those experiences (Spiegelberg, 1975, p. 70). Spiegelberg (1965, 1975) identified a three-step process for descriptive phenomenology: (1) intuiting, (2) analyzing, and (3) describing.

INTUITING
The first step, *intuiting,* requires the researcher to become totally immersed in the phenomenon under investigation and is the process whereby the researcher begins to know about the phenomenon as described by the participants. The researcher avoids all criticism, evaluation, or opinion and pays strict attention to the phenomenon under investigation as it is being described (Spiegelberg, 1965, 1975).

The step of intuiting the phenomenon in a study of quality of life would involve the "researcher as instrument" in the interview process. The researcher becomes the tool for data collection and listens to individual descriptions of quality of life through the interview process. The researcher then studies the data as they are transcribed and reviews repeatedly what the participants have described as the meaning of quality of life.

(*text continues on page 52*)

Table 4-1 Methodological Interpretations

Author	Procedural Steps

van Kaam (1959)	1. Obtain a core of common experiences
	2. List and prepare a rough preliminary grouping of every expression presented by participants
	3. Reduce and eliminate
	   Test each expression for two requirements:
	   A. Does it contain a moment of the experience that might eventually be a necessary and sufficient constituent of the experience?
	   B. If so, is it possible to abstract this moment and to label it, without violating the formulation presented by the participant? Expressions not meeting these two requirements are eliminated. Concrete, vague, and overlapping expressions are reduced to more exactly descriptive terms. Example: "I feel like I could pull my hair out by the roots" could be reduced to "feelings of frustration."
	4. Tentatively identify the descriptive constituents; bring together all common relevant constituents in a cluster labeled with the more abstract formula expressing the common theme
	5. Finally, identify the descriptive constituents by application; this operation consists of checking the tentatively identified constituents against random cases of the sample to see whether they fulfill the following conditions: Each constituent must:
	   (a) be expressed explicitly in the description
	   (b) be expressed explicitly or implicitly in some or the large majority of descriptions
	   (c) be compatible with the description in which it is not expressed
	   (d) if a description is found incompatible with a constituent, the description must be proven not to be an expression of the experience under study, but of some other experience that intrudes on it

Giorgi (1985)	1. Read the entire description of the experience to get a sense of the whole 2. Reread the description 3. Identify the transition units of the experience 4. Clarify and elaborate the meaning by relating constituents to each other and to the whole 5. Reflect on the constituents in the concrete language of the participant 6. Transform concrete language into the language or concepts of science 7. Integrate and synthesize the insight into a descriptive structure of the meaning of the experience
Paterson & Zderad (1976)	1. Compare and study instances of the phenomenon wherever descriptions of it may be found (putting descriptions in a logbook) 2. Imaginatively vary the phenomenon

3. Explain through negation
4. Explain through analogy and metaphor
5. Classify the phenomenon

Colaizzi (1978)

1. Describe the phenomenon of interest
2. Collect participant's description of phenomenon
3. Read all participant's descriptions of the phenomenon
4. Return the original transcripts and extract significant statements
5. Try to spell out the meaning of each significant statement
6. Organize the aggregate formalized meanings into clusters of themes
7. Write an exhaustive description
8. Return to the participants for validation of the description
9. If new data are revealed during the validation, incorporate them into an exhaustive description

van Manen (1984)

1. Turn to the nature of lived experience by orienting to the phenomenon, formulating the phenomenological question, and explicating assumptions and pre-understandings
2. Engage in existential investigation, which involves exploring the phenomenon: generating data, using personal experience as a starting point, tracing etymological sources; searching idiomatic phrases, obtaining experiential descriptions from participants, locating experiential descriptions in the literature, and consulting phenomenological literature, art, and so forth.
3. Engage in phenomenological reflection, which involves conducting thematic analysis, uncovering thematic aspects in life-world descriptions, isolating thematic statements, composing linguistic transformations, and gleaning thematic descriptions from artistic sources
4. Engage in phenomenological writing, which includes attending to the speaking of language, varying the examples, writing, and rewriting

Streubert (1991)

1. Explicate a personal description of the phenomenon of interest
2. Bracket the researcher's presuppositions
3. Interview participants in unfamiliar settings
4. Carefully read the interview transcripts to obtain a general sense of the experience
5. Review the transcripts to uncover essences
6. Apprehend essential relationships
7. Develop formalized descriptions of the phenomenon
8. Return to participants to validate descriptions
9. Review the relevant literature
10. Distribute the findings to the nursing community

ANALYZING

The second step is *phenomenological analyzing,* which involves identifying the essence of the phenomenon under investigation based on data obtained and how the data are presented. As the researcher distinguishes the phenomenon with regard to elements or constituents, he or she explores the relationships and connections with adjacent phenomena (Spiegelberg 1965, 1975).

As the researcher listens to descriptions of quality of life and dwells with the data, common themes or essences will begin to emerge. Dwelling with the data essentially involves complete immersion in the generated data to fully engage in this analytical process. The researcher must dwell with the data for as long as necessary to ensure a pure and accurate description.

DESCRIBING

The third step is *phenomenological describing.* The aim of the describing operation is to communicate and bring to written and verbal description distinct, critical elements of the phenomenon. The description is based on a classification or grouping of the phenomenon. The researcher must avoid attempting to describe a phenomenon prematurely. Premature description is a common methodological error associated with this type of research (Spiegelberg, 1965, 1975). Description is an integral part of intuiting and analyzing. Although addressed separately, intuiting and analyzing are often occurring simultaneously.

In a study on quality of life, phenomenological describing would involve classifying all critical elements or essences that are common to the lived experience of quality of life and describing these essences in detail. Critical elements or essences are described singularly and then within the context of their relationship to one another. A discussion of this relationship follows.

PHENOMENOLOGY OF ESSENCES

Phenomenology of essences involves probing through the data to search for common themes or essences and establishing patterns of relationships shared by particular phenomena. *Free imaginative variation,* used to apprehend essential relationships between essences, involves careful study of concrete examples supplied by the participants' experiences and systematic variation of these examples in the imagination. In this way, it becomes possible to gain insights into the essential structures and relationships among phenomena. Probing for essences provides a sense for what is essential and what is accidental in the phenomenological description (Spiegelberg, 1975). The researcher follows through with the steps of intuiting, analyzing, and describing in this second core step (Spiegelberg, 1965, 1975). According to Spiegelberg (1975), "Phenomenology in its descriptive stage can stimulate our perceptiveness for the richness of our experience in breadth and in depth" (p. 70).

PHENOMENOLOGY OF APPEARANCES

Phenomenology of appearances involves giving attention to the ways in which phenomena appear. In watching the ways in which phenomena appear, the researcher pays particular attention to the different ways in which an object presents itself. Phenomenology of appearances focuses attention on the phenomenon as it unfolds through dwelling with the data. Phenomenology of appearances "can heighten the sense for the inexhaustibility of the perspectives through which our world is given" (Spiegelberg, 1975, p. 70).

CONSTITUTIVE PHENOMENOLOGY

Constitutive phenomenology is studying phenomena as they become established or "constituted" in our consciousness. Constitutive phenomenology "means the process in which the phenomena 'take shape' in our consciousness, as we advance from first impressions to a full 'picture' of their structure" (Spiegelberg, 1975, p. 66). According to Spiegelberg (1975), constitutive phenomenology "can develop the sense for the dynamic adventure in our relationship with the world" (p. 70).

REDUCTIVE PHENOMENOLOGY

Reductive phenomenology, although addressed as a separate process, occurs concurrently throughout a phenomenological investigation. The researcher continually addresses personal biases, assumptions, and presuppositions and brackets or sets aside these beliefs to obtain the purest description of the phenomenon under investigation. Suspending judgment can make us more aware of the precariousness of all our claims to knowledge, "a ground for epistomological humility" (Spiegelberg, 1975, p. 70).

This step is critical for the preservation of objectivity in the phenomenological method. For example, in a study investigating the meaning of quality of life for individuals with type I (insulin-dependent) diabetes mellitus, the investigator begins the study with the reductive process. The researcher identifies all presuppositions, biases, or assumptions he or she holds about what quality of life means or what it is like to have diabetes. This process involves a critical self-examination of personal beliefs and an acknowledgment of understandings that the researcher has gained from experience. The researcher takes all he or she knows about the phenomenon and brackets it or sets it aside in an effort to keep what is already known separate from the lived experience as described by the participants.

Phenomenological reduction is critical if the researcher is to achieve pure description. The reductive process is also the basis for postponing any review of the literature until the researcher has analyzed the data. The researcher must always keep separate from the participants' descriptions what he or she knows or believes about the phenomenon under investigation. Therefore, postponing the literature review until data analysis is complete facilitates phenomenological reduction.

INTERPRETIVE OR HERMENEUTIC PHENOMENOLOGY

Interpretive frameworks within phenomenology are used to search out the relationships and meanings that knowledge and context have for each other (Lincoln & Guba, 1985). A phenomenological–hermeneutic approach is essentially the interpretation of phenomena appearing in text or the written word. Hermeneutics as an interpretive approach is based in part on the work of Ricoeur (1976). According to Allen and Jensen (1990),

> The value of knowledge in nursing is, in part, determined by its relevance to and significance for an understanding of the human experience. In order to obtain that understanding, nursing requires modes of inquiry that offer the freedom to explore the richness of this experience. Hermeneutics offers such a mode of inquiry. With this interpretive strategy, a means is provided for arriving at a deeper understanding of human existence through attention to the nature of language and meaning. (p. 241)

Heidegger (1927/1962) and Gadamer (1976) have been connected with hermeneutic analysis. Hermeneutic phenomenology is a "special kind of phenomenological interpretation, designed to unveil otherwise concealed meanings in the phenomena" (Spiegelberg, 1975, p. 57). Gadamer (1976) elaborated by noting that hermeneutics bridges the gap between what is familiar in our worlds and what is unfamiliar: "Its field of application is comprised of all those situations in which we encounter meanings that are not immediately understandable but require interpretive effort" (p. xii).

The theory of interpretation is closely tied to the concept of text (Ricoeur, 1981). Ricoeur (1976) described the interpretive process as a series of analytical steps. First, the researcher reads the text as a whole to become familiar with the text and begins to formulate thoughts about its meaning for further analysis. Structural analysis follows and involves identifying patterns of meaningful connection. This step is often referred to as an *interpretive reading*. Interpretation of the whole follows and involves reflecting on the initial reading along with the interpretive reading to ensure a comprehensive understanding of the findings. Several readings are usually required.

Ricoeur (1981) has addressed the difference between text and discourse, referring to these differences as distancing. The four principles of distancing are (1) the transcription itself and the meaning of the written word, (2) the relationship between what has been written and the intent of the person who wrote the text, (3) the meaning of the text beyond its original intent as well as the author's original intent, and (4) the new interpreted meaning of the written word and the audience. As described by Allen and Jenson (1990),

The hermeneutical circle of interpretation moves forward and backward, starting at the present. It is never closed or final. Through rigorous interaction and understanding, the phenomenon is uncovered. The interpretive process that underlies meaning arises out of interactions, working outward and back from self to event and event to self. (p. 245)

Allen and Jenson (1990) illustrated the application of hermeneutical inquiry in their exploration of what it means to have eye problems and to be visually impaired. Their example emphasizes the applicability of hermeneutics in the description and explanation of human phenomena. According to Allen and Jenson (1990),

The task . . . of modern hermeneutics is to describe and explain human phenomena (such as health and illness). The purpose of hermeneutical description and explanation is to achieve understanding through interpretation of the phenomena under study. It is the written description of the phenomena (text) that is the object of interpretation. (p. 242)

Interpretive phenomenology is a valuable method for the study of phenomena relevant to nursing education, research, and practice. Several investigations have used interpretive phenomenology in areas such as education evaluation (Diekelmann, Allen, & Tanner 1989), ethically difficult care situations (Anstrom, Jansson, Norberg, & Hallberg, 1993), research on aging (Ramhoj & de Oliveira, 1991), and the conduct of clinical interviews (Dzurec & Coleman, 1997).

Examples of the different interpretations describing phenomenology are outlined in Table 4-1. Applying any of these interpretations to a particular investigation will require a careful examination of the researcher's role, generation and treatment of data, and ethical issues connected with a phenomenological investigation. A discussion of these topics that relate to the selection of phenomenology as a research method follows.

Selection of Phenomenology as a Method

How do researchers decide to use the phenomenological method for a topic needing investigation? What phenomena important to nursing lend themselves to this type of qualitative investigation? The answers to these questions are grounded in nursing's philosophic beliefs about humans and the holistic nature of professional nursing.

Nursing encourages detailed attention to the care of people as humans and grounds its practice in a holistic belief system that cares for mind, body, and spirit. Holistic care and avoidance of reductionism is at the center of professional nursing practice. The holistic approach to nursing is rooted in the nursing experience and is not imposed artificially from without. Just as caring for only part of the client is inconsistent with nursing practice, so, too, is the study of humans by breaking them down into parts. The following example illustrates the nature of holistic nursing practice. When caring for a client who has had a mastectomy, the nurse not only addresses body image but also the effect the surgery may have on family, work, and psychologic well-being. The nurse might ask, "How are you feeling about your surgery?" or "What kinds of changes in your life do you anticipate as a result of your mastectomy?" These questions elicit more about the client as a person, with a life and feelings as opposed to a question such as, "Do you want to look at the scar?" That question deals only with the body part removed.

Because phenomenological inquiry requires that the integrated whole be explored, it is a suitable method for the investigation of phenomena important to nursing practice, education, and administration. Spiegelberg (1965) remarked that phenomenological method investigates subjective phenomena in the belief that essential truths about reality are grounded in lived experience. What is important is the experience as it is presented, not what anyone thinks or says about it. Therefore, investigation of phenomena important to nursing requires that researchers study lived experience as it is presented in the everyday world of nursing practice, education, and administration.

A holistic perspective and the study of experience as lived serve as foundations for phenomenological inquiry. A positive response to the following several questions will help researchers clarify if phenomenological method is the most appropriate approach for the investigation. First, researchers should ask, Is there a need for further clarity on the chosen phenomenon? Evidence leading researchers to conclude that they need further clarity may be that there is little if anything published on a subject, or perhaps what is published needs to be described in more depth. Second, researchers should consider the question, Will the shared lived experience be the best data source for the phenomenon under investigation? Because the primary method of data collection is the voice of the people experiencing a particular phenomenon, researchers must determine that this approach will provide the richest and most descriptive data. Third, as in all research, investigators should ask, What are the available resources, the time frame for the completion of the research, the audience to which the research will be presented, and my own personal style and ability to engage in the method in a rigorous manner?

Topics appropriate to phenomenological research method include those central to humans' life experiences. Examples include happiness, fear, being there, commitment, being a chairperson, being a head nurse, or the meaning of stress for nursing students in the clinical setting. Health-related topics suitable for phenomenological investigation might include the meaning of pain, quality of life with a particular chronic illness, or loss of a body part. Chapter 5 offers readers a selective sample of published research using phenomenological research methodology in the areas of practice, education, and administration.

Elements and Interpretations of the Method

RESEARCHER'S ROLE

As lived experience becomes the description of a particular phenomenon, the investigator takes on specific responsibilities in transforming the information. Reinharz (1983) articulated five steps that occur in phenomenological transformation as the investigator makes public what essentially was private knowledge. The first transformation occurs as people's experiences are transformed into language. During this step, the researcher, through verbal interaction, creates an opportunity for the lived experience to be shared (Reinharz, 1983). In the example of research on quality of life for individuals with type I diabetes mellitus, the researcher would create an opportunity for individuals living with this chronic illness to share their experiences related to the meaning of quality of life.

The second transformation occurs as the researcher transforms what is seen and heard into an understanding of the original experience. Because one person can never experience what another person has experienced in exactly the same manner, researchers must rely on the data participants have shared about a particular experience and, from those evelop their own transformation (Reinharz, 1983). In this instance, the her studying quality of life takes what participants have said and produces a description that lends understanding to the participants' original experiences.

Third, the researcher transforms what is understood about the phenomenon under investigation into conceptual categories that are the essences of the original experience (Reinharz, 1983). Data analysis of interviews addressing the meaning of quality of life would involve clarifying the essences of the phenomenon. For example, the data may reveal that quality of life for an individual with type I diabetes mellitus may center around freedom from restrictions in daily activities, independence, and prevention of long-term complications.

Fourth, the researcher transforms those essences into a written document that captures what the researcher has thought about the experience and reflects the participants' descriptions or actions. In all transformations, information may be lost or gained; therefore, it is important to have participants review the final description to ensure the material is correctly stated and nothing has been added or deleted (Reinharz, 1983).

Fifth, the researcher transforms the written document into an understanding that can function to clarify all preceding steps (Reinharz, 1983). The intent of this written document, often referred to as the exhaustive description, is to synthesize and capture the meaning of the experience into written form without distorting or losing the richness of the data. In other words, the exhaustive description of quality of life would reveal the richness of the experience identified from the very beginning of the investigation as perceived by individuals with type I diabetes mellitus.

In addition to the five transformational steps outlined by Reinharz (1983), the investigator must possess certain qualities that will permit access to data participants possess. The ability to communicate clearly and help participants feel comfortable expressing their experiences are essential qualities in a phenomenological researcher. The researcher is the instrument for data collection and must function effectively to facilitate data collection. The researcher must recognize that personal characteristics such as manner of speaking, gender, age, and other personality traits may interfere with data retrieval. For this reason, researchers must ask whether they are the appropriate people to access a given person's or group's experiences (Reinharz, 1983).

DATA GENERATION

Purposeful sampling is used most commonly in phenomenological inquiry. This method of sampling selects individuals for study participation based on their particular knowledge of a phenomenon for the purpose of sharing that knowledge. "The logic and power of purposeful sampling lies in selecting information-rich cases for study in depth. Information-rich cases are those from which one can learn a great deal about issues of central importance to the purpose of the research, thus the term purposeful sampling" (Patton, 1990, p. 169).

Sample selection provides the participants for the investigation. Researchers should contact participants, once they have agreed to participate, before the interview to prepare them for the actual meeting and to answer any preliminary questions. At the time of the first interview, the researcher may obtain informed consent and permission to tape-record if using this data-gathering instrument. Piloting interview skills and having a more experienced phenomenological researcher listen to the tape of an interview can assist in the development of interviewing skills. According to Benoliel (1988), an "effective observer–interviewer needs to bring knowledge, sensitivity, and flexibility into a situation. Interviewing is not an interpersonal exchange controlled by the interviewer but rather a transaction that is reciprocal in nature and involves an exchange of social rewards" (p. 211).

Researchers should help participants describe lived experience without leading the discussion. Open-ended, clarifying questions such as the following facilitate this process: What comes to mind when you hear the word *commitment?* What comes to mind when you think about quality of life? Open-ended interviewing allows researchers to follow participants' lead, to ask clarifying questions, and to facilitate the expression of the participants' lived experience. Interviews usually end when participants believe they have exhausted their descriptions. If interviews are not feasible, researchers may ask participants to write an extensive description of some phenomenon by responding to a preestablished question or questions. The concern with written responses versus tape-recorded interviews is that saturation may not be achieved. During the interview, researchers can help participants explain things in more detail by asking questions. This valuable opportunity is eliminated when participants write their descriptions.

The interview allows entrance into another person's world and is an excellent source of data. Complete concentration and rigorous participation in the interview process improves the accuracy, trustworthiness, and authenticity of the data. However, researchers must remember to remain centered on the data, listen attentively, avoid interrogating participants, and treat participants with respect and sincere interest in the shared experience.

Data generation or collection continues until the researcher believes saturation has been achieved, that is, when no new themes or essences have emerged from the participants and the data are repeating. Therefore, predetermination of the number of participants for a given study is impossible. Data collection must continue until the researcher is assured saturation has been achieved.

As noted in Chapter 2 of this text, Morse (1989) stated that saturation is a myth. She proposed that, given another group of informants on the same subject at another time, new data may be revealed. Therefore, investigators will be able to reach saturation only with a particular group of informants and only during specific times. "The long term challenge for the phenomenologist interested in generating theory is to interview several samples from a variety of backgrounds, age ranges and cultural environments to maximize the likelihood of discovering the essences of phenomena across groups" (Streubert, 1991, p. 121).

ETHICAL CONSIDERATIONS

The personal nature of phenomenological research results in several ethical considerations for researchers. Informed consent differs in a qualitative study as opposed to a quantitative investigation. There is no way to know exactly what might transpire during an interview. Researchers must consider issues of privacy. When preparing a final manuscript, researchers must determine how to present the data so that they are accurate yet do not reveal participants' identities. For an in-depth discussion of ethical issues in qualitative research, see Chapter 3.

DATA TREATMENT

Researchers may handle treatment of the data in a variety of ways. Use of open-ended interviewing techniques, tape recordings, and verbatim transcriptions will increase the accuracy of data collection. High-quality tape-recording equipment is essential. Researchers will also make handwritten notes. Adding handwritten notes to verbally transcribed accounts helps to achieve the most comprehensive and accurate description. A second interview may be needed, giving researchers an opportunity to expand, verify, and add descriptions of the phenomenon under investigation and assist participants in clarifying and expounding on inadequate descriptions. In addition, often participants will have additional thoughts about the phenomenon under study after the initial interview. Following an interview, researchers should immediately listen to the tape, checking that the interview made sense and verifying the need for a follow-up interview. Also, researchers should make extensive, detailed notes immediately following the interview in case the tape recording has failed.

When data collection begins, so, too, does data analysis. From the moment researchers begin listening to descriptions of a particular phenomenon, analysis is occurring. These processes are inseparable. Therefore, the importance of the reductive process cannot be overemphasized. Separating one's beliefs and assumptions from the raw data occurs throughout the investigation. Journaling helps in continuing the reductive process. Researchers' use of a journal can facilitate phenomenological reduction. Writing down any ideas, feelings, or responses that emerge during data collection supports reductive phenomenology. Drew (1989) has offered the added perspective that journaling that addresses a researcher's own experience can be "considered data and examined within the context of the study for the part it has played in the study's results" (p. 431).

Following data collection and verbatim transcription, researchers should listen to the tapes while reading the transcriptions for accuracy. This step will help to familiarize them with the data and begin immersing them in the phenomenon under investigation.

DATA ANALYSIS

Data analysis requires that researchers dwell with or become immersed in the data. The purpose of data analysis, according to Banonis (1989), is to preserve the uniqueness of each participant's lived experience while permitting an understanding of the phenomenon under investigation. This begins with listening to participants' verbal descriptions and is followed by reading and rereading the verbatim transcriptions or written responses. As researchers become immersed in the data, they may identify and extract significant statements. They can then transcribe these statements onto index cards or recorded in a data management file for ease of ordering later in the process. Apprehending or capturing the essential relationships among the statements and preparing an exhaustive description of the phenomenon constitute the final phase. Through free imaginative variation, researchers make connections between statements obtained in the interview process. It is critical to identify how statements or central themes emerged and are connected to one another if the final description is to be comprehensive and exhaustive.

Microcomputers and word processing software can make data storage and retrieval more efficient. Examining available software packages for qualitative data analysis may be an appropriate option, depending on researchers' personal preferences. See Table 2–2 for an overview of available software for data storage, retrieval, and analysis.

REVIEW OF THE LITERATURE

The review of literature follows data analysis. The rationale for postponing the literature review is related to the goal of achieving a pure description of the phenomenon under investigation. The fewer ideas or preconceived notions researchers have about the phenomenon under investigation, the less likely their biases will influence the research.

Once data analysis is complete, researchers review the literature to place the findings within the context of what is already known about the topic. Researchers may do a cursory review of the literature before fully developing the study to verify the need for the investigation.

TRUSTWORTHINESS AND AUTHENTICITY OF DATA

The issue of trustworthiness in qualitative research has been a concern for researchers engaging in these methods and is discussed at length in the literature (Beck, 1993; Krefting, 1991; Yonge & Stewin, 1988). The issue of rigor in qualitative research is important to the practice of good science.

The trustworthiness of the questions put to study participants depends on the extent to which they tap the participants' experiences apart from the participants' theoretical knowledge of the topic (Colaizzi, 1978). Consistent use of the method and bracketing prior knowledge helps to ensure pure description of data. To ensure trustworthiness of data analysis, researchers return to each participant and ask if the exhaustive description reflects the participant's experiences. Researchers should incorporate content added or deleted by participants into a revised description.

Requesting negative descriptions of the phenomenon under investigation is helpful in establishing authenticity and trustworthiness of the data. For example, in the study investigating the meaning of quality of life in individuals with type I diabetes mellitus, the researcher may ask, "Can you describe a situation in which you would feel that you did not have quality of life?" This question gives an opportunity to compare and contrast data. For additional discussion of issues surrounding reliability and validity in qualitative research, see Chapter 2.

Summary

Phenomenology is an integral field of inquiry to nursing, as well as philosophy, sociology, and psychology. As a research method, phenomenology is a rigorous science whose purpose is to bring to language human experiences. The phenomenological movement has been influenced by the works of Husserl, Brentano, Stumpf, Merleau-Ponty, and others. Concepts central to the method include intentionality, essences, intuiting, reduction, bracketing embodiment, and being-in-the-world.

Phenomenology as a method of research offers nursing an opportunity to describe and clarify phenomena important to practice, education, and research. Researchers selecting this approach for the investigation of phenomena should base their decision on suitability and a need for further clarification of selected phenomenon. They must give specific considerations to the issues of researcher as instrument, data generation, data treatment and authenticity, and trustworthiness of data. Investigations that use this approach contribute to nursing's knowledge base and can provide direction for future investigations.

The relevance of phenomenology as a research method for nursing is clear. Within the qualitative paradigm, this method supports " new initiatives for nursing care where the subject matter is often not amenable to other investigative and experimental methods" (Jasper, 1994, p. 313). Nursing maintains a unique appreciation for caring, commitment, and holism. Phenomena related to nursing can be explored and analyzed by phenomenological methods that have as their goal the description of lived experience.

REFERENCES

Allen, M. N., & Jenson, L. (1990). Hermeneutical inquiry, meaning and scope. *Western Journal of Nursing Research, 12*(2), 241–253.

Anstrom, G., Jansson, L., Norberg, A., & Hallberg, I. R. (1993). Experienced nurses' narratives of their being in ethically difficult care situations: The problem to act in accordance with one's ethical reasoning and feelings. *Cancer Nursing, 16*(3), 179–187.

Banonis, B. C. (1989). The lived experience of recovering from addiction: A phenomenological investigation. *Nursing Science Quarterly, 2*(1), 37–42.

Beck, C. T. (1993). Qualitative research: The evaluation of its credibility, fittingness, and auditability. *Western Journal of Nursing Research, 15*(2), 263–265.

Beck, C. T. (1994). Phenomenology: Its use in nursing research. *International Journal of Nursing Studies, 31*(6), 499–510.

Benoliel, J. Q. (1988). Commentaries on special issue. *Western Journal of Nursing Research, 10*(2), 210–213.

Blumensteil, A. (1973). A sociology of good times. In G. Psathas (Ed.), *Phenomenological sociology: Issues and applications.* New York: Wiley.

Cohen, M. Z. (1987). A historical overview of the phenomenological movement. *Image, 19*(1), 31–34.

Colaizzi, P. F. (1978). Psychological research as the phenomenologist views it. In R. Valle & M. King (Eds.), *Existential phenomenological alternative for psychology* (pp. 48–71). New York: Oxford University Press.

Diekelmann, N., Allen, D., & Tanner, C. (1989). *The NLN criteria for appraisal of baccalaureate programs: A critical hermeneutic analysis* (Pub. No. 15-2253). New York: National League for Nursing Press.

Drew, N. (1989). The interviewer's experience as data in phenomenological research. *Western Journal of Nursing Research, 11*(4), 431–439.

Dzurec, L. C., & Coleman, P. (1997). "What happens after you say hello?" A hermeneutic analysis of the process of conducting clinical interviews. *Journal of Psychosocial Nursing, 35*(8), 31–35.

Gadamer, H. G. (1976). *Philosophical hermeneutics* (D. E. Linge, Trans. & Ed.). Los Angeles, CA: University of California Press.

Giorgi, A. (1985). *Phenomenology and psychological research.* Pittsburgh, PA: Duquesne University Press.

Heidegger, M. (1962). *Being and time.* New York: Harper & Row. (Original work published 1927)

Husserl, E. (1931). *Ideas: General introduction to pure phenomenology* (W. R. Boyce Gibson, Trans.). New York: Collier.

Husserl, E. (1965). *Phenomenology and the crisis of philosophy* (Q. Laver, Trans.). New York: Harper & Row.

Jasper, M. A.(1994). Issues in phenomenology for researchers of nursing. *Journal of Advanced Nursing, 19,* 309–314.

Krefting, L. (1991). Rigor in qualitative research: The assessment of trustworthiness. *The American Journal of Occupational Therapy, 45*(3), 214–222.

Lincoln, Y. S., & Guba, E. G.(1985). *Naturalistic inquiry.* Beverly Hills, CA: Sage.

Merleau-Ponty, M. (1956). What is phenomenology? *Cross Currents, 6,* 59–70.

Merleau-Ponty, M. (1962). *Phenomenology of perception* (C. Smith, Trans.). New York: Humanities Press.

Morse, J. M. (1989). *Qualitative nursing research: A contemporary dialogue.* Rockville, MD: Aspen.

Munhall, P. (1989). Philosophical ponderings on qualitative research. *Nursing Science Quarterly, 2*(1), 20–28.

Munhall, P. L., & Boyd, C. O. (1993). *Nursing research: A qualitative perspective.* New York: National League for Nursing Press.

Natanson, M. (1973). *Edmund Husserl: Philosopher of infinite tasks.* Evanston, IL: Northwestern University Press.

Omery, A. (1983). Phenomenology: A method for nursing research. *Advances in Nursing Science, 5*(2), 49–63.

Paley, J. (1997). Husserl, phenomenology and nursing. *Journal of Advanced Nursing, 26,* 187–193.

Paterson, G. J., & Zderad, L. T. (1976). *Humanistic nursing.* New York: Wiley.

Patton, M. Q. (1990). *Qualitative evaluation and research methods.* (2nd ed.) Newbury Park, CA: Sage.

Ramhoj, P., & de Oliveira, E. (1991). A phenomenological hermeneutic access to research of the old age area. *Scandinavian Journal of Caring Science, 5*(3), 121–127.

Reinharz, S. (1983). Phenomenology as a dynamic process. *Phenomenology and Pedagogy, 1*(1), 77–79.

Ricoeur, P. (1976). *Interpretation theory: Discourse and the surplus of meaning.* Fort Worth, TX: Christian University Press.

Ricoeur, P. (1981). *Hermeneutics and the social sciences* (J. Thompson, Trans. & Ed.). New York: Cambridge University Press.

Rinaldi, D. M. (1989). The lived experience of commitment to nursing. *Dissertation Abstracts International.* (University Microfilms No. 1707)

Rose, P., Beeby, J., & Parker, D. (1995). Academic rigour in the lived experience of researchers using phenomenological methods in nursing. *Journal of Advanced Nursing, 21,* 1123–1129.

Schutz, A. (1970). *On phenomenology and social relations.* Chicago: University of Chicago Press.

Spiegelberg, H. (1965). *The phenomenological movement: A historical introduction* (2nd ed., Vol. 1–2). Dordrecht, The Netherlands: Martinus Nijhoff.

Spiegelberg, H. (1975). *Doing phenomenology.* Dordrecht, The Netherlands: Martinus Nijhoff.

Streubert, H. J. (1991). Phenomenological research as a theoretic initiative in community health nursing. *Public Health Nursing, 8*(2), 119–123.

van Kaam, A. (1959). A phenomenologicalal analysis exemplified by the feeling of being really understood. *Individual Psychology, 15,* 66–72.

van Manen, M. (1984). Practicing phenomenological writing. *Phenomenology and Pedagogy, 2*(1), 36–69.

Wagner, H. R. (1983). *Phenomenology of consciousness and sociology of the life and world: An introductory study.* Edmonton, Alberta: University of Alberta Press.

Yonge, O., & Stewin, L. (1988). Reliability and validity: Misnomers for qualitative research. *The Canadian Journal of Nursing Research, 20*(2), 61–67.

Zalon, M. L. (1997). Pain in frail, elderly women after surgery. *Image, 29*(1), 21–26.

Phenomenology in Practice, Education, and Administration

The acceptance of qualitative methods as legitimate approaches to the discovery of knowledge continues to grow as an increasing number of nurse–researchers apply qualitative methods to investigations that have as their phenomena of interest people's life experiences. Phenomenology as one approach to qualitative investigations has made a significant contribution to published research in the qualitative arena. As nurse–researchers continue to use qualitative methods to investigate nursing phenomena, the availability and quality of published research using qualitative methods will continue to grow. Qualitative methods allow exploration of humans by humans in ways that acknowledge the value of all evidence, the inevitability and worth of subjectivity, the value of a holistic view, and the integration of all patterns of knowing (Chinn, 1985).

This chapter provides an overview and critique of three phenomenological investigations, published as journal articles, in the areas of nursing education, practice, and administration. The article addressing a nursing practice problem is reprinted at the end of the chapter to provide readers with a sample of a phenomenological investigation while they use the critiquing guidelines. The chapter also offers examples demonstrating the applicability of phenomenological research for investigators interested in using this approach and amplifying the areas inherent in a phenomenological investigation on which readers should focus while critiquing a particular study.

The studies presented in this chapter were reviewed according to the "Critiquing Guidelines for Qualitative Research" (Streubert, 1998; see Box 5-1). These guidelines offer readers of qualitative investigations a guide to recognizing the essential methodological points of a published report. The guidelines also allow readers to examine how the research has contributed to the scientific base of nursing knowledge.

This chapter also provides readers with a variety of examples of published research using the phenomenological method. These examples are presented in Table 5-1, which summarizes significant points of selected phenomenological investigations. Examples of studies that use the method interpretations addressed in Chapter 4 are also included in Table 5-1 (Colaizzi, 1978; Giorgi, 1985; Munhall & Boyd, 1993; Spiegelberg, 1965,

(text continues on page 78)

BOX 5-1 CRITIQUING GUIDELINES FOR QUALITATIVE RESEARCH

STATEMENT OF THE PHENOMENON OF INTEREST

1. Is the phenomenon of interest clearly identified?
2. Has the researcher identified why the phenomenon requires a qualitative format?
3. Has the researcher described the philosophic underpinnings of the research?

PURPOSE

1. Has the researcher made explicit the purpose of conducting the research?
2. Does the researcher describe the projected significance of the work to nursing?

METHOD

1. Is the method used to collect data compatible with the purpose of the research?
2. Is the method adequate to address the phenomenon of interest?
3. If a particular approach is used to guide the inquiry, does the researcher complete the study according to the processes described?

SAMPLING

1. Does the researcher describe the selection of participants? Is purposive sampling used?
2. Are the informants who were chosen appropriate to inform the research?

DATA COLLECTION

1. Is data collection focused on human experience?
2. Does the researcher describe data collection strategies (i.e., interview, observation, field notes)?
3. Is protection of human participants addressed?
4. Is saturation of the data described?
5. Has the researcher made explicit the procedures for collecting data?

DATA ANALYSIS

1. Does the researcher describe the strategies used to analyze the data?

(*continued*)

BOX 5-1 CRITIQUING GUIDELINES FOR QUALITATIVE RESEARCH (CONTINUED)

2. Has the researcher remained true to the data?
3. Does the reader understand the procedures used to analyze the data?
4. Does the researcher address the credibility, auditability, and fittingness of the data?

CREDIBILITY

   a. Do the participants recognize the experience as their own?

AUDITABILITY

   a. Can the reader follow the researcher's thinking?
   b. Does the researcher document the research process?

FITTINGNESS

   a. Can the findings be applicable outside of the study situation?
   b. Are the results meaningful to individuals not involved in the research?
5. Is the strategy used for analysis compatible with the purpose of the study?

FINDINGS

1. Are the findings presented within a context?
2. Is the reader able to apprehend the essence of the experience from the report of the findings?
3. Are the researcher's conceptualizations true to the data?
4. Does the researcher place the report in the context of what is already known about the phenomenon?

CONCLUSIONS, IMPLICATIONS, AND RECOMMENDATIONS

1. Do the conclusions, implications, and recommendations give the reader a context in which to use the findings?
2. Do the conclusions reflect the study findings?
3. Does the researcher offer recommendations for future study?
4. Has the researcher made explicit the significance of the study to nursing?

From Streubert, H. (1998). Evaluating the qualitative research report. In J. Haber & G. Lobiondo-Wood (Eds.), *Nursing research: Methods, critical appraisal, and utilization* (4th ed., pp. 445–465). St. Louis, MO: C.V. Mosby. Adapted with permission.

TABLE 5-1 Selective Sampling of Phenomenological Research Studies

Author/Date	Domain	Phenomenon	Method	Sample	Date Generation	Findings
Aström, Jansson, Norberg, & Hallberg (1993)	Practice	Nurses' experiences in ethically different care situations	Hermeneutic analysis/interpretive phenomenology	18 experienced cancer nurses	Tape-recorded interviews, transcribed verbatim	"In complex situations the nurses reported that the ethical situations that arose were regarded either as overwhelming or at the other end of the spectrum, as possible to grasp, and they expressed either loneliness or togetherness, respectively. When reporting overwhelming situations, the nurses mostly referred to themselves by using the word "one," ie, "one would" and used "they" when referring to their co-actors. When narrating situations possible to grasp, they used the terms "I and we." The most important situational factor that was revealed in these narratives was whether or not the nurses had a support group in which to share their thoughts. Without the support group, they reported difficulties acting in accordance with their ethical reasoning and feelings" (p. 179).

Author (Year)	Focus	Purpose	Method	Sample	Data Collection	Findings
Ashworth & Hagan (1993)	Practice	The meaning of incontinence for nongeriatric urinary incontinence sufferers	Giorgi (1970/1985)	28 young or middle-aged women who suffered from urinary incontinence	Audiotaped interviews, transcribed verbatim	Incontinence was found to be a socially unacceptable topic of conversation; sufferers react with apathy, guilt, and denial
Baillie (1993)	Education	Factors influencing student nurses' learning in a community setting	Colaizzi (1978), with reference to the work of Knaack (1984) & Oiler (1982)	8 nursing students	Audiotaped interviews, transcribed verbatim	Factors affecting student learning included relevance of the learning experience, variety of experiences, role satisfaction, attitudes, and professional credibility; these factors were related to the students, mentor, and actual placements
Baillie (1996)	Practice	Phenomenological study on the nature of empathy as perceived by experienced registered nurses (RNs)	Colaizzi (1978)	9 experienced staff nurses working in surgical settings	Open, unstructured interviews, transcribed verbatim	Empathy was felt to be "beneficial, displayed both non-verbally and through the nurse's actions, and therefore the ability to empathize, and to feel empathy with the individual patient, needs supporting and promoting in nurses" (p. 1300).
Baumann (1993)	Practice	The meaning of the experience of being homeless as lived by 15 homeless women with dependent children	3-level phenomenology described by Ihde (1986) and Lanigan (1988)	15 homeless women	Semistructured interviews, no audiotaping, use of field notes to describe events and interviews	"A three level phenomenological methods was utilized: description, reduction, and interpretation. The descriptive level generates seven themes: boundaries, connections, fatigue/despair, self-respect, self-determination, privacy and mobil-

(continued)

TABLE 5-1   Selective Sampling of Phenomenological Research Studies (CONTINUED)

Author/Date	Domain	Phenomenon	Method	Sample	Date Generation	Findings
						ity. The reduction level reveals three ways of being homeless: physical, social and symbolic. The interpretation of the meaning of being homeless employs the metaphor of homelessness as a whirlpool" (p. 59).
Beck (1993)	Education	The meaning of a caring experience between a nursing student and a client	van Manen (1990a)	22 undergraduate students	Students wrote in-depth accounts	Five essential themes of a caring nursing student–client experience emerged: authentic presence, competence, emotional support, physical and positive consequences
Bottorff (1990)	Practice	Examination of the reality of persisting with breast feeding when other alternatives are available	van Manen (1990b)	3 mothers	Interview	The study identified a description of the meaning of continuing to breast-feed in relation to a mother's descision to breast-feed, the problems encountered, the relationship between mother and baby, being committed, and choosing a time to stop
Clarke & Wheeler (1992)	Practice	A view of the phenomenon of caring in nursing practice	Colaizzi (1978)	6 practicing nurses	Audiotaped interviews, transcribed verbatim	"Phenomenology was the chosen methodology, which facilitated the emergence of an essential structure of caring which incorporated four major categories de-

Author	Domain	Description	Framework	Sample	Data Collection	Findings
						scribed as 'being supportive,' 'communicating,' 'pressure' and 'caring ability.' It is suggested that, through gaining perspectives to enhance our understanding of the meaning of caring it will ultimately develop our understanding of nursing itself" (p. 1283)
Criddle (1993)	Practice	The experience of healing from surgery	Lincoln & Guba (1985)	9 postsurgical clients	Tape-recorded interviews, transcribed verbatim at 1 and 4 weeks posthospitalization	Healing included four overlapping themes: active participation, achieving balance, evolving beyond, and healing process
Daley (1997)	Education	A qualitative interpretivist study that analyzed the interrelationships between the knowledge gained through continuing nursing education programs and the context of nurses' clinical practice	Hermeneutic analysis/interpretive phenomenology	40 nurses from hospitals, nursing homes, and home care agencies	Semistructured tape-recorded interviews	"Findings indicated that nurses used information from continuing education programs to construct a knowledge base and that this process was affected by the structural, human resources, political and symbolic frames of the context in which nurses practice" (p. 102).

(continued)

TABLE 5-1   Selective Sampling of Phenomenological Research Studies (CONTINUED)

Author/Date	Domain	Phenomenon	Method	Sample	Date Generation	Findings
Diekelmann, Allen, & Tanner (1989)	Education	A hermeneutic analysis of the National League for Nursing (NLN) Criteria for the Appraisal of Baccalaureate Programs	Hemeneutic analysis/interpretive phenomenology	Text	Review of text	Analysis and recommendations related to the accreditation guidelines established by the NLN
Dobbie (1991)	Practice	A hermeneutical research study of the midlife spiritual experience of 10 women who are members of the United Church of Canada	Hermeneutic analysis/interpretive phenomenology and Giorgi's (1970/1985) descriptive phenomenology	10 women	In-depth face-to-face interviews	"The spiritual experience of these women in mid-life transition was organized within two simultaneous and interrelated experiences: an evolving consciousness of self and children, and an evolving consciousness of God. Five invariant themes emerged: trigger events, inferiority, essential loneliness, loving oneself and loving children" (p. 827).
Duke	Education	Qualitative investigation of the difficulties experienced by sessional clinical teachers of nursing	Phenomenology	18 clinical teachers	Unstructured interviews and written clinical scenarios	"Research findings indicate that although the sessional clinical teachers were skilled at identifying student problems, they were reluctant to make difficult evaluation decisions, due to low self-esteem, role conflict and their ethic of caring. It seems that gender

						socialization, patriarchal dominance and apprenticeship training had effected their confidence in their own decision making. The implications of such findings are of concern for the ongoing credibility and integrity of nursing courses, as clinical teachers have an influence on the nursing profession through the preparation of its practitioners" (p. 408).
Dzurec & Coleman (1997)	Practice	A hermeneutic analysis of the process of conducting clinical interviews	Hermeneutic analysis/interpretive phenomenology	9 students	Group interviews and field notes	Analysis revealed two major themes: the context of the interview and connecting with the interviewee; subthemes emerged under each category; interview content comprised the subthemes of role confusion, power gradients, language, and control; connecting with the interviewee comprised the subthemes of hearing interviewee issues and transcending the power gradient
Erickson & Henderson (1992)	Practice	Description of the lived experience of children as they accompany their mothers who are leaving abusive relationships	Giorgi (1970/1985)	13 children	Tape-recorded interviews using an unstructured interview guide	The experience of children as they accompany their mothers who are leaving abusive relationships include three main components: living with violence, living in transition, and living with mom

(continued)

TABLE 5-1 Selective Sampling of Phenomenological Research Studies (CONTINUED)

Author/Date	Domain	Phenomenon	Method	Sample	Date Generation	Findings
Girot (1993)	Education	The study examined the perception of clinical competence in nursing students from the perspective of experienced practitioners	Leininger (1985)	10 experienced nurses	Interview	Attributes of competence included trust, caring, communication skills, and knowledge/adaptability
Haase & Rostad (1994)	Practice	Exploration of the child's perspective of experiencing completion of cancer treatment	Colaizzi (1978)	7 children aged 5–18 years	Open-ended audiotaped interviews, transcribed verbatim	"Six theme categories were identified from the data: a gradual realization of normal; hierarchical and cyclical recurrence fears; completion embedded in the cancer experience; seeking a new normal; modifying relationships; and resolution and moving on. The themes were developed into an essential structure that indicated that the experience of completing cancer treatment has two faces—one of celebration and hope and one of uncertainty and fear" (p. 1483).

Jablonski (1994)	Practice	The study examined the primary recollections of clients who depended on mechanical ventilation	Colaizzi (1978)	12 participants: 5 males and 7 females	Face-to-face or telephone interviews using semi-structured interview technique; interviews were audiotaped, transcribed verbatim	15 themes were identified, 14 of which related to the experience of mechanical ventilation from intubation to extubation; the last offered client recommendations
King (1993)	Practice	Experiences of midlife daughters who were caring for their aging mothers	Giorgi (1970/1985)	7 daughters ranging in age from 42–69 years	Tape-recorded interviews, transcribed verbatim	A continuum of care framework was described that integrates the themes that emerged from the raw data; the themes included knowing mother and her needs; responding to mothers' needs; deferring to mothers' needs; recognizing, grieving, and identifying own fantasies
Morse, Bottorff, & Hutchinson (1994)	Practice	Identification of the ways clients achieve comfort	van Manen (1990b)	Clients who had experienced illness or injury	Interview	9 themes were identified: "The diseased body, the disobedient body, the vulnerable body, the violated body, the resigned body, the enduring body, the betraying body and the betraying (neurotic) mind. The process of achieving comfort is based on the patients' needs to live with illness or injury without being dominated by their bodies" (p. 189).

(continued)

TABLE 5-1 Selective Sampling of Phenomenological Research Studies (CONTINUED)

Author/Date	Domain	Phenomenon	Method	Sample	Date Generation	Findings
Pei-Fan & Tomlinson (1997)	Practice	The lived experience of parents following admission of their child to a pediatric intensive care unit	Colaizzi (1978)	10 families chosen from the Family Impact of Catastrophic Childhood Illness Project	Family interviews, tape recorded and transcribed verbatim	"The analysis uncovered a multidimensional and holistic phenomenon consisting of four organizing concepts: initial boundary ambiguity, parents' coping patterns, family resources, and functioning of the family boundary. These results provide evidence of a collective family level perception of stress when experiencing the health crisis of a child and support further use of family stress perception as a family level phenomenon that represents family meaning construction during critical illness of a child" (p. 608).
Nehls, Rather, & Guyette (1997)	Education	The lived experiences of students, preceptors, and faculty of record related to the preceptor model of clinical instruction	Hermeneutic analysis/interpretive phenomenology	31 senior-level undergraduate nursing students, 10 staff nurse preceptors, and 11 master's- and doctorate-prepared faculty-of-record	Extended private interviews using Heideggerian phenomenology	The authors identified common meanings, relational themes, and a constitutive pattern designated learning nursing thinking; Implications were offered for teaching practices that should be extended and those that should be altered

Source	Domain	Purpose	Method	Sample	Data	Findings
Paavi-lainen, & Astedt-Kurki (1997)	Practice	Examination of the ways the client and public health nurse cooperate	Hermeneutic analysis/interpretive phenomenology	11 public health nurses	Written essays	Successful collaboration requires an active and committed involvement by both the client and public health nurse; the goals must be shared, and there must be a trusting relationship; the client's well-being and the nurse's feeling of success depend on the relationship developed
Parsons (1997)	Practice	Care-giving for a family member with Alzheimer's disease	van Manen (1990b)	8 men: 5 spouses and 3 sons	Audiotaped interviews, transcribed verbatim	8 themes were identified: enduring, vigilance, a sense of loss, aloneness and loneliness, taking away, searching to discover, the need for assistance, and reciprocity; the three sons identified an additional theme of overstepping the normal boundaries
Rather (1992)	Education	The lived experience of the returning RN and descriptions of what is significant about schooling experiences	Hermeneutic analysis/interpretive phenomenology	15 returning RNs from 3 baccalaureate nursing programs	Extended, non-structured audio-taped interviews	Major finding was the constitutive pattern "Nursing as a Way of Thinking"
Ring & Danielson (1997)	Practice	Description of clients, experiences in the self-management of oxygen therapy	van Manen (1990a)	10 patients: 5 males and 5 females	Tape-recorded interview, transcribed verbatim	Findings indicated that clients need help with physiologic and psychologic difficulties and from social isolation; social isolation was a concern even when another family member was present in the household

1975; Streubert, 1991; van Kaam, 1959; van Manen, 1984). These examples are provided as a guide for readers interested in applying one of the various method interpretations. The author chose articles that could provide varied examples of method application; however, these articles serve only as a beginning point of reference. Nursing research articles are continually added to the wealth of data available; therefore, readers are encouraged to seek out most recently published examples. The examples provide readers with a sense of how the method can be used in nursing practice, education, and administration. Although phenomenology is appropriate for studying phenomena important to nursing administration, the approach has not been widely applied in this area.

Application to Practice

Many nursing interventions performed in clinical settings lend themselves to quantitative measurement. Examples include measurement of blood pressure, central venous pressure, or urine-specific gravity. However, nurses enmeshed in practice settings are well aware that much of what is done for clients is subjective and based on how nurses come to know their clients and the clients' life experiences. For example, caring, reassurance, and quality of life are phenomena central to nursing practice, but do not necessarily lend themselves to quantitative measurement. Therefore, subjective phenomena unique to the practice of professional nursing need investigative approaches suitable to their unique nature. Qualitative methods, which apply to the study of subjective interactive experiences, have been addressed in relationship to practice areas (Beck, 1990; Oiler, 1982; Omery, 1987; Pallikkathayil & Morgan, 1991; Paterson, 1971; Taylor, 1993). Phenomenology as a qualitative research method has been used to explore a variety of practice-related experiences such as postpartum depression (Beck, 1992), caring in acute care settings (Miller, Haber, & Byrne, 1992), the nature of empathy (Baillie, 1996), care-giving by men for family members with Alzheimer's disease (Parsons, 1997), and experiences with long-term oxygen therapy (Ring & Danielson, 1997).

One example of a phenomenological research study as applied to the practice setting is "Pain in Frail, Elderly Women After Surgery" by Margarete Lieb Zalon (1997). This article was reviewed using the guidelines presented in Box 5-1. When reviewing any piece of published research, consider that the readers of research are most often interested in the study findings as opposed to the literature review or method. Therefore, the findings are usually what will be published in the most detail, with only method and literature review highlights included. If readers are interested in more detail about the published research, it is often helpful to write directly to the authors.

The article by Zalon (1997) presents phenomenological research methodology in a comprehensive manner. She has been concise, yet detailed enough to allow readers to follow the method implementation in her discussion of the findings. Zalon served as Wallerstein Foundation for Geriatric Life Improvement Scholar for the study through a grant received from the American Nurses Foundation. The grant proposal is reprinted with permission following Chapter 15 for the purposes of allowing readers the opportunity to follow a funded qualitative research project from proposal to publication of the findings.

In her phenomenological investigation of pain in frail, elderly women, Zalon (1997) discovered that her participants endured pain and placed a high degree of trust in the nurses caring for them to provide pain-relief measures. Zalon captured the importance of her study to nursing practice in the statement, "Understanding pain from an elder's perspective can enhance nurses' abilities to relieve pain" (p. 21). Knowledge related to how frail, elderly women perceive pain contributes to nursing's substantive body of knowledge related to pain-relief practices.

Zalon (1997) made explicit for readers the phenomenon of interest— "the lived experience of postoperative pain in frail, elderly women" (p. 21)—and the rationale for a qualitative research format. Zalon emphasized that "the phenomenon of pain–that is, how people feel, understand, and interpret their pain–must be described before patterns of behavior and interactions can be understood" (p. 22). The phenomenological research method suited the investigation.

The philosophic underpinnings of the research by Zalon (1997) are supported by the work of Boyd (1993), Colaizzi (1978), Lincoln and Guba (1985), and Paterson and Zderad (1976). Zalon's reference to these qualitative researchers provided theoretical support for her investigation. Direction for implementation of phenomenological research methodology was provided by the procedural steps of Colaizzi (1978).

The purpose of the research was "to understand the lived experience of postoperative pain in frail, elderly women after surgery" (Zalon, 1997, p. 21). Zalon provided highlights of issues surrounding pain management and made clear her rationale for method selection. The investigation is an important phenomenological research contribution to the domain of nursing practice. Zalon noted a void in the research literature dealing with elderly people's pain perception. Her discussion of this void established for readers the need for the investigation and emphasized the appropriateness of phenomenology as the method choice for this research.

The phenomenological research method as described by Colaizzi (1978) guided Zalon's inquiry. Phenomenological methodology as identified by Colaizzi was appropriate for the investigation and provided direction for data analysis. Clearly, Zalon (1997) followed the procedural steps outlined by Colaizzi (1978) throughout the research process. A purposive sample of 16 hospitalized women aged 75 to 93 years who had undergone abdominal surgery were included in the study. *Purposeful (purposive) sampling* provides information-rich cases for in-depth study (Patton, 1990). Zalon provided demographic data related to age, type of surgery, and rationale for inclusion of women only:

> The study's purposive sample consisted of 16 hospitalized, frail, elderly women who had abdominal surgery and could discuss their postoperative pain; ages ranged from 75 to 93 years. Men were excluded because of possible gender differences concerning pain. Women who had abdominal surgery specifically for cancer were excluded because of possible differences in meaning attributed to pain. The types of surgeries were cholecystectomy (n = 7), repair of perforated cecum (n = 2), lysis of adhesions (n = 2), perforated ulcer (n = 1), perforated appendix (n = 1), iliac bypass (n = 1), antrectomy (n = 1), and drainage of renal abscess (n = 1). (p. 22)

The participants Zalon selected were appropriate to inform the research, given their immediate and personal experience with surgery and the consequent potential for postoperative pain.

Zalon (1997) conducted the data collection phase by completing personal audiotaped interviews that were transcribed verbatim. The interview format was that of an open-ended, unstructured interview, which allowed participants to speak freely and personally about their postoperative experiences. According to Zalon,

> Initially, participants were asked to describe what brought them to the hospital. Then a more specific question was asked, "What comes to mind when you think about the pain you had after your surgery?" (p. 22)

Although Zalon (1997) did not address data saturation in her article, she noted that she did not consider interviews complete until she had clarified all aspects of the interview with participants. Saturation of data is believed to occur when data begin to repeat themselves and no new themes emerge during the interview. Addressing saturation adds to the credibility of the study.

Zalon (1997) accomplished data analysis using the procedural steps described by Colaizzi (1978). The study reflected consistent use of the method for data analysis. Zalon reviewed transcripts in their entirety and extracted significant statements. By providing examples of theme clusters, Zalon allowed readers to follow her line of thinking in the data-reduction process. She integrated formulated meanings that emerged from the theme clusters into a description of pain in frail, elderly women after surgery. This procedural process is consistent with that described by Colaizzi (1978).

Credibility can be established by returning the exhaustive description to each participant and asking him or her to verify the accuracy of the material. Zalon (1997) established credibility of her findings by "providing participants with an opportunity to review and discuss the final results via home visits or telephone calls to determine if the description reflected their experience" (p. 22).

Auditability refers "to the ability of another researcher to follow the thinking, decisions and methods used by the original researcher" (Yonge &

Stewin, 1988, p. 64). Zalon (1997) provided a table that helped readers follow her line of thinking during data interpretation.

Fittingness of the research refers to how well the findings fit outside of the study situation. Zalon's findings regarding the perception of pain in frail, elderly women after surgery can be applied in a variety of contexts in which elderly people may encounter pain. Her findings may be applicable in hospitalized elderly people with arthritis, or in clients with cancer. Replication of the study would be beneficial to further confirm the fittingness of the findings.

Zalon's (1997) findings are presented in the context of the group studied. The data used both the informants' words and author's interpretations. From Zalon's report, readers get a sense of the needs of frail, elderly women in terms of pain relief following surgery. Furthermore, nurses are provided with direction for key assessments, an area in which to focus when caring for these individuals.

The conclusions focused on the importance of regaining a sense of control and

> a process of trying to restore one's place in the world, in life. The results suggest that nurses can facilitate restoration by exploring the significance that pain has for people in the context of their illness. This would enable nurses to individualize pain-relief strategies that support unique strengths and needs in order to enhance recovery from surgery. (Zalon, 1997, p. 25)

The study by Zalon (1997) is an example of the important contribution phenomenological research makes to nursing practice. Understanding the meaning of pain in frail, elderly people provides direction for assessment and intervention, and ultimately improved and more effective nursing care. Investigation of subjective phenomena unique to nursing practice is needed to expand nursing's body of knowledge and can provide the necessary background to guide quantitative investigations.

Application to Education

Nursing education also lends itself to objective and subjective research interests. Test construction and critical thinking are education-related examples that are appropriate for quantitative investigation, although not exclusively. The educational domain of nursing also lends itself to qualitative investigation in areas such as educational experiences, caring and the curriculum, or the effect of evaluation on student performance in the clinical setting.

Several authors have used qualitative methods to investigate phenomena unique to nursing education. An overview and critique of the study "Nursing Students' Experiences Caring for Dying Patients" by Beck (1997) are provided for this example of the phenomenological method applied to the educational domain of nursing.

Beck (1997) reported on a study important to nursing education that dealt with nursing students' experiences caring for dying clients. Six themes emerged from Becks' study:

> While caring for dying patients, nursing students experienced a gamut of emotions such as fear, sadness, frustration, and anxiety. Contemplation of the patient's life and death occurred as the students cared for their patients. In addition to providing physical, emotional, and spiritual support for dying patients, an integral part of nursing students' care involved supporting the patients' families. Helplessness was experienced by the students regarding their role as patient advocates. While caring for dying patients, nursing students' learning flourished. (p. 408)

The phenomenon of interest in the study was the meaning of undergraduate nursing students' experiences in caring for dying clients (Beck, 1997). Beck described nurse educators' efforts to use the most effective approach to prepare students to care for dying clients. She emphasized the importance of incorporating care of dying clients into the nursing curriculum and summarized the relevant research. She further noted that published research on nursing students' experiences with caring for dying clients has been conducted from a purely quantitative perspective.

Beck (1997) described the philosophic underpinnings of the research in relationship to the phenomenological methodology (Colaizzi, 1978; Husserl, 1970; Merleau-Ponty, 1962). She made explicit the purpose of the research and described the projected significance of the work to nursing education. Beck's purpose was to "describe the meaning of nursing students' experience caring for dying patients" (p. 409). A qualitative format suited the investigation because Beck was interested in studying lived human experience, making the choice of phenomenology appropriate to her investigation. This is an important contribution to the literature on nursing education and the responsibility of educators to prepare nursing students to care for dying clients.

The method of data collection was compatible with the purpose of the research and adequate to address the phenomenon of interest. Beck (1997) used the methodology described by Colaizzi (1978) and completed the study according to the processes that Colaizzi described.

The sample consisted of 26 sophomore and junior undergraduate nursing students enrolled in a nursing research course who had an experience caring for a dying client. Participation was voluntary and anonymous; the researcher obtained informed consent. Students responded in writing during an undergraduate research course to the following statement: "Please describe an experience you have had providing nursing care to a dying patient. Share all your thoughts, perceptions, and feelings you can remember until you have no more to write about the experience" (p. 410). Beck did not address data saturation. Although having participants write about their descriptions is clearly an option for data collection, there is at least one drawback. When participants write their descriptions, the researcher has no opportunity to use open-ended questions. Having the opportunity to ask additional questions to clarify and encourage expanded discussion is helpful to ensure exhaustive description and data saturation.

Data analysis proceeded according the steps outlined by Colaizzi (1978). The tables presented in the study offered examples of Beck's (1997) thinking process regarding themes. Examples of raw data further illustrated this process for readers.

Beck (1997) addressed credibility, auditability, and fittingness. She used peer debriefing and member checks to establish credibility. Furthermore, she noted that she bracketed her preconceptions and presuppositions before collecting data and during analysis. Beck further enhanced the trustworthiness of her findings by having a master's degree–prepared nurse, experienced in qualitative data analysis, follow the decision trail she used to analyze the data. Beck's (1997) conclusions, implications, and recommendations were related to the students' experiences with caring for dying clients and the implications for the nursing curriculum.

Application to Administration

There is limited literature on studies related to nursing administration that use a qualitative approach. This is a domain of nursing that is in need of further qualitative investigation and an area rich with important areas for investigation. An overview of the study "A Phenomenologicalal Approach to Understanding the Process of Deaning" by Stainton and Styles (1985) is presented as an example of the application of qualitative research in the area of nursing administration.

The phenomenon of interest, clearly identified in the study, focused on gaining an understanding of the process of "deaning." Stainton and Styles (1985) identified a specific rationale for using a qualitative format as well as the philosophic underpinnings of the research.

The purpose of the Stainton and Styles (1985) study was to gain insight into the deaning process. The rationale for use of a qualitative approach was as follows:

> First, there is little empirical evidence available that assists the novice in understanding the role of the dean. Second, deaning involves situational variables, management skills and personal knowledge that is gained through experience. And third, an expert dean will approach a situation with a host of unexamined or taken-for-granted meanings and practices that define what it means to be a dean in that situation. (p. 269–270)

The study makes a significant contribution to the understanding of the dean's work because it describes an interpretive, phenomenological approach to gaining a context-based understanding of the process of deaning (p. 269).

The method used to collect data was compatible with the research purpose and adequately addressed the phenomenon of interest. Stainton and Styles (1985) reported using an interpretive approach to discover the practical knowledge of an experienced dean. They presented the study as an interpretation of hermeneutic phenomenology whose aim is understanding through interpretation of the phenomenon under study. Stainton and Styles provided a clear rationale for their method choice:

> The many variables characteristic of academic settings generate idiosyncratic approaches to interpreting diverse goals and process. Governance structures (and administrative styles) therefore vary both within and among institutions. They are the result of the blend between the personal knowledge of the individual dean and the characteristics of the situational context in which the role is executed. . . . The successful interface and interplay between the organizational and interpersonal aspects of the dean's position require continuous interpretation of the individual and contextual variables, neither of which are static. Deans are situated in a specific academic organization and a social–economic–political milieu that provide a background of shared, implicit meaning in the context of which deaning takes place. Deaning, therefore, cannot be understood by objectively studying decanal [sic] behaviors alone. An expert dean will approach a situation with a host of unexamined or taken-for-granted meanings and practices that define what it means to be a dean in that situation. Judgments are not based on rule or steps but on a gestalt of the whole. (pp. 269–270)

From this rationale, the authors concluded that an interpretive approach was required to discover the practical knowledge of an experienced dean (p. 270).

The sample for the study included the two authors, identified as an expert dean and a novice dean. The research focused on understanding the process of deaning as explored through the mentorship relationship existing between the two authors. Given the interpretive approach used, the participants were appropriate to inform the research.

Stainton and Styles (1985) described participant and nonparticipant observation as the method of data collection. They made explicit the procedures for data collection, collecting data over a 2-year period to gain understanding of the dean's role. They did not address data saturation. They also did not specifically address credibility, auditability, or fittingness of the findings.

Stainton and Styles (1985) discussed how the findings might be applicable outside of the study situation. They concluded and recommended that

> a phenomenologicalal approach by means of the interpretive method used by expert and novice deans who can work in sympathetic tandem has potential for the preparation and orientation of some deans. This

approach may differ from the mentor or modeling approach, as it leads not to rules, imitation, or theoretical formulations, but to enculturation through understanding. Expert deans willing to have their practices studied in this manner by selected doctoral students or newly appointed deans could increase recruitment to and effectiveness in the decanal role. (p. 274)

The area of administration in nursing lends itself to phenomenological research. This is an area in which there is a need for more qualitative and, specifically, phenomenological investigations. Topics that may be appropriate to phenomenological investigation include the experience of being the chair, director of nursing, or head nurse and client care coordinators.

Summary

This chapter provided examples of phenomenological research applied to the areas of nursing practice, education, and administration. It offered critiquing guidelines suitable for use with phenomenological investigations and used these guidelines in the review of three phenomenological investigations. The chapter presented examples of phenomenological research using the method interpretations described in Chapter 4 to give phenomenological researchers examples they can review to help clarify method implementation. Finally, the chapter presented a selected sample of phenomenological studies.

Phenomenology as a research approach provides an avenue for investigation that allows description of lived experiences. The voice of professional nurses in practice, education, and administration can be a tremendous source of data that has yet to be fully explored. Identifying subjective phenomena unique to the domains of nursing education, practice, and administration is important to the ever-expanding body of nursing knowledge.

REFERENCES

Ashworth, P. D., & Hagan, M. T. (1993). The meaning of incontinence: A qualitative study of non-geriatric urinary incontinence sufferers. *Journal of Advanced Nursing, 18,* 1415–1423.

Astrom, G., Jansson, L., Norberg, A., & Hallberg, I. R. (1993). Experienced nurses' narratives of their being in ethically difficult care situations: The problem to act in accordance with one's ethical reasoning and feelings. *Cancer Nursing, 16*(3), 179–187.

Baillie, L. (1993). Factors affecting student nurses' learning in community placements: A phenomenological study. *Journal of Advanced Nursing, 18,* 1043–1053.

Baillie, L. (1996). A phenomenological study of the nature of empathy. *Journal of Advanced Nursing, 24,* 1300–1308.

Baumann, S. L. (1993). The meaning of being homeless. *Scholarly Inquiry for Nursing Practice, 7*(1), 59–72.

Beck, C. T. (1990). Qualitative research: Methodologies and use in pediatric nursing. *Issues in Comprehensive Pediatric Nursing, 13,* 193–201.

Beck, C. T. (1992). The lived experience of postpartum depression: A phenomenological study. *Nursing Research, 42*(3), 166–170.

Beck, C. T. (1993). Caring relationships between nursing students and their patients. *Nurse Educator, 18*(5), 28–32.

Beck, C. T. (1997). Nursing students' experiences caring for dying patients. *Journal of Nursing Education, 36*(9), 408–415.

Bottorff, J. L. (1990). Persistence in breastfeeding: A phenomenological investigation. *Journal of Advanced Nursing, 15,* 201–209.

Boyd, C. O. (1993). Toward a nursing practice research method. *Advances in Nursing Science, 16*(2), 9–25.

Chinn, P. (1985). Debunking myths in nursing theory and research. *Image, 17*(2), 171–179.

Clarke, J. B., & Wheeler, S. J. (1992). A view of the phenomenon of caring in nursing practice. *Journal of Advanced Nursing, 17,* 1283–1290.

Colaizzi, P. F. (1978). Psychological research as the phenomenologist views it. In R. Valle & M. King (Eds.), *Existential phenomenological alternative for psychology* (pp. 48–71). New York: Oxford University Press.

Criddle, L. (1993). Healing from surgery: A phenomenological study. *Image, 25*(3), 208–213.

Daley, B. J. (1997). Creating mosaics: The interrelationships of knowledge and context. *Journal of Continuing Education in Nursing, 28*(3), 102–113.

Diekelmann, N., Allen, D., & Tauner, C. (1989). *The NLN criteria for appraisal of baccalaureate programs: A critical hermeneutic analysis.* N.Y.: National League for Nursing, Pub. # 15-2253.

Dobbie, B. J. (1991). Women's mid-life experience: An evolving consciousness of self and children. *Journal of Advanced Nursing, 16,* 825–831.

Duke, M. (1996). Clinical evaluation—Difficulties experienced by sessional clinical teachers of nursing: A qualitative study. *Journal of Advanced Nursing, MDRV 23,* 408–414.

Dzurec, L. C., & Coleman, P. (1997). "What happens after you say hello?" A hermeneutic analysis of the process of conducting clinical interviews. *Journal of Psychosocial Nursing, 35*(8), 31–35.

Ericksen, J. R., & Henderson, A. D. (1992). Witnessing family violence: The children's experience. *Journal of Advanced Nursing, 17,* 1200–1209.

Giorgi, A. (1970). *Psychology as a human science: A phenomenologically based approach.* New York: Harper & Row.

Giorgi, A. (1985). *Phenomenology and psychological research.* Pittsburgh, PA: Duquesne University Press.

Girot, E. A. (1993). Assessment of competence in clinical practice: A phenomenological approach. *Journal of Advanced Nursing, 18,* 114–119.

Haase, J. E., & Rostad, M. (1994). Experiences of completing cancer therapy: Children's perspectives. *Oncology Nursing Forum, 21*(9), 1483–1492.

Husserl, E. (1970). *The crisis of European sciences and transcendental phenomenology: An introduction to phenomenological philosophy* (D. Carr, Trans.). Evanston, IL: Northwestern University Press.

Jablonski, R. S. (1994). The experience of being mechanically ventilated. *Qualitative Health Research, 4*(2), 186–207.

King, T. (1993). The experiences of midlife daughters who are caregivers for their mothers. *Health Care of Women International, 14,* 419–426.

Knaack, P. (1984). *Phenomenological research. Western Journal of Nursing Research, 6*(1), 107–114.

Leininger, M. (ed) (1985). Qualitative research methods in nursing. Grune & Stratton, Orlando, FL

Lincoln, Y. S., & Guba, E. G. (1985). *Naturalistic inquiry.* Beverly Hills, CA: Sage.

Merleau-Ponty, M. (1962). *Phenomenology of perception* (C. Smith, Trans.). New York: Humanities Press.

Miller, B., Haber, J., & Byrne, M. (1992). The experience of caring in the acute care setting: Patients and nurses' perspectives. In D. Gaut (Ed.), *The presence of caring in nursing* (pp. 137–156). New York: National League for Nursing.

Morse, J. M., Bottorff, J. L., & Hutchinson, S. (1994). The phenomenology of comfort. *Journal of Advanced Nursing, 20,* 189–195.

Munhall, P., & Boyd, C. O. (1993) *Nursing research: A qualitative perspective.* New York: National League for Nursing Press.

Nehls, N., Rather, M., & Guyette, M. (1997). The preceptor model of clinical instruction:

The lived experiences of students, preceptors, and faculty-of-record. *Journal of Nursing Education, 36*(5), 220–227.

Oiler, C. (1982). The phenomenological approach in nursing research. *Nursing Research, 31*(3), 178–181.

Omery, A. (1987). Qualitative research designs in the critical care setting: Review and application. *Heart and Lung, 16*(4), 432–436.

Paavilainen, E., & Astedt-Kurki, P. (1997). The client–nurse relationship as experienced by public health nurses: Toward better collaboration. *Public Health Nursing, 14*(3), 137–142.

Pallikkathayil, L., & Morgan, S. A. (1991). Phenomenology as a method for conducting clinical research. *Applied Nursing Research, 4*(4), 195–200.

Parsons, K. (1997). The male experience of caregiving for a family member with Alzheimer's disease. *Qualitative Health Research, 7*(3), 391–407.

Paterson, J. G. (1971). From a philosophy of clinical nursing to a method of nursology. *Nursing Research, 20*(2), 143–146.

Paterson, J. G., & Zderad, L. T. (1976). *Humanistic nursing.* New York: Wiley.

Patton, M. Q. (1990). *Qualitative evaluation and research methods* (2nd ed.). Newbury Park, CA: Sage.

Pei-Fan, M., & Tomlinson, P. (1997). Parental experience and meaning construction during a pediatric health crisis. *Western Journal of Nursing Research, 19*(5), 608–636.

Rather, M. L. (1992). "Nursing as a way of thinking"—Heideggerian hermeneutical analysis of the lived experience of the returning RN. *Research in Nursing and Health, 15,* 47–55.

Ring, L., & Danielson, E. (1997). Patients' experience of long-term oxygen therapy. *Journal of Advanced Nursing, 26,* 337–344.

Spiegelberg, H. (1965). *The phenomenological movement: A historical introduction* (2nd ed., Vols. 1–2). Dordrecht, The Netherlands: Martinus Nijhoff.

Spiegelberg, H. (1975). *Doing phenomenology.* Dordrecht, The Netherlands: Martinus Nijhoff.

Stainton, M., & Styles, M. M. (1985). A phenomenological approach to understanding the process of deaning. *Journal of Professional Nursing, 1,* 269–274.

Streubert, H. J. (1991). Phenomenological research as a theoretic initiative in community health nursing. *Public Health Nursing, 8*(2), 119–123.

Streubert, H. J. (1998). Evaluating the qualitative research report. In G. LoBiondo-Wood & J. Haber (Eds.), *Nursing research: Methods, critical appraisal and utilization* (4th ed., pp. 481–499). St. Louis, MO: C.V. Mosby.

Taylor, B. (1993). Phenomenology: One way to understand nursing practice. *International Journal of Nursing Studies, 30*(2), 171–179.

van Kaam, A. (1959). A phenomenological analysis exemplified by the feeling of being really understood. *Individual Psychology, 15,* 66–72.

van Manen, M. (1990a). *Researching lived experience.* New York State University of New York Press.

van Manen, M. (1990b). *Researching lived experience. Human science for an action sensitive pedagogy.* Althouse Press, London, Ontario.

van Manen, M. (1984). Practicing phenomenological writing. *Phenomenology and Pedagogy, 2,* 36–69.

Yonge, O., & Stewin, L. (1988). Reliability and validity: Misnomers for qualitative research. *Canadian Journal of Nursing Research, 20*(2), 61–67.

Zalon, M. L. (1997). Pain in frail, elderly women after surgery. *Image, 29*(1), 21–26.

RESEARCH ARTICLE

Phenomenological Approach: Pain in Frail, Elderly Women After Surgery

MARGARETE LIEB ZALON

Purpose: To describe the lived experience of postoperative pain in frail, elderly women.

Design: Colaizzi's (1978) phenomenological approach.

Sample, Method: 16 hospitalized women from ages 75 to 93, who had abdominal surgery. Unstructured, open-ended interviews were conducted in 1992.

Findings: Three major themes emerged: the immediate reality of pain, security, and dealing with pain. The immediate reality of pain consisted of the feeling, awareness, and past imposing on the present. Security consisted of comfort and trust. Dealing with pain consisted of endurance, control, and self-discovery of strategies, the most predominant of which was being still to relieve pain.

Conclusions: The frail elderly women in this study tended to endure pain and to trust nurses to provide pain-relief measures. Nurses should carefully assess pain and the desire of patients for control of pain-relief measures.

IMAGE: JOURNAL OF NURSING SCHOLARSHIP, 1997; 29(1) 21–26. ©1997, SIGMA THETA TAU INTERNATIONAL.

[Keywords: pain; aging; surgery; women]

Today, because of the aging population in the United States and advanced technology, an increased number of hospitalized patients are the frail elderly, over age 75. Unrelieved pain is prevalent among hospitalized patients (Miaskowski, Nichols, Brody, & Synold, 1994; Paice, Mahon, & Faut-Callahan, 1995). Research about pain has not always included the frail elderly perhaps partly because of the difficulties in recruiting subjects (Souder, 1992). Research about pain in the elderly is needed (Jacox, 1989).

Research on the effects of aging on the perception of pain has yielded mixed results. Harkins, Kwentus, and Price (1984) in a review of over 30 studies about pain concluded that age-related changes in pain and its perception are difficult to

Margarete Lieb Zalon, RN, CS, PhD, *Upsilon, Iota Omega*, is Associate Professor of Nursing at the University of Scranton. Dr. Zalon served as Wallerstein Foundation for Geriatric Life Improvement Scholar for this study through a grant received from the American Nurses Foundation. Funding for this study was also received from the University of Scranton. The author wishes to acknowledge Carla Mariano, RN, EdD, who was a consultant for this study; Marian Farrell, RN, CS, PhD, who provided additional assistance with data analysis; and Timothy Casey, PhD, who critiqued the manuscript. Correspondence to Dr. Zalon, Department of Nursing, University of Scranton, Scranton, PA 18510-4595.

Accepted for publication January 19, 1996.

document. Tolerance of experimentally-induced pain decreases with age (Woodrow, Friedman, Siegelaub, & Collen, 1972). However, experimentally-induced pain might be different from natural clinical pain and longitudinal data might yield different results.

Under-assessment and under-medication for pain are significant problems for hospitalized patients (Cohen, 1980; Zalon, 1993). Hospitalized elderly receive fewer pain prescriptions and analgesics (Faherty & Grier, 1984; Portenoy & Kanner, 1985). The elderly experience longer pain relief from analgesics (Kaiko, Wallenstein, Rogers, Grabinski, & Houde, 1986); however, older patients are more likely to have pain persisting beyond the first 4 days and find analgesics less helpful (Melzack, Abbott, Mulder, & Davis, 1987). Although, the elderly receive less medication for postoperative pain, it is not known whether their pain perception is decreased, pain tolerance is different, or pain relief is adequate. Errors to understand the experience of pain in hospitalized elderly are confounded by the lack of clarity in relationships among pain, analgesic administration, and confusion (Platzer, 1989). A recent study suggests unrelieved pain plays the more important role in such confusion among the aged (Duggleby & Lander, 1994).

Attitudes and beliefs of the elderly about pain might interfere with pain management (Hofland, 1992). Elders might be afraid to admit having pain (McCaffery & Beebe, 1989, p. 311). Little is known about elders' willingness to report pain, which may be compounded by caregivers' failure to discuss pain with their patients. Donovan, Dillon, and McGuire (1987) reported that only 45% of patients remembered discussing their pain with a nurse. Pain research in the elderly focusing on caregivers, analgesic administration, and experimental pain does not provide adequate information about the multidimensional nature of pain. Understanding pain from an elder's perspective can enhance nurses' abilities to relieve pain. The purpose of this study was to understand the lived experience of postoperative pain in frail, elderly women after surgery.

METHOD

The phenomenological method was used for data analysis in this exploratory study conducted in 1992 and 1993. Phenomenological description is an essential step in theory building (Paterson & Zderad, 1976, p. 83). Phenomenological research answers these questions: What is the phenomenon that is experienced and lived? What is its structure or commonalities in its many diverse appearances (Valle & King, 1978, pp. 15–17)?

The phenomenological method attempts to describe human experience in its context (Boyd, 1993, p. 103). The phenomenon of pain—that is, how people feel, understand, and interpret their pain—must be described before patterns of behavior and interactions can be understood.

The study's purposive sample consisted of 16 hospitalized, frail, elderly women who had abdominal surgery and could discuss their postoperative pain; ages ranged from 75 to 93 years. Men were excluded because of possible gender differences concerning pain. Women who had abdominal surgery specifically for cancer were excluded because of possible differences in meaning attributed to pain. The types of surgeries were cholecystectomy ($n = 7$), repair of perforated cecum ($n = 2$), lysis of adhesions ($n = 2$), perforated ulcer ($n = 1$), perforated appendix ($n = 1$), iliac bypass ($n = 1$), antrectomy ($n = 1$), and drainage of renal abscess ($n = 1$). Surgery was unplanned for all but one woman. Institutional review board approval was obtained. Prospective participants were approached on at least the fourth postopera-

TABLE A5-1   SELECTED EXAMPLES OF SIGNIFICANT STATEMENTS AND
CORRESPONDING FORMULATED MEANINGS

Significant Statement	Formulated Meaning
Theme Cluster: Endurance	
...hard enough. Like jabbing pains. It's when it's excessive that I ask.	She only asks for medication when jabbing pain becomes intolerable.
I have a pretty high level of tolerance for pain...And I've always been a fighter, so I've never been any different.	Describes herself as being able to tolerate pain. Her lifelong self-perception is that of a fighter.
I think about how long I have before I start thinking about it again.	She is reminded of the presence of pain by evaluating how much time she will have before the pain returns.
Theme Cluster: Comfort	
They were very attentive. Somebody around me. That seemed to help.	The attention provided by the nurses around her was helpful.
God is with me and I am with him...	God as a source of solace and comfort.
You tolerate it, and they encourage you and they talk to you...come on___, come on___let's move.	The nurses encouraged her to tolerate the pain of movement by talking with her.
Then they'd fix my pillow for me, hike it up. I turned over and go asleep again. And I wasn't up. I wasn't miserable all night. That was pretty good.	The nurses would help her get into a comfortable position which enabled her to sleep and kept her from feeling miserable.
I rested nice and everything and they made me comfortable and they'd sit me up, take me for a walk, head back and I was much better.	Being made comfortable and being helped when moving made her feel much better.

tive day and given an explanation of the study. Participants were alert and oriented when the consent forms were signed and during the interview. Pseudonyms were used when the interviews were transcribed.

Open-ended, unstructured interviews were conducted. Initially, participants were asked to describe what brought them to the hospital. Then a more specific question was asked, "What comes to mind when you think about the pain you had after your surgery?" Additional questions were only asked when necessary for clarification. When the participants described their experiences, and no further clarification was needed, the interview was considered complete. Interviews lasted from 20 minutes to 1 hour. The investigator's assumptions, derived from experience, the literature, and previous research, were bracketed or laid aside. These were listed before data collection and periodically as it progressed. Further literature review was suspended until data analysis was finished.

The interviews were tape-recorded and transcribed verbatim. Transcripts were compared with the tapes for accuracy. Colaizzi's (1978) method was used for data analysis. This involved reading the transcripts in their entirety. Significant statements about pain were then extracted and the meaning of each statement was formulated. Examples for two theme clusters appear in Table A5-1. Clusters of themes were organized from aggregated formulated meanings. The original transcripts were examined for each theme cluster. Finally, the results were integrated to yield a description of the pain after surgery.

Credibility was enhanced by providing participants with an opportunity to review and discuss the final results via home visits or telephone calls to determine if the description reflected their experience. Consultation was obtained from an expert on qualitative research who listened to portions of tapes and assisted with data analysis. A second doctorally-prepared nurse, experienced in phenomenological research, reviewed some of the transcripts and data analysis. Reliability and validity were addressed by procedures suggested by Lincoln and Guba (1985, pp. 289–331) to enhance trustworthiness of the data. Persistent observation was achieved by keeping notes about the analysis. Dependability and confirmability were achieved by keeping notes about the raw data, fieldnotes, and formulated meanings.

RESULTS

Pain in frail, elderly women after surgery is complex resulting in a unique experience. The data were clustered into three themes: (a) the immediate reality of pain, (b) security, and (c) dealing with pain. The immediate reality of pain consisted of the feeling, awareness, and past imposing on the present. Security consisted of comfort and trust. Dealing with pain consisted of endurance, control, and self-discovery of strategies to relieve pain. The themes manifested themselves in different forms among each of the participants. Relationships among the themes are illustrated in Figure A5-1.

The feeling of pain was central to the experience and set the stage for the thoughts, perceptions, and interactions that followed. But for some it was difficult to

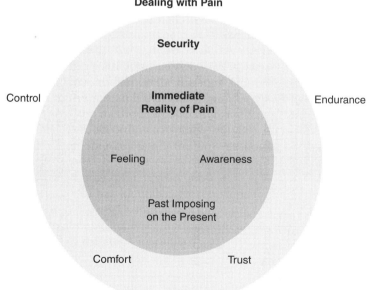

FIGURE A5-1. *Themes of the experience of pain in frail, elderly women after surgery.*

put into words. One woman said, "Well, how could you describe a pain, really?" The indescribability of pain suggests the perception that is a unique and solitary experience. This solitariness conveys a sense of loneliness as noted by the woman who said, "You don't expect anybody to know what that pain was, unless you have that experience yourself. It's beyond words." The indescribability of pain distanced the women from family, friends, and caregivers.

However, as the women talked more openly, they put their experience into words describing a variety of sensations: a dull ache, soreness, pressure, amazing discomfort, excruciating pain, and horrible pain. For some women, pain was not particularly intense at any time during the postoperative period. One said, "I refer to it as hurting, more than paining me." Women who had more intense pain used more descriptors that communicated a sense of vulnerability, a view of pain as an external object imposed upon them: "A hot poker in my belly"; "A needle"; "A knife." "A punch." Intense pain was all-encompassing. One participant said, "It was banging, all I do is feel the pain where they cut me." Intense pain created a need to monitor oneself and created a sense of distance between oneself and one's body. One woman said, "You couldn't even touch yourself there, you couldn't even sit or stand." Touching was a way to evaluate healing and recovery from surgery. Mild pain was described as pain leaving the body.

Awareness was a powerful moderator for interpreting the immediate reality of pain. A woman's sense of awareness was the degree to which she was fully aware of feelings, herself, and the environment. Several women described themselves as being fully aware almost immediately after surgery. Others described an altered sense of awareness. A strategy used by some women to deal with altered awareness was limiting pain medication. Haziness of perception was experienced by the five women over age 80. Lack of full awareness did not necessarily diminish the pain, but it altered the outward response to pain or memory of it. One woman commented, "The immediate days after, they kind of dissolved into the drug phase; I was acutely aware of excessive pain." Haziness of perception had an "other world" quality, being removed from reality and as one woman described it, being in "la la land."

The past imposed itself on the present for some of these women by providing a complexity of context by which to judge and ascibe meaning. This is a description by one woman, "I always think of pain in relation to the amount of pain I suffered with the neuropathy." The temporal nature of pain was highlighted by comparison with previous experiences, the most vivid of which was pain before surgery. Pain was the symptom that led all but one woman to seek medical attention. The time before surgery was characterized by uncertainty, waiting, and delaying—wishing and hoping the pain would dissipate. After surgery, pain for many of the women paled in comparison to their preoperative pain. One woman stated, "It wasn't as awful as I thought it would be." A woman with severe rheumatoid arthritis described postoperative pain as "temporary" and the pain of arthritis as "ongoing."

The past also influenced the relative importance of pain. One woman's mother died from a stroke shortly after a cholecystectomy at age 73. Another woman's brother died after surgery. For both, concerns about their own mortality superseded concerns about pain. The experiences of friends, family, and acquaintances created additional expectations. In summary, the women had a rich repertoire of personal experiences and a lifetime of experiences shared by others to provide a framework for the meaning of pain.

Feeling secure was manifest by seeking comfort and influenced by trust. Comfort was a state of experiencing emotional and physical solace that was obtained through interaction with others. The comfort of nursing care was valued. One woman said:

> First of all, they gave me medication, then they would come in and they'd give me a backrub which helped a lot really....It's just that they were being so nice, I guess, helped a great deal....If they don't listen, or if they seem like they're in a hurry, you sort of get frustrated.

Comfort was difficult to achieve independently but was facilitated by the demeanor, words, and actions of the nurses which conveyed expertise, availability, and reassurance. As one woman said, "When you have a good nurse and she has patience, she loves you." Roughness caused discomfort and exacerbated pain. Achievement of comfort led to a reduction in pain, although a distinction was made between comfort and pain relief. Family members and friends provided additional comfort by their mere presence and reliability.

Trust was being able to rely on others and one's own inner strength. Trust enabled the women to endure pain. It was manifest by the high regard that the women generally had for their physicians and nurses. The women trusted that their needs for pain management would be taken care of by physicians ordering medications and nurses providing pain medication. One said, "You couldn't get through it unless you were able to trust the people taking care of you." Trust had a spiritual dimension for five women. For them, trust in God was a lifelong pattern which helped in surviving surgery, enduring pain, and recovering.

Disconfirming experiences which eroded trust had the potential to exacerbate pain. One woman who had excruciating pain related how her anger about a bad experience after surgery affected her pain. Another woman, worried about getting the right medication, pointed to the sites of injections which relieved or didn't relieve pain. Her lack of trust resulted in fear which she handled by insisting that a family member stay with her.

Endurance, control, and self-discovery were subthemes related to dealing with pain. Endurance reflected lifelong patterns. Tolerating extreme pain before surgery, delay in seeking treatment, hope for a return to normalcy, and waiting for medication to be offered exemplified the women's capacity for endurance. The women described themselves as being able to tolerate pain. Medication was only for intolerable pain, "I only asked for another one [injection] when I couldn't cope any longer."

Pain was endured because it was a part of life. One woman said, "I try to take pain...I feel as though we have to have some pain." Suffering was described by some participants as a woman's role, "Men are no good [when it comes to tolerating pain]." Some women never asked for pain medication, expecting the nurses to know when medication was needed. Another noted that being demanding could adversely affect one's nursing care. The women did not like to take "narcotics." Fear of addiction in five of the women led to greater endurance of pain. "Fighting" or "battling" pain was a recurring metaphor. Reaching advanced age was indicative of one's endurance. If one could reach advanced age, then one was a survivor who could tolerate pain.

Control was experienced on a continuum between powerlessness and autonomy. Becoming sick and dependent before surgery and having severe unrelieved pain resulted in uncertainty and powerlessness. Reduction in pain after surgery led to a restoration of autonomy. Some women had no expectation of having control over how their pain was managed—trusting the staff to make pain-medication decisions.

Feeling in control was being able to ask for medication and having the nurses respond quickly to requests. Yet, for some, dependency on someone else for pain relief created a sense of powerlessness. One woman wondered why she was not given a patient-controlled analgesia (PCA) pump because, "If you are in control, you certainly ought to feel better about the whole thing."

Fear was manifestation of a loss of control but not experienced by all of the women. Fears included not recovering, not regaining mobility, the unknown, exacerbating pain with movement, and addiction. One 87-year-old woman's numerous fears about her survival, complications, and recovery were of far greater concern than pain. Five women were fearful of addiction, resulting in greater endurance of pain. Fear of addiction was a fear of the loss of control as described by one woman who "didn't want to become a victim of drug use."

The theme of self-discovery of strategies to decrease pain illustrates the independent nature of the women who called themselves survivors and fighters. One woman quickly discovered how to sleep through the night, "Before I go to bed, before I fall asleep, I say I need a shot so that I can sleep good." Pain relief was necessary for sleep which was essential to healing and recovery. Distraction relieved pain for one woman, "When you talk to someone it is not as painful." One woman didn't want to think about pain but about going home and recovery.

Lying still was the most common self-discovered strategy, enabling the women to endure pain and exert control over the unpredictable pain of movement. As one woman stated, "Well, you don't think you're making that move and you would never make it if you weren't made to make it. I couldn't believe it....You would never inflict that kind of pain on yourself." Lying still reduced pain, provided security, and decreased fears of doing harm. One woman commented about "The fear that somebody might bump you, cause if they did, you'd die." Although memory of details about the pain might have faded with time, pain associated with movement—particularly the first movement out of bed—was etched indelibly on these women's memories and was unequivocally the worst part of their experience.

DISCUSSION

The experience of pain in frail, elderly women after surgery is an interplay of themes related to (a) the immediate reality of pain: the feeling, awareness, and the past imposing on the present; (b) finding security: comfort and trust; and (c) dealing with pain: endurance, control, and self-discovery. The themes provide a link to the philosophical discussion of the nature of pain including chronic pain, research about uncertainty and control, and theoretical formulations about illness as well as direction for research and practice.

The uniqueness of the women's pain and the difficulty they had in sharing the experience indicates the solitary nature of pain. This is supported by philosophical analysis: "Whatever pain achieves, it achieves in part through its unsharability, and ensures its unsharability through its resistance to language" (Scarry, 1985, p. 4). The indescribable nature of pain provided the impetus for the development of the widely used McGill Pain Questionnaire (Melzack & Torgerson, 1971). The natural language of chronic pain has been called silence (Morris, 1991, p. 5). Hospitalized patients do not always report pain when first asked about it (Donovan, Dillon, & McGuire, 1987). The results of this study highlight the importance of taking adequate time to assess elders' pain.

CLINICAL SIDEBAR BY BARBARA PIEPER

In my outpatient wound practice, pain is the most difficult complaint I encounter. I can treat the venous ulcer no matter what its size. Yet, complaints of pain are often overwhelming. What medication will be most effective and usable given the patient's health history? How long can a medication be prescribed considering its major side effects? What nonpharmacologic approaches to pain management will the patient use? Frantically, I have searched the literature for answers. Surely, someone has studied pain and its management in a way that is useful for my patients. Yet, like Dr. Zalon, I find scant information.

Margarete Zalon studied the lived experience of postoperative pain in 16 frail, elderly women. The elderly are the fastest growing segment of American society. More of these women are undergoing major surgical procedures in the 1990s than in the past. Research about postoperative pain and its management for the elderly is lacking.

Dr. Zalon's findings are thought-provoking. Patients may have difficulty describing their pain; this does not mean that it isn't there. Past experience and the meaning a person ascribes to pain are important. If possible, perceptions of pain and its treatment should be discussed before surgery. Family members should be included in pain management so that they can provide comfort and reinforce teaching about pain control.

Nursing care was found to be a critical component of pain management. Nurses affected the patient's comfort and trust. Pain reduction enhanced the patient's autonomy. The women studied expected nurses to know when to give pain medication. The nurse studied was expected to listen with all of his or her senses and use the information gathered. What will happen to this level of pain assessment and management when registered nurses are replaced with less knowledgeable personnel?

Zalon's findings implied the need for patient education about pain management. Five patients feared becoming addicted. Besides medications, patients should be given information about nonpharmacologic methods of pain management. As these women experienced, one or several such methods may help to relieve pain.

Zalon's research is a beginning exploration of pain in frail, elderly women; themes have been identified. Replication may add to her findings.

Additional questions need to be explored. How effective are current postoperative pain management strategies for the elderly? With short hospitalization, what pain management strategies are safe when an elderly person will be home alone? How long postoperatively do the elderly experience surgical pain? What nonpharmacologic pain management strategies are most effective for the elderly?

Pain is a complex, subjective response. Nurses are continuously challenged in clinical practice to explore the many facets of pain and its reduction.

Although this study focused on acute postoperative pain which was relatively mild for most of the women, uncertainty and control were more important in the broader context of the entire experience of surgery. Preoperative pain was not only worse, but also associated with uncertainty creating stress and anxiety. The intensity of pain coupled with uncertainty added suffering to the experience. Postoperatively, uncertainties related to pain were diminished unless trust was eroded. Lack of trust creates uncertainty because of inconsistencies between expectations and experiences (Mishel, 1988). Pain after a myocardial infarction was a matter of experiencing pain, finding meaning, and taking action (Schwartz & Keller, 1993). Because postoperative pain had meaning and therefore less uncertainty, it provided an explanation for some of the women allowing the nurses to assume complete responsibility for pain relief.

The emergence of control as a theme illustrates the importance of determining how much control elderly women wish to exercise over pain relief. However, this may be problematic in the elderly because women with osteoarthritis most often used self-control as a coping strategy by keeping feelings to oneself and keeping others from knowing how bad things were (Burke & Flaherty, 1993). Perceived control in patients with chronic pain explains a significant portion of the variance in distress and disability (Wells, 1994). The results of the present investigation suggest further research is needed to determine the relationship between control over pre- and postoperative pain and recovery, particularly in light of the shift in uncertainty from pain to recovery. Self-discovery's emergence as a theme indicates elderly women might be successful in the use of pain-relief strategies that enhance control such as PCA pumps and biobehavioral methods, neither of which were employed in this sample. Improved postoperative analgesia has been reported for elderly men using PCA pumps (Egbert, Lampros, & Parks, 1993). However, the elderly use fewer opioids when provided with PCA pumps (MacIntyre & Jarvis, 1996). Replication of these studies would be useful.

The relative importance of postoperative pain in comparison with doubts about the return of mobility and functional status was striking. The illness-constellation model proposed by Morse and Johnson (1991, pp. 317–318) describes illness as affecting the sick person and significant others in four stages: uncertainty, disruption, striving to regain self, and regaining wellness. Uncertainty can be viewed as equivalent to the women's experience of pain before surgery when they knew something was wrong and tried to find out the cause of their symptoms. When the women sought medical care and early in the postoperative period, they can be characterized as being in a stage of disruption with a focus on the feeling, awareness, and past expectations about pain. This would explain the reliance on others for security provided through trust and comfort. Striving to regain their sense of self is manifest by the ways in which the women dealt with pain: endurance, control, and self-discovery. Thus, pain was decreased by lying still and using various strategies to achieve a sense of control and pain relief. The illness constellation model can be used to explain variations among the women as well as each woman's response to pain over time. Research is needed to determine whether the desire for control is an individual characteristic or a function of the stage of illness.

Pain has been described as a borderline experience between life and death (Arendt, 1958, p. 51). The experience of pain in these women can be viewed as a process of trying to restore one's place in the world, in life. The results suggest that nurses can facilitate restoration by exploring the significance that pain has for people in the context of their illness. This would enable nurses to individualize pain-relief strategies that support unique strengths and needs in order to enhance recovery from surgery.

Research article taken from: Zalon, M. L. (1997). Pain in frail, elderly women after surgery. *Image: Journal of Nursing Scholarship, 29*(1), 21–26. (reprinted with permission).

REFERENCES

Arendt, H. (1958). *The human condition.* Garden City, NY: Doubleday.

Boyd, C. O. (1993). Phenomenology: The method. In P. L. Munhall & C. O. Boyd (Eds.), *Nursing research: A qualitative perspective* (99–132). New York: National League for Nursing Press.

Burke, M., & Flaherty, M. J. (1993). Coping strategies and health status of elderly arthritic women. *Journal of Advanced Nursing, 18,* 7–13.

Cohen, F. (1980). Post-surgical pain relief: Patients' status and nurses' medication choices. *Pain, 9,* 265–274.

Colaizzi, P. (1978). Psychological research as the phenomenologist views it. In R. Valle & M. King (Eds.), *Existential-phenomenological alternatives for psychology* (48–71). New York: Oxford University Press.

Donovan, M., Dillon, P., & McGuire, L. (1987). Incidence and characteristics of pain in a sample of medical-surgical inpatients. *Pain, 30,* 69–78.

Duggleby, W., & Lander, J. (1994). Cognitive status and post-operative pain. Older adults. *Journal of Pain and Symptom Management, 9,* 19–27.

Egbert, A. M., Lampros, L. L., & Parks, L. L. (1993). Effects of patient-controlled analgesia on postoperative anxiety in elderly men. *American Journal of Critical Care, 2,* 118–124.

Faherty, B. S., & Grier, M. R. (1984). Analgesic medication for elderly people post-surgery. *Nursing Research, 33,* 369–372.

Harkins, S. W., Kwentus, J., & Price, D. D. (1984). Pain and the elderly. In C. Benedetti, C. R. Chapman, & G. Morrica (Eds.), *Advances in pain research and therapy: Vol. 7. Recent advances in the management of pain* (103–121). New York: Raven Press.

Hofland, S. L. (1992). Elder beliefs. Blocks to pain management. *Journal of Gerontological Nursing, 18*(6), 19–24, 39–40.

Jacox, A. K. (1989). Key aspects of comfort. In S. G. Funk, E. M. Tornquist, M. T. Champagne, L. A. Copp, & R. A. Wiese (Eds.), *Key aspects of comfort: Management of pain, fatigue, and nausea* (8–22). New York: Springer.

Kaiko, R. F., Wallenstein, S. L., Rogers, A. G., Grabinski, P. Y., & Houde, R. W. (1986). Clinical analgesic studies and sources of variation in analgesic response to morphine. In K. M. Foley, & C. E. Inturrisi (Eds.), *Advances in pain research and therapy: Vol. 8. Opioid analgesics in the management of clinical pain* (13–23). New York: Raven Press.

Lincoln, Y. S., & Guba, E. G. (1985). *Naturalistic inquiry.* Beverly Hills, CA: Sage.

MacIntyre, P. E., & Jarvis, D. A. (1996). Age is the best predictor of postoperative morphine requirements. *Pain, 64,* 357–364.

McCaffery, M., & Beebe, A. (1989). *Pain: Clinical manual for nursing practice.* St. Louis, MO: Mosby.

Melzack, R., Abbott, F. V., Zackon, W., Mulder, D. S., & Davis, M. W. (1987). Pain on a surgical ward: A survey of the duration and intensity of pain and the effectiveness of medication. *Pain, 29,* 67–72.

Melzack, R., & Torgerson, W. S. (1971). On the language of pain. *Anesthesiology, 34,* 50–59.

Miskowski, C., Nichols, R., Brody, R., & Synold, T. (1994). Assessment of patient satisfaction, using the American Pain Society's quality assurance standards on acute and cancer-related pain. *Journal of Pain and Symptom Management, 9,* 5–11.

Mishel, M. H. (1988). Uncertainty in illness. *Image: Journal of Nursing Scholarship, 20,* 225–232.

Morris, D. B. (1991). *The culture of pain.* Berkeley, CA: University of California Press.

Morse, J. M., & Johnson, J. L. (1991). Toward a theory of illness: The illness-constellation model. In J. M. Morse & J. Johnson, (Eds.), *The illness experience: Dimensions of suffering* (315–342). Newbury Park, CA: Sage.

Paice, J., Mahon, S. M., & Faut-Callahan, M. (1995). Pain control in hospitalized postsurgical patients. *Medsurg Nursing, 4,* 367–372.

Paterson, J. G., & Zderad, L. T. (1976). *Humanistic nursing.* New York: Wiley.

Platzer, H. (1989). Post-operative confusion in the elderly—A literature review. *International Journal of Nursing Studies, 26,* 369–379.

Portenoy, R. K., & Kanner, R. M. (1985). Patterns of analgesic prescription and consumption in a university-affiliated community hospital. *Archives of Internal Medicine, 145,* 439–441.

Scarry, E. (1985). *The body in pain: The making and unmaking of the world.* New York: Oxford University Press.

Schwartz, J. M., & Keller, C. (1993). Variables affecting the reporting of pain following acute myocardial infarction. *Applied Nursing Research, 6,* 13–18.

Souder, E. J. (1992). The consumer approach to the recruitment of elder subjects. *Nursing Research, 41,* 314–316.

Valle, R. S., & King, M. (1978). An introduction to existential-phenomenological thought in psychology. In R. S. Valle & M. King (Eds.), *Existential-phenomenological alternatives for psychology* (6–17). New York: Oxford University Press.

Wells, N. (1994). Perceived control over pain: Relation to distress and disability. *Research in Nursing and Health, 17,* 295–302.

Woodrow, K. M., Friedman, G. D., Siegelaub, A. B., & Collen, M. F. (1972). Pain tolerance: Differences according to age, sex and race. *Psychosomatic Medicine, 34,* 548–555.

Zalon, M. L. (1993). Nurses' assessments of patients' postoperative pain. *Pain, 54,* 329–334.

Grounded Theory as Method

Grounded theory is a qualitative research approach used to explore the social processes that present within human interactions. The roots of grounded theory can be found in the interpretive tradition of symbolic interactionism. Through application of the approach, researchers develop explanations of key social processes or structures that are derived from or grounded in empirical data (Hutchinson, 1993a). "Grounded theorists base their research on the assumption that each group shares a specific social psychological problem that is not necessarily articulated" (Hutchinson, 1993a, p. 185). Glaser and Strauss (1967) developed the method and published the first text addressing method issues: *The Discovery of Grounded Theory.*

Nursing has used the grounded theory to describe phenomena important to professional nursing (Beck, 1993; Benoliel, 1967; Hutchinson, 1992 & 1993a; Stern, 1981; Wilson 1977, 1986). Benoliel (1996) noted that grounded theory began to influence nursing knowledge development in the early 1960s. In her manuscript "Grounded Theory and Nursing Knowledge," she examined how the method has contributed to nursing's body of substantive knowledge from the 1960s through the 1990s. Benoliel (1996) suggested that the major focus of the contributions to nursing knowledge over these decades was on "adaptations to illness, infertility, nurse adaptation and interventions, and status passages of vulnerable persons and groups" (p. 406).

Grounded Theory Defined

Grounded theory as a method of qualitative research is a form of field research. *Field research* refers to qualitative research approaches that explore and describe phenomena in naturalistic settings such as hospitals, outpatient clinics, or nursing homes. "The purpose of field studies is to examine in an in-depth fashion the practices, behaviors, beliefs, and attitudes of individuals or groups as they normally function in real life" (Polit & Hungler, 1991, p. 195). The method systematically applies specific procedural steps to ultimately develop a grounded theory, or theoretically complete explanation about a particular phenomenon (Benoliel, 1996; Stern, 1980; Strauss & Corbin, 1990). Strauss and Corbin (1990) have explained grounded theory as follows:

A grounded theory is one that is inductively derived from the study of the phenomenon it represents. That is, it is discovered, developed, and provisionally verified through systematic data collection and analysis of data pertaining to that phenomenon. Therefore, data collection, analysis, and theory stand in reciprocal relationship with each other. One does not begin with a theory, then prove it. Rather, one begins with an area of study and what is relevant to that area is allowed to emerge. (p. 23)

The goal of grounded theory investigations is to discover theoretically complete explanations about particular phenomena. According to Strauss and Corbin (1990), grounded theory involves "systematic techniques and procedures of analysis that enable the researcher to develop a substantive theory that meets the criteria for doing 'good' science: significance, theory-observation compatibility, generalizability, reproducibility, precision, rigor, and verification" (p. 31).

Through an inductive approach, researchers using the method generate theory that can be either formal or substantive. *Substantive theory* is that developed for a substantive, or empirical, area of inquiry (Glaser & Strauss, 1967). Examples pertinent to nursing might include client care, hope for clients who are undergoing bone marrow transplantations (Ersek, 1992), or therapeutic touch (Heidt, 1990). *Formal theory* is developed for a formal, or conceptual, area of inquiry (Glaser & Strauss, 1967). Examples might include socialization to professional nursing or authority and power in nursing practice. Substantive and formal theory are considered to be middle-range theories in that both types fall between the working hypotheses and the all-inclusive grand theories (Glaser & Strauss, 1967).

Grand theories are complex, attempting to explain broad areas within a discipline as opposed to middle-range theory, which comprises primarily relational concepts (Marriner-Tomey, 1989). Grand theories are broadest in scope, frequently lack operationally defined concepts, and are unsuitable to direct empirical testing (Fawcett, 1989). *Partial theories* are the most limited in scope and utility, comprising summary statements of isolated observation within a narrow range of phenomena. Some partial or micro theories may be developed into middle-range theories with additional research (Fawcett, 1989).

Middle-range theories have a narrower scope than grand theories and encompass limited concepts and aspects of the real world (Fawcett, 1989). Middle-range theories have been purported to be most useful because researchers can empirically test them in a direct manner (Merton, (1957).

An important concept for new grounded theorists to recognize is that researchers do not begin with theory. Instead, researchers identify essential constructs from generated data; from these data, theory emerges. Procedural steps in grounded theory are specific and occur simultaneously (see Fig. 6-1). Because the information pertinent to the emerging theory comes directly from the data, the generated theory remains connected to or

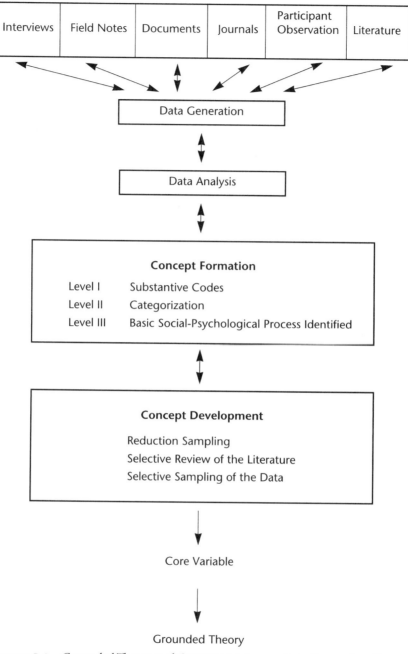

FIGURE 6-1. *Grounded Theory and Connections Among Data Generation, Treatment, and Analysis*

grounded in the data (Glaser & Strauss, 1967; Stern, 1980; Strauss & Corbin, 1990).

Stern (1980) differentiated grounded theory from other qualitative methodologies. There are five basic differences:

1. The conceptual framework of grounded theory is generated from the data rather than from previous studies.
2. The researcher attempts to discover dominant processes in the social scene rather than describe the unit under investigation.
3. The researcher compares all data with all other data.
4. The researcher may modify data collection according to the advancing theory; that is, the researcher drops false leads or asks more penetrating questions as needed.
5. The investigator examines data as they arrive, and begins to code, categorize, conceptualize, and write the first few thoughts concerning the research report almost from the beginning of the study (p. 21).

Methodological issues raised by more recent attempts to refine the process of generating grounded theory continue to be addressed in the literature (Baker, Wuest, & Stern, 1992; Keddy, Sims, & Stern, 1996; Robrecht, 1995; Wuest, 1995). Baker et al. (1992) discussed method slurring between grounded theory and phenomenology, which mixed steps from both methods, and addressed the importance of being specific about method. Robrecht (1995) proposed "dimensional analysis, described by Schatzman in 1991 as a method for the generation of grounded theory" (p. 169). Within a feminist framework, the grounded theory method incorporates diversity and change (Wuest, 1995).

Grounded Theory Roots

As a qualitative research method, grounded theory has been used extensively in the discipline of sociology. Nurse–researchers have widely recognized the significance of grounded theory as a method to investigate phenomena important to nursing, and continue to apply grounded theory as a qualitative research approach.

Benoliel (1996) examined the roots of grounded theory and its development over the past several decades. She identified the knowledge generation that occurred during this period as the Decade of Discovery, 1960–1970; Decade of Development, 1970–1980; Decade of Diffusion, 1980–1990; and Decade of Diversification, 1990 to present.

During the Decade of Discovery, 1960–1970, grounded theory emerged as a major research method within the field of sociology. As the method entered the Decade of Development (1970–1980), seminars for the continued development of grounded theorists emerged as well as funding for postdoctoral research training programs (Benoliel, 1996). The

Decade of Diffusion (1980–1990) resulted in even further expansion of the research method, and nursing became visible as a group of researchers who could explain and implement grounded theory method. Nursing journals gave more attention to grounded theory and university centers evolved that focused on grounded theory research in nursing (Benoliel, 1996). The Decade of Diversification (1990 to present) has resulted in the dissemination of the knowledge gained through grounded theory research.

Grounded theory is an important research method for the study of nursing phenomena. The method explores the richness and diversity of the human experience and contributes to the development of middle-range theories in nursing. This chapter reviews fundamental themes of grounded theory and addresses methodological issues specific to engaging in this qualitative research approach. The chapter also reviews the systematic techniques and procedures of analysis essential to grounded theory investigations. Additional reading of primary sources is necessary to grasp the method in a comprehensive manner.

Fundamental Characteristics of the Grounded Theory Method

Because Glaser and Strauss (1967) were the first to address grounded theory as a research method, they are consequently credited with the development and refinement of the method. Stern (1980) has written about the use of grounded theory in nursing and the importance of its use as a rigorous research method.

Grounded theory explores basic social processes. Symbolic interactionism theory, described by George Herbert Mead (1964) and Herbert Blumer (1969), is directly related to the grounded theory method. In *symbolic interactionism theory,* it is believed that people behave and interact based on how they interpret or give meaning to specific symbols in their lives, such as style of dress or verbal and nonverbal expressions. For example, the nurse's cap, which is seen less frequently, was a style of dress that gave meaning to some clients, which is apparent from statements such as, "How do I know you are my nurse if you do not wear your cap?" or "I liked it better when nurses wore caps—they looked more professional." Language can also have different meanings for different people. A common statement made by many nurses is, "I'm working on the floor today." Individuals familiar with the health care environment are likely to interpret that statement to mean that the nurse has been assigned to a specific unit in the hospital where he or she is providing nursing care to clients. Someone who is unfamiliar with the hospital setting or is from a different culture may interpret this statement differently. To them, "I'm working on the floor today" may mean cleaning or repairing the floor. Stern, Allen, and Moxley (1982) emphasized that "it is also through the meaning and value of which these symbols have for us that we try to interpret our world and the actors who interact with us. In this way, we try to read minds, and to act accordingly. Learning the meaning and value of interactional symbols is everyone's lifetime study, and no easy task" (p. 203). The study and exploration of the social processes that present within human interactions is grounded theory, are linked directly to symbolic interactionism.

Grounded theory methodology combines both inductive and deductive research methods (Glaser & Strauss, 1967; Stern 1980; Strauss & Corbin, 1990). From an inductive perspective, theory emerges from specific observations and generated data. The theory then can be tested empirically to develop predictions from general principles such as a deductive research method. Hutchinson (1993a) addressed an important difference between verificational research and grounded theory research. Her explanation is helpful in clarifying the inductive nature of grounded theory:

> In verificational research, the researcher chooses an existing theory or conceptual framework and formulates hypotheses, which are then tested in a specific population. Verificational research is linear; the researcher delineates a problem, selects a theoretical framework, develops hypotheses, collects data, tests the hypotheses, and interprets the results. On a continuum, verificational research is more deductive whereas grounded theory research is more inductive. Verificational research moves from a general theory to a specific situation, whereas grounded theorists aim for the development of a more inclusive, general theory through the analysis of specific social phenomena. (p. 183)

Constant comparative analysis is another fundamental characteristic that guides data generation and treatment. *Constant comparative analysis* of qualitative data combines an analytic procedure of constant comparison with an explicit coding procedure for generated data. "The constant comparative method is concerned with generating and plausibly suggesting many categories, properties, and hypotheses about general problems" (Glaser & Strauss, 1967). *Core variables* that are broad in scope interrelate concepts and hypotheses that emerge during data analysis. *Basic social psychologic processes* (BSPs) illustrate the social processes that emerge from the data analysis. A later section on the application of the grounded theory method explains these fundamental characteristics in greater detail.

Selection of Grounded Theory as a Method

The need for more middle-range theories in nursing that can be empirically tested is one reason for using grounded theory to conduct scientific investigations of phenomena important to nursing. Stern et al. (1982) further articulated the factors linking grounded theory to nursing: Nursing occurs in a natural rather than controlled setting, and the nursing process requires "constant comparison of collected and coded data, hypothesis generation, use of the literature as data, and collection of additional data to verify or reject hypotheses" (Stern et al., 1982, p. 201).

Grounded theorists embarking on a new investigation should ask themselves, Have I paid enough attention to this particular phenomenon in terms of the individual's viewpoint? Has empirical research and the published literature offered what seems to be an oversimplification of the concepts relevant to the phenomenon under investigation? Is there a need for a deeper understanding of specific characteristics related to a particular phenomenon? Has the phenomenon been previously investigated? Positive answers to these or similar questions can validate for grounded theorists that the method choice is appropriate. As in any type of research, grounded theorists must consider the issues of available resources, time frame, and personal commitment to the investigation.

Elements and Interpretation of the Method

Application of grounded theory research techniques to the investigation of phenomena important to nursing education, practice, and administration involves several processes. The following is a discussion on the development and refinement of the research question as well as on the sample, researcher's role, and ethical considerations in grounded theory investigations. Also described are the steps in the research process, including data generation, treatment, and analysis.

RESEARCH QUESTION

The main purpose of using the grounded theory approach is to explore social processes with the goal of developing theory. The research question in a grounded theory investigation identifies the phenomenon to be studied. More specifically, the question lends focus and clarity about what the phenomenon of interest is (Strauss & Corbin, 1990). Furthermore, researchers

> need a research question or questions that will give us the flexibility and freedom to explore a phenomenon in depth. Also underlying this approach to qualitative research is the assumption that all of the concepts pertaining to a given phenomenon have not yet been identified, at least not in this population or place; or if so, then the relationships between the concepts are poorly understood or conceptually undeveloped. (Strauss & Corbin, 1990, p. 37)

The nature of grounded theory methodology requires that investigators refine the research question as they generate and analyze the study data. Because the study focus may change depending on the data generated, the original question merely lends focus to the study. A truly accurate research question is impossible to ask before beginning any grounded theory study (Hutchinson, 1986).

An example of a grounded theory question that begins an investigation and lends focus to the study is, How do nursing faculty address unsafe skill performance by nursing students? The question is broad but adds focus to the investigation by clarifying that the study will explore faculty evaluation and feedback techniques as they relate to unsafe student clinical performance. As data collection and analysis proceed, the focus of the study may change, given the emerging theory. Hypothetically, the focus of the study could change to, What is unsafe skill performance? Researchers must begin with a broad question that also provides focus. Researchers should expect that they will refine the question throughout the research process.

SAMPLING

Just as it is impossible to finalize the research question before a grounded theory investigation, it is equally impossible to know how many participants will be involved. The sample size is determined by the data generated and their analysis. Grounded theorists continue to collect data until they achieve saturation. In terms of grounded theory, "saturation refers to the completeness of all levels of codes when no new conceptual information is available to indicate new codes or the expansion of existing ones. The researcher, by repeatedly checking and asking questions of the data, ultimately achieves a sense of closure" (Hutchinson, 1986, p. 125).

RESEARCHER'S ROLE

Stern (1980) emphasized that, in a naturalistic setting, it is impossible to control for the presence of the researcher. Investigators bring personal experience to a study to enhance understanding of the problem. According to Stern et al. (1982), in the conduct of naturalistic research, investigators do not attempt to remove themselves from the study. Rather, researchers openly recognize they have a role in the investigation. Stern et al. further delineated the grounded theorist's role as follows: "The grounded theory researcher works within a matrix where several processes go on at once rather than following a series of linear steps. The investigator examines data as they arrive, and begins to code, categorize, conceptualize, and to write the first few thoughts concerning the research report almost from the beginning of the study" (p. 205). The researcher is an integral part of the investigation and, consequently, must recognize the intimate role with the participants and include the implications of that role in the actual investigation and interpretation of the data.

Strauss and Corbin (1990) have identified skills needed for doing qualitative research: the ability "to step back and critically analyze situations, to recognize and avoid bias, to obtain valid and reliable data, and to think abstractly" (p. 18). Furthermore, "a qualitative researcher requires theoretical and social sensitivity, the ability to maintain analytical distance while at the same time drawing upon past experience and theoretical knowledge to interpret what is seen, astute powers of observation, and good interactional skills" (p. 18). To conduct a grounded theory investigation, researchers must possess excellent interpersonal skills, observational skills, and writing ability to put into words with a high degree of accuracy what they have learned.

ETHICAL CONSIDERATIONS

Researchers must also consider the ethical implications of conducting a grounded theory investigation or, for that matter, any qualitative investigation. Obtaining informed consent, maintaining confidentiality, and handling sensitive information are a few examples of ethical considerations researchers must address. Because it is impossible to anticipate what sensitive issues might emerge during data collection in a grounded theory investigation, researchers must be prepared for unexpected concerns. Chapter 3 provides an extensive discussion of ethical considerations pertinent to qualitative investigations.

STEPS IN THE RESEARCH PROCESS

Stern (1980) described five steps in the process of grounded theory research that compose the fundamental components of the method. They are (1) the collection of empirical data, (2) concept formation, (3) concept development, (4) concept modification and integration, and (5) production of the research report.

DATA GENERATION

Researchers may collect grounded theory data from interview, observation, or documents, or from a combination of these sources (Stern, 1980). Daily journals, participant observation, formal or semistructured interviews, and informal interviews are valid means of generating data.

Hutchinson (1992) described her data generation techniques in her article "Nurses Who Violate the Nurse Practice Act: Transformation of Professional Identity" as follows:

> data were gathered from phone and face-to-face in-depth interviews with a purposive volunteer sample of 30 nurses who went before the Florida Board of Nursing (BON), one attorney who worked with the BON, three members of the BON and the executive director, one member of the Probable Cause Panel and two nurse investigators who worked with the Department of Professional Regulation (DPR). Nurses ranged in age from 21–63, were Caucasian, Afro-American, Hispanic and Filipino; male and female. Their education ranged from the associate degree to the baccalaureate degree; some were trained as nurse practitioners, nurse anesthetists and certified nurse midwives. Interview questions for

the nurses were: 1. Tell me about your alleged "violation" of the Nurse Practice Act. What was the "problem?" How did it occur? How did you get reported to the DPR? After you were reported to the DPR what happened? 2. What was it like to go before the BON? Best/Worst things? 3. How could the BON experience be better? 4. What would you tell other nurses who have to go before the BON? 5. Where do you go from here? (p. 134)

Hutchinson (1992) further explained that her data collection included participant observation at six BON meetings and three administrative hearings as well as document analysis in which she read files on nurses who had appeared before the BON. This example should give readers a sense of the many methods researchers use to generate data in grounded theory investigations.

The researcher examines and analyzes the data gathered using field techniques, observational methods, documents, and publications through a system of constant comparison until the investigation generates a number of hypotheses. As investigators develop hypotheses, they consult the literature for previously developed theories that relate to the emerging hypotheses of the study in progress. The developed theory, consisting of related factors or variables, should be suitable for testing (Hutchinson, 1986; Stern, 1980; Strauss & Corbin, 1990).

DATA TREATMENT

The choice of data treatment and collection methods is influenced primarily by researcher preference. Researchers generally tape-record interviews and transcribe them verbatim. Researchers should transcribe and type double spaced field notes immediately. It is also helpful to leave at least a 2-in margin on one side of the transcribed data sheets for coding purposes. Table 6-1 provides readers with an example of a field note and Level I coding.

DATA ANALYSIS: GENERATING THEORY

The discovery of a core variable is the goal of grounded theory. "The researcher undertakes the quest for this essential element of the theory, which illuminates the main theme of the actors in the setting, and explicates what is going on in the data" (Glaser, 1978, p. 94). The core variable serves as the foundational concept for theory generation, and "the integration and density of the theory are dependent on the discovery of a significant core variable" (Hutchinson, 1993a, p. 193). The core variable has six essential characteristics:

1. It recurs frequently in the data.
2. It links various data.
3. Because it is central, it explains much of the variation in all the data.

TABLE 6-1   **Sample Field Note**

Field Note	Level-I Coding
2/18/98	
There are 7 students, 1 faculty member, and 3 staff members to care for 35 orthopedic clients. Each student has been assigned 1 client. The students are juniors in a baccalaureate nursing program. This is their <u>1st clinical experience</u> and their 4th week on the unit. The instructor is working with a student as she prepares an intramuscular injection. <u>The stu-</u>	Fear
<u>dent's hands are trembling.</u> The student drops the uncapped syringe on the floor, bends down, picks up the syringe to prepare to use the contaminated syringe to prepare the injec-	
tion. <u>The instructor asks her what is wrong with the way she</u>	Questioning
<u>is proceeding. The student does not know.</u> <u>Tears are welling</u>	Overwhelming
<u>up in the student's eyes.</u> <u>The instructor's face is flushed and</u>	Frustration
<u>she seems frustrated.</u> The instructor <u>explains</u> what is wrong,	Telling
<u>tells</u> the student she is unprepared for the experience, and	
<u>asks</u> a staff member to give the injection. The staff member	Asking
comments she doesn't have time. <u>The student leaves the</u>	
<u>medication room crying.</u> The instructor takes her to a confer-	Privacy
ence room to discuss the incident.	

4. It has implications for a more general or formal theory.
5. As it becomes more detailed, the theory moves forward.
6. It permits maximum variation and analyses (Strauss, 1987, p. 36).

BSPs are core variables that illustrate social processes as they continue over time, regardless of varying conditions (Glaser, 1978, p. 100). For example, in Hutchinson's (1992) article "Nurses Who Violate the Nurse Practice Act: Transformation of Professional Identity," the basic social process is the "transformation of professional identity that involves alterations in their ways of viewing themselves, their work and the profession of nursing" (p. 135). Emergence of the core variable is discussed later in the section Concept Development.

CONCEPT FORMATION
Grounded theory requires that researchers collect, code, and analyze data from the beginning of the study. "The method is circular, allowing the researchers to change focus and pursue leads revealed by the ongoing

data analysis" (Hutchinson, 1986, p. 119). Figure 6-1 illustrates the circular nature of data analysis in grounded theory.

CODING

During the conduct of a grounded theory investigation, the processes of data collection, coding, and analysis occur simultaneously. As they collect data through interviews, participant observation, field notes, and so forth, researchers begin to code data. They then examine data line by line, identify processes, and conceptualize underlying patterns. Coding occurs at three levels.

LEVEL I CODING. *Level I coding* requires that grounded theorists look for process. As they receive data, investigators apply a system of open coding, that is, they examine the data line by line and identify the processes in the data. It is critical to code each sentence and incident using as many codes as possible to ensure a thorough examination of the data. Researchers write code words in the wide margins of the field notes for easy identification.

In Level I coding, the codes are called substantive codes because they codify the substance of the data and often use the words participants themselves have used (Stern, 1980, p. 21). The two types of substantive codes are (1) those from the language of the people who were observed or interviewed and (2) implicit codes constructed by researchers based on concepts obtained from the data (Mullen & Reynolds, 1978).

From the beginning of the study, grounded theorists attempt to discover as many categories as possible and to compare them with new indicators to uncover characteristics and relationships. They discard early codes if those codes lack foundation in the data and may add more codes as data gathering progresses (Mullen & Reynolds, 1978).

LEVEL II CODING. *Level II coding* or *categorizing* requires use of the constant comparative method in the treatment of data. Researchers code the data, compare them with other data, and assign the data to clusters or categories according to obvious fit. Categories are simply coded data that seem to cluster and may result from the condensing of Level I codes (Hutchinson, 1986; Stern, 1980). Deciding on specific categories is facilitated by questioning what each Level I code might indicate and then comparing each Level I code with all other Level I codes. This process enables researchers to determine what particular category would be appropriate for the grouping of similar Level I codes. Researchers then compare each category with every other category to ensure the categories are mutually exclusive.

LEVEL III CODING. *Level III coding* describes BSPs, which essentially compose the title given to the central themes that emerge from the data. Questions suggested by Glaser and Strauss (1967) to describe BSPs include the following: What is going on in the data? What is the focus of the study and the relationship of the data to the study? What is the problem that is being dealt with by the participants? What processes are helping the participants cope with the problem? For example, in a study by Heidt (1990), participants offered the following when asked the proceeding questions:

> They were sick and wanted the help of the nurses to relieve their pain and or anxiety as well as to find ways to cope with their illness. Their energy fields could be characterized as being "closed" or depleted as a result of their illnesses. The nurses intentionally opened themselves to a healing energy that was within them and in the universe, and they acted as a "link for the flow of this energy to their patients. Through this helping relationship, the patients' field of energy opened, and their inner resources for healing were stimulated." (Heidt, 1990, p. 181)

CONCEPT DEVELOPMENT

Three major steps expand and define the emerging theory: reduction, selective sampling of the literature, and selective sampling of the data. Through these processes, the core variable emerges (Stern et al., 1982, p. 207).

REDUCTION

During data analysis, an overwhelming number of categories emerge that researchers need to reduce in number. Comparing categories allows researchers to see how they cluster or connect and can be fit under another broader category (Stern et al., 1982, p. 207). Category reduction is an essential component determining the primary social processes or core variables that trace the action in the social scene being investigated. The result of this reduction is a clustering of categories that, when combined, form a category of broader scope.

SELECTIVE SAMPLING OF THE LITERATURE

Stern (1980) has suggested that attempting a literature search before the study begins is unnecessary and perhaps may even be detrimental to the study. Reviewing the literature may lead to prejudgments and affect premature closure of ideas, the direction may be wrong. and available data or materials may be inaccurate (Stern, 1980).

Selective sampling of the literature is suggested and generally follows or occurs simultaneously with data analysis. The literature review helps researchers become familiar with works published on the concepts under study and fills in the missing pieces in the emerging theory. Referring to the example—How do nursing faculty address unsafe skill performance by nursing students?—that illustrated the development of the research question, investigators may review the published literature on the teaching of clinical skills, evaluation of those skills, or perhaps literature on what constitutes unsafe performance. Depending on what additional data emerge, researchers will also need to review literature pertinent to those new concepts.

As theory begins to develop, researchers conduct a literature review to learn what has been published about the emerging concepts. They use the existing literature as data and weave the literature into a matrix consisting of data, category, and conceptualization. Literature, carefully scrutinized, helps expand the theory and relate it to other theories (Stern et al., 1982). The literature can fill in gaps in the emerging theory and add completeness to the theoretical description.

SELECTIVE SAMPLING OF THE DATA

As the main concepts or variables become apparent, comparison with the data determines under which conditions they occur and if the concepts or variables seem central to the emerging theory. Researchers may collect additional data in a selective manner to develop the hypotheses and identify the properties of the main categories. Through selective sampling, saturation of the categories occurs (Stern et al., 1982).

EMERGENCE OF THE CORE VARIABLE

Through the process of reduction and comparison, the core variable for the investigation emerges. "The concept of core variable refers to a category which accounts for most of the variation in a pattern of behavior and which helps to integrate other categories that have been discovered in the data" (Mullen & Reynolds, 1978, p. 282). Heidt (1990) identified the core variable of her grounded theory investigation as "opening," "the core variable linking the experiences of nurses and patients in the process of giving and receiving therapeutic touch" (pp. 181–182).

Following the emergence of the core variable, researchers begin the steps of concept modification and integration. Through the use of theoretical codes, the conceptual framework moves from a descriptive to a theoretical level.

CONCEPT MODIFICATION AND INTEGRATION

Concept modification and integration are accomplished as researchers continue to analyze data. Theoretical coding provides direction and memoing preserves the researcher's thoughts and abstractions related to the emerging theory.

THEORETICAL CODING

Theoretical coding gives direction to the process of examining data in theoretical rather than descriptive terms (Stern, 1980). According to Stern (1980), this means applying a variety of analytical schemes to data to enhance their abstraction. Moving from descriptive to theoretical explanations, researchers examine all the variables that may affect data analysis and findings (Stern, 1980). During concept modification and integration, researchers use memoing to maintain their ideas pertinent to the emerging theory.

MEMOING

Memoing preserves emerging hypotheses, analytical schemes, hunches, and abstractions. Researchers must sort memos into cluster concepts to tie up or remove loose ends. They write memos on file cards or paper or store them in computer files. During the process, it becomes clear how concepts fully integrate with one another and which analytical journey extends beyond the focus of the research report. Investigators set aside memos that do not fit until they write another focus of the study. Sorted memos become the basis for the research report (Stern, 1980).

PRODUCTION OF THE RESEARCH REPORT

The research report for a grounded theory investigation presents the theory, which is substantiated by supporting data from field notes. The report should give readers an idea of the sources of the data, how the data were rendered, and how the concepts were integrated. A good report reflects the theory in ways that allow an outsider to grasp its meaning and apply its concepts.

Evaluation of Grounded Theories

Strauss and Corbin (1990) identified four criteria for judging the applicability of theory to a phenomenon: (1) fit, (2) understanding, (3) generality, and (4) control. If theory is faithful to the everyday reality of the substantive area and is carefully induced from diverse data, then it should fit that substantive area. If a researcher collected insufficient data and attempted closure too soon, then it is impossible to meet this criterion. Because it represents a reality, the grounded theory derived should be comprehensible to both the study participants and to practitioners with experience in the specific area studied. If the data on which the theory is based are comprehensive and the interpretations conceptual and broad, then that theory should be abstract enough and include sufficient variation so that it may apply to a variety of contexts related to the phenomenon under study, thus meeting the criterion of generality. The theory also should provide control with regard to action toward the phenomenon (Strauss & Corbin, 1990).

Summary

Grounded theory plays a significant role in the conduct of qualitative research. The fundamental characteristics and application of the approach include issues related to refinement of the research question; determination of the sample; and data generation, treatment, and analysis. Applied to the profession of nursing, grounded theory can increase middle-range substantive theories and help explain theoretical gaps among theory, research, and practice. Chapter 7 continues with the grounded theory method as it has been applied in nursing education, practice, and administration.

REFERENCES

Baker, C., Wuest, J., Stern, P. N. (1992). Method slurring: The grounded theory/phenomenology example. *Journal of Advanced Nursing, 17,* 1255–1360.

Beck, C. T. (1993). Teetering on the edge: A substantive theory of postpartum depression. *Nursing Research, 42*(1), 42–48.

Benoliel, J. Q. (1967). *The nurse and the dying patient.* New York: Macmillan.

Benoliel, J. Q. (1996). Grounded theory and nursing knowledge. *Qualitative Health Research, 6*(3), 406–428.

Blumer, H. (1969). *Symbolic intervention, perspective and method.* Englewood Cliffs, NJ: Prentice Hall.

Ersek, M. (1992). The process of maintaining hope in adults undergoing bone marrow transplantation for leukemia. *Oncology Nursing Forum, 19*(6), 883–889.

Fawcett, J. (1989). *Analysis and evaluation of conceptual models of nursing* (2nd ed.). Philadelphia: F.A. Davis.

Glaser, B. (1978). *Theoretical sensitivity.* Mill Valley, CA: Sociology Press.

Glaser, B. G., & Strauss, A. (1967). *The discovery of grounded theory: Strategies for qualitative research.* New York: Aldine.

Heidt, P. R. (1990). Openness: A qualitative analysis of nurses' and patients' experiences of therapeutic touch. *Image, 22*(3), 180–186.

Hutchinson, S. (1986). Grounded theory. The method. In P. L. Munhall & C. O. Boyd (Eds.), *Nursing research: A qualitative perspective* (pp. 111–130). Norwalk, CT: Appleton-Century-Crofts.

Hutchinson, S. A. (1992). Nurses who violate the Nurse Practice Act: Transformation of professional identity. *Image, 24*(2), 133–139.

Hutchinson, S. A. (1993a). Grounded theory: The method. In P. L. Munhall & C. O. Boyd (Eds.), *Nursing research: A qualitative perspective* (pp. 180–212). New York: National League for Nursing Press.

Hutchinson, S. A. (1993b). People with bipolar disorders quest for equanimity: Doing grounded theory. In P. L. Munhall & C. O. Boyd (Eds.), *Nursing research: A qualitative perspective* (pp. 213–236). New York: National League for Nursing Press.

Keddy, B., Sims, S. L., & Stern, P. N. (1996). Grounded theory as feminist methodology. *Journal of Advanced Nursing, 23,* 448–453.

Marriner-Tomey, A. (1989). Nursing theorists and their work, 2nd ed. Philadelphia. C. V. Mosby.

Mead, G. H. (1964). *George Herbert Mead on social psychology.* Chicago: University of Chicago Press.

Merton, R. K. (1957). *Sociological theory: Uses and unities.* New York: Free Press.

Mullen, P. D., & Reynolds, R. (1978). The potential of grounded theory for health education research: Linking theory and practice. *Health Education Monographs, 6*(3), 280–294.

Polit, D. F., & Hungler, B. P. (1991). *Nursing research: Principles and methods* (4th ed.). Philadelphia: J.B. Lippincott.

Robrecht, L. C. (1995). Grounded theory: Evolving methods. *Qualitative Health Research, 5*(2), 169–177.

Schatzman, L. (1991). Dimensional analysis: Notes on an alternative approach to the rounding of theory in qualitative research. In D. R. Maines (Ed.), *Social organization and social process: Essays in honor of Anselm Strauss* (pp. 303–314). New York: Aldine.

Stern, P. N. (1980). Grounded theory methodology: Its uses and processes. *Image, 12*(7), 20–23.

Stern, P. N. (1981). Solving problems of cross-cultural health teaching: The Filipino childbearing family. *Image, 13*(2), 47–50.

Stern, P. N., Allen, L. M., & Moxley, P. A. (1982). The nurse as grounded theorist: History, processes, and uses. *Review Journal of Philosophy and Social Science, 7,* 142, 200–215.

Strauss, A. (1987). *Qualitative analysis for social scientists*. New York: Cambridge University Press.

Strauss, A., & Corbin, J. (1990). *Basics of qualitative research: Grounded theory procedures and techniques*. Newbury Park, CA: Sage.

Wilson, H. S. (1977). Limiting intrusion—Social control of outsiders in a healing community. *Nursing Research, 26*(2), 103–111.

Wilson, H. S. (1986). Presencing—Social control of schizophrenics in an antipsychiatric community: Doing grounded theory. In P. L. Munhall & C. J. Oiler (Eds.), *Nursing research: A qualitative perspective* (pp. 111–114). Norwalk, CT: Appleton-Century-Crofts.

Wuest, J. (1995). Feminist grounded theory: An exploration of the congruency and tensions between two traditions in knowledge discovery. *Qualitative Health Research, 5*(1), 125–137.

Grounded Theory in Practice, Education, and Administration

This chapter examines method issues pertaining to grounded theory investigations as described in Chapter 6 in relationship to studies published in the areas of nursing practice, education, and administration. Two important questions guided the direction of this chapter: When should grounded theory be used? and How has the method been used to study issues in nursing education, administration, and practice? The chapter reviews three published studies using the guidelines for evaluating completed grounded theory research presented in Box 7-1. The chapter also provides readers with an overview of selected studies that highlight how nurse–researchers have used grounded theory in nursing practice, education, and administration (Table 7-1).

Critique Guidelines

Strauss and Corbin (1990) indicated that "a qualitative study can be evaluated accurately only if its procedures are sufficiently explicit so that readers of the resulting publication can assess their appropriateness" (p. 249).

> If a grounded theory researcher provides this information, readers can use these criteria to assess the adequacy of the researcher's complex coding procedure. Detail given in this way would be supplemented with cues that could, in longer publications, at least be read as pointing to extremely careful and thorough tracking of findings of conscientious and imaginative theoretical sampling. (Strauss & Corbin, 1990, pp. 253–254)

Furthermore, they suggested that, in reality, "there may be no way that readers can accurately judge how the researcher carried out the analysis" (Strauss & Corbin, 1990, p. 253). Therefore, guiding criteria for evaluating grounded theory investigations are provided. Criteria can assist reviewers of grounded theory studies to search out the critical elements of the method (see Box 7-1). When critiquing any published investigation, it is important to recognize that journal restrictions, page limitations, or other external forces beyond the author's control may have necessitated deletion of certain material, resulting in a limited critique of the research.

Readers of the present text who are interested in a more detailed discussion of method in a published study should contact the author.

Application to Practice

An excellent example of grounded theory research related to the practice arena is the study "Nurses' Experiences With Implementing Developmental Care in NICUs" by Shahirose S.J.E. Premji and Jacqueline S. Chapman (1997). This research report provides an example of the use of grounded theory in

---

BOX 7-1 GUIDELINES FOR CRITIQUING RESEARCH USING GROUNDED THEORY METHOD

STATEMENT OF THE PHENOMENON OF INTEREST

1. Is the phenomenon of interest clearly identified?
2. Has the researcher identified why the phenomenon requires a qualitative format?

PURPOSE

1. Has the researcher made explicit the purpose for conducting the research?
2. Does the researcher describe the projected significance of the work to nursing?

METHOD

1. Is the method used to collect data compatible with the purpose of the research?
2. Is the method adequate to address the research topic?
3. What approach is used to guide the inquiry? Does the researcher complete the study according to the processes described?

SAMPLING

1. Does the researcher describe the selection of participants?
2. What major categories emerged?
3. What were some of the events, incidents, or actions that pointed to some of these major categories?
4. What were the categories that led to theoretical sampling?
5. After the theoretical sampling was done, how representative did the categories prove to be?

DATA GENERATION

1. Does the researcher describe data collection strategies?
2. How did theoretical formulations guide data collection?

(continued)

BOX 7-1 GUIDELINES FOR CRITIQUING RESEARCH USING GROUNDED THEORY METHOD (CONTINUED)

DATA ANALYSIS

1. Does the researcher describe the strategies used to analyze the data?
2. Does the researcher address the credibility, auditability, and fittingness of the data?
3. Does the researcher clearly describe how and why the core category was selected?

EMPIRICAL GROUNDING OF THE STUDY: FINDINGS

1. Are concepts grounded in the data?
2. Are the concepts systematically related?
3. Are conceptual linkages described and are the categories well developed? Do they have conceptual density?
4. Are the theoretical findings significant? If yes, to what extent?
5. Was data collection comprehensive and analytical intrepretations conceptual and broad?
6. Is there sufficient variation to allow for applicability in a variety of contexts related to the phenomenon investigated?

CONCLUSIONS, IMPLICATIONS, AND RECOMMENDATIONS

1. Do the conclusions, implications, and recommendations give readers a context in which to use the findings?
2. Do the conclusions reflect the study findings?
3. Are recommendations for future study offered?
4. Is the significance of the study to nursing made explicit?

From Streubert, H. J. (1998). Evaluating the qualitative research report. In G. LoBiondo-Wood & J. Haber (Eds.), *Nursing research: Methods, critical appraisal and utilization* (4th ed., pp. 445–465), St. Louis, MO: C. V. Mosby; Strauss, A., & Corbin, J. (1990). *Basics of qualitative research: Grounded theory procedures and techniques*. Newbury Park, CA: Sage. Adapted with permission.

---

the investigation of phenomena important to nursing practice. Premji and Chapman's article conveys the intensity and rigor of grounded theory method and offers a clear example of the constant comparative method.

The phenomenon of interest for Premji and Chapman's (1997) grounded theory investigation was nurses' experience with implementing developmental care in neonatal intensive care units (NICUs). Because the authors were interested in generating new knowledge related to nurses'

(Text continues on page 128)

TABLE 7-1 Selective Sampling of Phenomenological Research Studies

Author/Date	Domain	Purpose	Sample	Data Generation	Findings
Baker & Stern (1993)	Practice	To investigate the evolution of readiness to self-manage a nonfatal chronic illness	Purposive sample of 12 individuals with a non-fatal chronic illness and the primary nurse caring for those individuals	Interviews	The key process in self-care readiness was finding meaning in chronic illness
Brecken-ridge (1997)	Practice	To investigate clients' perceptions of why, how, and by whom their dialysis treatment modality was chosen	22 participants from inpatient and outpatient renal dialysis units on the East Coast	Individual, focused, semi-structured in-depth interviews	"A grounded theory, 'Patients' Choice of a Treatment Modality versus Selection of Patient's Treatment Modality' emerged. The theory consisted of 11 themes that addressed the why, how, and by whom of decision-making: self decision; access-rationing decision; significant other decision; to live decision; physiologically dictated decision; expert decision; no patient choice in making decision; patient preference/choice; and switching modalities due to patient preference/choice" (p. 313).
Bright (1992)	Practice	To investigate the interaction among parents, grandparents, and first-born infants	3 families: 3 infants and their parents, and 6 grandparents	Interviews and participant observation	"Making place is defined as the process occurring in a family through which a newborn individual receives recognition as a member of that family. It is an integrative process in that it facilitates the creation of new relational connections

				within the family as well as giving new meaning to already existing ones" (p. 75).
Beck (1993)	Practice	To investigate the nature of the specific social–psychologic processes related to postpartum depression	Purposive sample of 12 mothers	Participant observation and in-depth audio-taped interviews	Loss of control was identified as the basic social–psychologic problem; women attempted to cope through a four-stage process of teetering on the edge, which included encountering terror, dying of self, struggling to survive, and regaining control
Biley (1992)	Practice	To determine how clients feel about participating in decision making about nursing care	8 clients	Informal interviews	Category saturation was not achieved; data suggest three categories that describe situations that affect client choice and participation in decision making: 1. If I am well enough . . . . 2. If I know enough . . . . 3. If I can . . . .
Byrne & Heyman (1997)	Practice	Nurses' perceptions of their work and clients and how communication is influenced	21 nurses	In-depth audio-taped interviews	"The core category was identified as defining the role of the accident and emergency department nurse. Two other categories also emerged and included 'Nurses' priorities and patients' anxieties' and 'Keeping the department running smoothly'" (p. 93).
Callaghan & Williams (1994)	Practice	Exploration of peoples' perceptions of living with diabetes	11 adults with type I (insulin-dependent) diabetes mellitus	Open-ended interviews, transcribed verbatim	Findings centered around the themes of management of diabetes, motivation, problems, and effect on life

(continued)

TABLE 7-1   Selective Sampling of Phenomenological Research Studies (CONTINUED)

Author/Date	Domain	Purpose	Sample	Data Generation	Findings
Cromwell (1994)	Practice	To explore elders' experience of forgetfulness	9 elder volunteers	Audiotaped interviews	"The personal or subjective experience of forgetfulness describes how elders, when faced with perceived forgetfulness, engage in a three-phase iterative process of self-assessment, coping, and reassessment. The goal of this process is the maintenance of a sense of self, or 'continuing to be who I am,' through actions aimed at maintaining identity continuity and personal competence" (p. 444).
Davies et al. (1996)	Practice	To begin to construct substantive theory about nurses' experience in caring for children who are dying after a prolonged illness	25 nurses	Individual, semistructured audiotaped interviews	"When nurses recognized that a child's death was inevitable, they struggled with both grief distress and moral distress. Their distress occurred within the context of the nurse–patient relationship" (p. 500).
Dewar & Morse (1995)	Practice	Examination of the circumstances that result in the breakdown of endurance following an illness	12 women and 8 men	Unstructured interviews, tape-recorded and transcribed verbatim	The experience of bearing catastrophic illness or injury involves encountering many difficult and undesirable events; major categories include holding on, building up, one last straw, and losing it
Diepeveen-Speeken-brink (1992)	Education	To discover the views of Dutch administrators of intramural health care	13 administrators	Semistructured audiotaped interviews	Three major themes emerged from data analysis: change, problems, and solutions

					institutions on the need for graduate nursing education and nursing research in the Netherlands
Dobos (1992)	Practice	To define risk as it pertains to clinical practice	3 registered nurses in clinical roles	Interviews	Risk in clinical practice was defined as uncomfortable and unavoidable role-related situations characterized by high unpredictability and negative or hostile overtones, dependency on others, high performance expectations, and health threats that extend beyond work hours; findings refuted the notion that nurses avoid risk and that risk requires strategies to minimize its negative effects
Ersek (1992)	Practice	Exploration of the processes of hoping in adults undergoing bone marrow transplantation	Purposive sampling of 10 men and 10 women, aged 20–58 years who had undergone bone marrow transplant	Audiotaped interviews	Core categories were dealing with it and keeping it in its place; the relationship between the two categories was explained by the dialectic of maintaining hope
Estabrooks & Morse (1992)	Practice	How do intensive care nurses (ICU) perceive touch and the process of touching? How do intensive care nurses learn to touch?	8 experienced ICU nurses	Interviews	Two substantive processes were revealed: the touching process and acquiring a touching style; the core variable, *cueing*, was defined as "the process by which, through symbolic interaction with others, one determines the need for and the appropriateness of touch" (p. 452).

(contin-ed)

TABLE 7-1 Selective Sampling of Phenomenological Research Studies (CONTINUED)

Author/Date	Domain	Purpose	Sample	Data Generation	Findings
Flaming & Morse (1991)	Practice	To examine what boys experience emotionally as they go through the physical changes of puberty	22 male participants	Audiotaped open-ended questions	A basic social–psychologic process emerged and was labeled "minimizing embarassment, with four stages: waiting for the change, noticing the change, dealing with the change, and feeling comfortable with the change" (p. 211).
Heidt (1990)	Practice	Exploration and description of client and nurse experiences in the process of giving and receiving therapeutic touch	14 nurses who had practiced therapeutic touch for a minimum of 3 years	Interviews and observations of one treatment session	The primary experience of therapeutic touch is opening to the flow of the universal life energy; this includes three major categories of experience: opening intent, opening sensitivity, and opening communication
Hinds & Moyer (1997)	Practice	To determine clients' experiences of support while receiving radiation therapy	12 patients undergoing radiation therapy	In-depth, semi-structured interviews, transcribed verbatim	"A substantive theory of support emerged which showed that support is an interpersonal process embedded in an array of social exchanges which involves encountering support, recognizing support and feeling supported. Three main types of support are encountered: being there, giving help and giving information. It is a multifaceted concept and all types of support are seen as important. Actions are interpreted within the norms and expectations of a relationship and labelled as supportive

				by the recipient. Family and friends are the principal sources of all types of support. Professional support is mainly informational" (p. 371).
Hutchinson (1992)	Practice	To explore and describe experiences of nurses who had been accused of violating the Nurse Practice Act	Purposive volunteer sample of 30 nurses	In-depth interviews, participant observation	The nurses experienced a transformation of professional identity that involved five phases: being confronted, assuming a stance, going through it, living the consequences, and re-visions
Lewis (1990)	Practice	To explore ward sisters'/charge nurses' perceptions of their responsibilities	10 hospital sisters from two large hospitals in southern England	Semistructured interviews	From the data analysis, substantive theory was developed that ward sisters act to gatekeep the professional nurses' function
Logan & Jenny (1997)	Practice	Description of clients' recollections of their experiences during mechanical ventilation and weaning	20 hospitalized patients who had recently undergone mechanical ventilation and weaning	Open-ended audiotaped interviews	"During ventilation and weaning, patients were engaged to various degrees in what they called 'work,' which consisted of their efforts to assist in their adjustment and recovery. This work had four themes: sense making, enduring, preserving self, and controlling responses. These themes represented activities by which patients dealt with their personal concerns and cooperated with the therapeutic plan" (p. 140).

(continued)

TABLE 7-1 Selective Sampling of Phenomenological Research Studies (CONTINUED)

Author/Date	Domain	Purpose	Sample	Data Generation	Findings
Ragsdale, Kotarba, & Morrow (1994)	Practice	To describe how people living with human immunodeficiency virus (HIV) and acquired immunodeficiency syndrome (AIDS) manage their illness in the hospital and at home	22 males and 1 female diagnosed with HIV/AIDS	Semistructured individual interviews	"The present investigation supports an early study that isolated six management styles used in the hospital; summarized in terms of general patient identities, they are the loner, the medic, the time keeper, the activist, the mystic, and the victim. This study discovered another strategy, the forced loner, that is common among those persons living with HIV; whose social environments or medical condition force them to curtail social engagements. The general tendency is toward the mystic management strategy as the conditions of PLHIV inevitably deteriorate and as previous efforts to exert control over the management and the course of their illness become futile" (p. 431).
Roe, Minkler, & Barnwell (1994)	Practice	To describe the experiences of African American women who have become the sole care-	71 African American women	Semistructured interviews, participant observation	Three patterns of the assumption of care-giving emerged: "sudden assumption, negotiated assumption, and inevitable assumption of the permanent care-

	givers for a grandchild or great-grandchild			giver role. Each pattern is described along six dimensions: Forewarning, initiation, the trigger event, the caregiver's goal, her assumed trajectory of the caregiving period, and her perceived influence on her own destiny" (p. 281).
Turner, Tomlinson, & Harbaugh (1990)	Practice	Convenience sample of 13 parents of 8 critically ill children	Interviews	A model of PICU uncertainty was derived that identified four areas in which ambiguity, conflicting information, or perceived inefficiency gave rise to uncertainty
Wigens (1997)	Practice/management	Examination of the conflict nurses confront that requires them to give holistic, individualized care in a new management environment	10 surgical nurses	Participant observation and interview	"Different interpretations by the key members of the 'new nursing' discourse have been identified. These have been termed the professional project discourse, the modernist discourse, and the traditionalist discourse. Various strategies are adopted by nurses to reduce cognitive dissonance caused by the two conflicting discourses. The most commonly use being rationalization about the need for emotional labour" (p. 1116).

use of a developmental care approach in an NICU, grounded theory method suited the investigation. According to Premji and Chapman, "The constant comparative method (Glaser & Strauss, 1967; Strauss & Corbin, 1990; Strauss, 1987) was used to generate a systematic, grounded, substantive theory of these nurses' experiences" (p. 99).

Premji and Chapman (1997) explained that the study purpose or aim was "to gain insight into nurses' (n = 8) experiences of working in a neonatal intensive-care unit (NICU) that incorporated the developmental-care approach" (p. 97). In discussing their rationale for the research in relationship to the available literature, the authors indicated that the developmental care approach in neonatal nursing practice has the potential to improve short- and long-term developmental outcomes for children. However,

> little attention has been directed toward the effect of its implementation on the NICU staff nurses. Existing reports in the literature are minimal and may not accurately reflect staff nurses' experience with DCA [developmental care approach]. Yet these nurses, being the infant's primary caretakers, are in a pivotal position to endorse or to reject developmental care. (p. 97)

The rationale for the study as confirmed by the literature supported the aim and purpose of the work and lent focus to the remainder of the study. The *sample* selection in this study is described as occurring in two phases. First

> Purposive sampling was used to recruit 4 subjects who were in favor of developmental care and 2 subjects who had previously represented the small minority of individuals who were strongly against developmental care. Purposive sampling was also used to make sure that 2 of the 4 pro-developmental-care subjects were among a group of 28 who, out of approximately 100 nurses in this NICU, had attempted certification in NIDCAP. (Premji & Chapman, 1997, p. 99)

Premji and Chapman (1997) combined purposeful sampling with theoretical sampling. Following the completion of interviews with the six nurses selected through purposeful sampling, they used theoretical sampling "to select additional subjects to collect further data in a selective manner for the purpose of filling gaps in the emerging theory" (p. 99). The final sample of eight nurses represented a variety of ethnic groups, levels of experience, and education.

Premji and Chapman (1997) clearly described data generation strategies. Following three information sessions and the signing of consent forms, they collected data through "tape-recorded, face-to-face, unstructured interviews" (p. 100). The researchers conducted the interviews after work hours either in their own homes or in a hospital meeting room. It is preferable to arrange interviews in locations unfamiliar to both researchers and participants. In addition, tape-recording interviews ensures that researchers will capture all the necessary detail and "[preclude] recall bias" (p. 100).

According to Premji and Chapman (1997), their data analysis strategies included verbatim transcription, use of open coding, axial coding, and selective coding to identify the core category or basic social process. They also addressed credibility and auditability in a section on strategies used to enhance credibility of the findings. The researchers wrote down their preconceptions before the study and later compared those notes with the results. "An independent audit of all transcripts by a second researcher demonstrated that comparable interpretations of the data were being made. Fittingness of the data was not addressed.

The basic social process or core category identified was "putting the baby first" (Premji & Chapman, 1997, p. 101). The major domains of "putting the baby first" included three phases: "learning, reacting and advocating/nonadvocating. Four concepts—encountering, appraising, supporting, and gaining sensitivity—were evidenced in each phase" (p. 101).

Premji and Chapman (1997) discussed their conclusions, implications, and recommendations in terms of their applicability to nursing practice and education. They also addressed the advantages and disadvantages of a developmental care approach in relationship to an infant and to the staff.

Grounded theory method suited the study because little research had been done on the topic at the time of the study. This important contribution to the literature can help improve nursing care to NICU infants.

Application to Education

An excellent example of the important contribution grounded theory can make to nursing education is the Burnard (1992) study "Student Nurses' Perceptions of Experiential Learning," published in *Nurse Education Today*. The study illustrates a good presentation of findings from a grounded theory investigation. There is little discussion of specific method issues, though, because of—as the author explained—space issues and article requirements. Frequently, journal publisher limitations prevent detailed discussion of method issues in qualitative research reports.

The purpose of Burnard's (1992) study was to identify student nurses' perceptions of experiential learning. He identified the need for a qualitative format to explore and clarify issues related to the topic. Burnard described the projected significance of the work to nursing as being related to the recommendation of experiential learning in nursing literature, particularly in the fields of psychiatric nursing and interpersonal skills training.

Burnard (1992) used a convenience sample of 12 student nurses in different parts of the United Kingdom. He collected data using in-depth interviews. He did not address theoretical sampling, perhaps because of journal limitations placed on method discussion. Also not addressed in the article were emergence of major categories and selection of a core category. Data collection appeared comprehensive given the presentation of the findings. Burnard did not address saturation, though, making a determination regarding conceptual density of the findings difficult.

Burnard (1992) reported that data analysis occurred in two ways: simple content analysis of themes and a modified grounded theory approach.

> There is not space in this paper to describe, in detail, the processes involved in analyzing the data. Suffice to say that a rigorous method of working through the interview transcripts was devised as were methods of coding and categorizing the data. Validity checks were maintained throughout the analysis by checking and rechecking the emerging categories with the respondents. The validity of the analysis method was also checked by having two disinterested research colleagues develop their own category systems from the data. In this sense, the category system was negotiated, although in the end (as with any method of analysis) the researcher has to take responsibility for the overall system of analysis. (p. 163)

A variety of categories emerged during data analysis; this section formed the heart of the report. Students found experiential learning to be something more than "just being taught" (Burnard, 1992, p. 164) and indicated they learned the most about nursing from working in a clinical setting. Although they valued classroom learning, they viewed it as less valuable than clinical learning. Burnard provided the following examples of student insights into the range of activities identified as contributing to experiential learning: "We have had role play, small group exercises, empathy exercises, ice-breakers, games, those sorts of things. We have done other things like being blindfolded and tied up and so forth and we've done role play and psychodrama. . . . We've done psychodrama and lots of exercises (p. 170).

The implications of the study findings for nursing education are specifically related to educators. How nurse–educators plan and use this type of learning in nursing education settings will prove important to educational outcomes. Students highly valued experiential learning, which provided opportunity for making connections between theory and practice. Although he did not offer recommendations for future study, Burnard (1992) concluded that

> these reviews of experiential learning offer a different perspective to the one traditionally offered in the literature on experiential learning. They have implications for the use and planning of experiential learning sessions in all branches of nursing. Nurse educators need to be clear about what they mean by the term "experiential learning" and also need to ensure that students are adequately prepared for any new learning situations that they bring to the learning arena. (p. 172)

Application to Administration

Severinsson and Borgenhammar's (1997) study "Expert Views on Clinical Supervision: A Study Based on Interviews" provides an example of grounded theory applied to nursing administration. They described the study purpose early in the article: "The aim of this study is to analyze views on clinical supervision held by a number of experts, and to reflect on the effects and value of clinical supervision in relation to public health" (p. 177). Severinsson and Borgenhammar have grounded the importance of the work in a comprehensive literature review and a sound rationale.

The sample for the investigation included

> seven well-known researchers from four Nordic countries: Norway, Denmark, Finland and Sweden. They are experts on "working conditions" and hold positions as associate professors and professors. Their fields are psychiatry, psychotherapy, psycho-social medicine, social medicine, social work, education, theology and nursing. Three are women and four are men. (p. 177)

The sampling procedure appeared to be purposeful, although the authors did not specify this in the article. Given the description provided, however, readers may assume that Severinsson and Borgenhammar selected participants specifically for their experience and ability to discuss the research topic.

The researchers conducted data analysis using the methodology of grounded theory construction. They followed three procedures to inductively generate categories grounded on data: (1) open coding (labelling phenomena for the discovery of structure); (2) axial coding (identification of patterns), and (3) selective coding (identification of core category).

A table in the article illustrated the authors' interpretations of the experts' views on how clinical supervision affects clients and professionals, thus giving readers a sense of how data analysis proceeded. The authors did not address credibility, auditability, and fittingness in the article; such discussion would have added to the presentation of the study and enhanced the meaning of the data.

Severinsson and Borgenhammar discussed the conclusions, implications, and recommendations in relationship to the data and literature presented. The results showed that clinical supervision is an integration process guiding a person from novice to expert by establishing a relationship of trust between supervisor and the individual being supervised. The study indicated that implementation of systematic clinical supervision may positively affect quality of care and client recovery, may create improved feelings of confidence in one's work, and may prevent burnout among staff. The reported negative aspect was the possibility of high "opportunity costs," that is, the time loss for client care by nurses participating in organized systematic supervision (p. 175).

Summary

Grounded theory as a qualitative research approach provides an excellent method of investigation for phenomena important to nursing. This chapter reviewed application of the method to areas important to nursing practice, education, and administration and offered new grounded theorists examples of research that apply the method described in Chapter 6. Recognizing the need for middle-range theory development in nursing, investigators should continue to apply this rigorous qualitative method to the investigation of phenomena important to nursing practice, education, and administration.

REFERENCES

Baker, C., & Stern, P. N. (1993). Finding meaning in chronic illness as the key to self care. *Canadian Journal of Nursing Research, 25*(2), 23–36.

Beck, C. T. (1993). Teetering on the edge: A substantive theory of postpartum depression. *Nursing Research, 42*(1), 42–48.

Biley, F. C. (1992). Some determinants that effect patient participation in decision-making about nursing care. *Journal of Advanced Nursing, 17,* 414–421.

Breckenridge, D. M. (1997). Patients' perceptions of why, how, and by whom dialysis treatment modality was chosen. *American Nephrology Nurses' Association Journal, 24*(3), 313–319.

Bright, M. A. (1992). Making place: The first birth in an intergenerational family context. *Qualitative Health Research, 2*(1), 75–98.

Burnard, P. (1992). Student nurses' perceptions of experiential learning. *Nurse Education Today, 12,* 162–173.

Byrne, G., & Heyman, R. (1997). Understanding nurses' communication with patients in accident and emergency departments using a symbolic interactionist perspective. *Journal of Advanced Nursing, 26,* 93–100.

Callaghan, D., & Williams, A. (1994). Living with diabetes: Issues for nursing practice. *Journal of Advanced Nursing, 20,* 132–139.

Cromwell,S. L. (1994). The subjective experience of forgetfulness among elders. *Qualitative Health Research, 4*(4), 444–463.

Davies, B., Cook, K., O'Loane, M., Clarke, D., MacKenzie, B., Stutzer, C., Connaughty, S., & McCormick, J. (1996). Caring for dying children: Nurses' experiences. *Pediatric Nursing, 22*(6), 500–507.

Dewar, L. A., & Morse, J. M. (1995). Unbearable incidents: Failure to endure the experience of illness. *Journal of Advanced Nursing, 22,* 957–964.

Diepeveen-Speekenbrink, J. C. (1992). The need for graduate nursing education and nursing research in The Netherlands: An exploratory study. *International Journal of Nursing Studies, 29*(4), 393–410.

Dobos, C. (1992). Defining risk from the perspective of nurses in clinical roles. *Journal of Advanced Nursing, 17,* 1303–1309.

Ersek, M. (1992). The process of maintaining hope in adults undergoing bone marrow transplantation for leukemia. *Oncology Nursing Forum, 19*(6), 883–889.

Estabrooks, C. A., & Morse, J. M. (1992). Toward a theory of touch: The touching process and acquiring a touching style. *Journal of Advanced Nursing, 17,* 448–456.

Flaming, D., & Morse, J. M. (1991). Minimizing embarrassment: Boy's experiences of pubertal changes. *Issues in Comprehensive Pediatric Nursing, 14,* 211–230.

Glaser, B. G., & Strauss, A. (1967). *The discovery of grounded theory: Strategies for qualitative research.* New York: Aldine.

Heidt, P. R. (1990). Openness: A qualitative analysis of nurses' and patients' experiences of therapeutic touch. *Image, 22*(3), 180–186.

Hinds, C., & Moyer, A. (1997). Support as experienced by patients with cancer during radiotherapy treatments. *Journal of Advanced Nursing, 26,* 371–379.

Hutchinson, S. A. (1992). Nurses who violate the Nurse Practice Act: Transformation of professional identity. *Image, 24*(2), 133–139.

Lewis, T. (1990). The hospital ward sister: Professional gatekeeper. *Journal of Advanced Nursing, 15,* 808–818.

Logan, J., & Jenny, J. (1997). Qualitative analysis of patient's work during mechanical ventilation and weaning. *Heart and Lung, 26,* 140–147.

Premji, S.S.J.E., & Chapman, J. S. (1997). Nurses' experiences with implementing developmental care in NICUs. *Western Journal of Nursing Research, 19*(1), 97–109.

Ragsdale, D., Kotarba, J. A., & Morrow, J. R., Jr. (1994). How HIV+ persons manage everyday life in the hospital and at home. *Qualitative Health Research, 4*(4), 431–443.

Roe, K. M., Minkler, M., & Barnwell, R. S. (1994). The assumption of caregiving: Grandmothers raising the children of the crack cocaine epidemic. *Qualitative Health Research, 4*(3), 281–303.

Severinsson, E. I., & Borgenhammar, E. V. (1997). Expert views on clinical supervision: A study based on interviews. *Journal of Nursing Management, 5,* 175–183.

Strauss, A., & Corbin, J. (1990). *Basics of qualitative research: Grounded theory procedures and techniques.* Newbury Park, CA: Sage.

Streubert, H. J. (1998). Evaluating the qualitative research report. In G. LoBiondo-Wood & J. Haber (Eds.), *Nursing research: Methods, critical appraisal and utilization* (4th ed., pp. 445–465). St. Louis, MO: C.V. Mosby.

Turner, M. A., Tomlinson, P. S., & Harbaugh, B. L. (1990). Parental uncertainty in critical care hospitalization of children. *Maternal Child Nursing Journal, 19*(1) 45–62.

Wigens, L. (1997). The conflict between "new nursing" and "scientific management" as perceived by surgical nurses. *Journal of Advanced Nursing, 25,* 1118–1122.

Grounded Theory Approach: Nurses' Experience With Implementing Developmental Care in NICUs

SHAHIROSE S.J.E. PREMJI • JACQUELINE S. CHAPMAN

The aim of this study was to gain insight into nurses' (N = 8) experience of working in a neonatal intensive-care unit (NICU) that incorporated the developmental-care approach. Although Als's model is family centered, the basic social process identified by nurses was putting the baby first. The process of putting the baby first was uncovered using grounded-theory methodology. The process included three phases: learning, reacting, and advocating/nonadvocating. In each of the phases, four main concepts—encountering, appraising, supporting, and gaining sensitivity—emerged from the data. Nurses appraised the advantages and disadvantages of this therapeutic approach not only to the infant but also to themselves.

Over the past decade neonatal nurses' responsibilities have become more complex and challenging as Als's (1986) developmental-care approach (DCA) has been introduced into neonatal nursing practice. The focus of this approach is the momentary state of neurobehavioral organization of a preterm infant (Gorski, Davison, & Brazelton, 1979). Initial, small sample studies (Als et al., 1986; Als et al., 1994; Becker, Grunwald, Moorman, & Stuhr, 1991, 1993) have demonstrated that DCA, as contrasted with traditional neonatal intensive-care unit (NICU) care, has the potential to improve both short-term and long-term developmental outcomes. Regardless of whether developmental care (Als, 1986) per se is effective, little attention has been directed toward the effect of its implementation on the NICU staff nurses. Existing reports in the literature are minimal and may not accurately reflect staff nurses' experience with DCA. Yet these nurses, being the infant's primary caretakers, are in a pivotal position to endorse or to reject developmental care.

CURRENT STATUS OF STAFF NURSES' INVOLVEMENT WITH DEVELOPMENTAL CARE IN NICUs

Very few professionals have attained the level of expertise required for certification to develop nursing-care plans based on developmental care's periodic, systematic behavioral observations. Such experts have completed the Neonatal Individualized Developmental Care and Assessment Program (NIDCAP) (Als & Gibes, 1986). NIDCAP-based or other types of developmental care usually have been implemented

Shahirose S.J.E. Premji, R.N., M.Sc.(N), Clinical Nurse Specialist-Nurse Practitioner, Chedoke-McMaster Hospitals; Jacqueline S. Chapman, M.S.N., Ph.D., Professor, Faculty of Nursing, University of Toronto.

through a program of nursing staff education accompanied by ongoing support. Expert consultation to staff nurses has been provided by NIDCAP-trained neonatal nurse clinicians and physical or occupational therapists (Becker et al., 1991; Tribotti & Stein, 1992).

Only two sets of investigators (Cole, Begish-Duffy, Judas, & Jorgensen, 1990; Tribotti & Stein, 1992) have commented on staff nurses' responses to implementation of the DCA in their workplace. In Tribotti and Stein's (1992) study, an inservice staff educational program based on developmental perspectives was implemented. Subsequently, nurses were given an investigator-devised Likert-type questionnaire. Only 42% of 84 potential subjects returned the questionnaire. Eighty-six percent of these respondents agreed with the item that the program had provided a "useful professional growth experience" (Tribotti & Stein, 1992, p. 39). Cole et al. (1990) introduced the DCA to their NICU through inservice/orientation programs, developmental rounds, developmental posters, seminars, and a NIDCAP-trained expert's one-to-one guidance with staff nurses. They reported that, subsequently, nurses "looked at babies differently" (p. 21), but they did not elaborate further on staff nurses' own responses to the program.

Although no randomized-control trial has been published to support the efficacy of the DCA, many centers in the United States have already adopted it (Oelberg, 1991), and its philosophy has gained acceptance in Canada. Yet few researchers have examined the effect of introducing the DCA on the staff nurses who are expected to implement it in their practice.

RESEARCH QUESTION

The researchers of this retrospective, qualitative study therefore addressed the following question: What was the experience of staff nurses working in an NICU that incorporated the DCA?

DESIGN

The constant comparative method (Glaser & Strauss, 1967; Strauss, 1987; Strauss & Corbin, 1990) was used to generate a systematic, grounded, substantive theory of these nurses' experiences. Data collected from interviews and observations were simultaneously analyzed, coded, and continuously compared to categories that emerged in previous data (Glaser & Strauss, 1967; Strauss, 1987).

SAMPLE

The target population included all nurses currently working full-time in a 48-bed NICU in a large metropolitan-area hospital. The concept of developmental care had been introduced to this unit 4 years previously. Purposive sampling was used to recruit 4 subjects who were in favor of developmental care and 2 subjects who had previously represented the small minority of individuals who were strongly against developmental care. Purposive sampling was also used to make sure that 2 of the 4 pro-developmental-care subjects were among a group of 28 who, out of approximately 100 nurses in this NICU, had attempted certification in NIDCAP. Therefore, some of the sample had completed formal training in developmental care, whereas others had only inservice education regarding it.

After these 6 subjects were interviewed, theoretical sampling (Glaser, 1978) was employed to select additional subjects to collect further data in a selective manner for the purpose of filling gaps in the emerging theory. Hence, a nurse with 10 years of experience on the unit, who would be able to compare and contrast care before and after the introduction of DCA, as well as an inexperienced nurse employed 1 year after DCA was implemented, were recruited. Theoretical sampling was terminated after these 2 additional subjects' data were analyzed and combined with the other 6 subjects' data because saturation of categories was then attained.

The final sample of 8 nurses represented a variety of ethnic groups. Some subjects were new graduates; others had worked in a NICU for many years. Some of these experienced subjects assumed the team-leader role; others were always assigned to patient care. Subjects' educational level ranged from registered nurse diploma to baccalaureate degree in nursing.

METHOD

Procedure

Three information sessions were held to describe the study to the nursing staff. A written summary with a tear-off sheet was provided to each attendee. Members of the nursing staff who wished to participate completed the information regarding their names and phone numbers and deposited the sheets in a manila envelope on the unit's bulletin board.

Before the initial interview all participants signed consent forms after agreeing to participate in two tape-recorded, face-to-face, unstructured interviews. Each subject was interviewed only once. Subsequent interviews were not found to be necessary because the nurses were very open in communicating their experiences during the first interview and because they did not feel the need to meet again. Interviews took place on subjects' off-duty time in their or the investigator's home or in a meeting room or the cafeteria at the hospital. All interviews proceeded without interruption. Length of interviews ranged from $\frac{1}{2}$ to 1 hour ($M = 45$ minutes) depending on how much information the nurses wished to share.

Analysis of Data

Each interview was transcribed as soon as possible after its completion. Strauss's (1987) paradigm of conditions, interactions, strategies, and consequences was used to provide structure for coding. With the first few interviews during open coding, labels were tentatively assigned to each event contained therein. Similarly, in each interview during axial coding, with the use of the paradigm, initial categories and subcategories were developed. Once all subjects were interviewed, categories were collapsed, phases of the process were suggested, and eventually selective coding was used to identify a core category or the basic social process (Strauss & Corbin, 1990).

Strategies Used To Enhance Credibility of Findings

Several of the strategies proposed by Lincoln and Guba (1985) were used to enhance the rigor of analysis and to lend credibility to the findings. The authors' preconceptions regarding these nurses' experiences with developmental care were written down prior to the study and later compared with the findings. Tape recording of all interviews precluded recall bias and allowed the interviewer to focus solely on the content of the interview. An independent audit of all transcripts by a second researcher demonstrated that comparable interpretations of the data were being made.

FINDINGS

The basic social process (Strauss, 1987) identified by the staff nurses working in this NICU that had incorporated the DCA was putting the baby first. As one nurse stated:

> I've become more sensitive to what the baby is trying to say. . . .I am more than willing now to adopt the whole idea of the darkened, quiet environment . . . and now it bothers me if I see somebody doing nursing care when I don't think they're always putting the well-being and the comfort of the infant first.

This process involves three recurring phases: learning, reacting, and advocating/ nonadvocating. Four concepts—encountering, appraising, supporting, and gaining sensitivity—were evidenced in each phase.

Each of these phases influences the others in a dynamic fashion. The phases are interactive in nature, not static. The phases continue endlessly, with each infant assignment eliciting a new process of learning, reacting, and advocating/nonadvocating, albeit over time, usually at a higher level of attainment. As the nurses' learning about the DCA becomes more sophisticated, they react to each infant's behavior in the context of a NICU where the DCA is promoted. The nurses current reactions modify their degree of either advocating or nonadvocating such care. As advocates they associate DCA with putting the baby first.

The Three Phases

Learning

The learning phases at the onset of the social process had more formal structure than those that came later. In the initial learning phases, all subjects were either formally trained in the performance of NIDCAP assessment or were given an introduction to the philosophy of the DCA. Education enabled nurses to increase their knowledge base about neonates and to develop the assessment skills necessary to carry out the DCA. Accordingly, nurses learned about the meaning of behaviors displayed by infants in response to their environment. One nurse remarked, "I didn't realize how much infants could tell you about how stressed out they were." By learning how best to match caregiving to each infant's behavioral repertoire, nurses began to adopt the new ideal of putting the baby first.

There was a noticeable difference in the levels of learning and understanding attained regarding developmental care between nurses who received NIDCAP training and those who did not. The initial knowledge discrepancy was a source of contention between nurses. A nurse explained:

> [I]f someone is telling them [how] to look after a baby developmentally supportively, they . . . interlink that with somebody telling them how to look after a baby technically . . . and they [the non-NIDCAP group] don't want somebody to tell them how to do that.

Thus in the learning phases, developmental care sometimes resulted in encountering; that is, in division and tension between nurses.

In the past, nurses' desire to "want to know" has been driven by the need to care for their patients (Fairman, 1992). Congruent with that historical precedent, nurses in this study sought knowledge about developmental care to enhance their practice. Even after the conclusion of structured programs, nurses still learned from others on the unit. Nurses often sought the guidance of those whom they felt were more competent. One nurse commented, "If I think it's something that is really questionable I always ask somebody. You know, like 'This is the way I found this baby positioned—Is this appropriate?'"

During the learning process, the nurses' appraisal of their ability to implement developmental-care perspectives led them to seek out appropriate resources that would support their attempts to learn developmental care. One nurse recalled the initial buddy system when she first started working on the unit. She said "[W]hen you got an assignment you were paired with somebody, so if I had questions about like [how] you had to settle the baby with the rolls around, somebody was there to help you."

Over time, nurses who became adept at implementing developmental-care perspectives supported those unaccustomed to DCA by serving as role models. Through these models' support, other nurses gained sensitivity to the subtleties of developmental care. As one nurse expressed it, "[T]here is a lot of support on the unit and you can get the help that you need. If there wasn't . . . people might not be so involved [with developmental care] especially to—you know—the degree most are."

Reacting

Learning about developmental care elicited certain thoughts and beliefs from nurses during the second phase—reacting. In the beginning, all of these nurses saw themselves as having a choice of being either for or against developmental care. The primary concern during early reacting phases was to appraise the effect of the DCA on the infant. A formerly anit-developmental care nurse said, "I think personally I didn't believe it [developmental care] would make a difference. I didn't think it would change the outcome for the children." Others initially reacted so that they "didn't look very kindly on it," and when DCA was introduced into the unit they wanted nothing to do with it. For instance, one subject stated, "I'll be—it may be fighting and kicking, sometimes, . . . you know people don't react well to change, and I'm one of those."

The primary force motivating nurses who reacted favorably was a positive appraisal of the outcomes of developmental care. Some nurses "bought into it [developmental care] right away" and believed that developmental care was "something positive and something good." Nurses gathered data regarding the outcomes of DCA from a variety of sources. One nurse revealed, "[N]urses who've been there longer than me—who've worked with both [no developmental care and developmental care]—they notice that the babies don't come back [to the follow-up clinic] as hyper because . . . of the hushed environment—and we try to reduce the amount of stimuli they get." One nurse, while reflecting on how she came to appreciate developmental care, stated: "But I can't even remember when I—like when—I really started to see that there was benefits to [the baby] . . . but bit-by-bit it made sense."

During the reacting phase, putting the baby first made sense to some nurses who, through observation of their own practice, noticed a difference in the behavior of the infant (e.g., being calmer, less irritable, etc.). One nurse stated the following:

> *Okay, basically what you like see in—as far as a[n] organized infant would be a baby who has not been extended in the extremities, who's sleeping— not agitated, . . . has rest periods in between . . . he's settled and he re- mains settled, he's not active and wasting a lot of his energy.*

Such nurses then acted as role models for other staff members. One nurse explained:

> *And I knew that you would see benefits from it [developmental care], and those nurses who were against . . . if they saw results—that the babies were coming out better, well organized, that they would eventually come around and use the same technique.*

If nurses who were prompting developmental care were successful, resistant nurses also gained sensitivity to the outcomes of developmental care and became believers.

Because of differences in appraisal of whether developmental care was of benefit to the infant, nurses continued encountering interpersonal conflicts. Whereas some nurses began implementing developmental-care perspectives, others reacted negatively and resisted such implementation. One nurse described the trajectory of different reactions to developmental care in the unit:

> *and then was a time—a period of change, a period of controversy . . . where some nurses would position their babies with foot rolls, and bundle them and then the next nurse on the next shift would come up and pull everything out of the isolettes.*

Advocating/Nonadvocating

The reacting phase of the process becomes merged with the third phase, advocating/ nonadvocating, as positive or negative feelings about developmental care manifest themselves in practice. Thus it is impossible to determine precisely when the reacting phase ends and the advocating/nonadvocating phase begins. The end of the reacting phase was marked by each nurse's serious consideration of advocating or not advocating the philosophy of developmental care. During this decision-making pro- cess, nurses carefully weighed not only the benefits to the infant but the risks to themselves. That is, nurses appraised the effect developmental care would have on them if they instigated it.

Some nurses reported that developmental care was a source of difficulty or conflict. First, they found that they could encounter self-frustration. For example, one nurse offered the following comment, "practicing that way means you have to take time out when the baby is stressed out instead of getting your work done and . . . see[ing] what they're [the babies] . . . trying to tell you." Second, barriers, such as risk to their interpersonal relationships, also threatened the nurses' initial willingness to engage in the DCA. When one nurse was asked what she did if someone was not implementing developmental care, she stated, "It depends . . . everybody has their own personality. . . . I do it [intervene] when I feel [it's] necessary, but I don't usually correct people because I can't be bothered to deal with that kind of nonsense [interpersonal conflict]." Nurses were nonadvocating when, in their perception, personal risks to themselves outweighed benefits to the infant.

Nurses, however, were reassured that there were certain benefits in developmental care for them as well. One nurse said that, "it might have to some extent lightened the workload because obviously you're [not] doing the baby up every 2 hours—every 3 hours instead of every 2 hours, you know you're not in there as much." The greatest advantage nurses perceived was their orientation toward the baby, that is, putting the baby first. One nurse summarized her feeling as follows, "I think one of the beneftis . . . for me was that . . . you begin to realize you're . . . working with babies, these aren't extensions of the equipment, these are babies, and they're not supposed to be tied down, strapped down." Another nurse explained that those who believed in developmental care were "always very eager to do anything [they] could to help the baby."

Nurses who were unwavering in their belief that developmental care had positive effects became advocates of developmental care. Advocates demonstrated their gained sensitivity toward facilitating the implementation of developmental care in the unit. One nurse explained:

> I don't think I've ever confronted anybody like—"I don't think I like the way you . . ."—you know, I wouldn't do that. I have dropped hints once in a while like—"My that's a lot of linen"—something like that you know.

Thus advocates of developmental care attempted to maintain rapport with the individuals they wished to influence by being flexible, biding their time, and offering insights, suggestions, and assistance.

If nurses wish to institute developmental care in NICUs, it is very important first to gain support for the DCA from the neonatologists, these nurses said. One nurse stated, "If you don't have the support of the neonatologist you're just out of luck." Advocating developmental care to rotating fellows and residents was viewed as important but not always easy. A nurse explained, "We get [doctors telling us] "Well at [the other hospitals] we do this.' We go, 'Well fine—here we do this.' You know, 'When in Rome do as the Romans do.' "

In their interaction with other health-care professionals, nurses once again weighed the benefits to the baby in relation to the risks of their own interpersonal relationships. Nurses reflected:

> Some people will be very . . . assertive when it comes to the doctors and they [the doctors] know they can't touch this child. . . . I mean there's always circumstances where—you know—things are too critical and you sort of have to throw that [developmental care] overboard and tend to what's necessary.

Further, the nurses using the DCA put the baby's not their colleagues' needs first. One nurse explained:

> it's not as if the nurse is not going to let them [other health professionals] see the baby but the nurse wants to work with the doctor, with any other health care professional to look after the baby the best way that we can.

Parents were no exceptions in that nurses also monitored the parents' interaction with their infant. A nurse commented:

Sometimes there is a bit of conflict with parents as far as them wanting to go into the isolette and touching the baby and to do things. But, our basic philosophy is to involve the parents as much as possible and . . . we explain the developmental care assessment to them.

For the most part, such strategies were successful in eliciting a "good response" from parents. There were certain instances, however, when parents would say, "This is my child and I will. . ." Once again, encountering occurred—it was not always easy to maintain rapport. In attempting to reconcile differences between nurses and parents regarding adherence to developmental care, nurses often "tr[ied] to tell [parents] . . . come at such and such a time if you want to visit because the baby will be up then." Nurses, where feasible, redirected the care to be given by parents. However, as advocates, nurses gave precedence to the needs of the baby rather than the demands of either parents or health professionals.

When the well-being of the infant was compromised, advocating nurses risked encountering conflict. As one nurse explained:

So you had to be aggressive in making sure . . . you control—like you could make up the time [schedules] when the doctor could go in to see [examine] that baby—that was probably the hardest to get used to—that you were the person that was in control.

Nurses have not, historically, asserted themselves in their practice; thus some nurses were more comfortable in the nonadvocacy role. According to Jacobson (1978), attachment to an infant and protective feelings toward an infant are great sources of emotional stress for neonatal nurses. These feelings of attachment and protectiveness toward an infant may have been the impetus for altering a nonadvocacy stance. The underpinnings of existential advocacy (Gadow, 1980) may be evident in the advocating/nonadvocating phase.

As nurses moved through each succession of the three phases, their perceptions guided their attitudes toward and practices regarding developmental care. These perceptions were based on their view of the advantages or disadvantages of developmental care both to themselves and to the infant. The entire process came to have the potential for changing attitudes and the way a nurse practices—that is, for putting the baby first. Although the trajectory of this individual and collective basic social process generally is forward moving, it may not always be linear.

DISCUSSION

Two important issues arise from this study's findings. First, why, when Als's model (1986) is family-centered, was the core category or basic social process these staff nurses experienced to put the baby first? Second, important new information is that these nurses appraise the advantages and disadvantages of what they perceived to be the DCA not only to the infant but also to themselves.

Als's (1986) model of developmental care suggests that nurses view the infant within the larger context of the family. Although the nurse subjects in this study were working in an NICU that was believed to incorporate the DCA, the findings of this study, based on these staff nurses' descriptions, clearly demonstrated that their interpretation of the DCA approach was to put the baby, not the family, first.

Although the authors scrutinized the data carefully, no clues to the answers to the following questions could be gleaned from the unstructured interview format used. Did these staff nurses reject the model? Was Als's (1986) model presented to them with an emphasis on the family, or was most of their teaching exposure about structural changes in the environment and about how to identify the infant's behavioral cues? Does the attachment Jacobson (1978) discusses of a primary nurse for "her" baby modify how these NICU nurses interpreted the DCA regardless of how the model was presented? Are the descriptions of this sample of nurses typical or atypical of other NICU staff nurses?

Consideration by these staff nurses of advantages and disadvantages to themselves of practicing the DCA was an unexpected finding. In each nurse's experience, she described how she learned about developmental care; what reactions she experienced, both to such learning and eventually to trying out the DCA; and how subsequently she came to make a decision to advocate or not advocate for the DCA. The underpinnings of existential advocacy (Gadow, 1980) are evident when exploring how nurses reached an ethical position of putting the baby first. In the advocating/nonadvocating phase, nurses believed that incorporating the DCA perspective into their practice would optimize the infant's outcome. The nurses sense of commitment and moral obligation to do good compelled some nurses to redirect the care of those who failed to adhere to principles of developmental care.

Gadow's (1980) philosophical conceptualization of the nurse-patient relationship within existential advocacy is adult focused. The NICU is a unique environment in that the patients, who are infants, have limited means of communication. As such, these patients demand "sensitive, involved, caring support" (Savage & Conrad, 1992, p. 65). Further, because the infants are not capable of regulating the nurses' level of intimacy and involvement, they have limited control over the nurse-patient relationship. In an NICU the nurse bears the sole responsibility of determining the level of commitment to the nurse-patient relationship and setting the limits of his or her involvement. In this study, some nurses invested heavily in the nurse-patient relationship. All of these subjects encountered conflict with other health professionals—especially doctors-in-training—and parents in trying to practice the DCA. They described how the ramifications of practicing DCA produced conflicting encounters for themselves with other nursing colleagues, health professionals, and parents.

In conclusion, in this preliminary small study, Als's (1986) model for the DCA did not relate to the reality of these staff nurses' perceptions in regard to the family's primacy. Several questions have been raised as to why this finding could have occurred. Second, the nurses appraised the effect of practicing the DCA approach not only on the infant but on the ramifications such a practice had on their interpersonal relationships with other professionals and parents.

Research article taken from: Premji, S. S. J. E., & Chapman, J. S. (1997). Nurses' experience with implementing developmental care in NICUs. *Western Journal of Nursing Research, 19*(1), 97–109. (reprinted with permission.)

REFERENCES

Als, H. (1986). A synactive model of neonatal behavioral organization: Framework for the assessment of neurobehavioral development in the premature infant and for support of infants and parents in the neonatal intensive care environment. *Physical and Occupational Therapy in Pediatrics, 6*, 3–53.

Als, H., & Gibes, R. (1986). *Neonatal and individualized care and assessment program (NIDCAP)*. Unpublished manual, Boston Children's Hospital, Cambridge, MA.

Als, H., Lawhon, G., Brown, E., Gibes, R., Duffy, F. H., McAnulty, G., & Blickman, J. (1986). Individualized behavioral and environmental care for the very low birth weight preterm infant at risk for bronchopulmonary dysplasia: Neonatal intensive care unit and developmental outcome. *Paediatrics, 78*(6), 1123–1132.

Als, H., Lawhon, G., Brown, E., Gibes, R., Duffy, F. H., McAnulty, G. B., Gibes-Grossman, R., & Blickman, J. G. (1994). Individualized developmental care for the very low-birth-weight preterm infant: Medical and neurofunctional effects. *Journal of the American Medical Association, 272*(11), 853–858.

Becker, P. T., Grunwald, P. C., Moorman, J., & Stuhr, S. (1991). Outcomes of developmentally supportive nursing care for very low birth weight infants. *Nursing Research, 40,* 150–155.

Becker, P. T., Grunwald, P. C., Moorman, J., & Stuhr, S. (1993). Effects of developmental care on behavioral organization in very low-birth-weight infants. *Nursing Research, 42*(4), 214–220.

Cole, J. G., Begish-Duffy, A., Judas, M. L., & Jorgensen, K. M. (1990). Changing the NICU environment: The Boston City Hospital model. *Neonatal Network, 9*(2), 15–23.

Fairman, J. (1992). Watchful vigilance: Nursing care, technology, and the development of intensive care units. *Nursing Research, 41,* 56–59.

Gadow, S. (1980). Existential advocacy: Philosophical foundation of nursing. In S. F. Spicker & S. Gadow (Eds.), *Nursing: Images and ideals: Opening dialogue with the humanities* (pp. 79–101). New York: Springer.

Glaser, B. (1978). *Theoretical sensitivity: Advances in the methodology of grounded theory.* Mill Valley, CA: Sociology Press.

Glaser, B., & Strauss, A. (1967). *The discovery of grounded theory: Strategies for qualitative research.* New York: Aldine De Gruyter.

Gorski, P. A., Davison, M. F., & Brazelton, T. B. (1979). Stages of behavioral organization in the high risk neonate: Theoretical and clinical considerations. *Seminars in Perinatology, 3*(1), 61–72.

Jacobson, S. (1970). Stressful situations for neonatal intensive care nurses. *American Journal of Maternal-Child Nursing (MCN), 3,* 144.

Lincoln, Y., & Guba, E. (1985). *Naturalistic inquiry.* Bevery Hills, CA: Sage.

Oelberg, D. G. (1991). Individualized neonatal developmental care plans [Editorial]. *Neonatal Intensive Care, 4*(6), 47.

Savage, T. A., & Conrad, B. (1992). Vulnerability as a consequence of the neonatal nurse-infant relationship. *Journal of Perinatal and Neonatal Nursing, 6*(3), 64–75.

Strauss, A. L. (1987). *Qualitative analysis for social scientists.* New York: Cambridge: University Press.

Strauss, A. L., & Corbin, J. (1990). *Basics of qualitative research: Grounded theory procedures and techniques.* Newbury Park, CA: Sage.

Tribotti, S. J., & Stein, M. (1992). From research to clinical practice: Implementing the NIDCAP. *Neonatal Network, 11*(2), 35–40.

CHAPTER 8

Ethnography as Method

Social scientists share an interest in and a commitment to discovery. Anthropologists, as a particular group of social scientists, are committed to the discovery of cultural knowledge. Early in the history of the social sciences, individuals interested in culture found that the ways of traditional science were inadequate to discover the nuances of people who live together and share similar experiences. This inadequacy led to the beginnings of *ethnography,* a means of studying groups of individuals' lifeways or patterns. Sanday (1983) has reported that ethnographic methods are not new. The ancient Greek Herodotus was an ethnographer who recorded variations in the cultures to which he was exposed. According to Sanday, Franz Boas's (1948) ethnographic examination of the Eskimo culture signaled the contemporary beginning of ethnographic study.

Anthropology is synonymous with the term *ethnography.* The product of anthropologists' work is ethnography (Muecke, 1994). As early as the 1960s, references can be found regarding the value of an ethnographic approach as a means to study nursing culture (Boyle, 1994; Leininger, 1970; Ragucci, 1972). Early nurse–ethnographers embraced the methods of anthropology to study phenomena they perceived were irreducible, unquantifiable, or unable to be made objective. Leininger (1985) went beyond the borrowing of ethnographic methods to develop what she called "ethnonursing research." This chapter explores the research method called ethnography and discusses common elements of ethnographic methodology, its uses, interpretations, and applications.

Ethnography Defined

According to Spradley (1980), "Ethnography is the work of describing culture" (p. 3). The description of culture or the cultural scene must be guided by an intense desire to understand other individuals' lives so much that the researcher becomes part of a specific cultural scene. To do this, Malinowski (1961) believed that researchers must learn the "native's point of view" (p. 25). Spradley, however, warned that ethnography is more than the study of the people; rather, "ethnography means learning from people" (p. 3). Spradley also pointed out that "the essential core of ethnography is this concern with the meanings of actions and events to the people [ethnographers] seek to understand" (p. 5).

Beyond Spradley's (1980) discussion of ethnography lies a long-standing debate about what constitutes ethnography. Muecke (1994) suggested "there is not a single standard form of ethnography" (p. 188). Boyle (1994) proposed that "the style and method of ethnography are a function of the ethnographer, who brings her or his own scientific traditions, training, and socialization to the research project" (p. 182).

According to Muecke (1994), the four major ethnographic schools of thought are (1) classical, (2) systematic, (3) interpretive or hermeneutic, and (4) critical. *Classical ethnography* requires that the study "include both a description of behavior and demonstrate why and under what circumstances the behavior took place" (Morse & Field, 1995, p. 154). This type of work requires considerable time in the field, constantly observing and making sense of behaviors.

The objective of *systematic ethnography* is "to define the structure of culture, rather than to describe a people and their social interaction, emotions, and materials" (Muecke, 1994, p. 192). The difference between classical and systematic ethnography lies in scope. Classical ethnography aims to describe everything about the culture. Systematic ethnography takes a focused look at the structure of the culture—what organizes the study group's lifeways. Systematic ethnography is the framework used by Spradley, whose method of ethnographic inquiry is explored fully in this chapter.

The aim of *interpretive* or *hermeneutic ethnography* is to "discover the meanings of observed social interactions" (Muecke, 1994, p. 193). According to Wolcott (cited in Muecke, 1994), "Ethnography is quintessentially analytic and interpretive, rather than methodological" (p. 193). Interpretive ethnographers are interested in studying the culture through analysis of inferences and implications found in behavior (Muecke, 1994).

Critical ethnography is another type of ethnography Muecke (1994) describes. It relies on critical theory (Fontana & Frey, 1994). Critical ethnographers do not believe there is a culture out there to be known but, rather, that researchers and members of a culture together create a cultural schema. Ethnographers subscribing to this tradition account for "historical, social and economic situations" (Fontana & Frey, 1994, p. 369) when reporting.

These four types of ethnographies represent a philosophic position. It is essential that researchers define their position before embarking on an ethnographic study. A researcher's philosophic stance determines what he or she will study as well as the framework for data collection and analysis.

Ethnography Roots

There is much debate about the historical beginnings of ethnography. Sanday (1983) proposed that ethnography began with Herodotus. Rowe (1965) has suggested that the Renaissance marked the initiation of ethnography as a research method. Still others have indicated that Malinowski's (1922) study of the Trobriand Islanders marked the beginning of ethnography. Atkinson and Hammersley (1994) offered that the contemporary beginning of ethnography occurred late in the 19th century as individuals began to acknowledge cultural differences or "deviations from norms" (p. 249) and became interested in studying these deviations. "The application of ethnographic method by Western anthropologists and sociologists to the investigation of their own societies has been a central feature of twentieth-century social science" (Cole, cited in Atkinson & Hammersley, 1994, p. 250). Atkinson and Hammersley (1994) identified two key phases in the development of ethnography in the 20th century: "the work of the founders of modern anthropology and that of the Chicago school of sociology" (p. 250).

Boas, Malinowski, and Radcliffe-Brown, the founders of modern anthropology (Atkinson & Hammersley, 1994), were committed to anthropology as a science. These ethnographers had the idea to chronicle their descriptions of primitive cultures. "The prime motivation on the part of all three founders was the rejection of speculation in favor of empirical investigation, a theme that has always been a central characteristic of empiricism, but not exclusive to it" (Atkinson & Hammersley, 1994, p. 250).

The Chicago school's most striking feature was its limited "questioning of the relevance of natural science as a methodological model for social research" (Atkinson & Hammersley, 1994, p. 250). One of the most important influences of the Chicago school was the attempt by many scientists in the school to connect scientific and hermeneutic philosophies with pragmatic philosophies such as the one espoused by Dewey (Atkinson & Hammersley, 1994). According to Woods (1992), these University of Chicago scientists laid the foundation for field research. They saw the city as a "social laboratory" (Woods, 1992, p. 338) that exemplified all forms of human behavior and activity. It was here that the idea of "native" was expanded to include social groups of local importance.

Beyond these early developments, ethnography has expanded and developed to meet the needs of scientists using its varied forms. Today, it is the quest to discover cultures and behaviors different from the researcher's that drives the use of this method. It is an exciting, interactive, decidedly qualitative approach that appeals to its followers. As Hughes (1992) pointed out, "What is quintessentially distinctive about anthropology [and thus ethnography] is just [its] *species-centeredness* and *holistic character*" (p. 442).

Fundamental Characteristics of Ethnography

Six characteristics are central to ethnographic research. Three could be claimed by other qualitative methods: (1) researcher as instrument, (2) fieldwork, and (3) the cyclic nature of data collection and analysis. The other three arguably could be said to be exclusive to ethnography: (4)

the focus on culture, (5) cultural immersion, and (6) the tension between researcher as researcher and researcher as cultural member, also called reflexivity. These characteristics should be considered foundational to ethnographic research.

RESEARCHER AS INSTRUMENT

The study of culture requires an intimacy with the participants who are part of a culture. Ethnography as a method of inquiry provides the opportunity for researchers to conduct studies that attend to the need for intimacy with members of the culture, which is precisely why the ethnographer becomes the conduit for information shared by the group. When anthropologists speak of researcher as instrument, they are indicating the significant role ethnographers play in identifying, interpreting, and analyzing the culture under study. The primary way that researchers become the instrument is through observation and the recording of cultural data.

More than just observing, researchers often become a participant in the cultural scene. Atkinson and Hammersley (1994) suggested that "participant observation is not a particular research technique but a mode of being-in-the-world characteristic of researchers" (p. 249). Participant observation demands complete commitment to the task of understanding. The ethnographer becomes part of the culture being studied to feel what it is like for the people in the situation (Atkinson & Hammersley, 1994; Boyle, 1994; Sanday, 1983).

Ethnographic researchers, despite becoming part of the cultural scene, will never fully have the insider's (emic) view. The emic view is the native's view, which reflects the cultural group's language, beliefs, and experiences. The only way ethnographers can begin to access the emic view is by collecting cultural group members' journals, records, or other cultural artifacts.

The strength of participant observation is the opportunity to access information from the outsider's (etic) view. The etic view is the view of the outsider with interpretation. The essence of ethnography is determining what an observed behavior is or what a ritual means in the context of the group studied. Ethnography is the description and interpretation of cultural patterns.

FIELDWORK

All ethnographic research occurs in the field. Researchers go to the location of the culture of interest. For example, Lipson and Omidian (1997) were interested in studying the culture of Afghan refugees in North America. The authors perceived this topic to be important for nursing. Lipson and Omidian participated in the informants' lives by visiting their homes, accompanying them to family and social events as well as religious services, and working with them in partnership community projects. Physically situating oneself in the environs of the study culture is a fundamental characteristic in all ethnographic work.

CYCLIC NATURE OF DATA COLLECTION AND ANALYSIS

In ethnographic research, a question about the differences in human experience found in a foreign culture leads researchers to determine those differences. As Agar (1982, 1986) has pointed out, one of the problems for ethnographers is that no clear boundaries exist between the similarities and differences in human experience. Therefore, data collected by ethnographers in the field to describe the differences and similarities lead to still other questions about the culture. Answering those questions leads to more questions. As Spradley (1980) and Spradley and McCurdy (1972) have indicated, the study ends not because a researcher has answered all of the questions or completely described the culture, but because time and resources do not allow continuation.

FOCUS ON THE CULTURE

Unique to ethnography is the focus on the culture. Ethnography is the only research method whose sole purpose is to understand the lifeways of individuals connected through group membership. As Boyle (1994) stated, "Ethnography focuses on a group of people who have something in common" (p. 161). It is essential that ethnographic researchers strive to discover and interpret the cultural meanings found within a connected group.

CULTURAL IMMERSION

Another characteristic of ethnography is the depth and length of participation ethnographers must have with the culture under study. The researcher's participation has been called *cultural immersion,* which requires that researchers live among the people being studied. For example, if a nurse–researcher is interested in studying the culture of families coping with human immunodeficiency virus in a family member, the researcher would need to immerse himself or herself in the life of the families studied. The researcher would observe how each family functions inside and outside of the home, studying as many facets of their lives as the participants would allow. Participant observation would take months, if not 1 year or more, to complete. Based on observation and most likely participation, the nurse–researcher would draw conclusions about the culture based on his or her discoveries while collecting data.

REFLEXIVITY

Reflexivity describes the struggle between being the researcher and becoming a member of the culture. Although conducting the research, on some level the researcher becomes a member of the culture. Through this type of participation, researchers must realize that they alter the culture and have the potential to be less objective. Because of the prolonged involvement as a researcher and participant in the group, it is extremely difficult to maintain a detached view.

This tension between researcher as pure researcher and researcher as participant has been discussed in many forums. How does one discover the emic—the insider's view—without becoming a part of the culture? The struggle for objectivity in collecting and analyzing data while being so intimately involved with the group is a characteristic unique to ethnography. More than just objectivity is of concern, however. Also of concern is the researcher's knowledge that just being present in the culture on some level affects its character.

Selection of Ethnography as Method

One of the goals of ethnography is to make explicit what is implicit within a culture (Germain, 1986). Cultural knowledge requires an understanding of the people, what they do, what they say, how they relate to one another, what their customs and beliefs are, and how they derive meaning from their experiences (Goetz & LeCompte, 1984; Spradley, 1980; Spradley & McCurdy, 1972; van Maanen, 1983). With these goals in mind, nurses interested in exploring cultures or subcultures in nursing or nurse-related cultures have the world available to them for study. Within the profession of nursing, there are many undiscovered cultures. An example of cultural practices within nursing that is implicit and has been made explicit through research (Wolf, 1988) is nursing rituals. Wolf discovered the rituals that nurses use to enable and protect them in their work with clients. Similarly, in Breda's (1997) research on nurses in professional unions, nurses are provided with a view of another implicit culture made explicit.

The use of the ethnographic approach provides nurses with the opportunity to explore the holistic nature of society and to ask questions relevant to nursing practice. The naturalistic setting in which ethnographic research is carried out supplies nurses with the view of the world as it is, not as they wish it to be. Fundamentally, entrance into the naturalistic setting in which the research participants live without interference from outside sources is a rich data source for exploring many nursing practice issues.

Nurses conducting ethnographic research must accept reflexivity as part of the research design. Reflexivity allows nurses to explore cultures within the paradigm of nursing, which values the affective and subjective nature of humans. The duality of being both researcher and participant provides opportunities to capitalize on insights derived from datum sources. "'Meaning' is not merely investigated, but is constructed by [the researcher] and informant through active and reciprocal relationships and the dialectical processes of interaction" (Anderson, 1991, p. 116). Anderson (1991) added that "field work is inherently dialectical; the researcher affects and is affected by the phenomena (s)he seeks to understand"

(p. 117). Reflexivity therefore leads to a greater understanding of the dynamics of particular phenomena and relationships found within cultures.

When choosing ethnography as the approach to study a particular culture or subculture, the nurse should ask several important questions. Do I have the time to conduct this study? Do I have the resources to carry it out? Will the data collected have the potential to bring new insights to the profession? If the nurse–researcher answers *yes* to these questions, then his or her study has the potential to contribute significantly to the nursing profession.

In addition to answering the preceding questions, nurses interested in ethnography should know why the approach may be useful. Spradley (1980) identified four primary reasons for using ethnography to study a particular culture. The first is to document "the existence of alternative realities and to describe these realities in [the terms of the people studied]" (p. 14). Much of what individuals know about other cultures they interpret based on their own culture. This way of thinking is limiting in that it promotes the idea that one truth—and thus, one reality—exists. For ethnographers, a description of alternative realities provides a rich and varied landscape of human life. Coming "to understand personality, society, individuals, and environments from the perspective of other than professional scientific cultures . . . will lead to a sense of epistemological humility" (Spradley, 1980, p. 15).

A second reason, according to Spradley (1980), for using the ethnographic approach is to discover grounded theories. Through a description of the culture, researchers are able to discover theories that are indigenous to the culture (Grant & Fine, 1992). Foundational to grounded theorists' research is a belief that the only useful theory is one that is grounded in the beliefs and practices of individuals studied. The principle that research should be based on the beliefs and practices of individuals (cultural groups) studied is also foundational to the work of ethnographers. The major difference between the conduct of ethnographic and grounded theory research is that ethnographers wishing to develop grounded theory will advance the description and interpretation of cultural observations to a level that yields a description of basic social–psychologic process. For a full discussion of grounded theory, see Chapter 6.

A third reason for choosing ethnography is to better understand complex societies. Early anthropologists believed that the ethnographic method was ideally suited to the study of non–Western cultures. Today, anthropologists see the value of using ethnography to study subgroups of larger cultures—both Western and non–Western. Examples can be found in nursing in the works of Anderson (1996) and Resnick (1996).

The fourth reason Spradley (1980) offered for using the ethnographic approach is to understand human behavior. Human behavior has meaning, and ethnography is one way to discover that meaning. Such discovery becomes particularly important when nurses look at the clients' health and illness behaviors. Understanding why cultural groups such as Hispanics, elderly people, abused women, or teenagers behave in health and illness situations can assist nurses who care for these groups to better provide interventions so they may potentiate the strategies already in use by the groups.

When nurses decide they will use ethnography to study a culture of interest, a parallel consideration will be whether they will conduct a micro- or macro-ethnographic study. Leininger (1985) called these study types "mini" or "maxi," respectively. Regardless of the terminology, the intent has to do with the scale of the study. A *micro-* or *mini-ethnography* is generally of a smaller scale and is narrow or specific in its focus. Preston's (1997) study of families whose membership included a "coronary sufferer" (p. 556) is an example of a micro study. The researcher interviewed and observed 12 adults in five family homes. The number of participants in the study was small, so the research focused on one small faction of a specific social group. Therefore, the study was considered a micro-ethnography because of the sample size and also the observation period, which was limited to 6 weeks.

A *macro-* or *maxi-ethnography* is a study that examines the culture in a broader context, extends over a longer period, and is most often reported in book form. Breda (1997) and Lipson and Omidian's (1997) ethnographies are examples of this type of study. These researchers observed a significant number of individuals over a period of several years and the scope was large.

Spradley (1980) further delineated the scope of ethnographic studies by placing them on a continuum. On one end are micro-ethnographic studies that examine a single social situation (nurses receiving report on one unit); multiple social situations (critical care nurses participating in a report on three intensive care units); or a single social institution (the American Cancer Society of Philadelphia). Moving on the continuum closer to macro-ethnographic studies, Spradley included multiple social institutions (American Cancer Societies of Northeastern Pennsylvania); a single community study (Chinatown in San Francisco); multiple communities (Hispanic communities in East Los Angeles); and a complex society (tribal life in Africa).

Elements and Interpretations of the Method

A number of individuals have described ethnographic research methods. Early ethnographic reports were written by individuals who documented their observations of the cultures they encountered. Although many of these individuals were not trained anthropologists, they gave rich and vivid accounts of the lives of the people they met. Sanday (1983) pointed out that these recorders were not participants in paradigmatic ethnography. *Paradigmatic ethnography* consists of the range of activities completed by a trained ethnographer, including observing, recording, participating, analyzing, reporting, and publishing experiences with a particular cultural group. Sanday offered three traditions within paradigmatic ethnography: (1) holistic, (2) semiotic, and (3) behavioristic.

The *holistic ethnographic interpretation* is the oldest tradition. The commitment of researchers in this tradition is to "the study of culture as an integrated whole" (Sanday, 1983, p. 23). According to Sanday, the ethnographers who ascribed to this approach included Benedict (1934), Mead (1949), Malinowski (1922), and Radcliffe-Brown (1952). Although all four ethnographers varied in their focus, their underlying commitment was to describe as fully as possible the particular culture of interest within the context of the whole. For instance, "Mead and Benedict were interested in describing and interpreting the whole, not in explaining its origin beyond the effect of the individual on it" (Sanday, 1983, p. 25). Radcliffe-Brown and Malinowski were not committed to the "characterization of the cultural whole but to how each trait functions in the total cultural complex of which it is part" (Sanday, 1983, p. 25). Although the focus of both sets of ethnographers was different, the underlying commitment to viewing the culture as a whole was preserved.

The *semiotic interpretation* focuses on gaining access to the native's viewpoint. Like the researchers committed to holistic interpretation, the major anthropologists in this tradition did not share epistemologies. The two major followers of this tradition are Geertz (1973) and Goodenough (1970, 1971). According to Sanday (1983), Geertz views the study of culture not as a means to defining laws but as an interpretative enterprise focused on searching for meaning. Furthermore, Geertz believes that the only way to achieve cultural understanding is through *thick descriptions,* large amounts of data (descriptions of the culture) collected over extended periods. According to Geertz, the analysis and conclusions offered by ethnographers represent fictions developed to explain rather than to understand a culture.

Goodenough (1970, 1971) is an ethnographer who embraces the semiotic tradition. He does so through what has been described as *ethnoscience,* "a rigorous and systematic way of studying and classify emic (local or inside) data of a cultural group's own perceptions, knowledge, and language in terms of how people perceive and interpret their universe" (Leininger, 1970, pp. 168–169). "Ethnoscience [is] viewed as a method of developing precise and operationalized descriptions of cultural concept" (Morse & Field, 1995, p. 29). Ethnoscience also is called ethnosemantics or ethnolinguistics to emphasize the focus on language.

According to Sanday (1983), Geertz's commitment is to the "notion that culture is located in the minds and hearts of men" (p. 30). Culture is described by writing out systematic rules and formulating ethnographic algorithms, which make it possible to produce acceptable actions such as the "writing out of linguistic rules makes it possible to produce acceptable utterances" (Sanday, 1983, p. 30).

"The differences between Geertz and Goodenough are not in aim but in the method, focus, and mode of reporting" (Sanday, 1983, p. 30). Both ethnographers are committed to the careful description of culture. Geertz's method and reporting are viewed as more of an art form compared with Goodenough's method in which the focus is on rigorous, systematic methods of collecting data and reporting findings.

The third interpretation is the *behaviorist approach*. Ethnographers using this approach are most interested in the behavior of members of a culture. The main goal "is to uncover covarying patterns in observed behavior" (Sanday, 1983, pp. 33–34). This approach is deductive. Ethnographers subscribing to this interpretation look specifically for cultural situations that substantiate preselected categories of data. Use of this interpretation deviates radically from the intent of the other two interpretations, which rely solely on induction.

Leininger (1978, 1985), a nurse–anthropologist, developed her own interpretation of ethnography: ethnonursing. *Ethnonursing,* according to Leininger, is "the study and analysis of the local or indigenous people's viewpoints, beliefs, and practices about nursing care behavior and processes of designated cultures" (Leininger, 1978, p. 15). The goal of ethnonursing is to "discover nursing knowledge as known, perceived and experienced by nurses and consumers of nursing and health services" (Leininger, 1985, p. 38). The primary function of Leininger's approach to ethnography is to focus on nursing and related health phenomena. This approach has been an important contribution to the nursing field. Many nurse–ethnographers subscribe to Leininger's philosophy and apply her suggested methods of inquiry.

SELECTING ETHNOGRAPHY

When individuals choose to conduct an ethnographic research study, usually they have decided there is some shared cultural knowledge to which they would like access. The way individuals access cultural knowledge is by making *cultural inferences,* which are the observer's (researcher's) conclusions based on what the researcher has seen or heard while studying another culture. Making inferences is the way individuals learn many of their own group's cultural norms or values. For instance, if a child observes another child being scolded for talking in class, the observer—without being told—concludes that talking in class can lead to an unpleasant outcome. Therefore, the child learns through cultural inference that talking in class is unacceptable. Ethnographers follow this same process in their observations of cultural groups. According to Spradley (1980), ethnographers use generally three types of information to generate cultural inferences: cultural behavior (what people do); cultural artifacts (the things people make and use); and speech messages (what people say).

A significant part of culture is not readily available. This information, called *tacit knowledge,* consists of the information members of a culture

---

**BOX 8-1 STEPS FOR CONDUCTING
ETHNOGRAPHIC RESEARCH**

1. Do participant observation.
2. Make an ethnographic record.
3. Make descriptive observations.
4. Make a domain analysis.
5. Make a focused observation.
6. Make a taxonomic analysis.
7. Make selected observations.
8. Make a componential analysis.
9. Discover cultural themes.
10. Take a cultural inventory.
11. Write an ethnography.

---

know but do not talk about or express directly (Hammersley & Atkinson, 1983; Spradley, 1980). In addition to accessing explicit or easily observed cultural knowledge, ethnographers have the responsibility of describing tacit knowledge.

UNDERSTANDING THE RESEARCHER'S ROLE

To access explicit and tacit knowledge, researchers must understand the role they will play in the discovery of cultural knowledge. Because the researcher becomes the instrument, he or she must be cognizant of what the role of instrument entails. The role of instrument requires ethnographers to participate in the culture, observe the participants, document observations, collect artifacts, interview members of the cultural group, analyze the findings, and report the findings. This role requires a significant commitment to the research that should not be taken lightly.

The step-by-step method of collecting, analyzing, and presenting ethnographic research, according to Spradley (1980), is presented to educate readers. Although Spradley is not the only ethnographic approach available, it is presented because of its explicitness, clarity, and utility for inexperienced ethnographic researchers.

Spradley (1980) has identified eleven steps in the conduct of ethnographic research. Box 8-1 summarizes these steps. The processes for data generation, treatment, analysis, and interpretation are discussed within the framework of the steps identified.

GAINING ACCESS

One of the first considerations when initiating an ethnographic study is to decide on the focus. Based on the focus of the inquiry, researchers can decide the scope of the project. Will the focus be micro- or mini-ethnography? A single social situation? Multiple social situations? A single social institution? Or will it be maxi- or macro-ethnography? Multiple social institutions? A single community study? Multiple communities? Complex societies?

Once researchers have decided on the scope of the project, their next step is to gain access to the culture. Because ethnography requires the study of people, the activities in which they are involved, and the places in which they live, to conduct the study, researchers will need to gain access to the culture. This may be the most difficult part of the study. Because researchers are not usually members of the group studied, individuals in the culture of interest may be unwilling or unable to provide the access required. In other instances, researchers may be studying social situations that do not require a group's permission. For instance, if researchers are interested in the culture of individuals who come to the local pharmacy to obtain their medications, permission may not be required. However, if they are interested in studying the culture of health professionals in an outpatient clinic, permission is necessary.

Access is easiest when researchers have clearly stated the study purpose and have shared how they will protect the participants' confidentiality. In addition, offering to participate in the setting may enhance researchers' ability to gain entry to the social situation. If, for example, a researcher wishes to study the culture of health professionals working in an outpatient clinic, his or her willingness to participate by offering "volunteer" services while in the setting may improve the chances of obtaining admission. As a "volunteer," the researcher not only has the opportunity to make observations but will become part of the culture after remaining on the scene for an extended period.

MAKING PARTICIPANT OBSERVATIONS

Actual fieldwork begins when researchers start asking questions about the culture chosen. Initially, the ethnographer will ask broad questions. Using the outpatient clinic as an example, the researcher might ask: Who works in the clinic? Who comes to the clinic for care? What is the physical setup of the clinic? Who provides the care to clients who come to the clinic?

In addition to asking questions, the researcher will begin to make observations. Three types of observations are descriptive, focused, and selective (Spradley, 1980). *Descriptive observations* start when the researcher enters the social situation. The ethnographer is trying to begin to describe the social situation, get an overview of the situation, and determine what is going on. After completing this type of observation, the researcher will conduct more focused descriptive observations. These observations are generated from questions the researcher asked during the initial descriptive phase. For example, while in the clinic the researcher discovers that nurses are responsible for health teaching. A *focused observation* is required to look specifically at the types of health teaching done by the nurses in the setting. Based on this focused observation, the researcher conducts a more *selective observation*. For example, the researcher observes that only two out of the seven nurses in the clinic conduct any health teaching with clients with acquired immunodeficiency syndrome (AIDS). A selective interview or observation involving the two nurses will address additional questions about why clinic staff members behave as they do.

Neophyte ethnographers should not be led to believe that they conduct observations and interviews in the linear manner just described. Rather, broad, focused, or selective questions may arise out of any observation. Furthermore, the intent of an observation is not to merely "look at" something. Rather, through observation, researchers look, listen, ask questions, and collect artifacts.

At any given time, ethnographers may be more or less involved in the social situation. For example, when the outpatient clinic is busy, the researcher as volunteer may be quite involved as a participant in the culture. At times of lesser traffic, the researcher may spend more time on observation. Explicit rules for when to participate and when to observe are unavailable. Researchers, the *actors* (members of the culture studied), and the activity determine the degree of participation in the social situation.

MAKING THE ETHNOGRAPHIC RECORD

On completion of each observation, ethnographers are responsible for documenting the experience. Documents generated from the observations are called *field notes*. Researchers may manage field notes by handwriting and storing them manually or by using computer programs to store and categorize data. A number of data storage, retrieval, and analysis software programs are available (see Chapter 2). Researchers who do not have a computer or are more comfortable documenting their observations in writing may use handwritten notes they organize in file boxes. These notes will chronicle what the researchers have seen and heard, answers to questions they asked, and created or collected artifacts.

In the clinic, for example, the researcher may observe the physical layout. Based on the observation, the researcher may ask questions related to what happens in each room. A floor plan (artifact) may become part of the record. The researcher may also take photographs to document the colors of the clinic or the decorations used. These artifacts may offer important insights as the study continues.

It is important throughout the study—but especially in the beginning—not to focus too soon and also not to assume that any comment, artifact, or interaction is incidental. Researchers should document experiences to create a thick or rich description of the culture. In the outpatient example, the researcher should document the colors of the clinic. This observation may seem incidental; however, if a staff member later reports that it is important to maintain a calm atmosphere in the clinic because of the types of clients seen, then the choice of the color blue for the walls may be an artifact that supports this belief system.

In addition to recording explicit details of a situation, ethnographers also will record personal insights. A wide-angle view of the situation will provide the opportunity to detail what participants have said and to share what may be implicit in the situation. Using a wide-angle lens to view a situation provides ethnographers with a larger view of what is actually occurring in a social situation. For example, if an ethnographer is interested in observing a change-of-shift report and attends the report with the purpose of investigating the nurses' interactions, the researcher may miss valuable information regarding the report. With a wide-angle approach, the ethnographer would observe all individuals, activities, and artifacts that are part of the social situation, rather than merely focus on the interactions between the nurses in the report. Attention to all parts of the social situation will contribute to a richer description of the cultural scene.

Spradley (1980) has offered three principles researchers must consider as they document their observations: "the language identification principle, the verbatim principle, and the concrete principle" (p. 65). The *language identification principle* requires that ethnographers identify in whose language the text is written. Spradley (1980) has pointed out that the most frequently recorded language is the *amalgamated language* (see Example 8-1), that is, the use of the ethnographer's language as well as the informants' language. For example, a nurse–ethnographer recording his or her observations of a clinic day might choose to mix the answers to questions with personal observations. Such mixing may create problems when data analysis begins because the researcher can lose sight of the cultural meaning of the observation. To minimize the potential of this happening, entries should identify the person making the remarks. Example 8-1 illustrates the correct way to record field notes. In Example 8-2, the record does not describe how the researcher obtained specific information. It is difficult to decipher whether the notes are the researcher's interpretations or whether the researcher obtained the information directly from the informants.

Although Example 8-1 is a limited notation, readers can get a sense of how researchers should report field notes to facilitate analysis. In this example, the receptionist's response gives the ethnographer clear information about the decorating. That the receptionist used the word *we* in Example 8-1 gives the researcher insight into the interactions occurring

---

Example 8.1

Field Note Entry No. 1   January 2, 1999

Ethnographer: Today when I visited the clinic, I noticed that the walls were painted blue. I asked the receptionist who had done the decorating.

Receptionist: "We had several meetings with the decorator."

Example 8.2

Field Note Entry No. 1   January 2, 1999

Today I observed the clinic waiting area. The area is painted in a pale blue. The chairs are wood and fabric. The fabric is a white-and-blue print, which contrasts with the wallpaper. The waiting area is very busy. The colors have an effect on the clients. They come in looking very harassed then they fall asleep. A decorator helped with the colors.

---

among staff members. Although Example 8-2 offers significant information, the researcher will find it difficult, after long months of data collection, to return to this note and distinguish his or her insights from factual information obtained from the informants.

The reporting of the receptionist's comments in Example 8-1 reflects the *verbatim principle,* which requires ethnographers to use the speaker's exact words. To adhere to this principle, researchers may use audiotaping, which not only offers ethnographers verbatim accounts of conversation but also affords them an extensive accounting of an interaction that will provide the material for intensive analysis. Documenting verbatim statements also provides researchers with a view of native expressions. In Example 8-1, the use of verbatim documentation allows the researcher to gain insight into the language. The receptionist's use of the word *we* to describe the activities with the decorator may provide valuable insights into the culture of the clinic.

The *concrete principle* requires that ethnographers document without interpretation what they have seen and heard. Generalizations and interpretations may limit access to valuable cultural insights. To reduce interpretation, researchers should document observations with as much detail as possible. Example 8-3 offers an example of concrete documentation without interpretation or generalization. In this example, all documentation is clear. The researcher has recorded facts and conversation verbatim.

MAKING DESCRIPTIVE OBSERVATIONS

Every time ethnographers are in a social situation, they generally will make descriptive observations without having specific questions in mind. General questions, which guide this type of observation, are *grand tour questions.* For example, a grand tour question that might initiate a study of a particular clinic is, How do people who live in this neighborhood receive health care? Remembering that the primary foci of all observations include the actors, activities, and artifacts will assist in the development of grand tour questions.

Spradley (1980) has identified nine major dimensions to any social situation:

Example 8-3

The clinic waiting area is painted ocean blue. The ladder-back chairs are light brown wood with upholstered seats. The fabric on the seats is an ocean blue-and-white checkered pattern. There are two small 2 ft by 3 ft by $2\frac{1}{2}$ ft brown wooden tables between the six chairs in the waiting room. There are two chairs along one wall with a table in the corner. Then, two chairs along the second wall with another table in the corner. The third wall has the two remaining chairs. The room is an 8 ft by 9 ft rectangle. Each table has a ginger jar lamp. The lamp base and shade are white. The fourth wall has a door and window on it. The draperies on the window are floor length and match the pattern on the chairs.

   Individuals enter the clinic, state their names to the receptionist, sit in the chairs, and close their eyes. Some patients snore.

   Ethnographer: "The colors in this room are great. Everything seems to go together so well. Who did the decorating?"

   Receptionist: "We had several meetings with the decorator."

---

1. *Space* refers to the physical place or places where the culture of interest carries out social interactions. In the outpatient clinic example, space would include the physical layout of the care delivery site.
2. *Actors* are people who are part of the culture under investigation. In the clinic example, the nurses, physicians, maintenance workers, secretarial/receptionist staff, and family members of clients in the clinic would be the actors.
3. The *activities* are the actions by members of the culture. In the clinic example, activities would include the treatments provided to clients and conversations between cultural group members.
4. *Objects* in the clinic example would include artifacts such as implements used for care, pamphlets read by clients, staff records, and meeting minutes. Any inanimate object included in the space under study may give insight into the culture.
5. Any single action carried out by group members is an *act*. An example of an act observed in the clinic would be the locking of the medicine cabinet.
6. An *event* is a set of related activities carried out by members of the culture. In the clinic example, the ethnographer one day may observe the staff giving a birthday party for a long-time client.
7. It is important that the researcher document the *time* he or she made observations and when activities occurred during those times. In addition to recording time, the researcher must relate the effect time has on all nine dimensions of social situations.

8. *Goal* relates specifically to what group members hope to achieve. In the clinic example, in painting the clinic blue, the staff may relate that their intention was to have a calming effect on clients, who often must wait long periods.
9. The researcher should also record *feelings* for each social situation, including the emotions expressed or observed. For example, during the staff-given birthday party for a long-time client, the ethnographer might observe tears from that client, cheers by the staff, and anger by a family member. Recording feelings provides a rich framework from which to make cultural inferences.

The nine dimensions can be useful in guiding observations and questions related to social situations. It is beneficial to plot the nine dimensions in a matrix (Spradley, 1980) to contrast each dimension. For example, in addition to describing the space where the culture carries out its interactions, researchers should relate space to object, act, activity, event, time, actor, goal, and feelings. What does the space look like?

> "What are all the ways space is organized by objects? What are all the ways space is organized by acts? What are all the ways space is organized by activities? What are all the ways space is organized by events? What spatial changes occur over time? What are all the ways space is used by actors? What are all the ways space is related to goals? What places are associated with feelings?" (Spradley, 1980, pp. 82–83).

Critical ethnographers would add the dimensions of social and political climate to Spradley's (1980) list. It is extremely important that researchers consider issues of power, social class, and politics to get a full view of the culture. In the clinic example, the researcher might ask the following questions: Why are women the primary care providers? Does the doctor ultimately make all the decisions? If so, why? Once researchers have collected data on all dimensions and have related each piece of data to other information, they can begin to focus further observations.

MAKING A DOMAIN ANALYSIS

Throughout data collection, ethnographers are required to analyze data. Analyzing data while in the field helps to structure later encounters with the social group of interest. Ethnographic data "analysis is a search for patterns" (Spradley, 1980, p. 85). These patterns make up the culture.

To begin to understand cultural meaning, ethnographers must analyze social situations they observe. A social situation is not the same as the concept of culture but, rather, "refers to the stream of behavior (activities) carried out by people (actors) in a particular location (place)" (Spradley, 1980, p. 86). Analysis of the social situation will lead to discovery of the cultural scene. *Cultural scene,* an ethnographic term, refers to the culture under study (Spradley, 1980). The first step in analysis is to do a domain

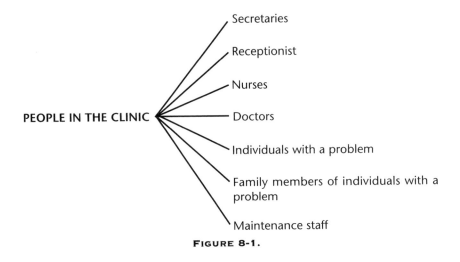

FIGURE 8-1.

analysis. Ethnographers doing a domain analysis focus on a particular situation.

In the outpatient clinic example, the category—people in the clinic—is the first domain the researcher must analyze. The researcher should ask, Who are the people in the clinic? Reviewing the field notes, the people in the clinic should be easy to identify (Fig. 8-1). Spradley (1980) has suggested it is important to identify the semantic relationships in the observations made. For example, x is a kind of y: nurses are kinds of people in the clinic. Furthermore, the researcher can do another analysis to explore the types of nurses who work in the clinic. Hammersley and Atkinson (1983) have approached analysis somewhat differently. They have recommended researchers generate concept categories, refining them further into subcategories. Regardless of the method used, it is essential that researchers work to discover the cultural meaning for people, places, artifacts, and activities. Creating as extensive a list as possible of categories will assist in discovery. To maintain inclusiveness, return to the dimensions described earlier in this chapter. Generating domain analyses leads ethnographers to ask additional questions and make further observations to explore the roles and relationships of the cultural group members.

MAKING FOCUSED OBSERVATIONS

Based on the completed domain analysis, ethnographers will need to make new observations and collect additional material. The domain analysis should be the trigger for the next round of observations. Researchers identify the domain categories that need development and then return to the research site. In the clinic example, based on the identification of different types of nurses in the clinic, the ethnographer would want to focus on the different types of nurses and discover their specific roles and activities. This information could provide important insight into the culture of the situation.

Making a Taxonomic Analysis

The taxonomic analysis is a more in-depth analysis of the domains researchers have chosen earlier. Researchers are searching for larger categories to which the domain may belong. In the clinic example, nurses in the clinic is a category identified in the domain analysis. Nurses are a type of people in the clinic. In addition, there are types of nurses. Nurses can be categorized based on their educational backgrounds: licensed practical nurses (LPNs), registered nurses (RNs), nurse–practitioners (NPs), and clinical nurse specialists (CNSs). These categories may be broken down further based on the focus of clients for whom the nurses care in the particular culture under study (see Fig. 8-2).

On completion of this analysis, ethnographers will look for relationships among the parts or relationships to the whole. Based on these new categories, researchers will make additional observations and ask more questions. In the clinic example, the researcher might ask, Why do the RNs have the primary responsibility for care of the clients with AIDS and Sexually Transmitted Diseases (STDs)? Are there different types of AIDS clients and are they cared for by specific RNs? Are AIDS clients treated differently from the clients with STDs? Are other nurses consulted regarding the care of these two groups of clients? Are the nurses able to select the types of clients for whom they care?

Clearly, the researcher has generated a number of questions from this taxonomic analysis of the concept *nurse*. In addition to using a reductive exercise, ethnographers should try to discover whether there are larger categories for which they have not accounted. In the clinic example, are the people in the clinic part of a larger system? If the clinic is affiliated with a hospital or public or private organization, then the answer is *yes*.

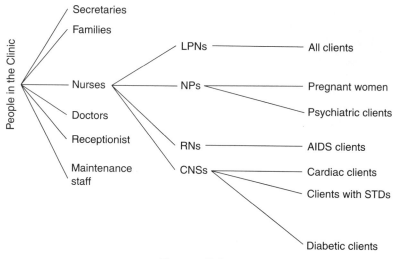

Figure 8-2.

The nurse–ethnographer will then need to ask further questions based on this association and conduct focused interviews to validate whether the previously derived larger or smaller categorizations are accurate.

MAKING SELECTED OBSERVATIONS

Through selective observations, researchers need to further refine the data they have collected. Selective observations will help to identify the "dimensions of contrast" (Spradley, 1980, p. 128). Spradley has offered several types of questions that will help researchers discern the differences in the dimensions of contrast. The *dyadic question* seeks to identify the differences between two domains. The question is, In what way are these two things different? In the clinic example, one of the questions the researcher should ask is, In what ways are NPs and CNSs different? *Triadic contrast questions* seek to identify how three categories are related. The researcher in the clinic example might ask, Of the three—NPs, CNSs, and RNs—which two are more alike than the third? *Card sorting contrast questions* allow ethnographers to place the domains on cards and sort them into piles based on their similarities. By identifying the similarities, the contrasts become easily recognizable. Asking these questions of the available data will lead ethnographers to the setting to ask still other questions.

MAKING A COMPONENTIAL ANALYSIS

"Componential analysis is the systematic search for attributes associated with cultural categories" (Spradley, 1980, p. 131). Boyle (1994) has indicated that componential analysis has two objectives: To specify the conditions under which participants name something and to understand under what conditions the participants give something a specific name. Componential analysis is language driven.

During this stage of analysis, researchers are looking for units of meaning. Each unit of meaning is considered an attribute of the culture. Again, researchers are searching for missing data. During componential analysis, they examine each domain for its component parts and ask questions to identify the dimensions of contrast. Based on the identification of missing data, the researchers will make selected observations. Table 8-1 is an example of simple componential analysis that illustrates dimensions of contrast based on the sorting of people who work in the outpatient clinic. In the clinic example, the ethnographer is able to determine that unlicensed personnel do not provide health care. This analysis helps the researcher to begin to identify a hierarchical structure. He or she must validate both hypotheses through selective interviews and observations. The purpose of using this process is to search for contrasts, sort them out, and then group them based on similarities and differences. This activity provides ethnographers with important information regarding the culture under study.

To fully carry out a componential analysis, ethnographers should

TABLE 8-1   **Dimensions of Contrast**

Domain	Dimensions of Contrast		
	Licensed	Supervised Personnel	Health Care Provider
Doctors	Yes	No	Yes
Nurses	Yes	Yes	Yes
Receptionist	No	Yes	No
Maintenance staff	No	Yes	No
Secretaries	No	Yes	No

move through the process in a sequential manner. The eight steps of the procedure are (1) select a domain for analysis (people who work in the clinic); (2) inventory previously discovered contrasts (some members are licensed, have supervisors to whom they report, and provide health care); (3) prepare the worksheet (this is called a *paradigm*); (4) classify dimensions of contrast that have binary values (licensed, yes or no); (5) combine related dimensions of contrast into ones that have multiple values (doctors and nurses are licensed personnel who provide health care); (6) prepare contrast questions for missing attributes (Are doctors the owners of the clinic because they appear not to have a reporting relationship?); (7) conduct selective observations and interviews to discover missing data and confirm or discard hypotheses; (8) prepare a complete paradigm (Spradley, 1980). "The final paradigm can be used as a chart in [the] ethnography" (p. 139). Although every attribute will not be discussed on the chart, important ones can be, allowing ethnographers to present a large amount of information in a concise and clear manner (Spradley, 1980).

PERFORMING DATA ANALYSIS

Although data analysis occurs throughout data collection, the next two stages—discovering cultural themes and taking a cultural inventory—focus solely on data analysis.

DISCOVERING CULTURAL THEMES

The discovery of cultural themes requires ethnographers to carefully examine the data collected and identify recurrent patterns. Whether tacit or explicit, the patterns constitute the culture.

To complete the theme analysis, researchers must become immersed in the data, which requires focused concentration over an extended period. The purpose of immersion is to identify patterns that have not become apparent at the particular point in the study or to explore patterns that may have been generated previously to assure their soundness. Spradley

(1980) has identified six universal themes that may be helpful during this stage of data analysis. These themes are not meant to explain all patterns, but they do provide a place to begin. The universal themes are (1) social conflict; (2) What types of conflicts are occurring between people in social situations? (cultural contradiction); (3) Is there information derived from the cultural group that appears contradictory? (informal techniques of social control); (4) Are there informal patterns of behavior that result in social control? (management of interpersonal relationships); (5) How do group members conduct their interpersonal relationships? (acquisition and maintenance of status); and (6) problem solving. Researchers then write an overview summary of the cultural scene to help identify themes they have not yet discovered.

TAKING A CULTURAL INVENTORY

Completing a cultural inventory is the first stage in writing an ethnography. The inventory provides the opportunity to organize collected data. A cultural inventory involves listing cultural domains; listing analyzed domains; collecting sketch maps, which are drawings of places or activities; listing themes; completing an inventory of examples; identifying organizing domains; completing an index or table of contents; completing an inventory of miscellaneous data; and suggesting areas for future study (Spradley, 1980). Once researchers have completed the inventory and interpreted the findings, they are ready to write the ethnography.

INTERPRETING THE FINDINGS

The purpose of an ethnographic study is to describe the culture. It is important to remember that no two researchers would likely describe a culture in the same way, because of issues within each researcher's culture, the period in which the study was conducted, and the information gathered by the researchers. Perhaps, some researchers would argue, these are reasons why qualitative methods and, in particular, ethnography can never be viewed as science. On the contrary, these are precisely the reasons why ethnography and other qualitative methods are science. What most qualitative methods of research seek to do is share a context-bound view of phenomena; in this case, the phenomenon is the culture of a group. Because culture is ever-changing and dynamic, the discoveries of today are applicable within context. These discoveries bring important insights but do not pretend to bring forward *the* truth but, rather, *a* truth. So, as ethnographers begin to write the study findings, they must remember that, if they used appropriate rigorous methods to collect and analyze data, then the product is one view of a truth.

WRITING THE ETHNOGRAPHY

The purpose of writing an ethnography is to share with people what the researcher has learned and to attempt to make sense out of the cultural patterns that present themselves. To do so, an ethnographer must ask,

For whom am I writing? Based on the answer to this question, the document will look different. If writing for a scholarly community, details will be important. If writing for the popular press, insights with exemplars will be most useful. If writing for an organization in the form of a formal report, the researcher must pay attention to those details that reflect the concerns that directed the inquiry.

One of the best ways to know what to write is to look for examples of what has been written. Ethnographers may choose to report natural history organized chronologically, spatially, or choose to organize information based on significant themes (Omery, 1988). A review of published texts that chronicle macro-ethnographies or scholarly journals that have published micro-ethnographies will provide good examples of how to organize the final ethnographic report. Every detail or idea may not be collapsible into one journal article or one book. Focusing on aspects of the research for several books or articles may be the only feasible way to report the findings of an ethnographic study.

Researchers may write several drafts until the document reflects the study. They may recruit colleagues to critique the work. Colleagues can help neophyte researchers discover whether the researchers have appropriately covered the topic.

MAKING ETHICAL CONSIDERATIONS

The protection of study participants is important regardless of the research paradigm, whether a qualitative or quantitative approach, phenomenology, grounded theory, ethnography, action, or historic. Because ethics is covered broadly in Chapter 3, this section shares unique ethical issues specific to ethnography.

When conducting ethnographic research, researchers by virtue of their roles as participant–observers are in a unique position to fit in. Researchers live among the people and therefore have the ability to be invisible at times in the researcher capacity. The invisible nature of researchers has significant value in data collection but can present potential dilemmas from an ethical standpoint. The important elements in conducting any type of research study are to inform participants fully about the matter to which they are consenting, inform participants they can withdraw from the study at any time for any reason, reduce all unnecessary risks, ensure that the benefits of the study outweigh the risks, and for the researchers who will be conducting the study to have appropriate qualifications (Lipson, 1994).

Informed consent is an ethical principle that requires researchers to obtain voluntary consent, including description of the potential risks and benefits of participation. Munhall (1988) has recommended "process consent" (p. 156) rather than the traditional consent signed in the beginning of most studies and not revisited unless participants question their obligations related to the study. *Process consent* or "consensual decision-making" (Ramos, 1989, p. 61) means that researchers renegotiate the consent as unforeseen events or consequences arise (Munhall, 1988; Ramos, 1989). By providing the opportunity to renegotiate the consent and be part of the decision making as the study develops, ethnographers afford participants the chance to withdraw or modify that to which they initially agreed.

Lipson (1994) has suggested that consent in the field becomes somewhat more difficult. For instance, the researcher secures consent before formal fieldwork begins. Some time passes and the researcher is in the field at the time an unexpected event occurs, such as the birth of a child. Although it is important that the researcher inform the group that he or she is chronicling this event for research purposes, it would be intrusive to address consent at that point. One way to handle this situation would be for the researcher to inform participants at a later time that the birth experience gave him or her insight into cultural values. If objections were to arise, it is obvious that the researcher could never erase the memory of the event; however, to protect the informants, it is imperative that he or she not formally include those data in the study. Covert participation in all research is highly regarded as a violation of individuals rights. Therefore, ethnographers should always be forthright with their objectives.

Risk is another major concern. Researchers should never put a participant group in danger to collect data. For example, the researcher in the field discovers that some young men are staging a gang fight in which they plan to use weapons. Believing that it would be important to learn more about conflict and how the group handles it, so the researcher plans to go as an observer. In this situation, the risk to the people involved far outweighs the goal to observe how the group handles conflict. Intervention is necessary. How the researcher intervenes should be determined by a number of factors. A research mentor is invaluable in helping the researcher sort out when and how to intervene. Too many variables are involved to offer a simple answer. The important principle is that the researcher does not engage in data collection to achieve his or her own goals when significant risk to research participants is involved.

Another principle described by Lipson (1994) is the researcher's qualifications. Usually, institutional review boards will assess the researcher's qualifications based on review of the submitted research proposal. An unqualified researcher can do substantial damage to a culture. It is essential that, even as a neophyte ethnographer, one clearly understands what it is he or she is doing and the potential risks in conducting a study without adequate sensitivity and knowledge.

It is essential that all qualitative researchers—but, in particular, ethnographers—be aware of and knowledgeable about their responsibilities to research participants. Specifically, because of the intimate nature of the relationships that develop when ethnographers live among study participants, these researchers have a significant duty to inform and protect informants.

Summary

This chapter discussed the ethnographic approach to research and presented issues related to selection of the method, interpretations of the approach, application of the approach, and interpretation of the findings. A thorough explanation of how to conduct ethnographic research has been shared to provide a framework from which to conduct the first ethnographic inquiry.

Ethnography offers a significant research approach to individuals interested in learning about culture, willing and able to report data in narrative format, comfortable with ambiguity, able to build trusting relationships, and comfortable working alone (Germain, 1986). The study of culture, whether in a well-known nursing unit or in a country whose health practices are unknown, offers exciting discovery opportunities. Nurse–researchers who choose to use this approach will find that the focus of the study will become an intimate part of their daily existence until they have fully explored, described, and interpreted that focus.

Chapter 9 provides a review of research that uses the ethnographic approach. It is hoped that the review will further assist those individuals interested in the approach to understand the method and will provide concrete criteria from which to judge the merits of published reports.

REFERENCES

Agar, M. H. (1982). Toward an ethnographic language. *American Anthropologist, 8*(4), 779–795.

Agar, M. H. (1986). *Speaking of ethnography.* Newbury Park, CA: Sage.

Anderson, J. M. (1991). Reflexivity in fieldwork: Toward a feminist epistemology. *Image, 23*(2), 115–118.

Anderson, N. L. R. (1996). Decisions about substance abuse among adolescents in juvenile detention. *Image, 28*(1), 65–70.

Atkinson, P., & Hammersley, M. (1994). Ethnography and participant observation. In N. K. Denzin & Y. S. Lincoln (Eds.), *Handbook of qualitative research* (pp. 248–261). Thousand Oaks, CA: Sage.

Benedict, R. (1934). *Patterns of culture.* New York: Houghton Mifflin.

Boas, F. (1948). *Race, language and culture.* New York: Macmillan.

Boyle, J. S. (1994). Styles of ethnography. In J. M. Morse (Ed.), *Critical issues in qualitative research methods* (pp. 159–185). Thousand Oaks, CA: Sage.

Breda, K. L. (1997). Professional nurses in unions: Working together pays off. *Journal of Professional Nursing, 13*(2), 99–109.

Fontana, A., & Frey, J. H. (1994). Interviewing: The art of science. In N. K. Denzin & Y. S. Lincoln (Eds.), *Handbook of qualitative research* (pp. 361–376). Thousand Oaks, CA: Sage.

Geertz, C. (1973). *The interpretations of culture.* New York: Basic Books.

Germain, C. P. (1986). Ethnography: The method. In P. L. Munhall & C. J. Oiler (Eds.), *Nursing research: A qualitative perspective* (pp. 147–162). Norwalk, CT: Appleton-Century-Crofts.

Goetz, J. P. & LeCompte, M. D. (1984). *Ethnography and qualitative design in educational research.* Orlando, FL: Academic Press.

Goodenough, W. (1970). *Description and comparison in cultural anthropology.* Chicago: Aldine.

Goodenough, W. (1971). *Culture, language and society.* Reading, MA: Addison-Wesley.

Grant, L., & Fine, G. A. (1992). Sociology unleashed: Creative directions in classical ethnography. In M. D. LeCompte, W. L. Millroy, & J. Preissle (Eds.), *The handbook of qualitative research in education* (pp. 405–446). San Diego, CA: Academic Press.

Hammersley, M., & Atkinson, P. (1983). *Ethnography: Principles in practice*. London: Tavistock.

Hughes, C. C. (1992). "Ethnography": What's in a word—Process? Product? Promise? *Qualitative Health Research, 2*(4), 439–450.

Leininger, M. (1970). *Nursing and anthropology: Two worlds to blend*. New York: Wiley.

Leininger, M. (1978). *Transcultural nursing: Concepts, theories and practices*. New York: Wiley.

Leininger, M. (1985). Ethnography and ethnonursing: Models and modes of qualitative data analysis. In M. Leininger (Ed.), *Qualitative research methods in nursing* (pp. 33–71). Orlando, FL: Grune & Stratton.

Lipson, J. G. (1994). Ethical issues in ethnography. In J. M. Morse (Ed.), *Critical issues in qualitative research methods* (pp. 333–355). Thousand Oaks, CA: Sage.

Lipson, J. G., & Omidian, P. A. (1997). Afghan refugee issues in the U.S. social environment. *Western Journal of Nursing Research, 19*(1), 110–126.

Malinowski, B. (1922). *Argonauts of the Western Pacific*. London: Routledge & Kegan Paul.

Malinowski, B. (1961). *Argonauts of the Western Pacific*. New York: Dutton.

Mead, M. (1949). *Coming of age in Samoa*. New York: New American Library, Mentor Books.

Morse, J. M., & Field, P. A. (1995). *Qualitative research methods for health professionals*. Thousand Oaks, CA: Sage.

Muecke, M. A. (1994). On the evaluation of ethnographies. In J. M. Morse (Ed.). *Critical issues in qualitative research methods* (pp. 187–209). Thousand Oaks, CA: Sage.

Munhall, P. L. (1988). Ethical considerations in qualitative research. *Western Journal of Nursing Research, 10*(2), 150–162.

Omery, A. (1988). Ethnography. In B. Sarter (Ed.), *Paths to knowledge: Innovative research methods for nursing* (pp. 17–31). New York: National League for Nursing.

Preston, R. M. (1997). Ethnography: Studying the fate of health promotion in coronary families. *Journal of Advanced Nursing, 25,* 554–561.

Radcliffe-Brown, A. R. (1952). *Structure and function in primitive society*. London: Oxford University Press.

Ragucci, A. T. (1972). The ethnographic approach and nursing research. *Nursing Research, 21*(6), 485–490.

Ramos, M. C. (1989). Some ethical implications in qualitative research. *Research in Nursing and Health, 12,* 57–63.

Resnick, B. (1996). Motivation in geriatric rehabilitation. *Image, 28*(1), 41–45.

Rowe, J. H. (1965). The Renaissance foundation in anthropology. *American Anthropologist, 67,* 1–20.

Sanday, P. R. (1983). The ethnographic paradigm(s). In J. Van Maanen (Ed.), *Qualitative methodology* (pp. 19–36). Beverly Hills, CA: Sage.

Spradley, J. P. (1980). *Participant observation*. New York: Holt, Rinehart & Winston.

Spradley, J. P., & McCurdy, D. W. (1972). *The cultural experience: Ethnography in complex society*. Prospect Heights, IL: Waveland Press.

van Maanen, J. (1983). The fact of fiction in organizational ethnography. In J. van Maanen (Ed.), *Qualitative methodology* (pp. 36–55). Beverly Hills, CA: Sage.

Wolf, Z. R. (1988). *Nurses' work, the sacred and the profane*. Philadelphia: University of Pennsylvania Press.

Woods, P. (1992). Symbolic Interactionism: Theory and method. In M. D. LeCompte, W. L. Millroy, & J. Preissle (Eds.), *The handbook of qualitative research in education*. San Diego, CA: Academic Press.

9

Ethnography in Practice, Education, and Administration

As a means of studying nursing and the cultural practices imbedded within it, ethnography creates unlimited opportunities for nurses interested in using this approach. The study of patterns within a culture provides an excellent opportunity to describe the practices of the people for whom nurses care, to understand the health-related phenomena of people within various cultures, and to examine nursing's own unique culture. Ethnography provides a chance to explore both the clinical aspects of nursing and its administrative and educative patterns and lifeways.

This chapter provides an overview of ethnographic studies that have explored cultures of interest to nursing. In addition, it critiques micro-ethnographic studies that reflect clinical nursing practice, nursing education, and nursing administration to provide readers with examples of published works and the contributions those works have made to the field. The ethnographic studies examined in this chapter have been critiqued using the guidelines in Box 9-1. The critiquing guidelines offer specific directives for determining the quality of the ethnographic works presented in this chapter and in the literature. The questions in Box 9-1 are specific to ethnographic research and reflect the most important aspects researchers must evaluate in an ethnographic study. A reprint of Lipson and Omidian's (1997) article, found at the end of this chapter, assists readers in understanding the critiquing process. Table 9-1 summarizes a recent series of ethnographic studies representing the areas of nursing education, administration, and practice.

Application to Practice

Ethnographic research methodology provides an exceptional opportunity for nurses interested in examining clinical practice issues. Whether the interest is in studying racism and health care access (Murrell et al., 1996) or Afghan refugee issues in the U.S. social environment (Lipson & Omidian, 1997), ethnographic research provides the framework for exploring the richness of nursing and nursing-related phenomena. Lipson and Omidian's (1997) study of Afghan refugees serves as the reference for critique in this section because of its scope. What they have reported to readers is one aspect of their study, which they conducted over a 6-year period. It is not unusual for researchers who publish an ethnography in a research journal to focus on only one facet of a larger study. Because of the significant amount of information generated in a long-term cultural study, many ethnographies are published as books. When researchers choose to publish their ethnographic work in a journal, the scope of the report must meet the page guidelines of the selected journal.

The Lipson and Omidian (1997) study clearly identifies the culture studied: Afghan refugees living in the San Francisco Bay Area. The reported scope of the study is a focused ethnography because of the specific nature of the inquiry: "the social context in which Afghan refugees find

---

BOX 9-1 CRITERIA FOR CRITIQUING ETHNOGRAPHIC RESEARCH

FOCUS

1. Has the researcher clearly identified the culture to be studied?
2. Are readers able to determine the scope of the study?
3. Has the researcher clearly stated the purpose of the study?

METHOD

1. Has the researcher appropriately selected the method to fulfill the purpose of the study?
2. Is the study conducted in the field?
3. Has the researcher reported established guidelines for participant consent?
4. Has the researcher protected study participants' rights?

SAMPLING

1. Is the group selected to inform the study appropriate?
2. Does the researcher discuss how key informants are selected and why?

DATA COLLECTION

1. Has the researcher clearly stated the strategies used to collect data?
2. Are the strategies selected appropriate to fully inform the study?
3. Has the researcher clearly described his or her role in the study?
4. Are multiple sources of data used (observation, interview, collection of artifacts)?
5. Is time in the field adequate to meet the purpose of the study?

(continued)

BOX 9-1 CRITERIA FOR CRITIQUING ETHNOGRAPHIC RESEARCH (CONTINUED)

DATA ANALYSIS

1. Does the researcher clearly state how data were analyzed?
2. Does the researcher demonstrate cyclic data collection or data analysis?
3. Based on the report, can another researcher follow the logic of the researcher's conclusions?

RIGOR

1. Has the researcher made clear how he or she maintains "objectivity?"
2. Has the researcher offered adequate documentation of data authenticity?
3. Have the informants participated in validating the researcher's findings?

FINDINGS

1. Do the findings make clear a description of the culture studied?
2. Are the findings offered within the appropriate context?
3. Are findings presented in a rich narrative format providing readers with a "feel" for the culture?
4. Do the findings go beyond the description to explain why particular aspects of the culture are as they are?
5. Are the findings reported in a systematic way, such as by themes?

CONCLUSIONS

1. Are the conclusions clear and do they relate to the study findings?
2. Does the researcher relate the relevance of the findings to nursing and offer how the results may be useful?

---

themselves, [specifically] describing perceptions of their interactions with mainstream American citizens and health and social service providers" (p. 110). The authors implicitly state the purpose of the study throughout the report. They clearly articulate that they studied the social context of Afghan refugees' "interactions with mainstream American citizens and health and social service providers" (p. 110).

The method used to conduct the inquiry is appropriate. Lipson and Omidian's (1997) use of ethnography to study the Afghan refugees living

(text continues on page 176)

TABLE 9-1 Selective Sampling of Micro-Ethnographic Studies

Author	Domain	Culture	Focus	Data Collection Strategies	Data Analysis
Breda (1997)	Administration	Professional nurses in unions	Realization of professional gains within the context of collective bargaining	Participant observation Interview	Not reported
Craig (1994)	Practice	Rural elderly population in a western plains community	Influence of communities on health	Participant observation Historical data Interviews	Analyzed for common categories
Cruise & Dunn (1994)	Practice	Low-income African American women susceptible to acquired immunodeficiency syndrome	Obtainment of face-to-face interactions	Focus groups	Not reported
Hall (1994)	Practice	Lesbians in alcoholic recovery	Help-seeking experiences, barriers to recovery	Semistructured ethnographic interviews	Constant comparative
Johnson, Primas, & Coe (1994)	Practice	Women who delivered without prenatal care	Reasons for not seeking prenatal care	Interview	Content analysis

Lipson & Omidian (1997)	Practice	Afghan refugees	Perceptions of interactions with mainstream American citizens and health and social services providers	Participant observation Interview	Not reported
MacDonald (1996)	Practice	Mothers of children afflicted with asthma	Meaning of asthma	Interview Participant observation	Spradley (1979)
Magilvy, Congdon, & Martinez (1994)	Practice	Frail elderly people living in rural areas and receiving home care	Description of service provision from the perspective of frail elderly people in rural areas	Interviews Participant observation Examination of artifacts	Ethnographic software
Paterson (1997)	Education	Clinical educators	Experiences of clinical educators as temporary systems	Interview Participant observation Document analysis	"Category generation" (p. 200) developed by Glaser & Strauss (1967)
Resnick (1996)	Practice	Elderly women	Factors involved in motivating elderly people's participation in rehabilitation	Interview Observation	Not reported
Thorne (1997)	Practice	Nurses espousing global consciousness	Description of experiences sources of global consciousness	Participant observation Interview	Constant comparative

in the San Francisco Bay Area demonstrates their intent to understand the culture. As Fetterman (1989) and Spradley (1980) have offered, ethnography is the work of describing culture. Clearly, this was Lipson and Omidian's goal. Lipson and Omidian report that they conducted their work in the field by participating and observing Afghan refugees. They visited homes of families; accompanied them to "weddings, concerts and other social occasions, and religious observances; . . . [and drove] individuals to appointments" (Lipson & Omidian, 1997, p. 114); advocated for the informants; and participated in community activities. The description distinctly identifies the location of the study—the field—where the people lived, worked, and socialized.

The Lipson and Omidian (1997) report does not include a description of consent or protection of the participants. In light of the close relationship ethnographers have with their informants, this is a serious omission. As stated in Chapter 8, it is extremely important to protect the rights of people who participate in ethnographic research studies. As Lipson (1994) has indicated, ethnographers are required to protect study participants in five ways: (1) inform participants fully about the matter to which they are consenting, (2) inform participants they can withdraw from the study at any time for any reason, (3) reduce all unnecessary risks, (4) ensure that the benefits of the study outweigh the risks, and (5) ensure that the researchers who will be conducting the study have appropriate qualifications.

Afghan refugees composed the culture studied and therefore were the primary study informants. Formally, they are the sample for the study. The report offers no clear description of how or why the researchers selected particular individuals. Rather, the report gives readers the impression that the researchers interviewed refugees who were available and willing to talk to them and, based on these interactions, the researchers invited these people to talk to others and to participate in additional activities involving the refugees. Although not stated, it appears that one of the two authors gained access to the group before assuming the role of ethnographic researcher, hence establishing trust within the group.

Lipson and Omidian (1997) clearly state that they used participant observation and formal and informal interviews to collect data. These excellent strategies allow researchers to move among group members as both researchers and advocates. However, there is the inherent danger, addressed by many authors, of "going native" when researchers become too involved without paying constant attention to their role as researcher. The reported findings do not give readers a sense that the researchers ever lost their perspective; rather, it appears the researchers moved within the culture as both sensitive participants and ethnographers.

An examination of the researcher's role criterion in the Lipson and Omidian (1997) study reveals that, as they report, the researchers participated in many activities as well as acted as advocates for the refugees.

They did not report maintenance of a journal as part of data collection. The use of a journal is a valuable tool for ethnographers. The journal can serve as a "reality check" of a researcher's motivation and role in participation within the culture's activities (Werner & Schoepfle, 1987).

Lipson and Omidian (1997) share their use of multiple data sources, including participant observation, interviews, and surveys in data collection. They do not mention the use of artifacts. Using multiple data sources provides for cross referencing of findings, thus helping to assure the validity of what researchers believe they are discovering. Lipson and Omidian also do not report how they maintained their objectivity throughout data collection. Data triangulation, including journaling (ie, keeping a journal), helps ethnographers regularly assess the truthfulness of their conclusions. Given that the researchers stayed in the field for more than 6 years, it is safe to assume that the time was adequate to describe the culture. Specifically, the data collection for the portion of the study reported in *Western Journal of Nursing Research* was carried out within a 1-year time frame.

Lipson and Omidian (1997) clearly identify the cyclic nature of data collection and analysis. They report that, "though the original intent of the study was to gather data on health and illness models, interviews invariably shifted to the topic of life in the United States and the problems of culture change as perceived by different generations" (p. 115). In this instance, the researchers identify that their plan was to focus on health and illness models used by the Afghan people. However, to get to the information they desired, it was necessary for them to ask questions and seek clarifications of activities important to the Afghan people. This was an appropriate shift in focus, reflecting the researchers' goal of fully describing the culture.

The research report does not explicitly demonstrate how Lipson and Omidian analyzed the data. The authors do report that they developed themes and categories based on observations and interviews. It is always helpful for researchers to state the specific process they used. Typically, ethnographers use the constant comparative method to analyze data. Because there is limited description of data analysis methods, readers are unable to determine whether the researchers' conclusions are logical. The study reads well, giving readers a rich sense of what it means to be an Afghan refugee in the United States. However, based solely on the report, it is difficult to determine whether the researchers' findings represent those of the people studied.

The researchers report the study findings in a context that allows readers to empathize with the frustrations of the people studied. Their interpretations of meaning and the narrative provide a view of refugee participation in a new culture. The authenticity of the report is difficult to determine, though, because the researchers do not describe participant confirmation of the findings. The researchers have greatly enhanced the level of understanding of the culture by going beyond the description to explain many of the situations Afghan people encounter. The research report is strengthened by its organization around recurrent themes.

Lipson and Omidian describe the need for health care reform based on the study findings. A recurrent topic throughout the study is the stress experienced by Afghan refugees; however, it is not the major focus. From the beginning of the report, the researchers describe the social context within which Afghan refugees live in the United States. Stress is a subtheme in the report. In the concluding remarks, the researchers call for health care reform to "eliminate the connections between public assistance and health care coverage" (p. 125). In the conclusion, the researchers describe the social stress Afghan refugees experience and relate this stress to cultural adjustment and U.S. service providers' lack of knowledge about Afghan refugees' needs, which consequently results in insensitive service provision. This conclusion, however, does not reflect the reported findings. Given the researchers' intimate knowledge of the culture, it appears they have drawn their conclusions from information other than that presented in the article. When making recommendations, it is extremely important that researchers report data that help readers understand the conclusions drawn.

Readers who have read the entire research report come away with a strong understanding the obvious struggles Afghan refugees experience in the United States. Lipson and Omidian have less clearly addressed the "so what" question of research, however. Although readers may empathize with the real obstacles Afghan people encounter, the researchers have not made explicit the relationship of these struggles to the nursing profession. This is not to suggest that social problems are not or do not have the potential to be nursing problems; rather, researchers are responsible for making the connection in a research report if they wish the findings to be applied in practice.

Application to Education

Nursing education presents another context in which nurse–researchers conduct ethnographic studies. The coming together of students and faculty for an educational opportunity creates its own culture. Few published studies have illustrated the lifeways of students and faculty. This context provides rich opportunities for nurses interested in nursing education research using the ethnographic approach. The article "The Negotiated Order of Clinical Teaching" (Paterson, 1997) serves as the reference for critique in this section. It was selected because it is the only education-focused ethnographic study published in recent years.

In the article, Paterson (1997) clearly identifies the focus of the study: clinical teachers as members of temporary systems. The author views clinical educators as members of a system in which they have no permanent attachment. Paterson further describes the scope of the presentation as "one aspect of a year-long exploratory and descriptive qualitative research study designed to explore and describe what takes place in the realm of clinical teaching in nursing education" (p. 197). Her statements lead readers to believe that the culture to be studied is nursing units, where clinical education occurs, although this idea is not stated explicitly. The purpose of the study also is implied rather than stated.

Early in the article, Paterson (1997) offers general statements about the qualitative methods she used to conduct the study. However, in the *Research Design* section, she clearly states that ethnography is the method she used "because it facilitates a description of events that may not be available or may be contradicted in self-reports by the subjects" (p. 198). Paterson indicates that, according to Boyle (1994) and Van Maanen (1995), this is a justification for using ethnography. She further identifies the nature of the field, indicating that a "total of 1,242 hours of participant observation occurred during the study" (p. 199). The study was conducted on "medical–surgical units in three urban Canadian hospitals" (p. 198). Unfortunately, there is no description of consent or protection of participants.

Six clinical teachers who volunteered composed the group studied within the clinical setting. Other than the statements about the volunteer nature of the informants, Paterson does not describe how or why she selected the individuals.

The researcher states that data collection occurred over a year-long period. This statement attests to the time in the field and represents a sufficient period in which to collect the type of data that interested her. Participant observation, one form of data collection in the study, encompassed more than 1,242 hours. In addition to participant observation, the researcher also used interviewing, concept mapping, and document analysis to inform the inquiry. As discussed in Chapter 2, there are levels of participant observation. In the Paterson study, the researcher has acted in the role of observer as participant. Her predominant activity apparently was as an observer who conducted interviews in the setting. She spent the majority of time in observation, however, to "fit" into the setting, completing some activities with the participants. The author does not report how she maintained objectivity throughout the study. One way many ethnographers maintain an objective stance toward data collected is to keep a journal. Journals may serve as a cross reference for researchers' interpretations during data collection and analysis.

According to Paterson (1997), she analyzed data "in the style of category generation developed by Glaser and Strauss" (p. 200). As expected, she analyzed data throughout the study. The researcher clearly describes the cyclic nature of data collection and analysis, as is exemplified in the following statement: "The data collection and the inductive analysis occurred concurrently, rather than as separate successive phases of the research process" (p. 200).

Paterson offers the study findings in a manner that provides a beginning understanding of clinical teaching from a clinical teacher's perspective. As a focused ethnography, the findings represent the cultural group of interest. The researcher reports the findings as themes and shares the findings in a narrative complete with interpretation and informant comments. The authenticity of the work is documented in the author's statements about the validation of emergent categories and their relationships to each other and with informants. An important inclusion in this report is the section on the "outlier" informant, whose experience was different from the other study informants.

The researcher clearly gives conclusions that relate to the study findings. Specifically, Paterson offers conclusions within the context of what is known about clinical teaching. Especially relevant is the author's suggestion that more research is needed based on the experience of the "outlier" informant. Paterson comments on the value of the research to the discipline, but those remarks are limited.

The Paterson study adds to the body of knowledge in the areas of clinical teaching and ethnographic methodology. She shares important information of value to nurse–educators and nursing service administrators.

Application to Administration

In the first edition of the present text, it was extremely difficult to find ethnographic studies that reflected the area of nursing service administration. Again, this is the case. There is a paucity of qualitative studies in the area of nursing service administration, making it an extremely fertile research area for qualitative researchers. Although not specifically an ethnographic study in nursing service administration, Breda's (1997) research on professional nurses organizing a collective bargaining unit was selected for critique because of the effects the topic has on the service sector.

The report identifies the culture as nurses employed within a "60-bed, private, not-for-profit psychiatric hospital in rural southern New England" (Breda, 1997, p. 99). The study is a focused ethnography, which specifically examines the union activities of nurses and the effects of those activities on the institution described. Breda clearly states that the "purpose of the study is to significantly add to the qualitative research literature on the topic by specifically examining how professional nurses in one hospital worked cooperatively in a labor union to realize gains in their professional standing" (p. 100). Because the purpose of the study is to explore activities carried out by a group, ethnography is an appropriate research method.

A question that arises about the design is, Why didn't the author consider action research as the method of choice? In the study, the researcher reports the activities nurses carried out within their collective bargaining unit that resulted in a change in their professional practice. That change is such an important part of the study that it offers a significant opportunity to use action research methodology, which has proven to be effective in creating change and empowering informants. However, Breda's description and interpretation of the actions carried out by the cultural group support ethnography as an appropriate study method.

Breda presents solid evidence that she conducted the study in the field. The researcher reports she was a participant and a researcher during 1992 and 1993, leading readers to believe the study occurred during a 1-year period. The actual time frame for the study is confusing in the report, however, because of the significant history of union activity presented. The report does not discuss consent or protection of participants.

The reported intent of the study was to examine how union activities assisted in the realization of professional gains. Given the focus, nurses both in and out of the union are appropriate informants for the study. The researcher does not share how she selected the informants; however, she appropriately interviews union and non-union nurses.

The researcher indicates she used participant observation and unstructured interviews to collect data. Although these strategies are useful, an examination of artifacts and documents is also important and should have been part of data collection. Documents in particular can provide essential information.

Breda states she was employed by the identified facility during a 9-year period. She reports that the study was conducted during 1 of the 9 years. The time in the field is certainly adequate; however, the length of the researcher's involvement in the institution before data collection occurred raises questions about the researcher's objectivity during data collection. It is difficult to imagine that a 9-year employee of an institution would not have developed significant biases about the institution during that time. Breda does report that she protected herself from "excessive bias . . . [by] periodically validating responses with both staff- and management-level nurses" (p. 101). The concern is whether co-workers would be comfortable raising questions about the researcher's conclusions given the relationship of the researcher to the informants. The literature is replete with references to "going native." In this case, the researcher was the native!

Breda does not report on data analysis, nor does she present any data that clearly represent the cyclic nature of data collection and analysis. The narrative is well written and gives a picture of the culture of union participation during the time of the study. The researcher does not present information that helps readers follow the logic of her conclusions.

From the findings, readers are able to follow the path of the nurses in their quest for professional autonomy. However, the significant background interspersed with the findings makes it difficult to determine which part of the article represents the research report and which part reflects the researcher's findings and interpretations. The study is definitely reported within context. The author, though, could have enriched the report by including information provided by management and nurses within the institution and by differentiating her knowledge of the institution as an employee with her knowledge as a researcher. Breda offers limited commentary by informants. She could have used more quotes to help readers get a better "feel" for people within the study culture and to offer a more rich description. The structure of the report does not permit readers clear insight into whether the headings presented are themes based on the findings or organizational writing categories derived by the researcher for publishing purposes. The researcher could have helped readers by describing data analysis and how she organized the findings.

The conclusions are explicit. Primarily, Breda relates the conclusions to the institution studied. She provides a limited discussion on how they relate to the discipline. Overall, Breda's study provides readers with an opportunity to obtain a view of the effect of collective bargaining on an institution. The culture of union organizations is an appropriate area of study.

Summary

This chapter reviewed samples of published ethnographic research in the areas of nursing practice, education, and administration. Each critique presents the strengths and limitations of reporting ethnographic research. The reviewed authors have contributed to the literature and provided readers with an opportunity to become part of the culture or subculture they studied.

Ethnographic research and the studies that use ethnography as a method add to the richness and diversity of the human experience by allowing readers to share in the lives of the people studied. As nurse-researchers become more comfortable with multiple ways of knowing and multiple realities, they will benefit by participating in the creation and dissemination of the knowledge imbedded in the cultural realities that enrich each person's life.

REFERENCES

Boyle, J. S. (1994). Styles of ethnography. In J. M. Morse (Ed.), *Critical issues in qualitative research methods* (pp. 159–185). Thousand Oaks, CA: Sage.

Breda, K. L. (1997). Professional nurses in unions: Working together pays off. *Journal of Professional Nursing, 13*(2), 99–109.

Craig, C. (1994). Community determinants of health for rural elderly. *Public Health Nursing, 11*(4), 242–246.

Cruise, P. L., & Dunn, S. M. (1994). Ethnography and AIDS: A methodology for identifying culturally relevant risk-reducing behaviors. *Journal of the Association of Nurses in AIDS Care, 5*(4), 21–27.

Fetterman, D. M. (1989). *Ethnography: Step by Step*. Newbury Park, CA: Sage.

Glaser, B. & Strauss, A. (1967). *Discovery of Grounded Theory*. Chicago, IL: Aldine Publishing Co.

Hall, J. M. (1994). Lesbians recovering from alcohol problems: An ethnographic study of health care experiences. *Nursing Research, 43*(4), 238–244.

Johnson, J. L., Primas, P. J., & Coe, M. K. (1994). Factors that prevent women of low socioeconomic status from seeking prenatal care. *Journal of the American Academy of Nurse Practitioners, 6*(3), 105–111.

Lipson, J. G. (1994). Ethical issues in ethnography. In J. M. Morse (Ed.), *Critical issues in qualitative research methods* (pp. 333–355). Thousand Oaks, CA: Sage.

Lipson, J. G., & Omidian, P. A. (1997). Afghan refugee issues in the U.S. social environment. *Western Journal of Nursing Research, 19*(1), 110–126.

MacDonald, H. (1996). Mastering uncertainty: Mothering the child with asthma. *Pediatric Nursing, 22*(1), 55–59.

Magilvy, J. K., Congdon, J. G., & Martinez, R. (1994). Circles of care: Home care and community support for rural adults. *Advances in Nursing Science, 16*(3), 22–33.

Murrell, N. L., Smith, R., Gill, G., & Oxley, G. (1996). Racism and health care access: A dialogue with childbearing women. *Health Care for Women International, 17,* 149–159.

Paterson, B. L. (1997). The negotiated order of clinical teaching. *Journal of Nursing Education, 35*(5), 197–205.

Resnick, B. (1996). Motivation in geriatric rehabilitation. *Image, 28*(1), 41–45.

Spradley, J. P. (1980). *Participant observation.* New York: Holt, Rinehart & Winston.

Thorne, S. (1997). Global consciousness in nursing: An ethnographic study of nurses with an international perspective. *Journal of Nursing Education, 36*(9), 437–442.

Van Maanen, J. (1995). An end to innocence: The ethnography. In J. Van Maanen (Ed.), *Representation in ethnography* (pp. 1–35). Thousand Oaks, CA: Sage.

Werner, O., & Schoepfle, G. M. (1987). *Foundations of ethnography and interviewing* (Vol. 1). Newbury Park, CA: Sage.

RESEARCH ARTICLE

Ethnographic Approach: Afghan Refugee Issues in the U.S. Social Environment

JULIENE G. LIPSON • PATRICIA A. OMIDIAN

Since Afghan refugees began coming to the United States in the early 1980s, the Afghan community of the San Francisco Bay Area has become the largest in the United States. This population copes with a number of stressors that negatively affect their health and psychological well-being. Based on an ethnographic study, we focus on the social context in which Afghan refugees find themselves, describing Afghans' perceptions of their interactions with mainstream American citizens and health and social service providers. The theme running through all such interactions is information—its scarcity, character, and cultural differences in type, purposes, and means of transmission. Quotes from interviews illustrate four types of problems: economic and occupational problems, health-care access, family and children's issues, and immigration issues/ethnic bias. Policy and program recommendations are applicable to other recent refugee populations that experience similar information problems with regard to the dominant society.

Refugees, by definition persons escaping persecution based on race, religion, nationality, or political stance (Scanlan, 1983), experience many types of stressors that can lead to anxiety, depression, physical health problems, or increased health risks. Afghan refugees in the United States experience stressors in three major areas: the traumas they faced in Afghanistan such as having observed atrocities, imprisonment and/or torture of self or family members, difficult escapes, and loss of family, property, culture, and social status (Anderson & Dupree, 1990; Omidian, 1996); daily concerns engendered by news and information from Afghanistan (Lipson & Omidian, 1996); and current resettlement and adjustment issues in U.S. society. The combination of these factors leads many Afghan refugees in the San Francisco Bay Area to describe the community's most prevalent health problems as mental health problems, mainly depression and physical symptoms related to high levels of stress from past refugee trauma and loss, current occupational and economic problems, culture conflict, and social isolation in the elderly (Lipson, Omidian, & Paul, 1995).

In this article we describe the third source of stressors: the ongoing everyday hassles and conflicts that characterized many interactions between Afghan community members and health and social service providers in the San Francisco Bay Area. Many of these conflicts are related to social marginality as this particular community attempts to maintain an Islamic identity and traditional tribalized social

---

Juliene G. Lipson, R.N., Ph.D., Professor, School of Nursing, University of California, San Francisco; Patricia A. Omidian, Ph.D., Lecturer, Department of Anthropology, California State University, Hayward.

relationships within the community itself. In addition, most Afghans feel that they are in exile and still hold some hope of returning to Afghanistan, at least to die there of old age if nothing else (c.f. Boesen, 1990, p. 160). Although this attitude is changing as more Afghans apply for U.S. citizenship, the feeling persists that one should maintain Afghan characteristics and lifestyle.

Interactions with non-Afghans are characterized by communication difficulties and mutual misunderstanding of Afghan and agency subcultures. The theme that runs through many of these difficulties is information—its scarcity, character, and cultural differences in type, purposes, and means of transmission. Quotes from interviews illustrate this theme through the daily hassles of coping with life in an unfamiliar sociocultural and legal system. In addition, inadequate English and lack of information affect the following realms: economic and occupational issues, health-care access, family and children's issues, and ethnic bias and immigrant issues.

REFUGEE HEALTH AND ADJUSTMENT

In examining refugee health and adjustment, researchers often focus either on premigration predictors of psychological stress, such as number of traumatic events, years in refugee camps, and family members who died; or they focus on such postmigration variables as employment, family income, public assistance, English ability, family size, culture conflict, or discrepancy between aspirations and opportunities (Chung & Kagawa-Singer, 1993; Rumbaut, 1985; Tran, 1987). Most refugee health studies search for statistical relationships between various stressors and depression or other symptoms. Qualitative studies usually interview small samples for the emic perspective or describe cultural characteristics to help health providers better understand their clients.

Neither approach captures the complexity of refugee adjustment in its daily social-environmental context, in which a refugee's interactions with people and agencies of the host culture often contribute to stress and health problems. Everyday hassles and annoyances—the mundane details of life—may contribute more to stress, illness, and depression than do major life event changes. Individuals vary in their subjective experience of a stressor and coping style, which contributes to the magnitude of their physical and emotional response. Generally, however, refugees experienced more traumatic events than did voluntary immigrants and more daily hassles accomplishing what American-born and acculturated immigrants hardly think about.

Finally, most refugees are socially marginalized on the basis of their experiences, identity, and lack of access to power and information. Growing xenophobia and new restrictive laws are further marginalizing refugees and immigrants in North America and Europe. They remain on the periphery in certain social settings, such as work, and often lack the power to improve their situations, which may be based on lack of information.

AFGHANS IN NORTHERN CALIFORNIA

After a 1979 coup and with the subsequent invasion by the former U.S.S.R., Afghans began leaving their country and continued to leave throughout 10 years of war. Since the withdrawal of former U.S.S.R. troops in 1989, Afghanistan has been unable to achieve peace and stability. At its peak, the Afghan refugee population was the largest in the world, numbering more than 6.5 million Afghans in Pakistan and Iran alone. Even in 1995, with 2.8 million refugees and 1 million internally displaced,

Afghan refugees are second only to Palestinians in number (U.S. Committee for Refugees, 1995) because ongoing civil war between political parties has discouraged them from repatriating.

Northern California has the largest population of Afghan refugees in the United States, some 15,000 to 25,000 people. The Afghan community has growth through chain migration; people were attracted to California by its weather and generous social-service system and by the flourishing flea markets. Whereas the first arrivals in the early 1980s were the urban, formerly wealthy, and highly educated elite, family reunification has brought middle-class relatives who are less educated. There is also a small but significant group of Afghans from rural areas who maintain a very traditional lifestyle; many are illiterate in their own language. Although the Afghan refugee community has one of the highest overall educational means of the refugee groups in the United States (means: women, 11 years, men, 17 years; Omidian, 1996, p. 32), many women and elders have had little or no formal education.

Although Afghans share nationality and religion, the community is strongly heterogeneous and divisive in politics, social class, ethnicity, and region as well as urban or rural origin in Afghanistan; this reflects Afghanistan's traditional tribal social structure (Barth, 1987). The community is further divided along gender and generational lines—the experience of men, women, and children raised in the United States and their elders are often strikingly different (Lipson & Miller, 1994; Omidian, 1996). The importance of this diversity within the whole community cannot be overstated, although space precludes addressing such diversity in each theme.

Afghans are staunch Muslims and strongly patriarchal. The most important social unit is the extended family. Because Afghans socialize almost exclusively with family members in the United States, American service providers often conclude that they are disinterested in community cohesive action (Lipson & Omidian, 1992). Recently, some Afghans have attempted to organize community efforts, but cooperation outside the extended family unit is rare. Afghans in the United States have not had time to build trusting relationships with non-kin; in Afghanistan, cooperation outside the family group was with people whose families were known to each other for generations.

In California, Afghan culture is in transition, with families ranging from quite traditional to more cosmopolitan based on their background and personal choice. Despite this range, however, language and cultural dissonance keep most Afghans from associating with Americans. Those who remain within their ethnic enclave base their views of American culture mainly on their observations of Americans in public, on TV, and on discussions with family members and Afghan friends. Although most employed Afghans work with Americans, they do not discuss their personal problems with nonfamily members; thus they have little access to information from American peers about dealing with public agencies and laws and so gain few opportunities to correct their stereotypes of American culture.

In addition, Afghans new to the United States tend to assume that people relate to government agencies as they did in Afghanistan. For example, business with the Afghan government was facilitated by demanding and giving bribes, and many Afghans still assume that the government's main occupation is obtaining money and services for its own uses. The cynicism of many Afghans increased in Pakistan as they observed corrupt administrators skimming off funds meant for refugee relief from the United Nations High Commissioner for Refugees (UNHCR) and nongovernmental organizations. Some of the problems resulting from the differences in orientation and communication are described next.

METHOD

We began ethnographic study of the health and adjustment of Afghan refugees in the San Francisco Bay Area in 1986. Methods have included participant observation as well as formal and informal interviewing on a broad range of topics. Participant observation included many visits to the homes of a number of families, accompanying them to weddings, concerts, other social occasions, and religious observances; driving individuals to appointments, at times acting as an advocate with health or social service providers; and working in partnership with a group of Afghans on several community projects, such as ESL (English as a second language) training, a community assessment, and a health fair.

We interspersed slow-paced participant observation over the past 10 years with three periods of intensive interviewing: (a) 1987–1988: 29 semi-structured interviews focusing on Afghan's perceptions of their health and refugee experiences and the Health Opinion Survey (Lipson & Omidian 1992), (b) 1990–1992: described in detail in the next paragraph, and (c) 1992–1993: a community health assessment including telephone interviews, seven community meetings, and a survey of 196 families (Lipson & Omidian, 1993; Lipson et al., 1995).

In the second (1990–1992) phase, we worked on separate projects but shared data and collaborated in writing. Working with the first author, two Afghan research assistants conducted open-ended interviews with 62 Afghans in Dari (Afghan Farsi) and Pashto, while the first author interviewed in English 30 bilingual Afghans and American health and social-service providers who work with Afghans (Lipson, 1993; Lipson & Miller, 1994; Lipson & Omidian, 1992). The research assistants, a female journalist and a male psychologist, were from different ethnic groups and cities. They drew on different networks to recruit interviewees to roughly represent the adult Afghan community in age (21–73 years), traditional/acculturated orientation, education (none to doctorate), and time in the United States (5 months to 14 years). The male research assistant interviewed 25 people (75% male), and the female research assistant interviewed 38 people (68% female). Each interviewer recorded interview data in Dari or Pashto and then translated the transcript into English. In conjunction with ongoing analysis of interview transcripts, the first author met frequently with each assistant to suggest further areas of questioning.

During this same period, the second author (Omidian, 1996; Omidian & Lipson, 1992) collected and analyzed data on intergenerational issues in Afghan refugee families, focusing on the elderly in an ethnically and religiously diverse sample. Extensive participant observation in homes, at concerts, religious gatherings, and weddings was facilitated by close friendship with four chief-informant families. The second author formally interviewed 49 people (19 males and 30 females), representing three generations, in Dari with the help of an interpreter. The interviews focused on relationships between generations in Afghanistan and the United States, health, and life satisfaction. Additionally, the second author visited and/or informally interviewed more than 50 other Afghans in various settings. Data were analyzed for themes and categories.

Although the original intent of the study was to gather data on health and illness models, interviews invariably shifted to the topic of life in the United States and problems of culture change as perceived by the different generations. Pervasive themes in every interview were how the person copes with life in California while maintaining his or her Afghan/Islamic identity and family conflicts generated by each generation changing at a different rate and for different reasons.

THE SOCIAL CONTEXT: "WE DON'T KNOW THE RULES"

Insufficient or accented English is at the root of many of the problems experienced by Afghans in Northern California. Problems with English are by no means uncommon, with 3.2 million new immigrants having settled in California in the past decade. One of every 11 Californians over 5 years of age (2.4 million people) does not communicate well in English (McLeod & Schreiner, 1993).

A large proportion of the Afghan community in the San Francisco Bay Area is not facile in English. Most of the non- or poor English-speakers are middle aged and older people and those who have been in the United States a shorter period of time. Even those who speak adequate English may not read it well enough to understand what is required of them from the public-health and social-service systems. In this information society, they have little access to the sources and means of obtaining information available to citizens and fluent English speakers. They struggle with trying to figure out appropriate agencies to meet their needs and deciphering the mass of red tape that characterizes such agencies. When they request services from the wrong place or person, they are treated rudely, which further discourages them.

Our informants illustrated problems associated with English:

We get official letters from social services and housing that inform you about things you must do, but our English is so weak we are not able to read them. We have to find someone to translate for us. It takes several days, which makes things difficult because some of the letters need answers soon. If we make a mistake, it affects everything. Believe me, we put ourselves in dangerous situations because of not knowing the rules and laws.

One woman saw a fire in her neighborhood. Her neighbor asked her something in English and pointed to her son. She thought she had asked if her son was the first to notice the fire and answered "yes." When the police inquired about her son, she answered "yes" to the same question. When they finally brought an Afghan to translate, he said, "Sister, your son makes real trouble for you; you confessed with your own lips that your son set the fire."

Some Afghans cope with English problems, and with not knowing the rules, in ingenious ways. For example, some have asked us to read and help them respond to agency forms and letters, which can be confusing and frustrating even for well-educated native-English-speaking Americans. Other coping strategies are illegal, but effective. For example, one man, the only member of his large family who reads English, revealed that he helps non-English-reading relatives obtain their driver's licenses by driving his relative to the Department of Motor Vehicles; they both take the written test and then secretly switch tests.

Money, Jobs, and Welfare

Financially, Afghans range from comfortable to destitute. Some Afghans have worked in the United States long enough to have bought a house and maintain a middle-class lifestyle. Others, such as a formerly wealthy family that owned three houses and had many servants in Afghanistan, now live in small and crowded apartments (e.g., nine family members in two bedrooms). Most of the educated Afghans are downwardly mobile. In contrast, Afghans from rural areas or who were less well off in Afghanistan perceive themselves as materially richer and more comfortable in the United States, even when public assistance is their only source of income.

One of the most significant resettlement challenges faced by refugees is earning a livelihood (Chichon, Gozdziak, & Grover, 1986). Because skills and status from the home country are rarely transferable to the host country, employment is a central issue. In particular, men experience stress and depression related to loss of status brought on by unemployment and changing family roles (Beiser, Johnson & Turner, 1993; Rahmany, 1992). The loss of their traditional breadwinner role is a severe blow to their self-esteem. Men from middle-class backgrounds are more willing to accept entry-level jobs than are well-educated or upper-class refugees, who are too proud to accept menial jobs. These professionals and former government officials do not qualify for the kinds of work they did in Afghanistan. Physicians exemplify this situation; most are unable to pass the licensure exam because of finances, English problems, or outdated medical training (Lipson & Omidian, 1992; Rahmany, 1992). Vocational counselors may inadvertently insult their Afghan clients by their lack of recognition of the importance of former social status. For example, a former director in Afghanistan's Ministry of Agriculture said:

I thought I could get a good job because I was American educated. I ran around to different cities and applied for every job I thought was appropriate for my education. The welfare department sent me letters saying I am capable of working and should take any job. Honestly, taking a job in a fast food restaurant is very humiliating for me, but being on welfare is even more humiliating.

In the opinion of some Afghan community members, 90% of the local Afghan families are supported by Aid to Families with Dependent Children (AFDC). This number is rapidly decreasing as young people move out of school and into the job market. Older Afghans themselves have strong and mixed feelings about the issue of public assistance. Most families think that they do not really have a choice, considering what jobs are available to them. One Afghan social worker said: "Afghans are not lazy. They want to work hard, but they cannot live on what they get paid. There is a problem with the job and without the job; there is not enough money either way." A former engineer with 10 children said, "I can't give up AFDC because if I pay medical bills from my own pocket, I won't have enough money for groceries or clothing."

In addition to the realistic fear of losing Medicaid coverage by giving up AFDC, many Afghans came to the United States believing that they are entitled to compensation because of their having lost everything in Afghanistan. A resettlement counselor noted that:

Some have the impression that welfare is a must for making it in this country. They are misinformed from the first day they arrive by people already here, and even before they arrive by family members who told them what to ask for.

Some Afghans make a livable income by working very hard and moonlighting. A small proportion of families have gained financial security through all adult and adolescent members working, even though none of the jobs pay well (e.g., gas-station attendant, hotel maid, or fast-food clerk). This kind of family cooperation has led to the excellent economic adjustment of Cuban immigrants in the United States; their relatively high family income level is due to proportionately more workers per family than is true of both the Hispanic and the U.S. populations (Perez, 1986). Among Afghans, this method of increasing family income is not without its costs, as expressed by one woman who worried that:

Young people need after-school sports like volleyball or baseball. Unfortunately, our children go after school to work, hard work, physical work. This kind of job makes them very exhausted. They are not able to do their homework like American students, and at school they are sleepy.

And another woman described:

You must work any shift you can get to make a living. Sometimes I go for cleaning, my husband goes to his job, and we leave the kids at home. During the duty you must think about the kids. What if something happens to them, what if they set a fire accidentally or something else?

Some Afghans live well through less-than-legal means, which is, of course, not unique to this ethnic/immigrant group. For example, we heard Afghans complaining about other wealthy Afghans who keep their money in Europe: "They have lots of red rugs and live on AFDC, SSI, and the flea market." Some under-the-table work (e.g., buying items at garage sales and selling them for profit at flea markets, or part-time cash work) supplements welfare nicely. Wealth is interpreted either as having money or as "having time to see friends and to be with people." Those who work are angry about those who do not and are jealous of the others having time to visit family and friends and to observe holy days without fear of losing their jobs. Thus it is difficult to determine the prevalence of supplementing welfare; we suspect that it might be true of only a small number of Afghans but is magnified by envious and widespread gossip.

Some educated Afghans who could obtain 9-to-5 office jobs prefer more flexible and independent, if lower status, work. For example, a former official prefers to buy, repair, and sell cars in the United States because he is his large family's only driver and needs the time to take his wife shopping, his children to school, and to maintain a vigorous schedule of socializing with family and friends. For the same reasons, there are a few highly educated Afghan taxi drivers in the San Francisco Bay Area, as well as in Washington, DC and New York City, although this is not as important in Northern California as it is in other parts of the country (Edwards, 1994).

It is important to emphasize differences in cultural norms of doing business in Afghanistan and the United States. Cleverness in business is respected in Afghanistan, as in the Middle East, and those who can work the system for their own gain are admired, if begrudgingly. Afghans' recent experiences were that their national government, political parties, and even refugee agencies in Pakistan were corrupt and run by bribes. U.S. agencies criticize Afghans' behavior. A social-service provider summed up Afghans' stance toward public agencies in this way:

Afghans seem to cheat a lot, but they are actually very honest people, except with the government. They had no experience with taxes or social services, and no positive experience with government offices in Afghanistan.

They do not see them the way Americans do—they do not have a western view of obligation about this.

Occasionally, the discovery of under-the-table income by the Internal Revenue Service (e.g., a highly profitable gambling spree in Nevada) leads to loss of public benefits. One Afghan stated his concern that the second generation will become California's next welfare subculture because "children do not learn Islam from their parents, only the flea markets and welfare." Yet this does not seem to be occurring as feared.

Health and Health Care

We have described elsewhere Afghans' health problems and access to care. Briefly, the major problems are stress; depression; and, for some, post-traumatic stress disorder (Lipson & Omidian, 1992). Afghans themselves comment on the prevalence of "mental problems" in their community: "The things they got from Afghanistan—murder, bombs—and the things they got here—children's freedom and not obeying—all together makes them mentally sick" (Lipson, 1993).

Afghans view health-care services far more positively than they do social services, but they have many problems with access to care and communicating their needs. Most Afghans in the San Francisco Bay Area have Medi-Cal (Medicaid), but very few local physicians accept Medi-Cal payments. There are almost no language- and culturally appropriate mental-health services available. Only the county public-health clinics and one county hospital where many Afghans seek care have full-time interpreters on staff.

Dental care poses a particular problem; for example, 64% of families in the community-assessment survey needed dental care (Lipson & Omidian, 1993). Afghans cannot get some specific needs met because of Medi-Cal restrictions. For example, a 40-year-old woman needed bridgework for some gaps where teeth had been pulled (some by herself), but Medi-Cal does not cover bridgework. It does cover extraction of all teeth and full dentures. Consequently, all her healthy teeth were extracted and she was fitted with dentures. The dentures do not fit correctly, however, and the woman cannot wear them, and Medi-Cal will not pay for another set.

Finally, making and keeping health-care appointments are difficult for those who speak little English and do not drive:

Any time a member of my family is sick, we don't know what to do. We can't make an appointment with the doctor, we can't find the addresses. It is really difficult to find someone to make an appointment for us and give us a ride, and someone to translate our needs and pains to doctor and from doctor to us. We ask some of our friends or sometimes neighbors. It is a great problem to tell our difficulty to someone.

Family and Children's Issues

Culture conflict is particularly evident in family relationships. Afghan traditional views on what constitutes proper family relationships and interactions between parents and children are at odds with American values and often lead to difficulties with the legal and social-service systems. For example, polygyny is commonplace and acceptable in Afghanistan, as long as the husband is able to support each wife equally. It is considered a crime in the United States, and INS restrictions have broken up several Afghan families in which there are cowives. For example, one man brought all his children to the United States but could bring only one wife; the third wife accompanied him and the other two stayed behind.

Afghans are highly family oriented and love their many children dearly, but life in the United States has created various conflicts between children and parents, such as the intergenerational clashes so common in immigrant families (Omidian, 1996; Sluzki, 1979). Children acculturate quickly in contact with their American peers, whom Afghan parents see as "having no respect" for their parents. Schools teach them independence and assertiveness, which contradict Afghan cultural values of family interdependence and strict obedience to elder family members, particularly to the father's authority.

Regulations and procedures of Child Protective Services also conflict with traditional Afghan culture. These agencies receive calls about "child abuse" in Afghan families from teachers or neighbors, some of which is physical punishment related to fathers' frustration with their children and life in general, but more of which is the customary way that Afghans discipline their children. In actuality, physical punishment of children is common everywhere in the world; the Human Relations Area Files reveal that 74% of 90 small-scale or peasant societies punish children physically, including spanking, slapping, beating, and pinching (Levinson, 1988). One Afghan man explained disciplinary practices by referring to a well-known Afghan expression, "If you don't hit the cows and donkeys they never obey you." He said:

> It is the same with small children; their habits are like animals and they don't know right from wrong. You must be very careful, and even if you need to punish them physically, it is good for their future, because when they get older and they don't accept your direction, they will be useless.

As a consequence of abuse-prevention education in the schools, children are now reporting physical punishment to their teachers, which may result in their being removed from the home. A young widow lost her three children for several weeks after her daughter told her teacher that "my mom hits me." Afghans react to this kind of incident with anger: "What right do strangers have to intrude in our family and judge our discipline? Our children are our responsibility." They perceive the laws as taking away their parental authority and responsibility. Others are so frightened by stories of children being taken out of the home that they are afraid to discipline their children in the Afghan way. Some children have learned to use the legal and social systems to manipulate their parents; indeed, some children have threatened their parents with calling the police if the parents do not give them the freedom they desire, and some of these parents yield to the demands because they do not know the laws.

Most Afghans see family matters as being strictly private: "The U.S. puts its nose where it is not to be." In fact, one antecedent of the 1978–1979 uprising against Afghanistan's Marxist government was its attempts to interfere in the domestic sphere. The following reported incident illustrates the culture clash between American standards of public care for children and an Afghan man's pride and anger about Americans invading his family privacy:

> Mr. Z's daughter had fallen and scratched her face. When the teacher asked her what had happened, she said she didn't know. Another teacher thought

that the father might have hit his daughter, so they informed Child Protective Services. When two social workers visited Mr. Z. and asked him what had happened to his daughter's face, he said he did not know. They lectured him about the evil of hitting one's children and cautioned him to be aware of where his children are at all times. They asked the girl again what had happened; she told them she had been playing and took them outside to show where she had fallen. The social workers asked why everyone said they didn't know what had happened when they actually did.

Ethnic Bias and Immigration Issues

The United States is currently experiencing another cycle of xenophobia as well as legislative efforts to decrease illegal immigration and restrict services to legal immigrants. Although the multicultural San Francisco Bay Area is more accepting than many areas in the United States, Afghans do experience anti-immigrant and anti-Muslim bias. When visiting the optometrist, for example, Mrs. A. was treated rudely by the receptionist. When she complained to the optometrist that her new prescription was too strong, making her dizzy and giving her headaches, he insisted that the glasses were fine; he implied that her headaches were from being "mentally unstable." She said, "We are treated this way because of our accent."

Many Afghans have come to expect biased treatment from mainstream agencies and cannot differentiate what is specific to their community from how "everyone" is treated (e.g., see Modica, 1994). For example, Mrs. B. asked one of us to go with her to the Department of Motor Vehicles, where for 6 months she had been attempting to obtain an identification card. She explained, "Americans get their cards right away."

Public expressions of anti-immigrant bias are most apparent in situations in which Afghans wear their traditional clothing. A 41-year-old father of six described a typical experience:

> *When I walk to the grocery store, people honk or yell at me from their cars. I don't know what they are saying, but it is embarrassing. I am proud to wear my own clothes and my hat that I wore in the JIHAD. My father and grandfather never wore pants! I wish I was martyred in Afghanistan!*

Even in the absence of blatant discrimination, many Afghans feel alienated:

> *We have no home here. Even if I could make myself a millionaire, I am just a foreign person here. If in our country I was sick and lost my job, at least there were a lot of people to help me. You were able to get help from your family, your relations, your friends, and even from neighbors. But here nobody knows you, nobody trusts you, nobody helps you.*

Recent tightening of Immigration and Naturalization Service guidelines has resulted in more undocumented Afghans having spent their entire assets in Afghanistan on false documents so that they could seek asylum in the United States. They experience the same problems as do other undocumented entrants, such as little access to health care and fear of deportation. One undocumented woman, for example, was apprehended and imprisoned in the United States for 2 years; she thinks this experience has made her "mentally ill" and said, "I must be single forever because no Afghan man will marry me; he is afraid of what might have happened to me in jail."

At an even deeper level, Islamic identity carries with it a potential for conflict with Euro-Americans. In the popular press and on television Muslims are portrayed as radical, America-hating terrorists with no concern for human life. Many Afghans cannot understand this portrayal because they are quite aware of "Christian terrorists" and other violence in U.S. society. When the federal building was blown up in Oklahoma, many Afghans feared retaliation because as Muslims, they would have been targeted had the government placed the blame on "Arab terrorists." Afghan students began telephoning one of us immediately after the incident and explicitly stated their fear that there would be a witch hunt against Muslims. They did not relax until a White militia group was identified and a suspect was arrested.

Recent anti-immigrant legislation has encouraged some Afghans to apply for U.S. citizenship. In the name of helping their community, a few Afghans generated income by setting up a citizenship test site with extra help for those who do not read English. Another Afghan with considerable experience with Americans angrily commented that "Some corrupt people in this community are giving the wrong information. They are not allowed to charge people $150 for that test; people do not realize that the test will be invalid when they go to get their papers."

DISCUSSION

Afghans, like other refugee populations, are excluded by language and lack of knowledge about common sources of information, and most have difficulty with newspapers in English. Transportation, language problems, and not understanding the system make gathering information by telephone or in-person agency visits very difficult. Afghans get the majority of their information about how to deal with the United States and its customs and rules from each other. In the Afghan community, information spreads rapidly even though it is often partial or erroneous. Sometimes the most valuable pieces of information are jealously guarded, used almost as a commodity, rather than openly shared; sometimes information is used as a weapon. These various themes in information are illustrated by a recent case:

> The S. family sought asylum in the United States 2 years ago. Other Afghans advised them that they had a better chance for asylum by saying that they had come directly from Pakistan and should not mention their several years in Germany. While waiting for their asylum hearing, a family who had helped the S. family requested that the young adult daughter become engaged to their oldest son. When the S. family refused, the other father alerted the INS to the "lie." The father and oldest daughter were jailed and the family faced deportation. The immigration attorney who had worked on their behalf dropped the case when she learned about "the lie."

Afghans' communication style and information transmission to each other and with non-Afghans and public agencies are strongly influenced by custom and worldview. Lack of general information and knowledge about "rules" are a source of problems experienced by Afghans and those in contact with them. Afghans also experience problems related to the source of information, accuracy and completeness of information, and its various uses. Sometimes, they are given useful information but do not trust it. An example is a man with an American master's degree in educational counseling who patiently kept applying for "appropriate" positions. After several years, with no job and significant health problems, he now admits that he did not understand America after all. After immigrating, his brothers and cousins had taken the first jobs they could get, slowly working their way into management, and had advised him to do likewise. Now his brothers are approaching retirement age in their own homes whereas his family still depends on AFDC and public housing.

While still dealing with traumatic experiences from the past and the ongoing tension of "bad news" from the continuing civil war in Afghanistan, most Afghan refugees in the San Francisco Bay Area need to deal with the challenges of functioning in a foreign society without English fluency and not fully understanding the rules. Only with family and close friends do people allow themselves to relax and let down their constant guard against potential situations that might surprise or hurt them. This level of tension varies with the individual, but we know many Afghans in whom such tension is expressed in such somatic symptoms as headaches, body aches, and hypertension.

In our research, Afghans have repeatedly linked their high stress levels and "mental health problems" with culture conflict and difficulties with language, laws, finances, and work. Although qualitative data gathered in 1991 is reported here, our recent Afghan community health assessment corroborated these findings with statistically significant relationships. For example, greater satisfaction with life in the United States was significantly related to speaking English, more income, and perception of better health ($p < .01$). Stress in a family member was significantly related to inadequate income, occupational problems, and loss of culture and traditions ($p < .001$) (Lipson, Omidian, & Paul, 1995).

That Afghans are upset may be inevitable and unavoidable, given the political conditions from which they came, what they have gone through, and the current cultural dissonance they experience. To address some of these problems, the number and availability of ESL programs should be increased, and these classes should integrate information about American culture, laws, and customs regarding public agencies, for example, child-abuse-reporting laws. Health-care reform is needed for access and to eliminate the connection between public assistance and health coverage. Finally, non-Afghan teachers, police, and social service and health care providers need education about Afghan culture and social stressors through in-service and cultural consultants (Budman, Lipson, & Meleis, 1992) because Afghans experience as much stress associated with service providers' insensitivity to their needs as from not knowing the rules.

NOTE

1. This is a revised and expanded version of a paper presented at the 1992 meeting of the American Anthropological Association. Special thanks to Asifa Etemadi, Khalil Rahmany, and Najia Hamid for their guidance and interviewing skills, as well as to the other Afghans who contributed directly or indirectly to this study. A UCSF Academic Senate grant supported part of the work on which this article is based.

Research article taken from: Lipson, J. G. & Omidian, P. A. (1997). Afghan refugee issues in the U.S. social environment. Western Journal of Nursing Research, 110–126. (Reprinted with permission).

REFERENCES

Anderson, E. W., & Dupree, N. H. (Eds.). (1990). *The cultural basis of Afghan nationalism.* New York: Pinter.

Barth, F. (1987). Cultural wellsprings of resistance in Afghanistan. In R. Klass (Ed), *Afghanistan: The great game revisited* (pp. 187–202). Boston: Freedom House.

Beiser, M., Johnson, P., & Turner, R. (1993). Unemployment, underemployment and depressive affect among Southeast Asian refugees. *Psychological Medicine, 23,* 731–743.

Boesen, I. W. (1990). Honour in exile: Continuity and change among Afghan refugees. In E. W. Anderson & N. H. Dupree (Eds.), *The cultural basis of Afghan nationalism.* (pp. 160–174). New York: Pinter.

Budman, C., Lipson, J., & Meleis, A. (1992). The cultural consultant in mental health care: The case of an Arab adolescent. *American Journal of Orthopsychiatry, 62,* 359–370.

Chung, R., & Kagawa-Singer, M. (1993). Predictors of psychological distress among Southeast Asian refugees. *Social Science in Medicine, 36,* 631–639.

Cichon, D., Gozdziak, E., & Grover, J. (1986). *The economic and social adjustment of non-Southeast Asian refugees.* Washington DC: U.S. DHHS, Office of Refugee Resettlement.

Edwards, D. (1994). Afghanistan, ethnography and the new world order. *Cultural Anthropology. 9,* 345–360.

Levinson, D. (1988). Family violence in cross-cultural perspective. In V. Van Hasselt, R. Morrison, A. Bellack, & M. Hersen (Eds.), *Handbook of family violence.* New York: Plenum.

Lipson, J. (1993). Afghan refugees in California: Mental health issues. *Issues in Mental Health Nursing, 14,* 411–423.

Lipson, J., & Miller, S. (1994). Changing roles of Afghan refugee women in the U.S. *Health Care for Women International, 15,* 171–180.

Lipson, J., & Omidian, P. (1992). Afghan refugees: Health issues in the United States. *Western Journal of Medicine, 157,* 271–275.

Lipson, J., & Omidian, P. (1993). Health among San Francisco Bay Area Afghans: A community assessment. *Afghanistan Studies Journal, 4,* 71–86.

Lipson, J., & Omidian, P. (1996). Health and the transnational connection: Afghan refugees in the United States. In A. Rynearson & J. Phillips (Eds.), *Selected papers on refugee issues: IV* (pp. 2–17). Washington, DC: American Anthropological Association.

Lipson, J. G. & Omidian, P. A. (1997). Afghan refugee issues in the U.S. social environment. *Western Journal of Nursing Research,* 110–126. (reprinted with permission).

Lipson, J., Omidian, P., & Paul, S. (1995). Afghan health education project: A community survey. *Public Health Nursing, 12,* 143–150.

McLeod, R., & Schreiner, T. (1993, May 13). One in 11 have trouble speaking California's official language. *San Francisco Chronicle,* p. A4.

Modica, L. (1994). The anthropologist as welfare recipient: Views from the inside. *Practicing Anthropology, 16*(4), 5–7.

Omidian, P. (1996). *Aging and family in an Afghan refugee community.* New York: Garland.

Omidian, P., & Lipson, J. (1992). Elderly Afghan refugees: Tradition and transition in Northern California. In P. DeVoe (Ed.), *Selected papers on refugee issues: I* (pp. 27–39). Washington, DC: American Anthropological Association.

Perez, L. (1986). Immigrant economic adjustment and family organization: The Cuban success story reexamined. *International Migration Review, 20,* 4–20.

Rahmany, K. (1992). *A long journey: The psychological adjustment of the Afghan refugees in the United States.* Ph.D. dissertation, Rosebridge Graduate School of Integrative Psychology, Concord, CA.

Rumbaut, R. (1985). Mental health and the refugee experience: A comparative study of Southeast Asian refugees. In T. Owan (Ed), *Southeast Asian mental health: Treatment, prevention, services* (pp. 433–486). Washington DC: NIMH.

Scanlan, J. (1983). Who is a refugee? Procedures and burden of proof under the Refugee Act of 1980. *In Defense of the Alien, 5,* 23.

Sluzki, C. (1979). Migration and family conflict. *Family Process, 18,* 379–390.

Tran, T. V. (1987). Ethnic community supports and psychological well-being of Vietnamese refugees. *International Migration Review, 21,* 833–844.

U.S. Committee for Refugees. (1995). *World refugee survey—1995.* Washington, DC: Immigration and Refugee Services of America.

Historical Research Method

Nursing care for clients includes acquiring a nursing history. If nurses did not collect background data, they would—through ignorance—greatly jeopardize decisions regarding a client's current health care needs and future chance of achieving a higher level of wellness. A historical understanding is crucial to providing nursing care because of nursing's essential holistic nature. Looking at the whole person requires recognition of multiple factors that influence the person. Similarly, decisions related to the nursing profession today, such as unionization, risk failure and inadequacy of response if the profession ignores history.

All knowledge has a historical dimension; conversely, historiography provides individuals with a way of knowing. Tholfsen (1977) explained that "the past is present in every person and in the cultural and institutional world that surrounds [them]" (p. 248). This means, Tholfsen continued, that historians must know the historical conditions of the period they are studying. Knowledge of the past helps to inform most other research designs that include explanatory background that establishes an understanding of the phenomenon under study. Selecting a historical research design as the methodology requires that researchers have an understanding of what history is; a knowledge of various social, political, and economic factors that affect events, ideas, and people; an interest in the subject; and creativity in approach (Christy, 1978; Rines & Kershner, 1979).

Historical Research Defined

Many definitions and explanations exist related to the meaning and nature of history. Austin (1958) defined *history* as "an integrated, written record of past events, based on the results of a search for the truth" (p. 4). Kruman (1985) explained history as "facts (ideas, events, social, and cultural processes) filtered through human intelligence" (p. 111). Kruman referred to an *objective relativism* that permits the objective reality of one historian to coexist with different historical interpretations of others, thus promoting change in ideas and advances in historical inquiry. Matejski (1986) conceived of history "as a past event, a record, or account of something that has happened" (p. 175). Furthermore, Matejski explained history as a field of study with its own set of criteria and methods that enables researchers to collect data and interpret findings. Having its own method that has often borrowed from other disciplines, historical inquiry examines the interactions of people, activities, and "multiple variables" (Matejski, 1986, p. 177) that affect human thought and activity. The narrative that results from a historian's findings must creatively weave the many factors into a readable and interesting story.

Historical research opens windows into the past, creating new ideas and reshaping human thinking and understanding. Ashley (1978) explained the crucial role historical research plays in the foundation of nursing scholarship by defining history as "the study of creative activity in human behavior [that] gives one the courage to create and respond to what is new without fear of losing one's identity with the whole of humanity" (p. 28). As Lynaugh (1996) suggested, history becomes "our source of identity . . . it helps us gain identity and personal meaning in our work, improves our comprehension and our planning, and validates social criticism" (p. 1).

Like nursing, history is an art and science. The discipline of history requires the use of scientific principles to study the interrelationship of social, economic, political, and psychologic factors that influence ideas, events, institutions, and people. Yet, to explain the findings of historical inquiry while balancing the rigors of scientific inquiry and the understanding of human behavior, historical researchers must revert to the "art of contemplation, speculation, and of interpretation" (Newton, 1965, p. 24).

Researchers who choose historical methods must exhibit more than just a curiosity about the past. Researchers formulate a thesis about the relationship among ideas, events, institutions, or people in the past. Chronologically ordering events over time does not explain the established links and ties. Probing for explanations between historical antecedents requires questioning, reasoning, and interpreting. Christy (1978) explained that "healthy skepticism becomes a way of life for the serious historiographer" (p. 6). Historiographers seeking to discover meanings in the past must sift through data and examine each piece closely for clues.

When studying the past, historical researchers use a variety of sources such as private letters, personal journals, books, magazines, professional journals, and newspapers. Researchers travel in time and explore these materials, seeking a relationship among ideas, events, institutions, or people. The purpose of such a study is not to predict but, rather, to understand the past in order to explain present or future relationships. From historical documents, historiographers derive insight from past lived experiences that they can adapt to generate new ideas (Barzun & Graff, 1985).

Researchers use a historical design if they believe something from the past will explain something in the present or the future. Conflict between what the researcher thinks and what he or she may have written about a particular topic also influences the decision to do historical research. For example, a misconception regarding nurses' participation in the late 19th-century women's movement led Lewenson (1990, 1996) to study the relationship between the women's suffrage movement and the four nursing organizations that had formed in America between 1893 and 1920. Lewenson (1990, 1996) conducted a historical inquiry to dispel the tension resulting from a contemporary understanding of the past, also called a present-mindedness, that omitted nursing's political response to the events of the late 19th and early 20th centuries. *Present-mindedness* refers to using a contemporary perspective when analyzing data collected from an earlier period. Such data analysis is stigmatized as unhistorical and leads to inaccurate conclusions when ideas and lived experiences of people in the past are compared with later events (Tholfsen, 1977, p. 247). Although Tholfsen has warned historians to be careful of absolutes and the dangers of present-mindedness, he has argued that "the best history is rooted in a lively interest in the present" (p. 247). Nevertheless, history refers to constant change, and it is this change that "produces the endless diversity characteristic of the historical world" (p. 248). Researchers must study each period within the context of its age to avoid judging or interpreting the past without respect to changes made over time. Hence, difference found in every age must "be understood in its own terms" (p. 248).

Nurses and history make a good match. Nurses come from rich, diverse backgrounds with many contacts they may use to better understand and explain human behavior. Nurses, who are adept at studying human behavior, are well suited to historical inquiry in which they study human behavior in the context of an event, a place, a person, an institution, or an idea in the past. Like historians, nurses identify and interpret patterns of behavior that occur over time.

Historical Research Traditions

Morse and Field (1995) have identified two traditions or schools of thought in historical research: the positivistic or neo-positivistic and the idealist schools. In the *neo-positivistic school,* historians take a more quantitative posture. The focus is on "reducing history to universal laws" (Morse & Field, 1995, p. 33). Historians use data analysis to verify or categorize information. "There is a strong effort to show cause–effect relationships" (Morse & Field, 1995, p. 33).

In the *idealist school,* historians are most concerned with getting inside an event and trying to understand the thoughts of individuals involved in the event while considering the time, place, and situations (Fitzpatrick, 1993; Morse & Field, 1995). The idealist school represents more closely the values of qualitative research as shared in the present text.

Regardless of the tradition observed by historical researchers, the intent is always the "interpretation and narration of past events" (Morse & Field, 1995, p. 33). Historical researchers must clearly identify the focus of the study and then make a commitment to a philosophic position.

Fundamental Characteristics of Historical Research

Although no single historical method exists, Lynaugh and Reverby (1987) have pointed out, essential guideposts and rules of evidence ensure the credibility and usefulness of the historian's findings. Lusk (1997) has identified several methodological stages: selecting "a topic and an appropriate theoretical framework, finding and accessing the resources, and analyzing, synthesizing, interpreting, and reporting the data" (p. 355). In search of an approach, Barzun and Graff (1985) wrote that, "without form in every sense, the facts of the past, like the jumbled visions of a sleeper in a dream, elude us" (p. 271). The next section offers beginning researchers a guide on how to develop a historical design. As in any process, researchers must allow fluidity between the steps of the guide, that is, they must easily move from one step to another, in both directions. For example, the data collected may direct the literature review and the literature review, in turn, may determine the thesis.

Selection of Historiography as Method

To understand the wholeness of the past, nurse–historians select a framework to guide the study. However, as Lynaugh and Reverby (1987) have warned, no one formula or specific method exists for doing historical research. Tholfsen (1977) has contended that "history lacks a coherent theoretical and conceptual structure" (p. 246). No one theoretical framework exists for the study of history. Although there is no "set methodology . . . some methodological consensus exists" (Lusk, 1997, p. 355). History is a discipline with many structures that Cramer (1992) has described as "permanent or semipermanent relations of elements that determine the character of the whole" (p. 6). Superimposed structure enables researchers to organize the data. For example, when using geography to frame a study, the researcher may write a regional history, or when using a particular topic to organize a study, the researcher may focus on women's work (Cramer, 1992).

Society asks historians to analyze an experience and use that experience to explain and prepare society for similar events in the future. For example, historians study the records of war so that society will learn what may help in future wars (Hofstadter, 1959). Writing for a specific function creates further tension between the dual nature that exists within the historian's role: the writing of a historical narrative and the writing of a historical monograph. According to Hofstadter, the historical narrative tells a story but often is disappointing in the analysis, and the historical monograph approximates a scientific inquiry but lacks literary style and frequently offers insufficient analytic data. However, both functions are enriched by interrelating social sciences and historical inquiry. Hofstadter believed that a combination of social sciences and historical research produces fresh ideas and new insights into human behavior.

Historians look at other disciplines to help inform and structure their work. To understand the development of nursing education in North America and to provide a theoretical framework, historians might use research from women's and educational history in the United States. Knowledge of U.S. labor history, which is important to nursing history because of nurses' apprenticeship role in hospitals, would also be a useful framework for historiographers to conceptually organize the data. To study history using a variety of approaches, such as philosophic, national, psychohistorical, or economic, allows researchers to explore a point in time with a conceptual guide from a particular discipline (Ashley, 1978; Matejski, 1986).

Nurse–historians ponder different theoretical frameworks that structure historical research. They may select from theoretical approaches such as biographic, social, and intellectual histories. A *biographical history,* the study of an individual, opens a wide vista to an entire period (Brown, D'Antonio, & Davis, 1991). Biography uses the story of a person's life to understand "the values, expectations, tensions and the conflicts of the time and culture within which he or she lived" (Brown et al., 1991). Interpretation requires historians to familiarize themselves with a period so that they may derive meanings from within the particular time frame rather than superimpose them from a later, contemporary distance. For example, to understand the life of the early 20th-century nurse and birth control activist Margaret Sanger, it is essential to understand society's beliefs about woman's roles and beliefs about procreation.

Social history explores a particular period and attempts to understand the prevailing values and beliefs by examining the everyday events of that period. Historian Vern Bullough described a strategy for doing a social history: Use specific quantitative data to understand the life experiences of "'ordinary' men and women" (Brown et al., 1991, p. 3). An analysis of census data, court records, and municipal surveys, for example, assists historians to go beyond the boundaries of class, ethnicity, economics, and race, hence, enabling them to gain a broader understanding of the study subject.

Intellectual history, in which "*thinking* is the event under analysis," lends itself to several approaches (Brown et al., 1991, p. 2). Historians may explore the ideas of an individual considered to be an intellectual thinker of a period; for example, they might study the ideas of public health nurse Lillian Wald. Or historians may explore the history of ideas over time, such as nursing leaders' ideas that influenced the development of U.S. nursing education. Another approach may be to explore the attitudes and ideas of people who are not considered intellectual thinkers of the period, such as the ideas of practicing nurses (Hamilton, 1991). However, historians must be aware that conflict may arise between the ideas and the contextual backgrounds that gave rise to them (Hamilton, 1993).

Historical researchers must be ready to "live in permanent struggle with conceptual ambiguities, missing evidence and conflicting viewpoints" (Lynaugh & Reverby, 1987, p. 4). Historians continually face a methodological polarity whereby tension exists between the "general and the unique, [and] between the particular and the universal" (Tholfsen, 1977, p. 249). However, this tension and ambiguity are essential to history because they mirror human experience with all of life's contradictions and ambiguities (Tholfsen, 1977). When approaching historical research, researchers must expect ambiguity of design as well as data. Researchers must decide on a particular theoretical framework and understand the conflicting views and ideas regarding the approach. Keeping this information in mind, historians can then begin to construct a creative design that addresses their research interest.

DATA GENERATION

DEVELOPING A FOCUS

To apply a historical design, researchers must first define the study topic and prepare a statement of the subject (Kruman, 1985). A clear, concise statement tells readers what researchers will be studying and their reasons for selecting the subject. Researchers must explain their interest in the topic and justify its relationship with other topics. In addition, researchers establish the purpose and significance to nursing and nursing research in the statement (Rines & Kershner, 1979). According to Lusk (1997), topics "should be significant, with the potential to illuminate or place a new perspective on current questions" (p. 355).

When selecting a topic, Austin (1958) has suggested that the subject be "part of a larger whole, and one which can be isolated" (p. 5). Isolating a part of the topic makes the study more manageable. For example, it may be easier to study the curriculum of three nurse training schools in 1897 than to tackle all of nursing education in the late 19th century.

Because historical study does not predict outcomes, there is no hypothesis. A researcher's interest and hunches about the topic guide the study and move the research toward a particular field or discipline. Researchers base their ideas on background information they have obtained. Patterns that emerge in the initial fact-finding and knowledge-building step aid in the creative formation of a thesis. For example, instead of predicting the effect of apprenticeship training on the development of nursing education, historians might identify themes or ideas about nursing education and use those themes to convey their ideas on the subject. An example is the Hanson (1989) study on the emergence of liberal education in nursing education.

To accomplish this important step, researchers must gather information regarding the period to be studied. They must have a working knowledge of the social, cultural, economic, and political climate that prevailed and how these factors influenced the subject. This knowledge helps researchers establish patterns and identify relevant points regarding the subject and justifies the selection of the historical method. Moreover, when selecting a topic, researchers need to be aware of the accessibility of the sources, the relevance of the topic to the audience, and its potential to enhance understanding (Lusk, 1997).

SELECTING A TITLE

Once historians have identified the focus of the study, it is helpful to delimit the project by titling it. The title tells readers what to expect from the study and narrows the topic for the historian. Typically, the title includes the time frame and purpose, for example, A Review of Critical Thinking in Nursing, 1990–2000.

Although the title appears first in a completed study and concisely describes the research topic, it may be the researcher's final step. The advantage of titling a study early in the project is to assist in focusing the work. Historians can always modify the title as the project develops and should be open to change based on data they uncover. A well-focused and delimited study will assist researchers in making the literature search effective and meaningful. It is essential, though, that historians do not prematurely close the literature search because the materials discovered are outside of the predetermined time frame. Rather, historians should continue their review of materials until they are comfortable that they have fully examined the thesis. It is easier to adjust the title than to risk having a poorly developed study.

CONDUCTING A LITERATURE REVIEW

A good starting point for a literature review is to identify major works published on the selected topic. If historians want to study the history of critical thinking, then they must assess what has been written on the subject and identify the themes and ambiguities related to critical thinking that exist in the literature. Part of the review includes identifying the problems connected with the topic, for example, the ambiguities that have arisen over time in defining and evaluating critical thinking. The anticipation of problems that may arise with methodology or with the interpretation of data allows historical researchers time to plan problem resolution. A search of the literature for references from several periods allows for a greater understanding of the subject. Various computer databases provide a means by which researchers may obtain some data needed in the literature review.

A literature review helps researchers formulate questions they need to address, delineate a time frame for the study, and decide on a theoretical framework. In addition, the review affords researchers an opportunity to learn what type of materials are available. For example, a researcher learns whether he or she can obtain primary sources or firsthand accounts of an event, such as the letters written by an individual living during the period of study. The researcher also learns of secondary sources or secondhand accounts of an event, such as histories or newspapers that have already been written on the particular study subject.

Based on the literature review, historians formulate questions regarding events that influenced the chosen subject. To elucidate the subject, researchers ask questions beginning with How, Why, Who, and What in light of the ideas, events, and institutions that existed and individuals who existed. If, for example, a researcher narrows a topic such as U.S. public health nursing to the study of public health nurses living at the Henry Street Settlement, then questions such as the following may guide the direction of the literature search: How did the Henry Street Settlement begin? Who began the Henry Street Settlement? What is a settlement house? Why was Henry Street the location? These questions may prompt the researcher to examine biographies of people who participated in the settlement house movement during the late 19th and early 20th centuries. Or to better understand life at that time, the historian might read city records regarding population statistics or examine published materials to understand another historian's perception of women's roles, education, work, and life during the study period. Newspaper accounts, written histories, proceedings of minutes, photographs, biographies, letters, diaries, and films may help historians seeking a greater understanding of a particular subject.

During the literature review, historians must develop an organizing strategy that will help them analyze the data. Some facts they had obtained may seem trivial in the beginning of the project, but may become crucial to explaining or connecting events learned later in the study. Thus, careful documentation using an index card filing system or a directory in a word processing program will help researchers retrieve the information at a later time (Austin, 1958; Barzun & Graff, 1985). The bibliographic entry should include the author, title, abstract, place of publication, date, and particular archive or library where the researcher found the information. Researchers must include any pertinent information in the notes so that, during data analysis, they will be able to easily retrieve important information or go back to the original source, if necessary.

During this phase of the project, historians begin to develop a bibliography. Using historical source materials from libraries, archives, bibliographies, newspapers, reviews, journals, associations, and the Internet, researchers begin to comprehend the extent of the subject under investigation (Matejski, 1986). To accomplish this important step, historians use collections in libraries and archives. Libraries and archives contain different types of reference materials that require different methods of storage and classification. To enable researchers to use each method appropriately, it is necessary they be familiar with both.

Libraries contain published materials that researchers often use as secondary materials. To locate materials, researchers use a card catalog, computerized catalog system, or computerized database that allows them to locate works. A call number, usually given in the catalog, designates the unique location of each volume in the library; volumes are usually arranged by subject. Libraries have purchased many of the books and thus permit them to circulate (Termine, 1993), whereas archival materials remain on-site.

Archives differ from libraries in their holdings, cataloging, and circulation policies. Archives contain unpublished materials that are considered primary source materials, such as the "official records of an organization or persons . . . [that] are preserved because of the value of the information they contain" (Termine, 1992). Instead of using a card catalog to find a book, researchers use a *finding aid,* a published book or catalog that lists what is in the archive or repository. The finding aid identifies a collection using a record group, a series, and a subseries. However, instead of being stored according to these designations, collections are stored haphazardly within aisles, shelves, and box numbers. Libraries contain a discrete number of volumes, whereas archives contain linear (cubic) feet of records. Archives acquire their material by collections. For example, many organizations cannot store or maintain their records and transfer this task to archives.

Unlike libraries, where books are circulated, archives require that researchers use the materials on-site. In most archives, researchers may only use pencil and paper to collect data; other archives permit the use of a laptop computer. Newer technologic advances have enabled researchers to use handheld scanners in conjunction with their laptop computers. Scanners provide a safe method for copying materials (Lusk, 1997). Archives usually require that researchers make appointments to discuss their project with an archivist. Besides offering researchers primary source references needed in historical research, archives provide materials and memorabilia researchers may use in exhibitions such as the history of an organization or a person. Because some of the primary source materials are fragile, archivists will only permit scholars engaged in historical research to use the collections (Termine, 1992).

Archivists and librarians assist researchers to access materials, thus rendering an important informational service. However, because of the differences between libraries and archives, the work of professional archivists and librarians varies. Whereas archivists work with the records, papers, manuscripts, and nonprinted materials found in the collections, librarians manage the books and publications (Termine, 1992). Table 10-1 summarizes the differences between libraries and archives.

DATA TREATMENT

IDENTIFYING SOURCES

Historic researchers must find some way to understand what actually occurred during an earlier period. To research historical antecedents, researchers must identify sources from the period. Primary sources give firsthand accounts of a person's experience, an institution, or of an event,

TABLE 10-1   Differences Between Libraries and Archives

	Libraries	Archives
Holdings	Published materials	Unpublished materials: records, manuscripts, papers
Locators	Card catalog	Finding aid
	Call number	Record group, series, subseries
	Unique location by subject	Haphazard location of "boxes" by aisle, shelf, box number
Stored	Volumes (titles)	Linear (cubic) feet
Acquired	Purchased by volume or issue	Donated or purchased collections
Use of materials	Circulation	Noncirculation; use of paper and pencil only or laptop computer to collect data

From Termine, J. (1992, March). Paper presented at the State University of New York, Health Science Center at Brooklyn, College of Nursing, Brooklyn, NY. Adapted with permission.

and may lack critical analysis. However, primary sources such as personal letters or diaries may contain the author's interpretation of an event or hearsay. Thus, researchers must analyze and interpret the meaning of the primary sources.

Ulrich (1990) wrote about Martha Ballard, an 18th century midwife from Hallowell, Maine. Using Ballard's diary as a primary source, Ulrich wrote a rich biographic account of Ballard as well as a historical rendering of everyday life during this period. Ballard's diary, which she kept daily for more than 27 years, connected "several prominent themes in the social history of the early Republic" (p. 27). More important, Ulrich explained, "It [the diary] transforms the nature of the evidence upon [which] much of the history of the period has been written" (p. 27). Earlier historians did not consider the potential the diary had for uncovering historical data about this period in the United States. Rather, they perceived Ballard's daily record as trivial and too filled with daily life to be of any importance because she documented the deliveries with which she assisted, the travel she endured to reach laboring women, the stories she wrote about other people, and the accounts of her own family. However, on viewing the same diary, Ulrich believed that it reached directly to the "marrow of eighteenth century life" (p. 33). The "trivia that so annoyed earlier readers provides a consistent, daily record of the operation of a female-managed economy" (p. 33).

Unlike primary sources that are written by people directly involved in an event, secondary sources are materials that cite opinions and present interpretations. Newspaper accounts, journal articles, and textbooks from the period being studied are secondary sources that place researchers within the context of a period. For example, newspaper accounts of the 1893 Columbian World Exposition held in Chicago added authenticity to the story about the founding of the American Society of Superintendents of Training Schools for Nurses (known today as the National League for Nursing). However, researchers may use secondary sources as primary sources, depending on the researchers' questions or the purpose of the study (Austin, 1958). For example, although newspaper articles from the late 19th century gave secondary accounts of what happened, they also offered insight into what was considered important during that period. Thus, if researchers are studying the insights of individuals present at a particular point in history, then they may use newspaper accounts as primary as well as secondary sources. Chaney and Folk (1993), for example, used cartoons found in the American Medical Association journal *American Medical News* as a primary source in the study "A Profession in Caricature: The Changing Attitudes Towards Nursing in the *American Medical News,* 1960–1989."

CONFIRMING SOURCE GENUINENESS AND AUTHENTICITY

When selecting primary sources, the genuineness and authenticity of those sources become important issues. Barzun and Graff (1985) have explained that historians are responsible for verifying documents to assure they are genuine and authentic. *Genuine* means that a document is not forged; *authentic* means that the document provides the truthful reporting of a subject (Barzun & Graff, 1985). Authenticating sources requires several operations, none of which is fixed in a specific technique. Researchers rely on "attention to detail, on common-sense reasoning, on a 'developed' field for history and chronology, on familiarity with human behavior, and on ever-enlarging stores of information" (p. 112). Authenticity of letters or journals becomes even more important when researchers find them in a nursing school attic or closet. More than likely, primary sources within archival collections have already been found to be genuine and have been authenticated by the institution in which they are housed. Nevertheless, researchers are responsible for the final authenticity of a document. A careful reading of the document, an examination of the type of paper and the condition of the material, and an extensive knowledge of the period can help researchers verify the document as authentic.

The validity of historical research relies on measures that address matters concerning external and internal criticism. *External criticism* questions the genuineness of primary sources and assures that the document is what it claims. *Internal criticism* of the data is concerned with content authenticity or truthfulness. Kerlinger (1986) has suggested that internal criticism "seeks the 'true' meaning and value of the content of sources of data" (p. 621). Researchers must ask, Does the content accurately reflect the period in which it indicates it is written? Do the facts conflict with historical dates, meanings of words, and social mores?

Spieseke (1953) has emphasized that, when determining the reliability of the contents, researchers must evaluate when authors of primary sources wrote their account—whether it was close to the event or 20 years later. Other questions researchers must ask are, Did a trained historian or an observer write the story? Were facts suppressed? If so, why? To ensure the accuracy of the writer, Spieseke has suggested that researchers check for corroborating evidence, look for another independent primary source that supports the data, and identify any disagreements between sources. Ulrich (1990), for example, authenticated Ballard's diary by corroborating some of Ballard's entries regarding feed bills with other sources from the town in which she lived.

What data researchers can validate externally as genuine, however, may be inconsistent when researchers examine the data contents. For example, an individual may have written letters in the 19th century, but the content may conflict with known facts of that period and pose serious questions regarding the truth of the content (Kerlinger, 1986). Nevertheless, external criticism "ultimately . . . leads to content analysis or internal criticism and is indispensable when assessing evidence" (Matejski, 1986, p. 189). Austin (1958) illustrated this point by explaining that learning the date of a source (external criticism) helps researchers determine if the content reflects the period in which it was written (internal criticism), and vice versa.

DATA ANALYSIS

Data analysis relies on the statement of the subject including the questions raised, purpose, and conceptual framework of the study. The themes developed by researchers direct the data analysis. Researchers frame the findings according to research questions generated by the thesis. According to Spieseke (1953), the purpose of the study often directs the data analysis. If researchers want to teach a lesson, answer a question, or support an idea, then they organize the selection of relevant data accordingly. How researchers analyze the material depends, in part, on the thematic organization of conceptual frameworks used in the study. Use of social, political, economic, or feminist theory will structure the data and enable researchers to concentrate on particular areas.

In data analysis, researchers must deal with the tension between the conflicting truths so that they may find interpretations or an understanding regarding the subject. In some way, researchers must strike a "balance between conflict" (Tholfsen, 1977, p. 246). They need to ask questions such as, Is the content found in the primary and secondary sources congruent with each other or are there conflicting stories? If a conflict does exist, is there supporting evidence to justify either side of the argument?

Another important aspect of analysis is researcher bias about the subject and the influence of that bias on data interpretation. Awareness of their bias helps researchers identify a particular frame of reference that may limit or direct their data interpretation. Self-awareness promotes a researcher's honesty in finding the truth and decreases the influence of bias on data interpretation (Austin, 1958; Barzun & Graff, 1985).

Through data analysis, researchers should develop new material and new ideas based on supporting evidence rather than just rehash ideas (Matejski, 1986). Researchers seek to discover new truths from the assembled facts. However, given the same data, individuals will analyze the data differently and thus contribute to the tentative nature of interpretation (Austin, 1958). To interpret the findings and get at a truth, historians must be conscious of the role ideology plays in analysis. Researchers must question how ideology, or any set of ideas, influences the analysis of a particular event. For example, a paternalistic ideologic view of the nurse's role in the health care system may starkly contrast with an interpretation of the same data using a feminist lens. Awareness of ideologic influence forces researchers to study the full effect ideas have on an event and to avoid accepting ideas on face value. Tholfsen (1977) argued that history will suffer if taught from any one ideologic stance; instead, its aim should be the "commitment to the disinterested pursuit of truth, accompanied by an openness to continuing debate and discussion" (p. 255). With this understanding, researchers analyze and sort out data and try to find new truths that the evidence produced by the data can support.

Analysis occurs throughout the process of data collection. Historians look for evidence to explain events or ideas. By interpreting primary and secondary documents, researchers form a picture of historical antecedents. However, these documents become part of history only when "they have been subjected to historiography that bridges the gap between lived occurrences and records" (Matejski, 1986, p. 180).

In their search of true meanings and in their attempts to bridge the gap, researchers must not only be aware of their own bias and that of ideology but also bias from the sources themselves that may impede interpretation. For example, in biographic research, the use of both informants through interviews and materials found in archival collections raises issues regarding the accuracy and validity of the data. Historians doing a biographic study need to be cautious of interviews that often present a biased or one-sided view of the individual being studied. Researchers may also suspect bias in archival holdings of an individual's papers, because the individual may have determined what to include in the collection (Brown et al., 1991).

An ethical concern regarding the use of an institution or individual's private papers is the right to privacy versus the right to know. Although discussion of this concern is beyond the scope of this chapter, it is important for historical researchers to be aware of this dilemma. Researchers must have a clear idea of the kinds of information they need to obtain from data. If they find the source in an archive, then the archivist is responsible for seeing that "policy, regulations, and rules—governing his action do exist and are effective" (Rosenthal, 1982, p. 4). However, scholars are ultimately responsible for using the data appropriately. If historiographers have as a goal to further the understanding of social, political, or economic relationships among individuals, institutions, events, or ideas, then they must question what purpose is served if they expose exploitative or embarrassing details. Historians who misuse data and generate sensationalism by "[presenting] conclusions regarding motives and behavior that transcend the evidence . . . [and] turn an ordinary book into a best seller" (Graebner, 1982, p. 23) are discouraging future access and preservation of primary sources. If this misuse involves the past, then only a historical reputation is damaged; however, if it involves people who are still living or their immediate ancestors, then it places at risk the right to access and future contributions of papers from other families or institutions. When determining how to use data, Graebner (1982) has suggested that "decisions, events, and activities which affect the public welfare or embrace qualities of major human interest—and thus add legitimately to the richness of the historical record—set the acceptable boundaries of historical search and analysis" (p. 23).

The confidentiality of source material has become more of an ethical concern for historians as researchers have placed greater emphasis on the lives of ordinary people (Lusk, 1997). Several professional organizations such as The American Historical Association (1987), American Association for the History of Medicine (1991), and Oral History Association (1988–1989) have developed ethical guidelines for historical research. Nurse–historians Birnbach, Brown, and Hiestand (1991), members of the American Association of the History of Nursing, have published ethical guidelines as well as professional standards for doing historical inquiry in nursing.

INTERPRETATION OF THE FINDINGS

The historical narrative is the final stage in the historical research process. During this stage, researchers tell the story that interprets the data and engages readers in the historical debate. Synthesis occurs and findings are connected, supported, and molded "into a related whole" (Austin, 1958, p. 9). Decisions regarding what to include and what to emphasize become important. In historical exposition, researchers explain not only what happened but how and why it happened. They explore relationships among events, ideas, people, organizations, and institutions and interpret them within the context of the period being studied. The political, social, and economic factors set a stage or backdrop from which to compare and contrast the historical data collected. Historical judgments, based on historical evidence, must pass through the filter of "human understanding of human experience" (Cramer, 1992, p. 7). To accomplish this task, researchers must be sensitive to the material; must show genuine engagement in the subject; and must balance the forces of self-interest, societal interest, and historical interest. Along with these attributes, researchers need creativity to achieve a coherent, convincing, and meaningful account (Ashley, 1978; Spieseke, 1953).

When writing the narrative, researchers are charged with creatively rendering the events, explaining the findings, and supporting the ideas. Researchers must possess discipline, organization, and imagination to accomplish this Herculean task. Historiographers must set aside time to write daily, find a quiet place to concentrate and contemplate the data, use a detailed outline to direct the writing of the manuscript, plan the story using the thematic framework established earlier in the study, and use time and place as landmarks to give balance and direct the flow of the story while critically interpreting the findings (Austin, 1958).

Historians weave together historical facts, research findings, and interpretations influenced by the conceptual framework into a coherent story. To guide them in the writing process, researchers may divide the narrative into chronologic periods. Or, they may use geographic places such as regional areas in the United States, thematic relationships, research questions, or political, social, cultural, or economic issues to organize the narrative. These ad hoc inventions are determined by each researcher and thus are subject to the researcher's interest, bias, and understanding of the historical method (Cramer, 1992; Fondiller, 1978).

Writers of history who want readers to hear the words spoken during the period studied may use direct quotations. Direct quotations also provide corroboration of and credibility to a researcher's interpretation. However, although authentic quotes are a useful narrative tool, researchers must avoid using too many direct quotations. It is better to paraphrase and use limited direct quotes to give the narrative the flavor of a person.

Historiography displays a researcher's creativity and imagination as the story unfolds. Creativity connects thoughts, quotes, and events into a readable story and gives birth to new ideas (Christy, 1978). The interpretations and response to the themes and questions rely on historians' ability to go beyond the known facts and develop new ideas and new meanings. No two historians who view the same data will respond in exactly the same way. The human filter through which all information passes will alter researchers' responses to the data and will provide the catalyst for the creation of new ideas (Barzun & Graff, 1985; Christy, 1978).

Summary

The nursing profession needs the infusion of new ideas, new meanings, and new interpretations of its past to explain its place in history and its future direction. Ashley (1978) confirmed that connection when she wrote, "With creativity as our base, and with strong historicalal knowledge and awareness, nurses can become pioneers in developing new types of inquiry and turn inward toward self-knowledge and self-understanding" (p. 36).

The historical method gives qualitative researchers tools to explore the past. Using certain guideposts along the way, historiographers formulate ideas, collect data, validate the genuineness and authenticity of those data, and narrate the story. However, to make the research meaningful, historians must relate the research questions and the findings to the present.

REFERENCES

American Association for the History of Medicine. (1991). Report of the committee on ethical codes. *Bulletin of the History of Medicine, 65*(4), 565–570.

American Historical Association. (1987). Statement on standards of professional conduct. *History Teacher, 21*(1), 105–109.

Ashley, J. (1978). Foundations for scholarship: Historical research in nursing. *Advances in Nursing Science, 1*(1), 25–36.

Austin, A. (1958). The historicalal method. *Nursing Research, 7*(1), 4–10.

Barzun, J., & Graff, H. F. (1985). *The modern researcher* (4th ed.) San Diego, CA: Harcourt Brace Jovanovich.

Birnbach, N., Brown, J., & Hiestand, W. (1991). *Ethical guidelines for the nurse historian. and Standards of professional conduct for historicalal inquiry into nursing.*

Brown, J., D'Antonio, P., & Davis, S. (1991, April). *Report on the Fourth Invitational Nursing History Conference.* Unpublished manuscript.

Bullough, V. (1991, April). *Social history.* Paper presented at the meeting of Fourth Invitational Conference on Nursing History: Critical Issues Affecting Research and Researchers, Philadelphia, PA.

Chaney, J. A., & Folk, P. (1993). A profession in caricature: The changing attitudes towards nursing in the *American Medical News,* 1960–1989. *Nursing History Review, 1,* 181–201.

Christy, T. (1978). The hope of history. In M. L. Fitzpatrick (Ed.), *Historical studies in nursing* (pp. 3–11). New York: Teachers College Press.

Cramer, S. (1992). The nature of history: Meditations on Clio's Craft. *Nursing Research, 41*(1), 4–7.

Fitzpatrick, M. L. (1993). Historical research. In P. L. Munhall & C. O. Boyd (Eds.), *Nursing research: A qualitative perspective* (2nd ed., pp. 359–390). New York: National League for Nursing.

Fondiller, S. (1978). Writing the report. In M. L. Fitzpatrick (Ed.), *Historical studies in nursing* (pp. 25–27). New York: Teachers College Press.

Glass, L. (1991, April). [Biographical history]. Paper presented at the meeting of Fourth Invitational Conference on Nursing History: Critical Issues Affecting Research and Researchers, Philadelphia, PA.

Graebner, N. A. (1982). History, society, and the right to privacy. In *The scholar's right to know versus the individual's right to privacy: Proceedings of the first Rockefeller Archive Center Conference, December 5, 1975* (pp. 20–24). Pocantico Hills, NY: Rockefeller Archive Center Publication.

Hamilton, D. (1991, April). *Intellectual history.* Paper presented at the meeting of Fourth Invitational Conference on Nursing History: Critical Issues Affecting Research and Researchers, Philadelphia, PA.

Hamilton, D. B. (1993). The idea of history and the history of ideas. *Image, 25*(1), 45–50.

Hanson, K. S. (1989). The emergence of liberal education in nursing education, 1893 to 1923. *Journal of Professional Nursing, 5*(2), 83–91.

Hofstadter, R. (1959). History and the social sciences. In F. Stern (Ed.), *The varieties of history* (pp. 359–370). New York: Meridan.

Kerlinger, F. N. (1986). *Foundations of behavioral research* (3rd ed.). New York: Holt, Rinehart & Winston.

Kruman, M. (1985). Historical method: Implications for nursing research. In M. M. Leininger (Ed.), *Qualitative research methods in nursing* (pp. 109–118). Orlando, FL: Grune & Stratton.

Lewenson, S. B. (1990). The woman's nursing and suffrage movement, 1893–1920. In V. Bullough, B. Bullough, & M. Stanton (Eds.), *Florence Nightingale and her era: A collection of new scholarship* (pp. 117–118), New York: Garland.

Lewenson, S. B. (1996). *Taking charge: Nursing, suffrage and feminism, 1873–1920*. New York: NLN Press.

Lusk, B. (1997). Historical methodology for nursing research. *Image, 29*(4), 355–359.

Lynaugh, J. (1996). [Editorial]. *Nursing History Review, 4,* 1.

Lynaugh, J., & Reverby, S. (1987). Thoughts on the nature of history. *Nursing Research, 36*(1), 4–69.

Matejski, M. (1986). Historical research: The method. In P. L. Munhall & C. J. Oiler (Eds.), *Nursing research: A qualitative perspective* (pp. 175–193). Norwalk, CT: Appleton-Century-Crofts.

Morse, J. M., & Field, P. A. (1995). *Qualitative research methods for health professionals* (2nd ed.). Thousand Oaks, CA: Sage.

Newton, M. (1965). The case for historicalal research. *Nursing Research, 14*(1), 20–26.

Oral History Association. (1988–1989). *Oral history evaluation guidelines* (Pamphlet No. 3) [On-line]. Available: www.baylor.edu/7Eoha/evaluationguidelines.html.

Rines, A., & Kershner, F. (1979). *Information concerning historicalal studies*. Unpublished manuscript. New York: Teachers College, Columbia University, Department of Nursing.

Rosenthal, R. (1982). Who will be responsible for private papers of private people? Some considerations from the view of the private depository. In *The scholar's right to know versus the individual's right to privacy: Proceedings of the first Rockefeller Archive Center Conference, December 5, 1975* (pp. 3–6). Pocantico Hills, NY: Rockefeller Archive Center Publication.

Spieseke, A. W. (1953). What is the historicalal method of research? *Nursing Research, 2*(1), 36–37.

Termine, J. (1992, March). *A talk about archives*. Paper presented at the State University of New York, Health Science Center at Brooklyn, College of Nursing, Brooklyn, NY.

Tholfsen, T. R. (1977). The ambiguous virtues of the study of history. *Teachers College Record, 79*(2), 245–257.

Ulrich, L. T. (1990). *A midwife's tale: The life of Martha Ballard based on her diary, 1785–1812*. New York: Vintage Books.

Historical Research in Practice, Education, and Administration

Using a historical method to study nursing practice, education, and administration provides a better understanding of relationships and allows us to view the world from a broader perspective. Lynaugh (1996) explained that "history yields self-knowledge by structuring a mind capable of imagining life beyond one's own life-span" (p. 1). Applying a historical methodology creates a synergy among the past, present, and future.

This chapter highlights how researchers in nursing practice, education, and administration apply historical methodology to understand patterns of our past and interpret those patterns to gain a better understanding of the current and future world. Included in the chapter are three critiques of historic research articles in the areas of practice, education, and administration. Based on criteria developed from the material discussed in Chapter 10, guidelines were created for critiquing historical research (see Table 11-1). A reprint of the Sandelowski (1997) article appears at the end of the chapter to assist readers to understand the critiquing process. Table 11-2 highlights a sampling of selected historical research publications.

Critique Guidelines

To critique historical research, historiographers need to understand what is expected in the process. This section reviews the essential components of doing historical research and suggests questions researchers might ask when using this design. Researchers may use these same questions—which have been applied to the three critiques in this chapter—to evaluate historic research.

Historiographers search for facts and evidence that will unveil the nature and relationships regarding historic events, ideas, institutions, or people. To accurately assess historical meanings, researchers must assure readers of external validity that confirms the source is what it claims. Simultaneously, researchers must establish the internal validity of the source, verifying the consistency between the genuineness of the primary source and the authenticity of the data. Historiographers may use a framework that helps to organize ideas and makes connections and, simultaneously, acknowledges personal and ideologic bias. To interpret the material

TABLE 11-1   Guidelines for Critiquing Historical Research

Data Generation

Title	1. How does it concisely reflect the purpose of the study?
	2. How does it clearly tell readers what the study is about?
	3. How does it delineate the time frame for the study?
Statement of the subject	1. Is the subject easily researched?
	2. What themes and theses are studied?
	3. What are the research questions?
Literature review	1. What are the main works written on the subject?
	2. What time period does the literature review cover?
	3. What are some of the problems that may arise when studying this subject?
	4. What primary sources can be identified?
	5. How was the subject narrowed during the literature review?
	6. What research questions were raised during the literature review?

Data Treatment

Primary sources	1. How were primary sources used?
	2. Were they genuine and authentic?
	3. How was external validity determined?
	4. How was internal validity determined?
	5. Were there inconsistencies between the external validity and internal validity?
	6. Does the content accurately reflect the period of concern?
	7. Do the facts conflict with historical dates, meanings of words, and social mores?
	8. When did the primary author write the account?
	9. Did a trained historian or an observer write the source?
	10. Were facts suppressed, and, if so, why?
	11. Is there corroborating evidence?
	12. Identify any disagreements between sources.
Secondary sources	1. What were the secondary sources used?
	2. How were secondary sources used?
	3. Do they corroborate the primary source?
	4. Can you identify any disagreements between sources?

(continued)

Table 11-1   **Guidelines for Critiquing Historical Research (CONTINUED)**

Data Analysis

Organization	1. What conceptual frameworks were used in the study? 2. How would the study be classified: e.g. intellectual, feminist, social, political, biographic? 3. Were the research questions answered? 4. Was the purpose of the study accomplished? 5. If conflict exists within the findings, was there supporting evidence to justify either side of the argument?
Bias	1. Was the researcher's bias identified? 2. Was analysis influenced by a present-mindedness? 3. What were the ideologic biases? 4. How did bias affect data analysis?
Ethical issues	1. Was there any infringement on a historical reputation? 2. Was there a conflict between the right to privacy versus the right to know? 3. Did the research show that decisions, events, and activities of an individual or organization affected the public welfare or embraced qualities of major human interest?

Interpreting the Findings

Narrative	1. Does the story describe what happened, including how and why it happened? 2. Were relationships among events, ideas, people, organizations, and institutions explained, interpreted, and placed within a contextual framework? 3. How were direct quotations used? (Too limited or too long) 4. Was the narrative clear, concise, and interesting to read? 5. Was the significance to nursing explicit?

and to make sense of the data as the story unfolds, researchers must possess clear narrative and explanatory skills.

Accuracy is extremely important to historiographers. The systems that researchers develop will help them maintain accuracy. How researchers collect data, organize the bibliography, and number the different drafts of the narrative assists in the accurate accounting of the story. Historiographers must organize the data and tell the story in a logical fashion. Furthermore, researchers must honestly address questions that arise from the data, trying to understand and explain what the data are describing. Researchers

(*text continues on page 220*)

TABLE 11-2 Selective Sampling of Historic Research Studies

Author/Date	Title	Findings
Care, Gregory, English, & Venkatesh (1996)	"A Struggle for Equality: Resistance to Commissioning of Male Nurses in the Canadian Military, 1952–1967"	"Prior to 1967, only female nurses were permitted to join the nursing division. A 25 year struggle by the Registered Nurses Association of Ontario (RNAO), its Male Nurses Committee (MNC), and the Canadian Nurses Association (CNA) was required to change this discriminatory policy. The struggle for equality on behalf of Canadian male nurses was successfully resolved because of the united stand taken by the MNC, the RNAO, and the CNA. The study also demonstrates the need to move beyond matriarchal history perspectives in nursing to more completely understand the evolution of the profession in Canada" (p. 103).
Hamilton (1996)	"The Seventh Star: Dorothy Ford Buschmann and the Founding of Sigma Theta Tau"	"This historical study examined the contributions of Dorothy Charlotte Ford Buschmann (1895–1953), a key advisor whom some might consider the seventh founding star. Findings suggest that Dorothy Buschmann believed that the foundations of professional nursing were love, honor, and courage and that the enduring value of nursing was its contribution to the social good. She played a vital role in designing Sigma Theta Tau's philosophy and constitution, extended membership throughout the Midwest, and served as the first national president from 1927–1934" (pp. 177–180).
Hektor & Touhy (1997)	"The History of the Bath: From Art to Task? Reflections for the Future"	The history of the bath is examined from Florence Nightingale through the 1920s along with thoughts on present-day practices. Key issues include bathing that has been reduced to a task rather than an opportunity for assessment and communication with the client when the professional nurse is no longer involved. Bathing has become routine, depersonalized, and, at times, harmful rather than a therapeutic and satisfying experience. The art of nursing as practiced in the past can help us to rediscover the meaning of the skillful and artful bath.
Lusk (1997)	"Professional Classifications of American Nurses, 1910–1935"	"The purpose of this historical study is to describe the official classification of American nurses as professional or nonprofessional, from 1910 to 1935. Labor legislation before World War I, military decisions during that war, and federal mandates during the Great Depression resulted in differing professional classifications of nurses. Although nurse

Reference	Title	
		leaders aspired to traditional criteria of professionalism, such as individual responsibility and a deep, distinct body of knowledge, these criteria were subsumed by political, financial, and gender issues. This study demonstrates that professional status cannot be assured by attainment of professional criteria alone, but is defined by more diverse, complex issues" (p. 227).
Mackintosh (1997)	"A Historical Study of Men in Nursing"	"This study outlines a brief history of men as nurses in the United Kingdom. History appears to indicate that men have had a place in nursing for as long as records are available, but their contribution has been perceived as negligible, largely because of the dominant influence that the 19th century female nursing movement has had on the occupation's historical ideology. The study indicates that men have an equally valid historical role within nursing, and that this should be acknowledged when considering male nurses' position within the nursing profession" (p. 232).
Newell (1995)	"Historical Perspective: Spondylolysis, an Historical Review"	"This historical review covers the earliest recorded findings and descriptions of lumbar spondylosis, as well as the century-old etiologic controversy regarding this condition. The importance of the work of Robert zu Coblenz in 1955 is recognized regarding the biomechanical and clinical understanding of the nature of spondylolysis" (p. 1950).
Olson (1996)	"Fundamental and Special: The Dilemma of Psychiatric–Mental Health Nursing"	"This article explores the tension between defining psychiatric–mental health nursing as fundamental to the discipline yet also special, an historic dilemma that continues to influence efforts to establish a secure place for the specialty. The findings of this research indicate that early reliance on interpersonal theory provided an uncertain basis for differentiating psychiatric–mental health nursing from other areas of nursing practice." (p. 3).
Russell (1997)	"An Oral History Project in Mental Health Nursing"	"The study confirms an assumption of the usefulness of oral history, as a record, additional to the written documents, which enriches the descriptions of historical processes" (p. 489).
Sarnecky (1997)	"Nursing in the American Army from the Revolution to Spanish-American War."	"The origin of the first permanent U.S. Army Nurse Corps dates back to 1901, but the history of nursing predates that formal beginning by almost 126 years. Since the start of the Revolutionary War in 1775, soldiers as well as civilian men and women have provided nursing care for the army during wartime. The nature of this caregiving evolved with each war, reflecting the changing models of disease causation, and the level of respect and responsibilities given to the nurses increased as their value became clear. Without the endowment of their spirit and contributions, the Army Nurse Corps of today would not exist" (p. 49).

must be prepared to answer questions such as, Did an event noted in a source actually happen? Could it have happened as it was noted in the primary source? Throughout the study, historiographers must be true to the data, allowing them to unfold and bring a better understanding of the subject. This process requires researchers to be aware of their own bias and degree of honesty in relationship to the findings. Does their own bias hinder discovery of new meanings that may be revealed? Essential to the historical method is imagination. Imagination lets researchers make connections in the data and create a story that assists in learning more of the truth (Barzun & Graff, 1985).

According to Spieseke (1953), historical researchers must be able to locate and collect data, analyze the reliability of the data, organize and arrange the data into a pattern, and express "it [the data] in meaningful and effective language" (p. 37). The narrative should show the successful attainment of these important skills, thus providing a method to evaluate the process. The narrative not only tells the story but it allows researchers (and others) to critique the study as well.

Table 11-1 organizes the data presented in Chapter 10 and suggests criteria to use when critiquing historical research. The criteria were used to critique published studies in the areas of nursing practice, education, and administration; these studies are presented later in the chapter. However, because published historical research should read as an interesting narrative, analysis using a specific instrument such as Table 11-1 may be inhibiting. Reviewers needs to know that such an instrument is just a guide—not an absolute rule. Headings in a published article may not clearly delineate primary or secondary sources or personal bias (as perhaps they might in a historical dissertation or in other forms of reported research). Nevertheless, used as a guide, Table 11-1 highlights important features of historical research and helps consumers critique its worth more effectively.

An answer to the question, What comes first: The chicken or the egg? epitomizes the dilemma in deciding whether to use the historical method first or to let the area of interest guide the decision regarding choice of method. Why select historical method in nursing practice, education, or administration when so many other methods are available to researchers? The research questions or conflicts that need historical explicating determine the selection of method. Armed with the appropriate tools, historical researchers venture into these areas and formulate specific questions. Following the selection of the subject, researchers must narrow the topic to enable them to study the area in depth. To build a body of knowledge requires teamwork or the linkage of several historical studies that eventually will fill gaps and offer a fuller understanding of history (Bloch, 1964). Historians probe historical antecedents in broad areas of nursing such as practice education, and administration, to explain relationships, ideas, or events that influenced nursing's professional development. A review of previous studies helps researchers determine their own course of study and stimulates imagination. Table 11-2 offers a sampling of historical research studies.

Application to Practice

During the early modern nursing movement, nursing education and nursing practice were so closely related that studying one often meant studying the other. During the late 19th century and well into the 20th century, hospitals relied heavily on student nurses to provide patient care. Changes in the traditional, apprenticeship educational model and the move to university-based educational settings dramatically and economically altered the delivery of care in hospitals and nursing practice. Before these changes, graduate nurses, on completing their training, were rarely hired to staff hospitals and were forced to look elsewhere for jobs. They worked outside of hospitals as private duty and public health nurses.

In 1928, Wolf (1991) addressed the National League of Nursing Education (now known as the National League for Nursing [NLN]) regarding the transition of graduate nurses employed by hospitals. Wolf explained how graduate nurses who provided client care—as opposed to student nurses—would be advantageous to hospital administrators, nursing educators, and to the graduate nurses. Aside from stabilizing nursing service, providing an excellent service, and profiting the employer and employee, Wolf argued that hiring graduate nurses would improve the value society placed on nursing service. Wolf believed that graduate nurses faced undue criticism from hospital administrators, who believed that student nurses were more "buoyant, resilient, and enthusiastic" (Wolf, 1991, p. 140) than graduates. Yet, Wolf argued that "the graduate nurse sees more to be done for a patient than a student, she knows better what to do" (p. 140).

Wolf's (1991) speech provides historians with a perspective of someone personally involved in the changes in nursing practice history that had profound effects on the shape of things to come. Historical research in the development of nursing practice might examine nursing practice in hospitals, private duty, or in public health. External factors such as wars, economic depressions, and advances in medicine and science affected the development of the nursing profession and pose an infinite number of ways to approach the study of nursing practice. Researchers can find primary and secondary sources in published nursing textbooks, hospital manuals, speeches presented at various professional meetings, minutes of professional meetings, and graduation addresses. Archives of hospitals, schools of nursing, and visiting nurse services contain data that tell the story of nursing practice.

Discussions in the literature that have defined nurses' roles, specialization, and society's value of care find their origins in history. Bullough (1992) explained that "clinical specialization started in the early twentieth century as nurses with advanced knowledge and training were needed to care for groups of patients with special needs" (p. 254). Specialties emerged in nursing such as nurse–anesthetist, nurse–midwifery, public health nursing, and critical care nursing that demanded additional education, practical experience, and, in some instances, certification. Unanswered questions about the development of different specialties and the needed qualifications for each lend themselves to historical inquiry.

CRITIQUE OF A STUDY IN PRACTICE

In the study "'Making the Best of Things': Technology in American Nursing, 1870–1940," Sandelowski (1997) explores the changing definition of technology and its effect on nursing practice in the United States. This topic has been largely unexplored in nursing. Sandelowski addresses pertinent issues and dilemmas nurses have encountered in the use of technology. As the title indicates, the time frame for the study was 1870–1940. The modern nursing movement began during the 1870s and marks the beginning period of study. The year 1940 marks the beginning of World War II and the end of the period that Sandelowski refers to as the "World of the Tool" (p. 15). Following the war, the "World of the Screen" began and technology drastically changed. Sandelowski's use of the phrase *"making the best of things"* (p. 11) sets the tone of what was expected of nurses and describes the intimate hands-on relationship they had developed with technology.

The statement of the subject is embedded throughout the opening discussion about the meaning of technology and the purpose of the article. Sandelowski directs readers through the different concerns technology has posed in nursing over time. She organizes the study by dividing nursing practice into the world before technology (before 1940) and the world after its introduction. Although in the post–World War II era the increasing technology created ethical dilemmas, Sandelowski contends that nursing historically had been concerned about the use of technology and its effect on nursing practice. Even before the use of high technology, nurses grappled with issues such as how the use of devices helped or hindered their nursing practice. Did equipment separate them from actual patient care or did it enhance that care? Furthermore, Sandelowski raises the issue about how the use of technology affected the public's image of nursing "as an academic and caring profession involving intellectual and empathic skills" (p. 4). The researcher suggests the use of technology was central to nursing's discussion about whether it was an art, a science, or a craft.

Sandelowski (1997) defines *technology* as "the use of material objects to achieve practical human ends" (p. 4). She clarifies the definition: although the history of technology is "historically and culturally 'context dependent'" (p. 4), technology is shaped by the use of material items rather than defined by human nature. Craft technology, which is different from a machine or automated technology, was the primary type of technology available to nurses between the 1870s and 1940s. Craft technology required a person to use and to direct. During this period, physicians introduced the use of thermometers, stethoscopes, microscopes, and x-ray and electrocardiograph machines, which ultimately distanced them from patients and further delineated the separation of nursing and the medical profession. During this same period, however, nurses used other types of equipment to enable them to provide direct patient comfort and care.

Sandelowski (1997) carefully identifies the primary sources used, such as advice journals and instructional literature, hospital and training school manuals, photographs, drawings, ephemera, hospital correspondence, and student lecture notes. Secondary sources were found in the "history of nursing and medical technology" (p. 5). Although Sandelowski clearly identifies the primary source materials, she does not clearly identify the secondary sources; consequently, they are more difficult to determine.

Throughout the narrative, Sandelowski (1997) leads readers through changes in nursing practice as a result of technology. The story is interesting and Sandelowski never leads readers too far from the subject of the article. Nursing practice and the technology that nurses use to practice remain the central theme of the article. Sandelowski creatively tells the story of nursing and delineates categories of technology nurses used over time. One of the categories, "in-the-flesh" (p. 5) techniques, highlights elements of nursing practice, such as observation, positioning, and lifting. Nurses were expected to use their trained senses in touch, smell, and sight as well as to use their voices to soothe clients. Another technology category, "device-mediated procedures" (p. 6), includes aspects of care such as administering medications or applying poultices. Anything that required an appliance, utensil, implement, or other material object composed this category of technology.

Sandelowski (1997) explicates the different meanings technology had in nursing practice and the central role it has played in delineating the relationship between nurses and physicians. The explanation also highlights the nurse's closeness to patients mediated through the objects that assisted nurses to provide care. For example, the researcher points out that the literature frequently addresses the bed—a common device that demanded nurses' "painstaking attention" (p. 6). Nursing practice until the 1930s warranted the use of noninvasive procedures, such as the application of heat or cold, splints, or bandages, and wound care. With the introduction of more invasive types of technologic devices, nurses incorporated into their practice the use of inhalers, suction tubes, irrigation, and catheterization. Their work brought them inside the patient's body—into an intimate zone.

The researcher traces the origins of technologic equipment such as the hypodermic needle and describes the resultant changes to medical and nursing practice. For example, it was not until the 1930s that it became acceptable for nurses to administer intramuscular injections. Yet, physicians still maintained control over other invasive skin-piercing treatments, such as beginning an intravenous instillation. Nurses were expected to know everything about, and assisted physicians with, skin-piercing procedures but were unable to incorporate the procedures into their routine practice until much later. Sandelowski interprets the control of technology as a means of maintaining a clear line between medical and nursing practice. The determination of who could use technology further delineated the authority medicine maintained over nursing.

The study raises other issues in nursing practice. Nurses were expected to use what they had, make good, or make the best of things. "Making the best of things," the phrase in the article title, so aptly describes the expectation that nurses could and should adapt their skills and equipment to provide comfort and care to clients. Nurses were to be conscious of preserving resources and not to inadvertently increase the cost to patients (clearly an issue nurses contend with in the 1990s). Sandelowski suggests that nurses received little, if any, reward for the devices they invented to save time, money, and discomfort. Furthermore, she explains, nurses were either never aware of the option of royalties or were kept in the dark by manufacturers that never offered that option.

The researcher carefully interprets her findings throughout the narrative and uses the various source materials to support her interpretations. Sandelowski uses frequent quotes and direct references to illustrate nurses' use of devices in client care, a subject widely discussed in the source materials. For example, nurses were evaluated on the use and the "appreciation of equipment" (Sandelowski, 1997, p. 14). Any breakage would constitute misuse of the resources and hospitals would judge the offending nurse poorly. Sandelowski pointed out that some hospitals posted on bulletin boards statistics on broken and misused equipment to teach the proper care of hospital equipment. Hospitals expected nurses to revere equipment and be ever mindful of the economic implications of breakage and misuse.

The concluding section of the article is a synthesis of findings, made relevant to the 1990s. Before World War II, during a period Sandelowski (1997) labels as the "world of the tool" (p. 15), nurses used technology that required a close, hands-on approach. Technologic devices brought them closer to patients rather than separated them from patients, as happened with physicians. Sandelowski contrasts the period under study with the world following the 1940s—the second half of the century that she labels the "world of the screen" (p. 15). During this period, technology separated nursing from direct patient care. Consequently, interpretation of data on technologic tools becomes more relevant to practice. The idea that technology in the 1990s has separated nursing from patient raises questions that nursing must address. The history of technology in nursing practice provides important insights into the practice arena that previous research has not highlighted. Sandelowski encourages further research into technology and into the issues raised by its use today.

Sandelowski studied the interplay of technology and nursing practice over time. Her report is but one example of a historical study of nursing practice. In each area of nursing practice, a history exists that researchers may study and use to explain an important aspect of that practice today.

Application to Education

Researchers interested in nursing education are concerned with varied aspects of this subject, such as an analysis of nursing texts (Davis, 1988b), the entry into practice dilemma (Leighow, 1996), the history of accreditation in Canada (Richardson, 1996), the development of university education in nursing (Baer, 1992), or the biography of an important figure in nursing education (Downer, 1989). Using historic frameworks, researchers may address topics in nursing education ranging from curriculum design to control of education. This approach not only provides background descriptive information but answers relevant questions regarding issues that concern nursing today.

Currently, topics such as adult learners, critical thinking, and cultural diversity concern nursing educators. However, historians may question whether adult learners is a new idea in nursing education and may attempt to understand this topic by studying nursing students of the past. Historians may examine past records of nurse training schools or professional studies of nursing. For example, the 1923 Goldmark (1923/1984) study *Nursing and Nursing Education in the United States* indicated that, in 1911, about 70% of the training schools required students to be aged 20 or 21 years old for admission; however, within 7 years, the age requirement had dropped to ages 18 or 19 years. Why did the admission age drop at that time and why did training schools initially believe older women would be better training school candidates? What teaching strategies worked better with older women than with younger ones? Both questions address the past and yet relate to current, pertinent issues related to adult learners.

Another contemporary issue, encouraging critical thinking among nursing students, has its roots in nursing's history. For example, in 1897, Superintendent of Bellevue Training School [Agnes] Brennan addressed the Superintendent's Society:

> An uneducated woman may become a good nurse, but never an intelligent one; she can obey orders conscientiously and understand thoroughly a sick person's need, but should an emergency arise, where is she? She works through her feelings, and therefore lacks judgment. (Brennan, 1991, p. 23)

Was Brennan referring to critical thinking when she reasoned that nurses needed to have the knowledge and theory regarding pathology to understand the appropriate care of sick people? Brennan suggested it was equally important for nurses to spend time in clinical practice learning the "character of the pulse in different patients or finding out just why some nurses can always see at a glance that this patient requires her pillow turned" (p. 24). She firmly believed that a trained nurse required both theoretical and practical knowledge and that, without both, something would be missing in the nursing care provided. As she pointed out, "Theory fortifies the practical, practice strengthens and retains the theoretical" (p. 25). Brennan discussed clearly her views on the theory–practice dichotomy that still baffles nursing educators today. However, Brennan firmly believed that nurses must be educated to think so they may practice.

Historiography has addressed the contemporary issue of cultural diversity by studying racial tensions in nursing and in society and offering researchers a better understanding of the inherent conflicts. Historians may question, Was there cultural diversity in nursing? From where did the nursing student at the beginning of the 19th century come? What socioeconomic–political background did the student bring to nursing? In the book *Black Women in White: Racial Conflict and Cooperation in the Nursing Profession, 1890–1950,* Hine (1989) described the opening of nurse training schools for African Americans who had been excluded from most of the existing U.S. nurse training schools. Of the schools that did not racially discriminate, many admitted African Americans using quotas. The very origin of the National Association of Colored Graduate Nurses (NACGN) in 1908 speaks to the early exclusion of African Americans from the first two national nursing organizations: American Society of Superintendents of Training Schools for Nurses (renamed the National League of Nursing Education in 1912) and the Associated Alumnae of the United States and Canada (renamed the American Nurses Association [ANA] in 1911). Historians need to look at what was, as well as what was not, to better understand historic events. For example, How did nursing handle cultural diversity? When did the profession welcome people of a different race, color, and creed into the profession? Who were the advocates of an integrated society?

Historians who search for answers may learn that nursing political activist Lavinia Dock spoke out against prejudicial treatment of any professional nurse. Dock (1910) cited the need for nursing to demonstrate practical ethics and ardently hoped that the nursing association (ANA) would not ever "get to the point where it draws the color line against our negro sister nurses" (p. 902). She believed that the nursing association was one place in the United States where color boundaries were not drawn. However, as the ANA expanded, Dock witnessed evidences that made her remark "that this cruel and unchristian and unethical prejudice might creep in here in our association" (p. 902). Dock said that, under no circumstances, should nurses emulate the cruel prejudices displayed by "men" and urged nurses to treat each nurse of color "as we would like to be treated ourselves" (p. 902). She supported black nursing leader Adah Thomas, who became president of the NACGN and a politically active nursing leader who, in 1929, wrote the history of African American nurses in the book *The Pathfinders* (Davis, 1988a).

Questions raised by conflicting ideas in the data and the omission of information in the narrative suggest new areas for historic inquiry. An example is Mosley's (1992) historical doctoral dissertation "A History of Black Leaders in Nursing: The Influence of Four Black Community Nurses on the Establishment, Growth, and Practice of Public Health Nursing in New York City, 1900–1930." Mosley included a section specifically addressing institutional racism as it existed in nursing during the first 30 years of the 20th century. To understand the prejudice experienced by African American nurses, Mosley focused on the lives and contributions of four leaders in public health nursing: Jessie Sleet Scales, Mabel Staupers, Elizabeth W. Tyler, and Edith M. Carter.

CRITIQUE OF A STUDY IN EDUCATION

In "An Experiment in Leadership: The Rise of Student Government at Philadelphia General Hospital Training School, 1920–1930," Egenes (1998) examines the successful initiation of a student government at the Philadelphia General Hospital Training School (PGH) between 1920 and 1930. The title clearly informs readers of the time frame and subject. Although the researcher has not specifically identified primary and secondary sources in the article, Egenes does use and clearly reference them throughout the text. For example, some of the primary sources include periodicals of the period such as *The National Hospital Record* and *The American Journal of Nursing;* reports such as the *Annual Report of the Bureau of Charities of the City of Philadelphia for the Year Ending December 31, 1919,* located in the Center for the Study of the History of Nursing; and archival material from the PGH collection and minutes of PGH Student Government Association student council meetings. Secondary sources that support the narrative include historiographies by researchers such as Kalisch and Kalisch (1986), Rosenberg (1992), and Reverby (1987). Egenes uses the historians' work to provide the contextual setting for the article, and references them appropriately. For example, Reverby's (1987) work explained how women in the 1920s had more opportunities available to them other than nursing. Jobs with considerably shorter working hours, less of the perceived drudgery, and more independence competed with careers in nursing. Egenes uses Reverby's account to explain the social context of the 1920s and its effect on recruitment of educated middle-class women into nursing. Egenes examines the establishment of self-government at PGH as a way of inducting new recruits into the profession.

The opening paragraph of Egenes's (1998) study clearly presents the purpose of the study. Despite the perceived notion that the period under study was "considered a time of little progress in nursing education (p. 71)," an experiment in reforming the authoritarian nature of training schools was underway. Egenes explains that nursing schools were under public scrutiny for the poor care of students' health. In 1906, the *Ladies Home Journal* published an account of how training schools failed to adequately nourish their nurses. Letters from nurse graduates of training schools who had undergone some of the hardships of training supported these allegations. Other articles also deplored the strict, authoritative, and militaristic-type training. Nursing leaders acknowledged and recognized this criticism as barriers to recruiting intelligent middle-class women into the ranks of the nursing profession. Egenes uses the important Rockefeller Foundation's Goldmark (1923/1984) report published in 1923 to support the need to reform nurse training. The researcher explains that the Committee for the Study of Nursing Education—the authors of the Goldmark report—called for the introduction of student government to "broaden the educational experience of training school students" (p. 72).

Egenes (1998) analyzes the data in the context of the prevailing social, political, and economic climate of the 1920s. To attract college-educated women into nursing during World War I, nursing leadership had initiated the Vassar Training Camp. The Vassar Training camp recruited college-educated nurses into nursing; the nurses received their preliminary training in 1918 at Vassar and their clinical experience at various hospital-based programs. By 1921, following the armistice, Vassar Training Camp students who had remained to complete their training met to discuss how to improve nurse training and attract other women like themselves into the profession. Egenes intersperses interesting comments from the graduates who identified the need for student government. Those women viewed student government as a means to improve morale, allow for self-expression, and recruit better students into nursing.

In addition to pointing out the nursing leadership who supported the notion of student government, Egenes (1998) also includes the ideas of opponents. Egenes explains that detractors of student government believed that "student input on nursing service issues was deemed inappropriate" (p. 74). Egenes introduces PGH by identifying the excellent reputation it held in the 1920s. PGH was considered a reputable and progressive training school: the Vassar Training Camp and the Army School of Nursing selected PGH to offer clinical courses and the Committee for the Study of Nursing Education selected PGH to serve as part of the sample for its study. PGH proved to be an excellent place to carry out an experiment in student government. In addition, the leadership of PGH under nursing leader, S. Lillian Clayton furthered the chance for the successful implementation of a student government. Clayton argued for students' personal rights on several occasions and was not adverse to identifying the poor living conditions and ways to improve them.

Egenes (1998) clearly sets the background for the experiment in student government at PGH. The story slowly unfolds and Egenes narrates it articulately. The researcher presents and appropriately documents several examples of student government outcomes. From the PGH Student Government Association student council meeting minutes, Egenes weaves a story that supports the success of such an association. Initially, the idea of such an association was considered "revolutionary and frightening" (p. 77); however, it eventually became part of the fabric of the school and served as a model for other schools. Committees were formed that addressed some of the problems students confronted at PGH, such as wearing collars that were too high on uniforms, or gaining access to late passes, or receiving "gentlemen callers." Activities increased over time to include students' varied concerns and interests, such as glee clubs, book review clubs, and basketball teams. In the 1930s, according to Egenes, the activities of PGH shifted from student government toward the organization of student activities.

The conclusion of the report contains several succinct comments that support PGH's move toward creating a more progressive environment for nursing education between 1920 and 1930. Having a viable student government at a nurse training school meant that students would have increased opportunities for learning; be able to develop leadership skills; be responsible for enforcing rules of the nurses' home (which would free administrators from that task); create an empowered student body; facilitate cooperation between faculty and students; and serve as an excellent place to learn organizational skills that the students could apply to their work in professional organizations. The school and its administrative leadership created the right environment for the experiment in student government. In contrast to the commonly held belief that most schools of nursing were considered to be "too insular and impermeable" (Egenes, 1998, p. 82) to outside forces, PGH stood as an excellent example of change brought on by progressive nursing education administrators. Egenes suggests that the experiment had a substantial effect on the development of nursing education, supporting this comment with the National League of Nursing Education 1937 publication of a revised curriculum, which encouraged nursing schools to form a student organization. The final sentence in Egenes's study, "The noble experiment of PGH promoted student development and fostered a more humane environment in hospital training schools" (p. 82), remains an important idea today. Schools of nursing, especially in the 1990s, could benefit from the promotion of student development and the fostering of a more humane educational environment.

Application to Administration

By now, it should be clear to readers that doing historical research requires creativity. Researchers may select a topic of interest and study it using different approaches. Studying the history of nursing organizations founded by nursing leaders provides researchers with a fertile field of study. An example of a nursing administration research study is one on the beginnings of the NLN, an organization that epitomizes the efforts of nurse–administrators to organize and control nursing education and practice (Birnbach & Lewenson, 1991). The NLN began in 1893 when a group of nursing superintendents in charge of nurse training schools met in Chicago at the Canada and Columbian Exposition. Superintendents throughout the United States met and founded the American Society of Superintendents of Training Schools for Nurses. In 1912, this organization became the National League of Nursing Education, and, in 1952, became the NLN. Superintendents started this organization so they could collectively address the issues confronting the developing profession. They advocated reforms such as improving educational standards, developing uniform training school curricula, decreasing working hours, and increasing the number of years of training. Through their efforts, the organization developed needed educational reforms in nursing and fostered the control of practice.

To study nursing administration, researchers might use biographies of nursing leaders. A biography offers insight into the characteristics of people as well as their role. Biographies of leaders before the modern nursing movement, such as the one done by Griffon (1998) on Mary Seacole, give a different perspective on women who contributed to establishing independent practice and setting the stage for future nurses. A biography need not be limited to one person but may compare and contrast the relationships among a group of leaders, such as the study by Poslusny (1989): "Feminist Friendship: Isabel Hampton Robb, Lavinia Lloyd Dock, and Mary Adelaide Nutting." The following section discusses the biographic study of Mary Seacole to demonstrate a critique of a study related to nursing administration.

CRITIQUE OF A STUDY IN ADMINISTRATION

The often unheard of contribution by Mary Seacole to nursing history is recorded in the Griffon (1998) study "A Somewhat Duskier Skin: Mary Seacole in the Crimea." Griffon researched Mary Seacole's life and explains why the British did not accept her in the same way they did Florence Nightingale. Both women served as nurses during the Crimean War and both earned the respect of the people for whom they cared. Despite some similarities between the two women, the differences blocked Seacole from sharing in the same historic fame. Griffon analyzes four reasons why Seacole was overlooked in the history of medicine and uses them to explain that omission. First, although Seacole was from British–ruled Jamaica, the English did not consider her British. Second, Seacole lived in a patriarchal society and was expected to stay within the bounds of female domesticity. Third, Seacole's background or her "duskier skin" (p. 122) kept her from being considered respectable in the eyes of many of the British upper class. Fourth, Seacole's knowledge of medical remedies was considered unacceptable for women of that period and kept her from being fully accepted and acknowledged by the British power elite.

The article title uses Seacole's own words to describe her mulatto background and her experiences in the Crimea. Although the title does not delineate a time frame, dates of Seacole's life and the events in the Crimea are interspersed throughout the report. Griffon uses Seacole's autobiography *The Wonderful Adventures of Mrs. Seacole in Many Lands* and articles published in *The Times* in 1854 as some of the primary sources. To explain the context in which Seacole lived, Griffon relies heavily on several secondary sources: historiographies by Rendall (1991), Summers (1988), Lorimer (1978), and Baly (1986). Griffon uses the primary and secondary materials to weave the history of Seacole's life, beginning with her birth in Jamaica in 1805. Seacole's father was an army officer from Scotland who was stationed in Jamaica. Her mother, a free black slave, ran a boarding house frequented by British soldiers and their families. Seacole's mother practiced the "Creole medical art" and taught Seacole many of the African herbal remedies as well as the practice of midwifery (Griffon, 1998, p. 116).

Griffon (1998) explores the social context in which Seacole was raised. During the 1800s, women were expected to stay at home and not venture out to cure ill people. In defiance of these restrictions, Seacole traveled extensively, freely offering her medicinal treatments. After a brief marriage, Seacole successfully managed her mother's hotel and, like her mother, became known for her work caring for sick people. During a yellow fever epidemic in 1853, the authorities asked Seacole to "take charge of the nursing arrangements at the military encampment" (p. 116).

The narrative is interesting; it explains the poor condition the British army found themselves in at beginning of the Crimean War. Griffon suggests that the British army in 1854 was unprepared to handle day-to-day operations and care for sick and wounded soldiers. Griffon explains how the army had been depleted during the 40 years that followed the Napoleonic Wars. Within 1 month of the arrival of 27,000 British soldiers, 8,000 had died of cholera or malaria. The Crimea lacked medical staff and nursing personnel as well as bandages to dress wounds.

The desperate conditions in the Crimea were reported in Britain; the reports resulted in widespread public concern about the soldiers' safety and support for the troops. Florence Nightingale offered her expertise to lead a group of women to care for wounded soldiers. Because of her political connections, Nightingale was appointed as the superintendent of the Female Nursing Establishment of the General Hospitals in Turkey. Among the women who volunteered to serve with Nightingale in the Crimea was Mary Seacole. However, Nightingale turned Seacole away, as did several other military offices where she had applied.

In the compelling text, Griffon compares Nightingale's work and her well-known heroic efforts to nurse the troops with the lesser known efforts of Mary Seacole. Griffon points out that one of the differences between

Nightingale and Seacole was that Nightingale spent much of her time as an administrator of the military hospital in Scutari, whereas Seacole was on the battlefield providing nursing care. In addition, Nightingale served as an emissary of the British government, whereas Seacole sponsored her own travel and had set up a hotel where she provided nursing care to wounded soldiers. Griffon (1998) indicates that the research reveals many soldiers remembered Seacole for her life-saving activities. Even Nightingale eventually acknowledged Seacole's contributions.

When the war ended in 1856, Seacole left the Crimea and returned penniless to England. Griffon describes how Seacole lived through difficult financial times, reporting that benefactors who recognized her heroic efforts during the war frequently supported her. Little is known about Seacole's later years; she died in 1881.

In "Analysis," one of the final sections of the report (Griffon, 1998, p. 21), Griffon presents the four reasons for Seacole's omission from "the history of medicine" (p. 21). It is unclear why Griffon uses medical history instead of nursing history as a framework, other than because of Griffon's own bias, background, or interest. How researchers interpret the findings as well as the type of lens they use to interpret the findings, such as a medical history framework or nursing history framework, set the tone for the narrative and the analysis of the material.

Griffon (1998) refers to Seacole's work more in terms of the medical services Seacole the "doctress" (p. 122) provided, rather than as a provider of nursing care. Griffon contends "that the very style of Creole medicine may also have caused friction" (p. 123) for Seacole. Griffon reasons that perhaps Nightingale denied Seacole's offer to serve with the Nurses' Enlistment Centre because Nightingale may have been uncomfortable with Seacole's use of Creole medicine and may have felt the use would have jeopardized the nurses' work.

Particularly interesting are Griffon's (1998) conclusions, which provide further insight into why Nightingale was remembered rather than Seacole and others who had served as nurses during the Crimean War. Griffon attributes Nightingale's fame to her continued efforts to improve and reform health care throughout her lifetime. Nightingale's work far exceeded her heroic efforts in the Crimea. Her prolific writings about hospital administration, sanitary measures, architecture, and statistics contributed to her legendary stature. Seacole, on the other hand, was known for her work in the Crimean War on what Griffon describes as a "local basis" (p. 124). Seacole chose to live a more retiring life than Nightingale and therefore did not build on her brief fame. In addition, Griffon suggests that the British xenophobic ethnocentrism contributed to Seacole's entry into anonymity.

Griffon's (1998) historical study about Seacole also concludes that the politics of Victorian culture kept Nightingale and Seacole apart, even though they both had stepped out of their prescribed female roles. In one insight, Griffon speculates that, if Mary Seacole had been accepted by the

Nurses' Enlistment Centre, she might not have opened her own hotel or functioned in such an independent capacity.

Mary Seacole was an administrator of her own hotel and her own practice; therefore, her life history enlightens us. The historical study of her life provides a way to understand nursing administration at a crucial point before the beginning of the modern nursing movement.

Summary

In nursing practice, education, and administration, historians have an opportunity to study different facets of nursing. Creativity, an open mind, and fortitude assist historical researchers to find new sources to study; make connections among events, ideas, and people; and critically analyze the findings. No less important to this process is the ability to write an interesting narrative that holds readers' attention and permits the flow of ideas. Insights from historical studies such as technology in nursing, experiments in leadership, and the life of Mary Seacole contribute to nursing knowledge and thus provide us with another way to evaluate contemporary issues in nursing.

REFERENCES

Annual Report of the Bureau of Charities of the City of Philadelphia for the year ending December 1919 (1920) Philadelphia: City of Philadelphia 9-19. Center for the study of the History of Nursing, School of Nursing. University of Pennsylvania (hereafter cited as CNHN) Accession #1993-14.

Baer, E. (1992). Aspirations unattained: The story of the Illinois Training School's search for university status. *Nursing Research, 41*(1), 43–48.

Baly, M. (1986). *Florence Nightingale and the nursing legacy.* London: Croom Helm.

Barzun, J., & Graff, H. F. (1985). *The modern researcher* (4th ed.). San Diego, CA: Harcourt Brace Jovanovich.

Birnbach, N., & Lewenson, S. (Eds.). (1991). *First words: Selected addresses from the National League for Nursing 1894–1933.* New York: National League for Nursing Press.

Bloch, M. (1964). *The historian's craft.* New York: Vantage Books.

Brennan, A. (1991). Comparative value of theory and practice in nursing. In N. Birnbach & S. Lewenson (Eds.), *First words: Selected addresses from the National League for Nursing 1894–1933* (pp. 23–25). New York: National League for Nursing Press. (Original speech presented 1897)

Bullough, B. (1992). Alternative models for specialty nursing practice. *Nursing and Health Care, 13*(5), 254–259.

Care, D., Gregory, D., English, J., & Venkatesh, P. (1996). A struggle for equality: Resistance to commissioning of male nurses in the Canadian military, 1952–1967. *Canadian Journal of Nursing Research, 28*(1), 103–117.

Davis, S. (1988a). Adah Belle Samuels Thomas. In V. Bullough, O. M. Church, & A. P. Stein (Eds.), *American nursing: A biographical dictionary* (pp. 313–316). New York: Garland.

Davis, S. (1988b). *Evolution of the American nursing history text: 1907–1983* (University Microfilm International Order No. PUZ8906485). New York: Columbia University, Teachers College.

Dock, L. (1910). Report of the thirteenth annual convention. *American Journal of Nursing, 10*(11), 902.

Downer, J. L. (1989). *Education for democracy: Isabel Stewart and her education, 1878–1963* (University Microfilm International Order No. PUZ9013541). New York: Columbia University, Teachers College.

Egenes, K. J. (1998). An experiment in leadership: The rise of student government at Philadelphia General Hospital Training School, 1920–1930. *Nursing History Review, 6,* 71–84.

Goldmark, J. (1984). *Nursing and nursing education in the United States.* New York: Garland. (Original work published 1923)

Griffon, D. P. (1998). "A somewhat duskier skin": Mary Seacole in the Crimea. *Nursing History Review, 6,* 115–127.

Hamilton, D. B. (1996). The seventh star: Dorothy Ford Buschmann and the founding of Sigma Theta Tau. *Image, 28*(2), 177–180.

Hecktor, L. M., & Touhy, T. A. (1997). The history of the bath: From art to task? Reflections for the future. *Journal of Gerontological Nursing, 5,* 7–15.

Hine, D. C. (1989). *Black women in white: Racial conflict and cooperation in the nursing profession, 1890–1950.* Bloomington: Indiana University Press.

Kalisch, P., & Kalisch, B. (1986). *The advance of American nursing* (2nd ed.). Boston: Little, Brown.

Leighow, S. R. (1996). Backrubs vs. Bach: Nursing and the entry-into-practice debate, 1946–1986. *Nursing History Review, 4,* 3–17.

Lorimer, D (1978). *Colour, class and the Victorian.* Leicester, England: Leicester University Press.

Lusk, B. (1997). Professional classifications of American nurses (1910–1935). *Western Journal of Nursing Research, 19*(2), 227–242.

Lynaugh, J. (1996). Editorial. *Nursing* History Review, *4,* 1.

Mackintosh, C. (1997). A historical study of men in nursing. *Journal of Advanced Nursing, 26,* 232–236.

Mosley, M. O. P. (1992). A history of blacks in nursing: The influence of four black community health nurses on the establishment, growth, and practice of public health nursing in New York City, 1906–1930. (Doctoral dissertation, Columbia University, 1992).

National League for Nursing Education Committee on Curriculum (1937). A curriculum guide for schools of nursing. New York: NLNE.

Newell, R. L. M. (1995). Historical perspective: Spondylolysis, an historical review. *Spine, 20*(17), 1950–1956.

Olson, T. (1996). Fundamental and special: The dilemma of psychiatric–mental health nursing. *Archives of Psychiatric Nursing, 10*(1), 3–10.

Poslusny, S. (1989). Feminist friendship: Isabel Hampton Robb, Lavinia Lloyd Dock, and Mary Adelaide Nutting. *Image, 21*(2), 64–68.

Rendall, J. (1991). *Women in an industrializing society: England 1750–1880.* Oxford, England: Basil Blackwell.

Reverby, S. M. (1987). *Ordered to care: The dilemma of American nursing, 1850–1945.* New York: Cambridge University Press.

Richardson, S. (1996). The historical relationship of nursing program accreditation and public policy in Canada. *Nursing History Review, 4,* 19–41.

Rosenberg, C. (1992). *Explaining epidemics and other studies in the history of medicine.* New York: Cambridge University Press.

Russell, D. (1997). An oral history project in mental health nursing. *Journal of Advanced Nursing, 26,* 489–495.

Sandelowski, M. (1997). "Making the best of things": Technology in American nursing, 1870–1940. *Nursing History Review, 5,* 3–22.

Sarnecky, M. T. (1997). Nursing in the American Army from the Revolution to the Spanish American War. *Nursing History Review, 5,* 49–69.

Seacole, M. (1998). The wonderful adventures of Mrs. Seacole in many lands (reprint). New York: Oxford University Press.

Spieseke, A. W. (1953). What is the historical method of research? *Nursing Research, 2*(1), 36–37.

Summers, A. (1988). *Angels and citizens. British women as military nurses, 1854-1914.* London: Routledge & Kegan Paul.

Sutherland, J. A. (1995). Historical concept analysis of empathy. *Issues in Mental Health Nursing, 16,* 555–556.

Wolf, A. (1991). How can general duty be made more attractive to graduate nurses? In N. Birnbach & S. Lewenson (Eds.), *First words: Selected addresses from the National League for Nursing, 1894–1933* (pp. 138–147). New York: National League for Nursing Press. (Original speech presented 1928)

RESEARCH ARTICLE

Historical Research Approach:
"Making the Best of Things"
Technology in American Nursing, 1870–1940

MARGARETE SANDELOWSKI
School of Nursing
University of North Carolina at Chapel Hill

It has become commonplace in contemporary nursing literature to describe, laud, or lament the impact of technology on nursing.[1] Whether appearing as the main subject matter of a text or only in a passing reference, *technology* is usually depicted as a critical and explanatory event in nursing history. The effect of this is to divide nursing history into two periods: (1) before World War II and (2) after, with the incorporation of "high" or "modern" technology, such as vital function monitoring and assisted ventilation systems. The implication here is either that there was no technology in nursing before the advent of critical or intensive care nursing, or that the impact on nursing of whatever technology existed before the 1960s was essentially unremarkable. Julie Fairman found that nurses who worked in the first special care units in the late 1950s did not think of familiar equipment, such as sphygmomanometers, chest tubes, tracheotomy tubes, and catheters as technology, but rather reserved this term for such new devices as dialysis machines and cardiac monitors.[2] Feminist critics of technology studies have noted a Western and masculinist cultural tendency to think of only the most modern, spectacular, and dramatic equipment (often of primary interest to men) as technology or as significant technology.[3]

The technology that nurses began to incorporate into their practice after World War II was, in many respects, very different from the technology that prevailed in nursing before that time, and it engendered problems, especially ethical dilemmas, for nurses who had not previously encountered it. But there are also important technology issues that have not changed in American nursing history. Nursing concerns about the nature and use of devices and about what devices mean for the care of patients and for the advancement of nursing have not been confined to encounters with "high" technology. Nurses have always sought to understand and to make the best of the things that have increasingly and paradoxically both defined and blurred the definition of their practice. They have advised and admonished each other about the use and abuse of devices and the problems of simultaneously "nursing the equipment" and nursing the patient.[4] They have also been concerned about how the use of these things has contributed to or detracted from the image of nursing as an academic and caring profession involving intellectual and empathic skills. Indeed, devices have always been central to debates concerning the relationship between the hands and the mind and spirit of the nurse and whether nursing is best understood as primarily an art, a science, or a craft.[5]

Nursing History Review 5(1997):3–22. Copyright © 1997 by The American Association for the History of Nursing.

In this article, I describe the technology of American nursing and some of the issues and problems nurses encountered around this technology, from the appearance of the first trained nurses in the 1870s to the beginning of World War II. I use the term "technology" to refer primarily to the use of material objects to achieve practical human ends. Although the meaning of technology is historically and culturally "context dependent" and encompasses much more than things,[6] the essence of technology can nevertheless be said to lie in things. The means, ends, and expressions of technology are physical or material.[7] Accordingly, I only allude here to such issues of critical importance in nursing history as the transformation of nursing work and thought and the altered social relations and division of labor resulting from the delegation, or transfer, of technology from medicine to nursing.

Between the 1870s and the 1940s, craft (as opposed to machine or automated) technology prevailed in nursing practice. Craft technology may be differentiated from other technology by the individualized (as opposed to standardized) use of implements that require human energy and direction (as opposed to external sources of energy and direction).[8] Although medical practice in this same time period was transformed by devices such as the thermometer, stethoscope, microscope, and X-ray and electrocardiograph machines, which placed a new emphasis on diagnosis and served to distance physicians from patients,[9] nursing practice (or those techniques nurses performed themselves on their own initiative or under orders from the physicians) remained focused on patient comfort and continued to be characterized by techniques and devices that maintained intimate physical contact with patients.[10]

The primary sources I used included advice and instructional literature for nurses (i.e., textbooks and professional journal articles), hospital and training school procedure manuals, medical trade and advertising ephemera, photographs and drawings, and a miscellaneous collection of materials, such as hospital correspondence and student lecture notes. I also had the opportunity to see and handle in museum collections certain implements used in practice in the late nineteenth and early twentieth centuries, such as glass cups and metal scarifiers for wet cupping. Many of the devices used then (e.g., glass thermometers, enema cans with rubber tubing, manually operated beds) were still in use when I began to practice as a nurse in the late 1960s. The secondary sources I used were in the history of nursing and medical technology. Together, these sources offer a basis for understanding continuity and change in the history of technology in nursing, a story that remains largely untold.

"COMMON UTENSILS AND APPLIANCES"

From the appearance of the first trained nurses in the 1870s through the 1930s, American nursing practice was largely concerned with providing for the physical needs and comfort of, administering physical therapies to, and managing the physical environment of ailing patients and childbearing women.[11] Nursing work comprised two large categories of techniques. The first category included "in-the-flesh" techniques,[12] such as observation, positioning, and lifting, which involved only (or primarily) nurses' "trained" senses of sight, hearing, smell, and touch; deft and gentle hands; and strong back and limbs. Nurses were taught to cultivate their senses for the close observation that made nursing a scientific profession, as opposed to a merely mechanical practice. Yet their hands were singled out for the development of the manual dexterity and sure, swift, and sensitive touch that made trained nursing indispensable to patients and physicians.[13] Although nurses were cautioned to "use [their] eyes and ears, but not the tongue,"[14] they were to use their voices to soothe patients. Indeed, one of the reasons nurses were initially viewed as ideal to give anesthesia was because the feminine voice calmed the patient for an easier induction; nurse anesthesia was often referred to as "vocal anesthesia."[15] Nursing practice was also physically arduous, requiring nurses to push, pull, lift, and carry heavy patients and objects. In short, the body of the nurse was the critical element in ministering to the body of the patient.

The second category of techniques included the device-mediated procedures, such as medication administration, the application of poultices, catheterization, and purgation, which involved or required the use of a variety of appliances, utensils, implements, and other material objects. Even with the increasing availability of utilities such as electricity and central plumbing, which reduced physical labor, these objects relied for their use largely on the manipulations and muscle power of the nurse. The physical world of the nurse typically involved familiar and everyday objects, or "common utensils and appliances,"[16] generally found in the home and not at all exclusive to nursing or medical care. Indeed, nursing practice included a wide range of household and domestic work and therefore included cooking, housekeeping, and child care crafts.[17] Examples of such everyday objects were the materials, implements, and chemical solutions used for bed-making, bathing, bandaging, feeding, cleaning, and the implementation of various water and mechanical therapies. Watches, safety pins, needles and threads, ice picks, and matches were included among the "equipment of the nurse's bag."[18] Early anesthesia, for which nurses were often largely responsible, involved no more than a "bottle and rag."[19]

The bed, in particular, was portrayed as an object demanding the painstaking attention of the nurse: the "greatest part of her work is around, about, and with the bed,"[20] and patients were often "condemned to weeks of imprisonment in bed."[21] Dozens of kinds of beds were differentiated in instructional texts for nurses according to cases (e.g., surgical versus obstetric), therapeutic intent or purpose (e.g., for resting versus a pelvic examination), and the primary therapeutic modality employed (e.g., air versus water beds).[22] Nurses expressed preferences for what they viewed as the best materials out of which to construct beds (e.g., brass, iron, or wood) and bedding (e.g., linen, straw, rubber) to achieve the various purposes for which they were used and to facilitate maintenance and hygiene. Dozens of kinds of bandages, poultices, and other external remedies, as well as cleansing and therapeutic baths, were also important foci of didactic literature for nurses, with instruction including the materials and containers needed to make, apply, or provide the most functional, effective, and aesthetically pleasing treatments.[23]

Fewer of the objects that nurses used in practice, such as the hypodermic syringe and the urinary catheter, distinctively signaled nursing, or a kind of specialized work. Nurses shared the use of these objects with physicians. Even in the many cases where nurses were the primary and probably (by virtue of greater use) more proficient users of these things and in the better position to determine when and under what conditions they should be used, they were viewed as medical (as opposed to nursing) objects, to be used only by order or under the direction of physicians. In theory, if not actually, nurses worked as agents for physicians. Indeed, physicians viewed nursing care as a kind of medical therapy and increasingly became dependent on nurses to harness the benefits of technological advances in diagnosis, medical therapeutics, anesthesia, and surgery.[24]

The devices nurses typically used in their practice generally extended their (and, nominally, physicians') reach over and into the patient's body. Most nursing practice through the 1930s involved ministrations to the outside of the body, including applications of heat and cold, poultices and dressings, and splints and bandages. Typical courses of training included the application of cups and leeches, dressing bedsores and wounds, and applying friction, fomentations, and other irritants and counterirritants.

Fewer techniques involved the use [of] devices to enter body orifices, but those that did increasingly characterized nursing as opposed to medical practice. Nurses instilled and removed air and gases, fluids, and substances for various cleansing, nutritional, and other therapeutic purposes. They used inhalers and tents for various kinds of respiratory and oxygen therapies, rubber or glass tubing to suction, gavage, lavage, administer enemas, douche, irrigate, and catheterize. These kinds of bodily entries emphasized the viscerality and "dirty work" of everyday nursing practice,[25] which involved handling human excrement and waste and bound nurses and patients in the most intimate and often embarrassing of human contacts.

Even fewer nursing procedures involved needles, such as the hypodermic injection and hypodermoclysis. Although nurses gave hypodermic injections in the nineteenth century and hypodermoclysis injections in the early twentieth century (both involving insertion of needles in tissue just beneath the skin), it was not until well into the 1930s that it was considered appropriate for a nurse to administer intramuscular injections.[26] Intravenous instillations of substances and the removal of blood remained controversial as nursing functions until well into the 1960s.[27] Many activities that involved deep piercing of the body with a needle or other implement were seen as exclusively in the physician's domain, with nurses only assisting. Yet assistance here typically meant doing everything involved in the procedure except the discrete act of piercing the skin. That is, whether assisting physicians to perform a paracentesis or lumbar puncture or surgery, nurses were expected to have the knowledge to prepare and set up the equipment, prepare the patient and the room, and care for the patient and equipment after the procedure, which included watching for untoward treatment effects and cleaning up. This kind of division of labor, in which nurses did "everything but" (in the case of needle therapies, everything but the act of penetration), often characterized the process by which the use of devices was delegated to nurses. That is, the transfer of technology from medicine to nursing was controlled to maintain a line between medicine and nursing and even the dominance and authority of physicians over nurses.

Because of the design and purposes of the devices nurses commonly used, the kinds of devices available, and the strict controls placed on nurses by physicians, few devices extended either the senses or interpretive capacities of the nurse. That is, few devices entailed an embodiment relationship between nurse and machine,[28] helping them see, hear, or feel better or differently. Nurses did not routinely use such sense extenders as microscopes and stethoscopes. Taking the blood pressure with a sphygmomanometer and stethoscope did not become part of routine nursing practice until the 1930s.[29]

Moreover, few devices entailed hermeneutic relationships with devices.[30] That is, few devices demanded that nurses interpret the texts produced by instruments or machines. When the thermometer first made its way into nursing practice in the late nineteenth century, nurses were only responsible for reading and recording the number registered at the top of the column of mercury. Only physicians were obligated and even deemed capable of interpreting the meaning of that number and initiating clinical action on the basis of that interpretation. Indeed, an argument apparently offered for why it might be acceptable to delegate the use of the thermometer, a medical "instrument of precision,"[31] to nurses was that they would not be distracted by everything physicians knew about the science of clinical thermometry and thus make mistakes in reading it.[32]

"A MANIA FOR ADAPTING AND INVENTING"

In addition to using familiar household objects and objects exclusive to nursing or medical care, nurses also transformed everyday objects into implements for comfort and healing. They used bedside tables to relieve dyspnea,[33] and they fashioned bed supports out of broom handles.[34] The innovative use of the broom handle not only provided comfort to the patient, but it was also labor-saving; it saved nurses from the physical exertions of tugging and lifting patients who were constantly sliding down in their beds. Moreover, as exemplified by the bedside table and the broom handle, relatively few of the objects nurses used in practice had, or were restricted because of their design to, only one purpose. In the hands of nurses, everyday objects often became "technological objects" in the domain of nursing.[35]

Indeed, a prevailing theme in instructional and advice literature for nurses was the need to improvise and to use their ingenuity in using, fashioning, and transforming existing objects to provide nursing care.[36] Private duty nurses in the home, who were faced with "a deficient supply of things" available to hospital nurses for whom "everything is at hand,"[37] were especially encouraged to improvise and were counseled on how to use the implements they had for a variety of purposes. A 1935 photograph, taken in the home of a Maternity Center Association patient, shows the nurse how to set up a room for a home delivery by making good use of articles normally found there. This improvised room, which featured a soft bed, newspapers, linens, jars, and basins, stood in sharp aesthetic contrast to the hard metal furnishings and equipment shown in a photograph of a delivery room at New York Hospital.[38] But it demonstrated how nurses could "imitate hospital conditions in the home" by using the "utensils and materials . . . at hand."[39]

Nurses were repeatedly admonished not to waste the resources nor add to the expenses of their patients, no matter whether their parents were economically advantaged or disadvantaged, by having them buy unnecessary implements. Public health nurses, who also had limited access to the latest hospital equipment and for whom "tools [were] as necessary for doing a good piece of public health work as [were] the hundred and one mechanical appliances in a machinist's kit,"[40] were similarly encouraged to use their ingenuity in making and adapting devices in the home.

As one nurse summarized it, nursing involved "making the best of things."[41] With "fire, water, salt, and newspapers, [the nurse] will seldom be embarrassed in any emergency."[42] Instead of a fountain syringe, a nurse could use a funnel and rubber tubing.[43] Instead of forceps, a nurse could use a clothespin. Nurses could refashion teapots and flower sprinklers into enema cans.[44] They could turn miners' pails into stupe kettles.[45] They could use paper bags as inhalers.[46] The "nursing appliances" exhibited at the 1903 meeting of the American Society of Superintendents of Training Schools for Nursing demonstrated the interest nurses had in devices,[47] the value they placed on ingenuity, and even somewhat of "a mania for adapting and inventing."[48] Nurses were encouraged to see the things around them in new ways and not be easily or unnecessarily taken in by the latest inventions.

Indeed, it was easy to be seduced by new appliances. One student nurse, on a tour of her hospital in 1930, wrote in her log that the instruments in a sterilization room "took my eye immediately." She found the infant respirator, one of only four such machines in the country, "the most interesting part of the whole trip."[49]

Nurses were encouraged to be inventive by adapting ready-to-hand objects, but they were also, if not as frequently, cautioned not to ignore the inventions that were not so ready to hand and even to invent these kinds of devices themselves. Nurses were invited to publicize their improvisations and inventions. Professional nursing journals, such as the Trained Nurse (and later the Trained Nurse and Hospital Review) and the American Journal of Nursing, regularly featured articles about, photographs and drawings of, and brief written descriptions on the latest "remedies and appliances" either invented for use by nurses or invented by nurses themselves.[50]

Although improvisation constituted an important and often unrecognized kind of invention, nurses were encouraged to move beyond simply making do with what they had and to collaborate with manufacturers to place new inventions of primary usefulness to nurses on the market. The invention and manufacture of the Good Samaritan Infusion Radiator, featured in a 1931 American Journal of Nursing article, was offered as an example of the successful collaboration possible between a nurse inventor and manufacturer.[51] The New York City Board of Health adopted another nurse's invention of a new plug for infant bottles.[52]

As one nurse argued, instead of "grumbling" about the inadequacies of hospital furniture, nurses needed to study this furniture with a view toward "chanc[ing] on a remunerative invention."[53] Nurses were intimately concerned with hospital furnishings and were therefore in the best position to create equipment that conserved the time and energy of the nurses (and others) who had to use it. Patients could not be well served if the people around them were struggling with poorly designed equipment. Nurses were advised of the opportunities and even the obligation they had to participate in "original work in the improvement of hospital appliances."[54] There were no persons better suited to this work than the women who daily struggled with the problems and impediments to patient care the poorly designed appliances presented. Indeed, one nurse lamented that, even in hospitals boasting complete operating rooms, X-ray departments, laboratories, and the latest equipment for hydrotherapy and electrotherapy, there was no satisfactory equipment for nursing. Using the same object for different purposes could actually harm patients and impede efficient practice, as when infectious organisms were transferred on basins used for both clean and dirty procedures and when the overuse of devices contributed to their early destruction.[55]

Nurses applauded labor-saving products and utilities, such as the electric pad that warmed solutions to be administered internally to patients, beds and carts with rubber wheels, and a central water supply to fill bathtubs. Much of the nurses' work obligated them to carry heavy objects to and from designated areas while maintaining the proper temperature and cleanliness of these items. As one nurse noted about the electric warming pad, "only nurses who have, quite literally, spent hours in filling and carrying hot water bags intended to keep solutions warm, can appreciate fully the simplicity of this carefully worked-out device."[56]

Although "necessity [was] the mother of invention," nurses had to anticipate needs, rather than wait for "dire necessity" to occur.[57] Not only might nursing intervention be impeded by too much improvisation (or too great a readiness to make do), it was also thwarted by the lack of recognition of nurses' contributions to the design of equipment. The "individuality of the inventor [was often] totally lost."[58] Either nurses were unaware of the commercial opportunities available to them or manufacturers deliberately contributed to their ignorance by preferring that "royalties never [be] considered."[59]

"BUY THE BEST"

Instructional texts for nurses emphasized improvisation, or *making the best of things*, and, less frequently, invention, or *making the best things*. Yet a third emphasis was on *buying the best things*. Instructional, but primarily promotional, literature advised nurses that the effectiveness of their work and their reputation in the eyes of physicians depended, in part, on buying the best equipment. Indeed, as one text addressing the "ethics of nursing" promised: "The doctor will see at a glance if your instruments are just what they should be, that you know how to keep them, and the inference will be that you know how to use them."[60] One physician encouraged nurses in private practice to always buy the best thermometers, scissors, forceps, and dressing instruments. He also suggested adding to nurses' instrument collection manometers (to determine the specific gravity of urine), litmus paper, and an 8-ounce graduated glass measure, since physicians could not carry all of these items from house to house, and it was easier for the nurse to include them as part of her outfit.[61]

Attention was given in didactic literature to the devices that should be included in the nurse's outfit, nursing bag, or pocket case.[62] Advertising literature also featured such containers. For example, the Chicago Nurse's Case (made of the "best Morocco leather" and selling for $10), shown in a 1918 catalog of surgical instruments and supplies, included vials, glass syringes and needles, forceps, thermometer, scissors, knife, probes and directors, baby scales, metal and rubber catheters, a scarifier, and razor.[63] Outfits including such items were promoted as suitable gifts for nurses.[64]

Promotional literature also included testimonials by nurses on behalf of the thermometers and other implements they favored. In 1914, in the third edition of her popular nursing text, Clara Weeks-Shaw described the clinical thermometer as "this now familiar instrument [that] is indispensable to every nurse."[65] Becton, Dickinson, and Company (B-D) featured the B-D Clinical Thermometer as the one having "found much favor among the Nursing Profession."[66] Judson Pin Company advertised the Capsheaf Safety Pin as "highly endorsed by trained nurses."[67] Meinecke and Company printed a nurse's testimonial for their Ideal Douche Pan.[68] The Lister Surgical Company claimed that nurses who used Lister's Towels preferred them to any other pads for women.[69] These advertisements, placed in nursing journals, made nurses aware of products to buy (or to recommend to physicians and hospitals for purchasing). A note from the "Publisher's Desk" of the *Trained Nurse and Hospital Review* encouraged nurses to send for sample of the products they saw advertised in the journal. Assured that the journal permitted only advertisements of reputable products, nurses were encouraged to see these ads as being as "valuable" as the other reading matter in the journal.[70]

The advertisements also appealed directly to nurses by emphasizing the value of their products for both patient comfort and safety and nursing efficiency. Moreover, they offer clues about the problems devices themselves may have posed for nurses in practice. For example, a B-D ad for clinical thermometers suggested problems with reading the markings, resetting the mercury, and preventing breakage.[71] A Taylor Instrument Companies ad, showing a drawing of a nurse with a thermometer in a Tycos Safety Case pinned to her apron, suggested that nurses often lost thermometers.[72] Judson Pin Company promised nurses a safety pin that "cannot catch in the fabric."[73] The Lister Surgical Company promised a gynecological towel that was more absorbent, did not need to be washed, and, in general, saved "time, money, and annoyance."[74] Meinecke and Company's douche pan was "ideal" because (by virtue of being "anatomically correct in shape") it did "not hurt," had a "capacious interior," and was easy to maintain "in a sanitary condition."[75]

Medical trade catalogs, although largely oriented toward the physician consumer, promoted products that solved problems nurses had in promoting patient comfort and safety and that promised to make practice safer, less laborious, and even more aesthetically pleasing. Becton, Dickinson, and Company, in their 1918 *Physician Catalog*, advertised the HY-JEN-IC thermometer as filling the requirements of nurses (and others) whenever "economy is a factor," and the Olympian thermometer as popular with nurses (and others) "preferring strength, legibility, and 'easy shakers' to quick registration."[76] Greeley Laboratories promised to meet and conquer common objections to administering medicines via hypodermic injection. These objections were caused by poorly designed syringes and needles that became clogged, stuck, slipped, leaked, and permitted breaks in aseptic technique.[77] In the Hospital Supply Company of New York 1913 *Catalogue of Sterilizers*, ad copy acknowledged the "unjustifiably disagreeable duty on nurses" to make do with the "obnoxious prevailing method of emptying bed pans into open sinks." The Climax Combined Bedpan Sterilizer and Washer made this job less disagreeable and reduced hospital odors.[78] The same company advertised the Climax Dressing Sterilizer as preventing injury to the nurse because of poor design. As pictured and described in the ad, the nurse used to be forced to "pass her arm past a hot Sterilizer and manipulate the valves in the constricted space between the apparatus and the wall."[79] A new design feature eliminated this potential hazard.

"NURSING THE EQUIPMENT"

Nurses regularly discussed the problems they encountered in using devices, whether they were as simply constructed as rubber tubing or as complex an apparatus as an oxygen tent. A procedure involving as ostensibly simple a device as the rubber tube used for an enema or colonic irrigation could be hazardous to patients and a problem for nurses; hard tips could puncture delicate membranes and rubber goods were difficult to clean and preserve.[80]

Nurses described the many nursing problems, ignored in the medical literature, that oxygen therapy caused. Physicians might order this therapy, but nurses had to administer it. That is, they had to find ways to maintain the appropriate dose or concentration of oxygen in a tent or chamber while simultaneously providing other kinds of care that allowed oxygen to escape, as when nurses bathed patients.[81] Although many of the objects nurses used routinely in practice were simply constructed, they were not necessarily simple to use and did not produce simple outcomes. As one prominent nurse author observed, applying a compress to the eyes might appear simple, but the patients' eyesight was still at stake.[82] An ostensibly simple device such as a glass thermometer was much more complicated than it seemed. Formal analyses of nursing tasks, which became increasingly common in the 1920s and 1930s, showed the complexity of even the most "elementary nursing procedures."[83]

Devices were increasingly central components of these procedures, making "nursing the equipment" as important in practice as nursing the patient.[84] Didactic texts typically emphasized the articles required for procedures both the nurse and physician performed, including the increasingly equipment-embodied domains of physical and laboratory diagnosis, surgery, anesthesia, and orthopedics. They also emphasized the before and after care of equipment, which involved selecting and then arranging devices on trays; cleaning, disinfecting, or sterilizing equipment; mending and otherwise maintaining the integrity of equipment; and preventing their destruction. A key feature of instructional literature and visual displays was the variety of specialized "trays" of equipment for the procedures nurses performed themselves or for those they assisted physicians to perform.[45] Nurses also held positions as keepers of equipment in central supply rooms in hospitals.

Nurses were evaluated not only on their technical abilities, but also on their "appreciation of equipment."[86] A nurse could be judged as extravagant and as misusing equipment. The breaking of glass syringes required a written incident report. The need to preserve glass thermometers inspired friendly rivalry among wards as to which ward had the lowest incidence of breakage.[87] In an effort to "teach care of hospital equipment," some hospitals had bulletin boards displaying the number of various devices used and destroyed in a year, how they were ruined, and the cost to replace them.[88] In the era before the widespread use of disposable devices, nurses had to develop a reverence for the things they used, if only for the sake of economy.

Nurses were also to use devices in ways that contributed to their professional mission of creating an environment most conducive to patient recovery. For example, one nurse advised that medical and surgical appliances ought not to be visible in the sick room.[89] Nurses were also concerned with the noise caused by handling the glass- and enamelware that constituted many of the devices they used.[90]

CONCLUSION: THE "WORLD OF THE TOOL"

Technological devices are a source of information about both the empirical and aesthetical dimensions, or content and form, of nursing practice.[91] These devices also entail different kinds of human engagements with and experiences of the world.[92] Indeed, the diversity of the devices used by nurses over time has in part shaped the world in which nurses practice.

The "world of the tool" in which nurses practiced prior to World War II seems to have entailed a very different engagement with technology than the "world of the screen" in which nurses now practice.[93] In the older world of the tool, nurses were typically preoccupied with the manual complexities and even physical labor of manip-ulating simply constructed yet often unyielding, fragile, and hard-to-clean items. They were also concerned with the artful and scientifically principled integration of these devices into nursing care. Yet for all of the difficulties they encountered in bending sometimes unpliable items to their will, nurses seemed to have a close and, by necessity, hands-on relationship with the tools of their trade, which, in turn, kept them in close physical contact with their patients. While physicians were increasingly looking at their patients through microscopes and X-rays, listening to them through stethoscopes, and interpreting their conditions via laboratory assays and electrocardiograms, nurses continued to maintain more direct sensory and other physical contact with their patients.

In contrast, in the contemporary world of the screen, nurses appear more physically removed from both patient and machine. They are increasingly preoccu-pied with the hermeneutic complexity of interpreting machine-generated texts (such as rhythm strips on monitor screens or numerical data in digital displays and computer printouts). Instead of problems of hand manipulation, the technology making up the world of the screen poses largely interpretive problems of distinguishing true representations from artifactual misrepresentations of patient conditions. Instead of the tool-world problem of too much physical manipulation or touching, screen technology seems to have created the new problem of not literally and figuratively touching patients enough or in the right way. Technology no longer seems to incorporate the touch of the nurse so much as it stands in physical and even paradigmatic opposition to it.[94] Although more detailed investigation is needed in the history of technology in nursing to warrant any conclusions about continuity and change, in the world of the screen, devices appear heavy because of the epistemological and even moral freight they carry. Technology now often appears at odds with the mission and ethic of nursing care. In the world of the tool, devices often seemed to be just plain heavy or hard to handle.

The renewed call for nurses to invent equipment, to forge relationships with engineers, and to be better educated concerning the making and using of devices evokes the earlier call for nurses to adapt, invent, and reinvent the world to promote nursing goals.[95] There is still a concern that nurses, because of knowledge deficits in the engineering, physical, and other scientific and technological principles and theories underlying the operations of devices, are leaving the design and development of the material world of practice to others less equipped to understand that world. In the modern calls for technological expertise, we can still hear the invitation to nurses to make the best of things, for themselves and for the patients in their care.

Margarete Sandelowski, PhD, RN, FAAN
Professor and Chair
Department of Women's and Children's Health
School of Nursing
University of North Carolina at Chapel Hill
7460 Carrington Hall
Chapel Hill, N.C. 27599

Acknowledgments
This study was supported by a Lillian Sholtis Brunner Fellowship from the Center for the Study of the History of Nursing at the University of Pennsylvania in Philadelphia. I am especially grateful to Joan Lynaugh, director of the center, for her astute advice and gentle counsel, and to Margo Szabunia, curator, and Betsy Weiss, administrative assistant, at the center for facilitating access to relevant collections. I also gratefully acknowledge the assistance of Gretchen Worden, curator at the Mutter Museum, and John Parker, reference assistant, Charles Greifenstein, reference librarian, and Keven Crawford, manuscript curator, at the Historical Services Division of the Library of the College of Physicians of Philadelphia.

Research article taken from: Sandalowski, M. (1997). "Making the best of things": Technology in American Nursing, 1870–1940. *Nursing History Review, 5,* 3–22 (reprinted with permission).

NOTES

1. See, for example, Carolyn Cooper, "The Intersection of Technology and Care in the ICU," *Advances in Nursing Science* 15, no. 3 (1993):23–32; Sally Gadow, "Touch and Technology: Two Paradigms of Patient Care," *Journal of Religion and Health* 23, no. 1

(1984): 63–69; Virginia Henderson, "The Essence of Nursing in High Technology," *Nursing Administration Quarterly 9*, no. 4 (1985):1–9; G. Laing, "The Impact of Technology on Nursing," *Medical Instrumentation* 16, no. 5 (1982): 241–42; Margarete Sandelowski, "A Case of Conflicting Paradigms: Nursing and Reproductive Technology," *Advances in Nursing Science* 10, no. 3 (1988): 34–45; J. K. Schultz, "Nursing and Technology," *Medical Instrumentation* 14, no. 4 (1980): 211–14; and Sallie Tisdale, "Swept Away by Technology," *American Journal of Nursing* 86, no. 4 (1986): 429–30 (hereafter cited as *AJN*).

2. Julie Fairman, "Watchful Vigilance: Nursing Care, Technology, and the Development of Intensive Care Units," *Nursing Research* 41, no. 1 (1992): 56–60.

3. Autumn Stanley, *Mothers and Daughters of Invention: Notes for a Revised History of Technology* (New Brunswick, N.J.: Rutgers University Press, 1995), xxxi–xxxii, and Judy Wajcman, *Feminism Confronts Technology* (University Park: Pennsylvania State University, 1991), 16–17, 137.

4. M. R. Smith, "What Are We Doing to Improve Nursing Practice, II: Through Improvement of Nursing Methods," *AJN* 32, no. 6 (1932): 685–88. Quote on p. 687.

5. See, for example, Mary M. Roberts, "Modification of Nursing Procedures as Demanded by Progress in Medicine," *Hospital Progress* 12, no. 9 (1931): 390–93, and Isabel M. Stewart, "The Science and Art of Nursing," *The Nursing Education Bulletin* 2, no. 1 (1929): 1–4.

6. Carl Mitcham, *Thinking Through Technology: The Path Between Engineering and Philosophy* (Chicago: University of Chicago Press, 1994), 152.

7. Brooke Hindle, "The Exhilaration of Early American Technology: An Essay," in *Early American Technology: Making and Doing Things from the Colonial Era to 1850*, ed. Judith A. McGraw (1966; reprint, Chapel Hill: University of North Carolina Press, 1994), 10–18.

8. Mitcham, 162, and I. R. McWhinney, "Medical Knowledge and the Rise of Technology," *The Journal of Medicine and Philosophy* 3, no. 4 (1978): 293–304.

9. See Audrey B. Davis, *Medicine and Its Technology: An Introduction to the History of Medical Instrumentation* (Westport, Conn.: Greenwood Press, 1981); Joel D. Howell, ed., *Technology and American Medical Practice, 1880–1930; Anthology of Sources* (New York: Garland Press, 1988); Stanley J. Reiser, *Medicine and the Reign of Technology* (Cambridge, U.K.: Cambridge University Press, 1978).

10. As itemized in Ethel Johns and Blanche Pfefferkorn, *An Activity Analysis of Nursing* (New York: Committee on the Grading of Nursing Schools, 1934) 150–66, even with the increasing use of electric power, the vast majority of devices nurses used in this period were nurse powered. See also Theodore J. Berry, *The Bryn Mawr Hospital, 1893–1968* (Bryn Mawr, Pa.: Bryn Mawr Hospital, 1969), 132–42; Kathleen H. McIlveen and Janice M. Morse, "The Role of Comfort in Nursing Care: 1900–1980," *Clinical Nursing Research* 4, no. 2 (1995): 127–48; and Ruth Sleeper, "The Two Inseparables: Nursing Service and Nursing Education," *AJN* 48, no. 11 (1948): 678–81.

11. See, for example, *A Handbook of Nursing for Family and General Use* (New Haven: Connecticut Training School for Nurses, 1878); *A Manual of Nursing Prepared for the Training School for Nurses Attached to Bellevue Hospital* (New York: Putnam, 1878); Annual Report, January 1878, Records of Women's Hospital of Philadelphia, Center for the Study of the History of Nursing, University of Pennsylvania School of Nursing (hereafter cited as CSHN); Carolyn V. Van Blarcom, *Obstetrical Nursing*, 1st–3d eds. (New York: Macmillan, 1992, 1928, and 1936); Joseph B. DeLee, *Obstetrics for Nurses*, 5th and 10th eds. (Philadelphia: W. B. Saunders, 1917 and 1933); Joseph B. DeLee and Mabel C. Carmon, *Obstetrics for Nurses*, 11th ed. (Philadelphia: W. B. Saunders, 1937); Minnie Goodnow, *The Technic of Nursing* (Philadelphia: W. B. Saunders, 1928); Isabel A. Hampton, *Nursing: Its Principles and Practice*, 2d ed. (Cleveland: E. C. Koeckert, 1903); Bertha Harmer, *Textbook of the Principles and Practice of Nursing*, 1st–3d eds. (New York: Macmillan, 1922, 1928, 1934); Bertha Harmer and Virginia Henderson, *Textbook of the Principles and Practice of Nursing*, 4th ed. (New York: Macmillan, 1939); Anna C. Maxwell and Amy E. Pope, *Practical Nursing: A Textbook for Nurses*, 2d ed., rev. (New York:

Putnam, 1910); Clara S. Weeks-Shaw, *A Textbook of Nursing: For the Use of Training Schools, Families, and Private Students,* 3d ed. (New York: D. Appleton, and Company 1914); and Henry L. Woodard and Bernice Gardner, *Obstetric Management and Nursing* (Philadelphia: F. A. Davis, 1936).

12. I borrowed this phrase from Don Ihde, *Technics and Praxis* (Boston: Dordrecht, 1979), 18.

13. See, for example, Harmer (1922), 7, 45; *Nursing Procedures*, Philadelphia General Hospital School of Nursing, 1924, p. 120, CSHN; Lecture no. 1, 1902, p. 4, Chautauqua School of Nursing Lecture Notes, CSHN.

14. Lecture, 17 November 1887, Mary U. Clymer Papers, CSHN.

15. Maurine Ligon, "Psychology and Suggestive Therapy in Anesthesia," *Trained Nurse and Hospital Review 96,* no. 3 (1936): 260–62. Quote on p. 260.

16. Marie Koeneke, *Nursing Procedures: The Lankenau Hospital*, 1927, Lankenau Hospital School of Nursing Records, CSHN.

17. As noted on p. 470 in the editorial "Anybody Can Nurse!" *Trained Nurse and Hospital Review* 105, no. 6 (1940): 470–72, nursing practice did not lend itself to definite lines of demarcation, with some tasks bordering on housework while others absorbed the latest medical techniques, such as blood transfusions.

18. Emily A. M. Stoney, *Practical Points in Nursing for Nurses in Private Practice*, 2d ed. (Philadelphia: W. B. Saunders, 1897), 25.

19. Martin S. Pernick, *A Calculus of Suffering: Pain, Professionalism, and Anesthesia in Nineteenth-Century America* (New York: Columbia University Press, 1985), 223.

20. Harmer (1922), 33.

21. Lecture no. 13, circa 1904, p. 4, Chautauqua School of Nursing Lecture Notes, CSHN.

22. Forty-three varieties of beds and bed-making were listed in an unpublished study referred to in Johns and Pfefferkorn, 25.

23. See, for example, citations listed in note 11 above and K. L. Milligan, "Bandaging," *Trained Nurse and Hospital Review* 41, no. 5 (1908): 299–302; E. M. Simpson, "The Bath as a Healing Agent," *AJN* 3, no. 5 (1903): 333–37.

24. William R. Houston, *The Art of Treatment* (New York: Macmillan, 1937). See also Jo Ann Ashley, *Hospitals, Paternalism, and the Role of the Nurse* (New York: Teachers College Press, 1976); Joan E. Lynaugh and Claire M. Fagin, "Nursing Comes of Age," *Image: Journal of Nursing Scholarship* 20, no. 4 (1988): 184–90; and Barbara Melosh, *"The Physician's Hand": Work Culture and Conflict in American Nursing* (Philadelphia: Temple University Press, 1982).

25. Nurses do "dirty work" in the literal and sociological sense, as introduced in Everett C. Hughes, *Men and Their Work* (Glencoe, Ill.: Free Press, 1958), 49–53.

26. See, for example, Harmer (1928), 448–68; Harmer and Henderson (1939), 565–97; and Bertha Harmer and Virginia Henderson, *Textbook of the Principles and Practice of Nursing*, 5th ed. (New York: Macmillan, 1955), 712–65.

27. See, for example, J. R. Anderzon, "Emerging Nursing Techniques: Venipuncture," *Nursing Clinics of North America*, 3, no. 1 (1968): 165–78; Jules K. Joseph, "Should We Permit Qualified Nurses to Administer Intravenous Therapy?" *Hospital Management* 64, no. 1 (1947): 65–68; "Nursing Practice and Intravenous Therapy," *AJN* 56, no. 5 (1956):572–73; "Should Nurses Do Venipunctures?" *AJN* 51, no. 10 (1951): 603–4; J. A. Willan, "How the States Stand on IV Administration by Nurses," *Hospital Topics* 40, no. 7 (1962): 41–45.

28. For a fuller explanation of embodied human-machine relations; see Ihde (1979) and Don Ihde, *Existential Technics* (Albany: State University of New York Press, 1983) and *Technology and the Lifeworld: From Garden to Earth* (Bloomington: Indiana University Press, 1990).

29. See the Harmer and the Harmer and Henderson series of textbooks cited above in note 11. The Philadelphia General Hospital School of Nursing included this technique for the first time in their 1948 procedure book. See *Nursing Procedures,* 1948, p. 40, Philadelphia General Hospital School of Nursing, CSHN.

30. For a fuller explanation of hermeneutic human-machine relations, see Ihde (1979, 1983, 1990).

31. S. Weir Mitchell, *The Early History of Instrumental Precision in Medicine*, an address before the Second Congress of the American College of Physicians and Surgeons, 23 September 1891 (New Haven, Conn.: Tuttle, Morehouse, and Taylor, 1892).

32. Reiser, 117.

33. Harmer (1922), 59.

34. "A Practical Point," *Trained Nurse and Hospital Review* 40, no. 1 (1908): 17.

35. Ihde (1990), 70.

36. See, for example, Lyla M. Olson, *Improvised Equipment: In the Home Care of the Sick*, 1st–3d eds. (Philadelphia: W. B. Saunders, 1928, 1933, 1939); A. H. Ross, "Ingenuity and Private Nursing," *AJN* 5, no. 12 (1905): 873–75; Emma V. Skillman, "Improvisations in Private Duty Nursing," AJN 26, no. 4 (1926); 269–70; and Stoney.

37. Lecture, 17 November 1887, Mary U. Clymer Papers, CSHN.

38. Louise Zabriskie, *Mother and Baby Care in Pictures* (Philadelphia: J. B. Lippincott, 1935), 64–65.

39. DeLee and Carmon, 19.

40. Louise B. Nichols, "For the Limited Budget," *Public Health Nurse* 20, no. 8 (1928): 416–18.

41. E. M. Rice, "Making the Best of Things," *Trained Nurse and Hospital Review* 41, no. I (1908): 22–24.

42. Ibid., 24.

43. Ross, 874.

44. Olson (1939), 100.

45. Pauline Carlson, "The Evolution of a Stupe Kettle," *AJN* 37, no. 6 (1937): 584–85.

46. As shown in *AJN* 26, no. 11 (1926): 846.

47. Carolyn C. Van Blarcom, "Appliances Exhibited at the Meeting of the American Society of Superintendents of Training Schools for Nurses in Pittsburgh," *AJN* 4, nos. 6 and 9 (1904): 436–37, 681–84.

48. Ross, 875.

49. Log, 4 November 1930, Charlotte Tyson Rath Papers, CSHN.

50. See, for example, the picture of a practical croup tent, shown on p. 472, *AJN* 26, no. 6 (1926); E. Berends, "An Improvised Funnel," *Trained Nurse and Hospital Review* 96, no. 3 (1936): 223; and, N. E. Cadmus, "Some Hospital Devices and Procedures," *AJN* 16, no. 7 (1916): 589–605.

51. M. Theodore, "The Good Samaritan Infusion Radiator," *AJN* 31, no. 11 (1931): 1267–68.

52. "An Interesting Device," *AJN* 26, no. 4 (1926): 280.

53. Martha M. Russell, "Hospital Furnishings," *AJN* 26, no. 11 (1926): 841–46. Quote on p. 841.

54. Nancy P. Ellicott, "Opportunities for Original Work in the Improvement of Hospital Appliances," *AJN* 14, no. 10 (1914): 843–45.

55. Amy M. Hilliard, "Equipment for Nursing Procedures," *AJN* 21, no. 7 (1921): 728–31.

56. Mary L. Duchesne, "A Labor-Saving Device," *AJN* 23, no. 3 (1923): 470–72. Quote on p. 472.

57. Ellicott, 845.

58. Ibid., 844.

59. Ibid., 843.

60. "Ethics of Nursing, No. IV: The Doctor," *The Trained Nurse* 3, no. 1 (1889): 80–85. Quote on p. 85.

61. P. C. Remondino, "The Trained Nurse in Private Practice," *The Trained Nurse* 32, no. 2 (1904): 77–82.

62. See, for example, "Bag Equipment for Rural Nursing," *Public Health Nurse 21,* no. 7 (1929): 352; J. E. Hitchcock, "The Story of Our Bag," *Public Health Nursing* 27, no. 1 (1935): 29–31; Ruth W. Hubbard, "Bag Technic and the Hourly Nurse," *AJN* 28, no. 6. (1928): 557–59.

63. Frank S. Betz Company, *Surgical Instruments and Supplies*, 1918, p. 37, Medical Trade Ephemera Collection, College of Physicians of Philadelphia (hereafter cited as MTEC).

64. See the ad for a "nurse's outfit" on the back of the March 1929 table of contents in *AJN* 29, nos. 1–6 (1929).

65. Weeks-Shaw, 58.

66. See the ad for B-D Clinical Thermometers in *Trained Nurse and Hospital Review* 66, no. 1 (1921): 73.

67. See the ad for Capsheaf Safety Pin in *Trained Nurse and Hospital Review* 35, no. 6 (1905).

68. See the ad for the "Ideal" Douche Pan, *Trained Nurse and Hospital Review* 32 (1904).

69. See the ad for Lister's Towels, *Trained Nurse and Hospital Review* 33, no. 6 (1904).

70. "Publisher's Desk," *Trained Nurse and Hospital Review* 32, no. 2 (1904): 152.

71. See note 66 above.

72. See the ad for Tycos Fever Thermometer, *Trained Nurse and Hospital Review* (1915).

73. See note 67 above.

74. See note 69 above.

75. See note 68 above.

76. Becton, Dickinson, and Company, *Physician Catalog*, 1918, p. 14; MTEC.

77. Greeley Laboratories, *Greeley Hypodermic Unit*, circa 1906, p. 8, MTEC.

78. Hospital Supply Company of New York, *Catalogue of Sterilizers*, 1913, p. 41, MTEC.

79. Ibid., 10.

80. See, for example, G. W. Aurt, "Perforation of the Rectum With Enema Tips," *Transactions—American Proctologie Society* 40 (1 September 1939): 203–13; and H. H. Rayner, "Injury of the Rectum Caused by the Faulty Administration of an Enema," *British Medical Journal* 1 (5 March 1932): 419–21.

81. See, for example, Harmer and Henderson (1939), 603, and Margaret J. Hawthorne et al., "Oxygen Therapy: A Study in Some Nursing Aspects of the Operation of an Oxygen Tent," *AJN* 38, no. 11 (1938): 1203–16.

82. Harmer (1928), vi.

83. See, for example, Martha E. Erdmann and Margaret Welsh, "Studies in Thermometer

Technique," *Nursing Education Bulletin* 2, no. 1 (1929): 8–33; S. M. Therese, "Why the Nurse Needs Sound Education: Analysis of Elementary Nursing Procedures," *Trained Nurse and Hospital Review* 95, no. 6 (1935): 557–62.

84. Smith, 687.

85. See, for example, the Harmer and the Harmer and Henderson textbooks cited in note 11 above; "Comparative Nursing Methods: Lumbar Puncture, Hypodermoclysis, and Intravenous Infusion Trays," *AJN* 30, no. 3 (1930): 253–60; Photo Collection of Equipment Trays and *Procedure Books*, 1924–1954, Philadelphia General Hospital School of Nursing, CSHN; "Student Experience Record of Central Surgical Service," 1935, Albert Einstein Medical Center (formerly Jewish Hospital) School of Nursing Records, CSHN.

86. "Evaluation of Nursing Care," 1935, Albert Einstein Medical Center School of Nursing Records, CSHN.

87. Harriet M. Gillette, "A Practical Thermometer Tray," *AJN* 26, no. 11 (1926): 840.

88. Charlotte J. Garrison, "Teaching Care of Hospital Equipment," *AJN* 27, no. 10 (1927): 823–26.

89. Weeks-Shaw, 16.

90. See, for example, "Bulletin," 1936, Albert Einstein Medical Center School of Nursing Records, CSHN, and the note on "noisiness," *The Trained Nurse* 2, no. 1 (1888): 27.

91. I. Katims, "Nursing as Aesthetic Experience and the Notion of Practice," *Scholarly Inquiry for Nursing Practice* 7, no. 4 (1993): 269–78; and H. Schnadelbach, "Is Technology Ethically Neutral?" in *Ethics in an Age of Pervasive Technology,* ed. Melvin Kranzberg (Boulder, Colo.: Westview Press, 1980), 28–30.

92. Ihde (1979, 1983, 1990).

93. Mitcham, 191.

94. See, for example, Leah L. Curtin, "Nursing: High-Touch in a High-Tech World," *Nursing Management* 15, no. 7 (1984): 7–8; and Sally Gadow, "Touch and Technology: Two Paradigms of Patient Care," *Journal of Religion and Health* 23, no. 1 (1984): 63–69.

95. See, for example, June C. Abbey and Marvin D. Shepherd, "Nursing and Technology: Moving into the 21st Century," *Dean's Notes* 10, no. 3 (1989): 1–2; Marianne Neighbors and Evelyn E. Eldred, "Technology and Nursing Education," *Nursing and Health Care* 14, no. 2 (1993): 96–99; and "Nursing and Technology: Redefining Relationships," *Biomedical Instrumentation and Technology* 25, no. 2 (1991): 89–98.

Action Research Method

Action research emerged decades ago as an answer to the gap between theory and practice. For years, practitioners in many different fields had found it difficult to implement research findings in their practice. The founders of action research believed the answer to the practitioners' problems lay in implementation. Accordingly, they developed a new form of research that included implementation of a change or new idea in the practice setting as an integral part of the research process. The belief was that if researchers included implementation of change as part of a research project, practitioners would more likely incorporate the change as a continuing part of their practice. Over the years, researchers in many different practice disciplines have used action research, refining and improving on it in the process. Currently, English and Australian nurse–researchers most often engage in action research.

This chapter provides an overview of action research, its roots, and fundamental characteristics. It also provides guidelines for selecting action research as a method for nursing research. The chapter also provides readers with the basic tools for designing an action research study in nursing.

Action Research Defined

Action research is a method of research that involves taking action to improve practice and systematically studying the effects of the action taken. Action researchers study a particular practice setting to identify and describe problems or areas needing change. Then they identify possible solutions to the problems and take action to implement those solutions in the problem setting. The researchers carefully evaluate the process and also the outcomes of the change to be certain the change has had its desired effect. The aim of action research is to derive relevant solutions applicable to specific practice settings. Thus, the purpose of an action research study would be to generate solutions to practice problems that are relevant to a particular hospital or practice setting. Action research would not seek generalizable solutions to problems that apply to a number of similar practice settings because its solutions are designed for the particular setting in which the research occurs.

Action research leads to the generation of *practical knowledge,* knowledge that relates directly to the problems and concerns specific to a setting. Practical knowledge is useful in a particular setting because it ultimately improves practice. As an indirect result of action research, practitioners learn about their practice and about themselves within a setting and also learn to implement change to improve their own practice. Practitioners who collaborate in an action research study become committed to the desired change and thus are more likely to include the change as a permanent part of their practice when the study is finished.

Action Research Roots

Researchers created action research in the 1940s to effect change in practice and to contribute to the body of scientific knowledge about organizational behavior. Collier (1945) and Lewin (1946) were the earliest contributors to this creation. Collier first used teams of researchers, administrators, and laypeople to devise strategies or actions for improving race relations. His idea of using research teams to produce change remains a basic premise in contemporary action research studies. Kurt Lewin developed action research as a method of helping social workers improve their practice. He promoted action research as a method of interacting with or participating in a system for the dual purposes of learning about and creating change in the system. He believed that interaction with a system also contributed to the body of scientific knowledge about the system. Thus, according to Lewin, action researchers serve both theory and practice. From his studies, Lewin developed a body of scientific knowledge about change that is familiar to many researchers. However, action research is different from change theory because it uses principles of change theory to change a system and then systematically studies the change process and outcome.

Varied disciplines have adopted action research strategies since their introduction in the 1940s, especially organization and management, psychology, sociology, nursing, and education researchers. Researchers in each of these disciplines have used Collier's (1945) and Lewin's (1946) basic ideas and added nuances of their own to mold action research methodology to the needs of their discipline. As a result, although contemporary action research takes many different forms, it has retained fundamental characteristics common to all forms.

Fundamental Characteristics of Action Research

All action researchers strive to find solutions for practical practice problems by implementing changes in practice and then closely observing and evaluating the changes during implementation. Four fundamental characteristics are common to action research: (1) a search for solutions to practical practice problems, (2) collaboration between researchers and practitioners, (3) the implementation of changes in practice, and (4) the development of theory (Holter & Schwartz-Barcott, 1993).

All action research studies seek solutions to practical practice problems. In nursing, researchers classify problems as *practical* when they pertain to a particular practice situation or setting. Because problems are practical, researchers do not attempt to generalize them across settings. The purpose is to find solutions by implementing and evaluating the success of changes identified in a specific practice. Action researchers in nursing have studied practical problems ranging from adoption of new nursing practice roles to improving the health of communities.

Another identifying characteristic of action research is the collaboration between researchers and practitioners. When nursing practitioners have identified a need for change, they form a collaborative action research team with one or more nursing research experts. Nursing practitioners offer practice expertise or local knowledge to the research team as well as insight into the nuances of the practice and its historic development. They also contribute their practice expectations. Nurse–researchers bring research and nursing theory expertise to the research team. The extent of collaboration between researchers and study participants varies among action research studies. The levels of collaboration range from the review of the problem and diagnosis only to full collaboration at all subsequent stages of the research process. Action researchers who facilitate collaboration at all stages are able to obtain the most practical solutions to the problems they identify (Holter & Schwartz-Barcott, 1993; Whyte, Greenwood, & Lazes, 1991).

Participatory action research is one form of action research that places prime importance on collaboration with research participants by including them as co-researchers throughout the entire research process (Argyris & Schon, 1991). Participatory action researchers believe that collaboration with participants helps to verify that outcomes validly represent the lived experience and truly represent reality. Another benefit is that participation in the research study will likely empower participants in the process (Reason, 1994). Thus, in participatory action research, the inquiry includes direct involvement of the practitioners as co-researchers in all phases of the study.

Another defining characteristic of action research is implementation of change as a vital stage in the research process. In traditional research, researchers discover solutions to problems through research projects. Following the conclusion of a research project, researchers publish their results; practitioners then read the results and translate them to specific practice settings for implementation. Action research studies, in contrast, include implementation of solutions as an actual part of the research process. In action research, there is no delay between the study completion and the implementation of solutions. Researchers implement solutions as part of the research process so they may carefully study the implementation process. This stage alleviates the problems inherent in traditional research associated with translating solutions to particular practice settings. Action researchers evaluate both the change and the process of change. In the evaluation process, if the co-researchers identify a need to revise the change in practice, they will do so and continue to evaluate the implementation of the revised change.

The development of theory is another characteristic of action research. Theory developed by action researchers is called local theory (Argyris & Schon, 1991) or grounded practice (Rolfe, 1996). *Local theory* is produced by action researchers in the field to explain the situation under study. Action researchers primarily use *reflection* to make theory explicit (Argyris & Schon, 1991); that is, they help practitioners reflect on their practice as the research project progresses. Through this reflection, practitioners gain insight into the tacit forces that influence their behavior. Reflection makes the obscure obvious. It allows practitioners to uncover many factors influencing their practice and discover which factors facilitate and which inhibit that practice (Reason, 1994). Insight into behavior frees practitioners to change their behavior, their organization, or their community. Insights gained become local theories. As the research progresses, researchers test the theory in the field by constructing interventions that place the theory in action. They then evaluate the intervention and refine the theory accordingly. The research may continue in a cycle of theorizing, acting, evaluating, and theorizing until the practice reaches its desired level.

Although not its main function, action research can also contribute more broadly to existing change theory or lead to the formulation of new theories of change. The theories developed are considered potentially generalizable. Knowledge uncovered in action research that pertains to the change process can help practitioners in many settings to implement change (Tolley, 1995).

Selection of Action Research as Method

Nurse–researchers choose to use action research methodology when they want to change nursing practice. They begin by articulating a specified purpose for conducting the research study. Identified purposes may include bringing about a measurable change in behavior, helping practitioners to overcome resistance to change, changing nursing practice, or empowering practitioners (Hart & Bond, 1996). Any single research project may include only one of these purposes or incorporate several or all of them. Inherently, action research projects are neither static nor linear. They are dynamic processes that progress through cyclical stages. The purpose of the intended project may grow and change as the study progresses.

Nurses in practice may approach nurse–researchers for help in planning and implementing an action research project; alternately, nurse–researchers might identify a solution for a common problem and approach nurses in practice to implement an action research study. The goals and beliefs of the major players in the change will guide the form the action research takes. If researchers' major goal is to implement a change and empower practitioners in the process, a form of participatory action research will be the choice.

Action research is a useful methodology in today's rapidly changing health care environment because it provides the mechanism for changing practice and simultaneously evaluating the success of the change. Practitioners save time and energy by implementing and evaluating change simultaneously. They learn about the process of change. They gain personal insight into its challenges and rewards. They engage in the challenge of making the change work. As a result, they more readily adapt to and accept the change. Thus, action research has the potential for teaching practitioners survival skills for a rapidly changing health care environment (Hayes, 1996).

Nurses often find themselves on the front lines of change. They are asked to participate in downsizing and cost-cutting. These changes may bring about expected efficiencies but also create unexpected results. For instance, nurse job satisfaction may decline as the result of changes in practice or quality of client care may suffer in the process. Implementing changes through action research makes it possible for nurses to discover innovative methods for dealing with unanticipated results. Participation makes it possible for nurses to identify phenomena in need of further study (Hayes, 1996).

A change to participative management, implementation of new methods for staff orientation, or a change in methods of surveying client populations for high-risk behaviors are examples of changes in nursing practice amenable to action research. Choosing action research will facilitate the implementation of practical solutions to current health care challenges. Practical solutions will more likely succeed (Martin, 1997).

Because of its dynamic and often collaborative nature, action research is not easy to implement. Researchers cannot always identify in advance the details of the method. Collaborative problem solving takes time and energy. The research team will need to choose methods of data generation throughout the project. If solutions are not working, the team may need to revise them. Rapid staff turnover may mean new participants join the team (Meyer, 1993). Participation in the study may not be voluntary for these newcomers, because the unit has already begun the study. The result is a study that may require more time and energy than anticipated. However, the outcome may certainly be worth the effort. If carried to completion, the results of an action research study create lasting improvements in nursing practice.

Elements and Interpretations of the Method

Action researchers do not provide highly prescriptive methodological guidelines. The aim of learning through action for action research remains paramount, whereas the choice of method depends on the peculiarities of the situation. Action researchers describe their craft as a cyclical process involving planning, acting, reflecting, and evaluating (Waterman, et al., 1995).

Researchers differ in their approach as to which comes first—analysis or implementation. If analysis comes first, the action research process begins with a review of the problem situation. The process then progresses to diagnosis and planning for change. Implementation and evaluation of the effects of the change follow. This conception of the action research process closely parallels the steps of the nursing process, and is thus most easily understood by nurses. If implementation comes first, the researchers implement the change and carefully evaluate its effects. Evaluation always includes reflection to facilitate the uncovering of intentions behind behavior. Evaluation is often followed by more planning and revisions to the implementation.

Data are generated during all stages of the action research cycle using a variety of methods. Researchers should choose data generation techniques to gain as much detailed information as possible. Researchers need to probe for the reasons or intentions behind actions without threatening or constraining practitioners (Argyris, et al., 1985). To achieve the goal of understanding the reasons for certain actions, action researchers combine interview with observation and qualitative with quantitative methods. Data generation needs to be meticulous, with detailed record keeping to facilitate a deep understanding of practice (Winter, 1989).

PLANNING

Data generation during the planning stage of the action research process will vary, depending on whether the study begins with analysis or implementation. If researchers intend to begin with analysis, then the purpose of initial planning is to generate detailed data about the situation as it exists before a change is implemented. For example, imagine you are planning an action research study focused on implementation of a new teaching method for nursing students at risk for failure. Planning begins with a detailed analysis of the current learning situation, which might give specifics such as student learning styles, student level of anxiety, placement of the learning in the curriculum, the physical learning environment, and teacher qualities and style. Each of these factors is amenable to different techniques of data generation.

Members of the research team then begin data generation by developing surveys of attitudes, preferences, or experiences. Practitioners on the team provide valued insight into the survey content based on their experiences in the setting, whereas researchers on the team contribute expertise in survey development. In a clinical practice setting, nurse–clinicians, nurse–administrators, other health professionals, and clients complete the surveys. In educational settings, educators, administrators, and students complete the initial surveys. The goal of the initial surveys is to gain an overall impression of the details of the situation, particularly the important factors that require additional investigation.

Data generation in the planning stage might also include observation of practitioners as they carry out their work over several days. To assure objectivity, researchers who are not practitioners in the setting are the observers. Researchers also interview key players in the situation to gain a greater understanding of the intentions behind the observed actions. For example, an action research team working with teenage members of a community to improve the teenagers' health observe that many of the teenagers smoke as they wait outside school for classes to begin. Key players would be the smokers. By interviewing the smokers, the researchers could determine factors motivating the teenagers to smoke. Additional data generation techniques might include keeping detailed diaries containing subjective impressions of interactions with practitioners and field notes of meetings. Also, researchers might use documents relating to a situation, such as nurses' notes, time sheets, or nursing-care plans.

Data generation begins in a broad, comprehensive way at first. As the research progresses, emerging insights guide and focus successive data generation. Data generated include facts and interpretations or explanations of those facts. Interpretations and explanations are authoritative and accurate because they are grounded in practice. Often, explanations include judgments about relevance and causation. When practitioners and researchers collaborate to generate and analyze data, the interpretations and impressions they have formed are likely to be more accurate (Winter, 1989). Expert researchers on the team provide professional authority to the interpretations, whereas the commonsense experiences of individuals living the situation provide practical authority.

In the initial planning stage, co-researchers decide which methods of data generation are valuable for a particular situation. Nurse–researchers serve as a valuable resource to participants at this stage. Co-researchers begin to form tentative data generation techniques as they begin planning. The researchers and participants together determine techniques for recording data, such as tape recordings, video recordings, note taking, or photographs and slides. The choice depends on the intrusiveness of the technique and the level of accuracy and detail it produces. Tape recording and videotaping are generally more intrusive, but provide greater accuracy of detail. Note taking and photographs are less intrusive, although they provide less accurate detail.

Co-researchers should plan to use at least three different methods of data generation so that each method "can partly transcend its own limitations by functioning as a point of comparison with another" (Winter, 1989, p. 22). Two methods of data generation might result in polarized opinions or insights; however, a third method might allow for an interpretation that reconciles the polarization. Hence, through triangulation of data generation techniques, researchers and participants establish more meaningful problem solving (see Chapter 14 for a more detailed discussion on the triangulation approach to research).

Throughout the action research cycle, researchers serve as the experts in data generation techniques. Researchers have a detailed understanding of a variety of techniques and their applications. However, the decisions about data generation will remain collaborative, with the researcher serving in the role of expert facilitator. A team of nurse–researchers generally is the most effective way to provide the needed expertise. It is difficult to find a single nurse–researcher expert in the many different types of data generation needed for an action research study.

After generating data, the co-researchers analyze the data following the specific guidelines for each data generation technique used. They analyze quantitative data using traditional statistical methods and qualitative data using qualitative methods. The *constant comparative method* developed by Glaser and Strauss (1967) lends itself well to analysis of the qualitative data generated in an action research study. To do constant comparative data analysis, researchers read through the data set to identify *units of data,* which may be as small as a few words or a sentence to as large as a paragraph or two. After identifying units in the data set, researchers assign the units to categories. In this effort, it is vitally important that the researchers compare each successive unit with previously identified units. Researchers proceed through the data until they have assigned all units to categories. Next, they review and refine the categories. Then the researchers identify themes in the categories, which may result in the development of grounded theory. Refer to Chapter 6 for a more detailed discussion of grounded theory methodology.

Researchers on the team take the lead in analyzing data, but they include practitioners in the final interpretation and explanations. Practitioner input is crucial at this stage to establish that the resulting interpretations accurately represent the reality of the situation. Co-researchers meet—often on more than one occasion—to discuss the findings. They probe interpretations, discuss details, identify inconsistencies, and seek explanations. Often, they discover more than one explanation for a behavior observed. The co-researchers discuss the data and suggest possible explanations until the members reach consensus. Then the co-researchers are ready to create an *action plan,* which details the descriptions of the change, process for implementation, plan for facilitating reflection, and evaluation plan. The action plan details the intended role for each player in the planned change and describes the methods for executing the roles. The evaluation plan includes a description of data generation and data analysis techniques and both process and outcome measurements. If the action research does not include an analysis of the current situation, the study begins with action planning. Whether action planning is the first or second stage of the research cycle, the co-researchers complete a detailed plan before acting. As in assessment, action planning requires meetings among the co-researchers to discuss and plan the details. Researchers keep detailed notes of meetings and write a report of the final plan.

Consider the example of implementing a new teaching method to meet the learning needs of at-risk nursing students. The co-researchers would thoroughly assess the current teaching situation using surveys of teacher and student attitudes and experiences. They might observe several classes and take detailed field notes. They might interview both groups of students and faculty to determine their perceptions of the learning situation, tape recording all interviews for analysis. The researchers on the team then would analyze all data and meet with student and faculty representatives to discuss and probe the interpretations. After several meetings, the team might decide to change teaching methods from lecture format to methods that include active student participation in the classroom. The team then would meet to create an action plan for active student participation. Such a plan would include a detailed description of new roles for faculty and students as well as a plan for evaluation. The plan also would include the role that educational administrators should take in implementing the change and would create a time line for implementation.

An action plan may further indicate that researchers should facilitate student and faculty representatives' reflection during the implementation phase. The plan would include strategies for researchers, students, and faculty to keep detailed notes of planning meetings and diaries of their personal reactions. The plan also might provide for biweekly team meetings with student and faculty representatives to facilitate further reflection. Any action plan would include a means for evaluation, such as student course grades, surveys of student and faculty responses to the course and the learning environment, and focus groups with students and faculty. When an action plan reaches completion, the change is ready for implementation.

ACTION

The action stage of the action research process involves the actual implementation of the new idea or change. Implementation occurs following action planning over a specified period. In the example of implementing a new teaching method for nursing students at risk for failure, the researchers might suggest that the new method of active student participation in the classroom occur over one semester in an adult health nursing course. Students taking the course and the faculty teaching the course would continue as co-researchers throughout the entire implementation. *External researchers* on the team take no active role in the implementation itself.

They remain present during the implementation to guide and facilitate reflection that occurs simultaneously with the implementation. *Internal researchers,* however, do have a role in the implementation because they are members of the group in the practice setting.

REFLECTION

Reflection is an important step in the action research cycle that occurs during implementation of the new idea. Reflection provides insight into the process of implementation and the effect the change has on the key players. To engage in reflection, the key players think about how the new practice is affecting them while they are acting. Diaries, team meetings, and interviews aid the process of reflection. Data recorded during reflection are important contributions to the theory that emerges from the action research study.

Occasionally, reflection points to a problem in the planned implementation. The research team discusses the problem area and may or may not decide to adjust the implementation plan as a result. If they do make adjustments, then the co-researchers will keep careful records of the adjustments and the reasons for making them. These midcourse adjustments can be important to the success of a planned implementation. If the research experts on the team are outside researchers, they are more detached from the setting and able to provide objectivity to adjustment decisions. Co-researchers should be cautious not to make adjustments in haste, but should carefully analyze behavior and responses while keeping in mind normal reactions to the change process.

Reflexive critique (Rolfe, 1996; Winter, 1989) and dialectic critique (Winter, 1989) can also be useful aids for reflection. Used during group discussions, each serves to focus reflection to uncover underlying influencing factors. *Reflexive critique* is based on an understanding that all statements made during data generation—including participants and researchers' written and verbal language—are subject to reflexivity. Reflexivity describes the belief that the language individuals use to describe an experience reflects that particular experience and also all other experiences in each individual's life. Knowing that observations and interpretations are reflexive creates two assumptions for action researchers: (1) a rejection of the idea of a single or ultimate explanation for an event or observation and (2) the belief that offering various explanations for an experience explicitly increases understanding of the experiences.

When engaging in reflexive critique, the researchers and participants probe for the reflexive basis of the data generated. They make explicit the alternative explanations or interpretations, the goal being to establish that a number of alternative explanations can be relevant and equally important. Reflexive critique facilitates discussion between researchers and participants, providing a path to greater insight. For example, suppose action researchers have implemented a new method of nursing-care deliv-

ery in an intensive care unit (ICU). The researchers evaluate implementation of the new method by interviewing ICU nurses to determine their
degree of satisfaction with the new method. Several nurses state they
do not find the new method helpful. The researchers then engage the
participants in reflexive critique by asking them to discuss the reasons
they do not find the new technique helpful. Several nurses say they do
not like the new technique because it is time-consuming. Further probing
reveals that, for some nurses, the new technique is time-consuming because they lack several necessary basic skills. Other nurses say they find
the method time-consuming because they have to stop and think about
what they are doing, unlike the old method of care, which was automatic.
It is imperative that both researchers and participants engage in reflexive
critique to reveal the multiple explanations for a phenomenon. They might
decide on the most likely explanation, or they might uncover several
competing or complementary explanations.

In contrast, *dialectic critique* aids reflection by probing data to make
explicit their internal contradictions rather than complementary explanations. By probing the discrete elements of a phenomenon and exposing
its contradictory nature, the researchers and participants come to a clearer
understanding of the nature of change inherent in a particular phenomenon. Consider the previous example of the implementation of a new
nursing-care delivery method in an ICU. Using dialectic critique, the researchers reflecting on the implementation of that method would meet
with the participants to discuss the time needed to implement the new
method. The researchers would probe the participants for conflicting
information related to time. In doing so, they might discover that inexperienced nurses say the new technique takes too much time to implement,
whereas experienced nurses say the new technique takes less time than
old methods. Or, they might discover that the new technique takes more
time to implement on the day shift than on the night shift. Discussing and
probing these opposites would give the co-researchers insight into the
complex factors influencing implementation of the new method.

EVALUATION

Evaluation occurs at the conclusion of the implementation or at specified
intervals throughout the implementation, as designated in the action plan.
Co-researchers plan evaluation carefully. An evaluation of the implementation process includes the data generated during reflection as well as
additional data. The evaluation process, which often follows a process
similar to the initial assessment, should include triangulation of data generation techniques to validate meaningfulness and accuracy. Methods of
data generation will depend on the evaluation questions asked. Most
studies require qualitative and quantitative techniques of data generation.
Researchers may choose from reflective diaries, critical incident analysis,
interviews, and observation to evaluate the implementation process. They

might measure outcomes of the implementation using surveys, interviews, and objective measures.

Expert researchers on the team guide the evaluation process in consultation with the practitioners on the research team. The researchers prepare and distribute tools or they might ask key practitioners to distribute tools. Researchers interview key players and conduct evaluation meetings. As in the first stage of the research, data analysis proceeds following the guidelines of the specific type of data gathered. The researchers analyze the quantitative data using statistical techniques and the qualitative data using methods such as constant comparative analysis. Researchers meet with practitioners to present their interpretations for discussion and verification. As in the analysis stage, these discussions are necessary to establish practical authority and more meaningful evaluation.

The co-researchers then write a study report. Remember that the result of a data analysis is a plurality of explanations for phenomena observed. The report includes many explanations and also questions for further consideration. The report is not intended to be a prescription for action. Instead, the purpose is to provide its consumers a springboard for dialogue. The co-researchers discuss the report and determine additional action, if needed. The practitioners suggest additional courses of action with guidance from the researchers. Practitioners then implement the action and continue to evaluate its effectiveness, with or without the continued guidance of the researchers (Whyte et al., 1991).

ETHICAL CONSIDERATIONS

Obtaining participants' informed consent is not as straightforward in an action research study as in other forms of research (Meyer, 1993). The dynamic and ever-changing nature of action research means that participants are not always well informed of all the research details when they consent to participate in a study. In an action research study, the consent form should include a statement about the participant's willingness to participate in a broadly defined project and to cooperate with the researchers and other participants in the process. The consent form should state that the nature of the proposed change emerges as the study progresses. It should state that the participant agrees to contribute toward planning, implementing, and evaluating the change.

Action researchers have difficulty guaranteeing that participants may withdraw from an action research study once the study has begun (Meyer, 1993). In action research, a group of individuals commits to carrying out the project. As a result of this commitment, group pressure, whether explicit or implicit, may make it difficult for individual participants to withdraw from a study without consequences. Whenever researchers implement change, they should expect conflict between group members and some member dissatisfaction. One or more members may become so dissatisfied with the process that they refuse to participate in some sessions or consider withdrawing from the study. Participants who withdraw risk rejection by other group members. This pressure is inherent in any action research study and should be a point of discussion as the researchers plan the study. Reflection sessions should allow participants to discuss dissatisfaction. Members should include plans for considering group member dissatisfaction and design coping strategies to lessen the possibility of participant withdrawal.

The process of action research may place participants in a vulnerable position. Often, because a project may proceed over several years, the research team members become close. Working together as a closely knit team results in numerous frank and open discussions. If researchers on the team are outside researchers and not working members of the practice team, participants may come to view those researchers as confidants. The researchers, in the process, may gain detailed personal knowledge about group members and gain power in the group. The researchers will need to strive for neutrality in the group and minimize the vulnerability of group members.

Risks to group members in an action research project include breaches of confidentiality and anonymity (Titchen & Binnie, 1993). The researchers gain close and personal knowledge of the practice group; however, when writing the final research report, it is paramount that researchers do not reveal participants' identities. They must maintain the participants' confidentiality and anonymity.

Summary

Action research can be an effective method for implementing change in today's health care environment. Its major advantage is that it creates practical solutions to everyday nursing practice problems. Because it involves implementation and evaluation of new ideas, action research also provides an answer to the gap between theory and practice. Action research is a dynamic process that involves cycling among analysis, action, reflection, and evaluation. Participants in action research are active members of the research team, participating in the planning, implementation, and evaluation of the action taken. When used appropriately, action research can result in lasting change that creates a more meaningful nursing practice.

REFERENCES

Argyris, C., Putnam, R., & Smith, D. M. (1985). *Action science.* San Francisco: Jossey-Bass.
Argyris, C., & Schon, D. A. (1991). Participatory action research and action science compared: A commentary. In W. F. Whyte (Ed.), *Participatory action research* (pp. 85–96). Newbury Park, CA: Sage.
Collier, J. (1945). United States Indian administration as a laboratory of ethnic relations. *Social Research, 12,* 277–294.
Glaser, B. G., & Strauss, A. (1967). *The discovery of grounded theory.* Chicago: Aldine.

Hart, E., & Bond, M. (1996). Making sense of action research through the use of a typology. *Journal of Advanced Nursing, 23,* 152–159.

Hayes, P. (1996). Is there a place for action research? *Clinical Nursing Research, 5,* 3–5.

Holter, I. M., & Schwartz-Barcott, D. (1993). Action research: What is it? How has it been used and how can it be used in nursing? *Journal of Advanced Nursing, 18,* 298–304.

Lewin, K. (1946). Action research and minority problems. *Journal of Social Issues, 2*(4), 34–46.

Martin, J. (1997). Observations on the neglected concept of intervention in nursing research. *Journal of Advanced Nursing, 25,* 23–29.

Meyer, J. E. (1993). New paradigm research in practice: The trials and tribulations of action research. *Journal of Advanced Nursing, 18,* 1066–1072.

Reason, P. (1994). Three approaches to participative inquiry. In N. K. Denzin & Y. S. Lincoln (Eds.), *Handbook of qualitative research* (pp. 324–339). Thousand Oaks, CA: Sage.

Rolfe, G. (1996). Going to extremes: Action research, grounded practice and the theory–practice gap in nursing. *Journal of Advanced Nursing, 24,* 1315–1320.

Titchen, A., & Binnie, A. (1993). Research partnerships: Collaborative action research in nursing. *Journal of Advanced Nursing, 18,* 858–865.

Tolley, K. S. (1995). Theory from practice for practice: Is this a reality? *Journal of Advanced Nursing, 21,* 184–190.

Waterman, H., Webb, C., & Williams, A. (1995). Parallels and contradictions in the theory and practice of action research in nursing. *Journal of Advanced Nursing, 22,* 779–784.

Whyte, W. F., Greenwood, D. J., & Lazes, P. (1991). Participatory action research: Through practice to science in social research. In W. F. Whyte (Ed.), *Participatory action research* (pp. 19–55). Newbury Park, CA: Sage.

Winter, R. (1989). *Learning from experience: Principles and practices in action-research.* Philadelphia: Falmer Press.

Action Research in Practice, Education, and Administration

The primary purpose of action research is to implement a change to solve a nursing practice problem. Nursing practice problems amenable to action research may be related to clinical nursing practice, education, or administration. This chapter presents sample action research studies in each of the nursing practice domains. The criteria for critical review of action research studies presented in Box 13-1 guided the critique of each study. The purpose of the guide for critical review is to aid readers in critically reviewing the merits of the studies presented in the research reports, both in terms of practical application and contribution to the body of scientific knowledge.

In addition, Table 13-1 provides an overview of selected research studies in clinical nursing practice, education, and administration. Currently, U.S. nurse–researchers do not commonly use action research. Most often nurse–researchers in England, other parts of Europe, and Australia use action research. For that reason, the table identifies the country of origin of the research studies presented. A reprint of Manley's (1997) article found at the end of this chapter assists readers in understanding the critiquing process.

Application to Practice

Clinical nursing practice problems are complex and multifaceted. They often include both technologic aspects and human system factors. In the current climate of rapidly changing health care practices, it is vitally important to identify and solve clinical nursing practice problems. Solving problems means implementing changes in practice settings over time; therefore, including implementation through an action process ensures the use of changes in practice. Nurse–researchers have used action research in clinical nursing practice to benefit client care in many ways, such as through changes in methods of client care delivery, changes in the overall health status of a community, and development of new nursing roles. Multiple study outcomes have included improvements in the practice itself and in practitioners by way of self-empowerment and the creation of tools for more effective practice.

Action research studies in clinical nursing practice only rarely involve health care recipients. In the United States, an initiative called Healthy

Cities used action research to involve community members in planning and implementing health-promotion strategies for their community (Flynn et al., 1994; Rains & Ray, 1995). As another example, a worldwide effort to promote breast-feeding has involved community members and health care providers in an action research project ("Global Participatory Action Research [GLOPAR]," 1995).

More commonly, researchers have undertaken action research in clinical practice to change methods of client care delivery and develop new

---

BOX 13-1 CRITIQUING GUIDELINES FOR ACTION RESEARCH

PLANNING

1. Does the study begin with an analysis of the practice situation or does it begin with implementation of the action?
2. Analysis of the practice situation
   a. Is the practice setting described in sufficient detail?
   b. What methods of data generation are used to describe the practice situation?
      - Are qualitative techniques used to study human qualities?
      - Are quantitative techniques used to study nonhuman factors?
   c. Are procedures for selecting participants described?
   d. What is the extent of collaboration between researchers and participants during the analysis of practice phase?
   e. Are strategies for data analysis described?
   f. Are participants involved in the interpretation?
   g. Does the description reflect understanding of the practice situation?
3. Action planning
   a. Is the planned change described in detail?
   b. Are methods of implementing the planned change described?
   c. Are methods for evaluating the planned change described?
   d. Are participants included in action planning?

ACTING

4. Is the planned change implemented in the practice setting where the problem occurred?
5. Is the period for implementation specified?

(continued)

BOX 13-1 CRITIQUING GUIDELINES FOR ACTION RESEARCH (CONTINUED)

REFLECTING

6. Are methods for facilitating reflection specified?
7. Are the results of reflection described?

EVALUATING

8. Are strategies for evaluating the change described?
9. Are the process for implementing the change and the outcomes of the change evaluated?
10. Are data evaluation methods appropriate to factors evaluated?
    a. Are qualitative techniques used to evaluate human factors?
    b. Are quantitative techniques used to evaluate technologic factors?
11. Are participants included in the evaluation?
12. Are appropriate methods used to analyze evaluation data?
13. Does the research address validity and reliability of quantitative findings and trustworthiness of qualitative findings?

CONCLUSIONS, IMPLICATIONS, AND RECOMMENDATIONS

14. Do the conclusions reflect the findings?
15. Is a theory formulated from the findings?
16. Are implications described in sufficient detail?
17. Has the researcher discussed ethical and moral implications of the study?
18. Are recommendations for research and practice included?
19. Does the researcher describe the benefits participants gained from the study?

nursing practice roles. An excellent example of an action research study to develop a new nursing practice role is Manley's (1997) "A Conceptual Framework for Advanced Practice: An Action Research Project Operationalizing an Advanced Practitioner/Consultant Nurse Role." The following review of Manley's research report is provided to assist readers in critiquing action research reports. Criteria for critical review of action research in Box 13-1 guided the critique.

Manley (1997) completed her action research study to operationalize and evaluate an advanced practitioner/consultant nurse role. In England, the advanced practitioner/consultant nurse role is much like the clinical

(*text continues on page 272*)

TABLE 13-1 Selective Sampling of Action Research Studies

Author	Domain	Purpose	Sample	Date Generation Methods	Results
Bellman (1996) *England*	Practice	Implement and evaluate the Roper, Logan, and Tierney model of clinical nursing practice	Nursing staff on 1 surgical client care unit	Self-rating scale, semi-structured client interviews, care plan analysis, collaborative action planning, group reflection on practice, client and multidisciplinary team feedback, change process evaluation tool	Outcomes included personal and client-centered enhancement of nurses on the unit, improved team cohesion, and a greater sense of empowerment of the nursing staff
Breda et al. (1997) *USA*	Administration	Implement changes to increase autonomy of nurses in the workplace	Nursing managers and nursing staff of a psychiatric hospital	Reflective discussion through a study group, initiation of action plans, and qualitative evaluation	Autonomy among the nursing staff increased throughout the institution; nurses took increased ownership for their practice, changed their nursing approach to emphasize wellness and healing, and began to treat clients as partners
Hyrkas (1997) *Finland*	Education	Improve teaching for clinical practice in schools of nursing	Clinical practice educators in 6 clinical practice settings, stu-	Diaries, time logs, and survey questionnaires for assessment and eval-	Specific plans for clinical teaching were developed and initiated; the authors do not describe the plans

					in detail
			dents in the clinical groups, and nurses of the units in which learning took place	uation, and action plan development and initiation	
Jones (1996) *England*	Practice	Examine if the emergency nurse practitioner role could be an effective addition to a pediatric emergency department	6 nurses and 26 clients seeking help in the emergency department during 1 month	Comparison of the nurses' treatment plans with physician treatment plans for the same clients; nurses completed the research diaries	Nurses did make accurate diagnoses and treatment plans; time for clients was decreased; nurses' confidence in treating and diagnosing grew with each client seen; nurses were satisfied with the nurse practitioner role
Manley (1997) *England*	Practice	Develop, initiate and evaluate an advanced practitioner/consultant nurse role in an ICU	All nursing staff on the unit	Values clarification, observation, diary, initiation of action plan, focus group evaluation	Detailed role description was given for an advanced practitioner/consultant nurse; a conceptual framework highlighted preparation of advanced practitioner/consultant nurses
Nicoll & Butler (1996) *England*	Education	Determine the causes of anxiety in student nurses taking biology and initiate and evaluate an action plan to reduce the anxiety	66 nursing students	Delphi technique to identify causes of anxiety; 10-student quality circle for action planning; focus group evaluation of changes made	Action research was an effective method of course evaluation; students' anxiety was decreased and students reported that their participation in the process was valued by the faculty; faculty also benefited from the positive changes in students' attitudes and behavior

(continued)

TABLE 13-1 Selective Sampling of Action Research Studies (CONTINUED)

Author	Domain	Purpose	Sample	Date Generation Methods	Results
Rains & Ray (1995) *USA*	Practice	Enable community members to identify health promotional needs and implement a health promotional program	Committee of community members representing many sectors of the city	Survey, action plans, unspecified methods for evaluating change	The community members identified smoking, exercise, alcohol abuse, mental health, and dietary choices as the priority health promotion issues and implemented programs to promote health in these areas; the action research process empowered community members for effecting change in the health status of its members
Rolfe & Phillips (1995) *England*	Practice	Develop and refine the role of an advanced practice nurse in dementia	42 health care and medical professionals (hospital managers, hospital and community nurses, occupational therapists, social workers, and physicians)	Semistructured group interviews; action planning; evaluation through reflective diaries; critical incident analysis; in-depth interviews with nurses, clients, and other members of the health team	Development and initiation of a role for an advanced practice nurse were grounded in the needs and requirements of practitioners
Street & Robinson (1995) *Australia*	Administration	Initiate a new second-line manager role—associate charge nurse—on a hospital unit and ex-	5 associate charge nurses, the unit manager, and clinical nurses from 1 nursing unit	In-depth interviews; action, analysis, reflection cycle	The group worked through a number of action plans that fostered cultural shifts in the clinical nursing practice on the unit and facilitated the initiation of the new role;

	Focus	Purpose	Sample	Method	Findings
		plore issues associated with the role			specific cultural shifts included inadequate preparation for new roles, tensions between clinical and management functions in the role, culture of supportiveness among the nursing staff, and continual interruption
Titchen & Binnie (1993) *England*	Practice	Analyze and document a change in practice style from team nursing to primary nursing	Nursing staff and administrator of 1 patient care unit	Workshop for action planning; reflective diaries and conversations; participant observation; interviews with staff nurses; informal, recorded conversations for evaluation of initiation of action plans	Enabled staff to clarify and implement new nursing roles; facilitated staff's personal and professional development in problem solving
Titchen & Binnie (1995) *England*	Administration	Develop, test, and refine 3 strategies for clinical supervision to educate unit nurses for primary nursing roles	Nursing staff and unit manager of a client care unit	Participant observation, in-depth interviews, reflective conversations, and document review	3 clinical supervision strategies were developed to help unit leaders; each strategy involved learning from clinical practice; in the first strategy, the leader facilitates the staff nurses' reflection on a practice situation; in the second strategy, the leader reflects with the staff nurse on the leader's clinical practice; in the third strategy, the staff nurse and leader share a practice experience and reflect on it together

nurse specialist role in North America. It is an expert nursing practice role that includes educator, researcher, and consultant functions. The purpose of the advanced practitioner/consultant nurse role is to improve client care through clinical, strategic, and policy initiatives.

Manley's study is an excellent example of an empowering type of action research. The study used staff participation and collaboration with the researcher throughout all phases to attain the goal of staff emancipation. All unit nurses were study participants for the 3-year period of implementation.

The study begins with an analysis and description of the clinical practice setting and also describes the context of advanced practice roles in England at the time of the study. Manley—as an outside researcher—initiated the study in 1989 at the time of the Nursing Development Unit (NDU) movement. The study took place on a five-bed intensive care and NDU unit (ICU) was implemented with unit staff participation. The researcher used values clarification as the methodology for gaining an understanding of the clinical practice setting in which a change was desired. The author provides no information about specific techniques for data generation or analysis during the values clarification, although she does reveal that she used reflection in the process. In addition, the author indicates that an open and nonhierarchical management approach facilitated the environment for the study.

Following the values clarification exercises, the nursing staff identified five priority areas for the client care unit: (1) staff development, (2) education, (3) research, (4) practice development, and (5) quality assurance. Action planning began with a thorough review of advanced nurse practice literature. With the researcher acting as facilitator, the nurses decided to implement an advanced practitioner/consultant nurse role on their unit, and the plan included a job description for this role. Interestingly, the staff recruited the researcher to assume the advanced practitioner/consultant nurse role. With the assumption of this new role, the researcher became an inside researcher, rather than an outside facilitator. One might question the objectivity of the researcher when her role changed from outside to inside researcher.

The researcher/practitioner and the nursing staff engaged in reflection throughout implementation of the role. The researcher/practitioner kept a diary to facilitate her reflection. She describes the theoretical outcomes of her reflection in great detail, mainly from her own perspective. Although she facilitated staff reflection using focus group discussion, she does not provide primary data from the focus groups in her report. Readers can only assume that the nurses' personal thoughts and feelings were part of the reflection and thus influenced the resulting conceptual framework for an advanced practitioner/consultant nurse role.

The researcher describes the study implementation as cycling between action, reflection, evaluation, and planning. Collaborative reflection among staff members and the researcher/practitioner facilitated refinement of the role description. Cycling to implement following the refinement allowed the staff to evaluate its effectiveness.

Manley's evaluation strategies included her working diary, her field notes, and the focused group discussions with teams of nurses. As an additional strategy, the nurses participated in the performance review of the advanced practitioner/consultant nurse. The researcher first analyzed her diary using a thematic analysis of work activities. She placed the work activities into 22 categories and grouped these categories into themes. She gave the categorized work activities list to the nursing staff, who discussed them in the focus group sessions. At the conclusion of the study, the researcher completed an in-depth thematic analysis of the work categories. The thematic analysis resulted in seven themes. She then cross-analyzed all categories for processes and theoretical underpinnings. The result is a conceptual framework for the advanced practitioner/consultant nurse role. The conceptual framework has three sections: (1) a description of the context in which the advanced practitioner/consultant nurse functions; (2) a description of the subroles, skills, and processes used by the advanced practitioner/consultant nurse; and (3) a description of the outcomes resulting from implementation of the advanced practitioner/consultant nurse role.

In the report, Manley does not describe the context of the study in sufficient detail to facilitate transference of findings to other settings. She suggests in her description of context that the nursing staff and the advanced practitioner must share values and beliefs for the role to be successful. Furthermore, she indicates that an open, nonhierarchical management style is necessary for success. The researcher points out that, to achieve successful role implementation, the advanced practitioner must have legitimate authority and be a contributing member of the management team. Clearly, these factors contributed to successful implementation of the role in the study. However, it is unclear if these same factors would ensure success in other practice settings.

Manley presents a dynamic description of the subroles and related processes and theoretical underpinnings. She points out that, unlike how they may appear in the description, the subroles are neither static nor linear. In implementing the role, the advanced practitioner/consultant nurse varies the emphasis placed on different subroles, depending on the changing needs of the unit and its clients. This insight reflects the value of action research. By studying the role implementation in action, the researcher gained insight into its dynamic nature. The researcher describes the role in intricate detail that should be useful to other practitioners who are attempting to implement such a role. Of particular help is the researcher's discussion of the skills and processes used to implement the role. This description gives readers keen insight into the how-to of the advanced practitioner/consultant nurse role. The author writes exclusively from the perspective of the advanced practitioner/consultant nurse. Unfortunately, she does not include the perspective or reactions of the nursing staff regarding the processes and skills used. The perspective of nursing staff would be a useful addition to the conceptual framework.

The existing conceptual framework also only superficially addresses the outcomes of the implementation. The researcher suggests that she achieved the expected outcomes, pointing out that the action research improved client care and empowered staff. However, she does not present any data to support these claims. Noting that other studies focused on linking subroles with quality outcome indicators, the researcher focused her research on the processes used by advanced practitioner/consultant nurses. The study would have been strengthened had the researcher included measurement of quality indicators. The inclusion of objective data gained through quality indicators would have provided necessary support for the study claims of success.

The research report does contain an excellent discussion of the study implications. Manley discusses the limitations of implementing the role in other settings and suggests strategies that might aid such implementation. She discusses practice implications, particularly in relation to the education and accreditation of advanced practitioner/consultant nurses. The report does not include recommendations for further refinement of the role, nor does it address the ethical and moral implications of the study.

Application to Education

Although most recent action research studies in nursing have related predominantly to clinical practice, early action research tended to focus on nursing education. Action research remains a viable method for implementing and evaluating change in nursing education. Researchers can use action research to change faculty or student practices. As in other settings, if used collaboratively with research participants, action research in nursing education can be empowering to students and faculty alike. An example of action research in nursing education designed to empower students is the Nicoll and Butler (1996) study "The Study of Biology as a Cause of Anxiety in Student Nurses Undertaking the Common Foundation Programme" (Table 13-1).

Nicoll and Butler (1996), biology teachers in a college of nursing in England, noticed that students frequently commented in course evaluations that the biology course caused them increased anxiety. In response, Nicoll and Butler designed an action research study to determine the major causes of anxiety and identify methods for reducing the anxiety.

The study begins with an analysis of the extent and character of the anxiety experienced by students currently enrolled in the biology course. Sixty-six students in one course voluntarily participated in the study. The researchers used a Delphi technique to gain information about students' perceptions of the causes of their anxiety. The researchers intended to actively involve participants from the start to commit them to the research and its success. However, the researchers provide no detailed information about how they conducted the Delphi technique. In addition, the researchers do not describe how they analyzed the data generated from the Delphi technique. The report does provide a list of data categories sorted into five themes. The categories describe the students' perceptions of the causes of their anxiety, learning context, student factors, and curriculum factors.

Next, the researchers solicited 10 students from the group to form an action planning group. Students in the group used the data generated from the Delphi technique to formulate suggestions for change. The planning group reported back to the whole group on several occasions to gain their input into the emerging action plan. The faculty were present during the action planning, but the researchers do not describe the level of their participation at this point. The students completed and presented a list of suggestions to the faculty. The faculty then met to incorporate the suggestions into the final action plan. The faculty included all but one of the students' suggestions in the final plan. The research report does not include details on the implementation of the action plan.

The faculty implemented the action plan changes in the remaining 10 months of the biology course. The researchers chose focus group sessions as the method of evaluating the changes. Given that seven students volunteered for the focus group session, the focus group method proved effective in stimulating open discussion and reflection among the group members. The faculty members were present during the focus group sessions and recorded field notes following the sessions. Recording field notes is a less intrusive, but more inaccurate, method of recording data. Although the researchers do not indicate how they analyzed the data, they do describe the evaluation in detail. The students recognized that the course would always generate some level of anxiety and reported that some changes actually increased, rather than decreased, their anxiety. The report describes how other changes were successful in decreasing anxiety. Although the evaluation is exclusively qualitative, some complementary quantitative data, such as anxiety scales and course or exam grades, would have strengthened the results. The authors do not address trustworthiness in the report.

The researchers conclude that the action research method was particularly effective for course evaluation. In their evaluations, the students indicated they preferred the action research method for course evaluation because they enjoyed the benefits of the changes recommended. This result differs from the norm in that faculty usually implement student recommendations for change only in subsequent courses. In addition, the researchers point out that the action research method was helpful to them as teachers, but acknowledged the method can be threatening to teachers because students may criticize their methods. Furthermore, some faculty resisted the changes proposed because implementing them would increase faculty workload. However, the researchers noted positive behavior and attitude changes in faculty as the study progressed. The researchers also indicate that involving the students in a research study provided unexpected but welcomed benefits.

The Nicoll and Butler (1996) report, like the Manley (1997) study previously critiqued, presents purely local theory. The value in reporting the study in the literature is that it describes a form of course evaluation that benefits students and faculty alike. The study demonstrates to others the potential value of action research as a form of course evaluation.

Application to Administration

Nurse–researchers use action research studies in nursing administration to initiate new nursing administrative roles (Street & Robinson, 1995) and to initiate new methods of nursing administration (Titchen & Binnie, 1993). An excellent example demonstrating the usefulness of action research to initiate new methods of nursing administration is the article "Enhanced Nursing Autonomy Through Participatory Action Research" (Breda et al., 1997). The researchers conducted the study to explore issues of autonomy and improve the administrative practices in a small, rural, psychiatric hospital. A group of staff nurses, supervisors, and one external researcher had observed that the nurses in their hospital were not autonomous because of hospital policies, procedures, and regulations. They believed the policies sometimes conflicted with professional norms and restrictive policies and regulations sometimes prevented the nurses from making autonomous clinical decisions.

This action research study begins with an analysis of the practice setting in the hospital. Analysis consisted mainly of consciousness-raising that began at a retreat for staff nurses and management. Following a presentation on the attributes of a professional, several nurses in the group observed they were not practicing autonomously. At this point, these nurses became co-researchers in an action research project with the external researcher. The observation led to a consciousness-raising session in which the researchers discussed autonomy and began to identify the factors that constrained their autonomy. The investigators concluded at the end of the consciousness-raising session that they were members of an oppressed group. This insight stimulated them to want to change to a more autonomous practice.

Next, the researchers formed a study group to discuss autonomy further, learning from each other in the process. The study group methodology facilitated additional consciousness-raising and knowledge generation about the lack of autonomy in the setting. The authors do not provide any details about how they recorded data. They also provide little detail about the knowledge generated. Their focus is mainly on the process of consciousness-raising and how that process freed the nurses to take action. This portion of the study points to an important function of action research: Working as a group to discuss and describe the perceived problem—autonomy—led to action for the purpose of problem solving. The process worked because the consciousness-raising sessions empowered the nurses to take action. The authors used two techniques to analyze their practice setting: consciousness-raising and study group.

The study group invited all nurses in the hospital to attend their initial sessions. Participation was purely voluntary. A core group of 12 staff nurses and supervisors completed the initial analysis and formulated an action plan. At the conclusion of their analysis, the investigators realized that gaps in their knowledge and skill base impeded their professional autonomy. Their action plan was to prepare for and take the American Nurses Association certification examination. The authors do not provide additional details about the action plan.

The researchers implemented the plan and engaged in reflection during the implementation. They continued to cycle between implementation, reflection, and planning for 1 year. In the process, they increased their knowledge and gained self-confidence as they learned. They began to question some of their practices and made plans to change those practices. As their confidence continued to increase, physicians and administrators began to notice the changes in the nurses' behavior. Planning and implementation continued as the researchers tried a variety of independent nursing interventions in their practice. The group met throughout the process and continued to reflect on their practice, particularly in terms of autonomous decision making.

The final action item the group implemented was a retreat for all nurses in the hospital to share the outcomes of their action research study. They discussed interventions they had tried and they also shared their insights about professional autonomy. The researchers evaluated the retreat using a formal exit evaluation and informal verbal comments. The retreat was helpful to the researchers in gaining the remainder of the hospital staff's support.

Each time the core research team met, they recorded their conversations for later analysis and evaluation. The research team used a process of reflection and categorization to analyze the data and identify three emergent themes. The themes describe the changes in the nurses' practice that resulted in increased autonomy. The authors do not discuss trustworthiness of findings.

The researchers conclude their participation in the study was a powerful and freeing experience, a catalyst for them to achieve professional autonomy. They also point out the constraining forces present in their environment that limited their autonomy. The researchers conclude that active participation in the hospital system allowed them to change that system and they recommend action research for other practice settings where nurses desire change.

Readers might ask why the Breda et al. study is classified as an administrative study. In reality, the administrators gave tacit approval and support to the researchers to undertake the study. Administrators also supported the group meetings and the changes in practice, and first- and second-level administrators participated in the study. Although the staff nurses generated the study, the administrators' responses allowed the study to flourish. Although the authors do not describe the study as such, they could well have described it as an action research study for participative governance.

This action research study (Breda et al., 1997) reports local theory rather than broad, generalized, theoretical formulations. However, the study has potential application to similar nursing practice settings. The authors of the report provide excellent insight into the process of action research used in the study. They present an excellent example of nurses who acted and learned from their actions. In the study, the researchers emphasize self-growth and the creation of change within a system. They make no attempt to add to our theoretical knowledge of change or autonomy; rather, the theory generated in the study is purely a local theory.

Summary

Currently, nurse–researchers in the United States rarely use action research because they do not regard it as a rigorous form of research. Each of the studies critiqued was successful in following the action research cycle. Each analyzed the current situation and created action plans. Researchers implemented and evaluated the changes in the studies. For the most part, the researchers used appropriate methods of data generation throughout the studies. The studies are less rigorous than they could have been because the researchers did not provide for trustworthiness of qualitative data and validity and reliability of quantitative data. However, serious nurse–researchers should make increased use of action research in clinical nursing practice, education, and administration. This method can be an effective tool for implementing change. Attention to rigor in action research would help it to receive more widespread recognition as a valuable research tool.

REFERENCES

Bellman, L. M. (1996). Changing nursing practice through reflection on the Roper, Logan, and Tierney model: The enhancement approach to action research. *Journal of Advanced Nursing, 24,* 129–138.

Breda, K. L., Anderson, M. A., Hansen, L., Hayes, D., Pillion, C., & Lyon, P. (1997). Enhanced nursing autonomy through participatory action research. *Nursing Outlook, 45,* 76–81.

Flynn, B. C., Ray, D. W., & Rider, M. S. (1994). Empowering communities: Action research through Healthy Cities. *Health Education Quarterly, 21,* 395–405.

Global participatory action research (GLOPAR). (1995). *Journal of Human Lactation, 11,* 262.

Hyrkas, K. (1997). Can action research be applied in developing clinical teaching? *Journal of Advanced Nursing, 25,* 801–808.

Jones, S. (1996). An action research investigation into the feasibility of experienced registered sick children's nurses (RSCNs) becoming children's emergency nurse practitioners (ENPs). *Journal of Clinical Nursing, 5,* 13–21.

Manley, K. (1997). A conceptual framework for advanced practice: An action research project operationalizing an advanced practitioner/consultant nurse role. *Journal of Clinical Nursing, 6,* 179–190.

Nicoll, L., & Butler, M. (1996). The study of biology as a cause of anxiety in student nurses undertaking the common foundation programme. *Journal of Advanced Nursing, 24,* 615–624.

Rains, J. W., & Ray, D. W. (1995). Participatory action research for community health promotion. *Public Health Nursing, 12,* 256–261.

Rolfe, B., & Phillips, L. (1995). An action research project to develop and evaluate the role of an advanced nurse practitioner in dementia. *Journal of Clinical Nursing, 4,* 289–293.

Street, A., & Robinson, A. (1995). Advanced clinical roles: Investigating dilemmas and changing practice through action research. *Journal of Clinical Nursing, 4,* 349–357.

Titchen, A., & Binnie, A. (1993). What am I meant to be doing? Putting practice into theory and back again in new nursing roles. *Journal of Advanced Nursing, 18,* 1054–1065.

Titchen, A., & Binnie, A. (1995). The art of clinical supervision. *Journal of Clinical Nursing, 4,* 327–334.

A Conceptual Framework for Advanced Practice: An Action Research Project Operationalizing an Advanced Practitioner/Consultant Nurse Roles

MANLEY, KIM, BA, MN, RGN, DipN, RCNT, PGCEA
Lecturer in Nursing/Course Director MSc in Nursing, RCN Institute, Royal College of Nursing, 20 Cavendish Square, London WIM OAB, UK. Accepted for publication 20 November 1996

SUMMARY

- *A preliminary conceptual framework for an advanced practice/consultant nurse role is presented which links the role to its context and outcomes.*
- *The conceptual framework was developed in the process of analysing data from a 3-year action research study involving the operationalization of an advanced practice/consultant nurse in a Nursing Development Unit.*
- *The skills and knowledge base of consultancy, underpinned by a strong nursing foundation, augmented by strong leadership and combined with the educator and researcher functions, are presented as the attributes of the advanced practitioner/consultant nurse.*
- *The facilitation of a transformational culture is highlighted as central to the skills and processes used within the role.*
- *Implications for the preparation and accreditation of the advanced practitioner/consultant nurse are highlighted.*

Keywords: action research, advanced practice, conceptual framework, consultant nurse, practice development, transformational culture.

INTRODUCTION

This paper presents a preliminary conceptual model for advanced practice developed in the process of analysing data from a 3-year action research study involving the operationalization of an advanced practice/consultant nurse role, in which I was the action researcher. One of the hallmarks of action research is that analysis occurs in practice during each phase in the action research cycle. Hence there is a preliminary conceptual framework resulting from the early research. Deeper analysis of data collected to inform action will be used to further refine the model at a later date.

The terms advanced practitioner and consultant nurse are used interchangeably in this article. The reason for this is that currently there appear to be two schools of thought concerning the essence of advanced practice (Manley, 1996a) (28). One school sees advanced practice as relating to the new clinical posts developing at the nursing–medicine interface. Many of these, although retaining nursing values, are associated with taking on what were previously considered to be medical tasks. Such posts serve an important function in enabling nursing to respond to changing health care needs, but I see them as primarily specialist posts, rather than advanced practitioner posts. The other school of thought (to which I subscribe) is associated with advancing nursing practice, rather than medical practice. This view encompasses expert nursing practice (as a generalist or specialist), but it is more than that, as it also integrates the subroles of educator, researcher and consultant. Such posts are multidimensional and their purpose is to promote and develop clinical nursing from clinical to strategic and policy levels, whilst simultaneously creating and maintaining a culture in which nurses and nursing strive for more effective patient and health care services.

BACKGROUND: THE CONTEXT IN WHICH THE POST DEVELOPED AND RELATED CONTEMPORARY ISSUES

The post was developed within the context of the early Nursing Development Unit (DNU) movement and followed 2 years of developmental work between 1989 and 1991 (Manley, 1990; Warfield & Manley, 1990; Jenkins, 1991; Clayton & McCabe, 1991) (26, 41, 21, 5). I facilitated this development work using a values clarification approach with the all-qualified nursing staff of a five-bedded intensive care unit. A number of practice developments resulted which were congruent with the values and beliefs shared. These core values and beliefs centred on nursing, collaboration, change, the value of the individual and teamwork. An open and nonhierarchical management approach further facilitated an environment for development (Salvage, 1989; Jenkins, 1991) (32, 21).

In 1991 a second values clarification exercise was undertaken in preparation for the unit's application to the King's Fund for financial support. This resulted in staff identifying what they wanted to achieve in forthcoming years and also how they wished any funding to be used. Priority areas identified included staff development, education, research, practice development and quality assurance activities. Staff perceived the need for someone to help them with these areas and decided that any financial support obtained should be used for that purpose.

At the time, a number of posts designed to achieve similar objectives existed in Britain and the USA. Within Britain, there was the consultant nurse (Wright, 1991) (42) and the lecturer–practitioner (Vaughan, 1987, 1989) (38, 39). In 1991, both lacked a detailed role description, although both roles have subsequently developed. Within the USA, the clinical nurse specialist and nurse–practitioner roles predominated, both being promoted as advanced practice roles (Kitzman, 1989) (22). The role description for the clinical nurse specialist was the most developed in terms of its explicit four subroles, its skills and competencies and the primary criteria required by the post-holder; these are outlined in (Table 1) (Hamric, 1989) (13). Nurse–practitioners were considered to have primarily a unidimensional focus to their role (providing direct services) whereas the clinical nurse specialist was multidimensional (providing both direct and indirect services as represented by a combination of direct and indirect practice and the other subroles) (Kitzman, 1989) (22). Kitzman considered that the differing role dimensions of the clinical nurse specialist and nurse–practitioner reflected their respective purposes. For nurse–practitioners, their stated purpose was "to provide patient care" (Ford & Silver, 1967) (8), and for clinical nurse specialists it was "to improve patient care" (Crabtree, 1979; Holt, 1984) (6, 19). Today, in contemporary American practice, there has been some amalgamation of the two roles (Hickey et al., 1996) (17). Both are beginning to share

TABLE I   THE SUBROLES, SKILLS AND COMPETENCIES AND PRIMARY
CRITERIA OF THE AMERICAN CLINICAL NURSE SPECIALIST HIGHLIGHTED
BY HAMRIC (1989)

Subroles

Expert practitioner
Educator
Researcher
Consultant

Skills and competencies

Change agent
Collaborator
Clinical leader
Role model
Patient advocate

Primary criteria

Master's/doctorate prepared
Client-based practice
Certification through meeting expert criteria in practice

---

similar attributes, with the nurse–practitioner moving towards the multidimensional focus of the clinical nurse specialist

In Britain, the title clinical nurse specialist was beginning to be used in the late 1980s and early 1990s, but British roles were very different to the American roles and the title was inconsistently applied (Manley, 1993) (27). British nurses with the title of clinical nurse specialist primarily fulfilled a specialist practice role in the areas of stoma nursing, diabetic nursing and infection control (Wade & Moyer, 1989) (40). Some aspects of the educator and consultant roles were evident but these were superficial and underdeveloped compared with their American counterparts. Nurse–practitioners, also beginning to develop in the UK in similar ways to the USA, tended in contrast to encompass direct practice totally, with little involvement with the other subroles.

Contemporary views on the nature of advanced practice in Britain are reflected in the UKCC's statement on advanced practice, which seems to suggest a multidimensional rather than unidimensional focus to such posts:

> Advanced nursing practice is concerned with adjusting the boundaries for the development of future practice, pioneering and developing new roles responsive to changing needs, and with advancing clinical practice, research and education to enrich professional practice as a whole (UKCC, 1994, p. 8) (37)

Such a view seems to imply achievement as an expert practitioner within an area of nursing, be that generalist or specialist, and highlights the other dimensions of the role necessary to facilitate development of other practitioners and nursing practice.

THE POST AND ITS EVALUATION

Through values clarification the staff of the NDU discussed in this article had identified the need for an advanced practice type post. They also identified eight future objectives, one of which reflected their wish to fulfill what they considered an important responsibility—the evaluation of such a post. This objective was particularly important, as the proposal was being developed at a time when other senior clinical posts were being lost within NHS restructuring exercises throughout Britain, and the value of a clinical career structure for nursing needed to be demonstrated, particularly to senior managers nationally.

The funding proposal was successful and unit staff asked me to undertake the new role so as to continue the work achieved collaboratively. The role description outlined by Hamric (1989) (13) was used as a starting point to develop what was then a unique role in Britain. The job description was structured around the four subroles identified by Hamric (1989) (13) for 4 days a week, and then combined with the responsibilities of a lecturer in higher education (Course Director to the MSc in Nursing) for the remaining day.

I fulfilled all the primary criteria outlined by Hamric (1989) (13), but their relevance to the British context had not yet been established. There had, however, been European moves for Master's prepared nurses in practice (Casey, 1990) (3).

In relation to evaluation, the possession of theoretical and practical knowledge implied by the primary criteria, skills competencies and subroles (Figure 1) had already been linked to quality outcome indicators (Georgopoulus & Christman, 1990) (10). Georgopoulus & Christman, in a 2-year longitudinal study, compared practitioners who possessed these criteria with two other groups: those attributed the same title but not possessing all of the identified skills and competencies, and those who were conventional nurse ward managers. A significant impact on over 100 outcome indicators was demonstrated in practitioners who possessed all the criteria, compared with the other two groups who did not. This seems to suggest that practitioners, with both theoretical and practical knowledge to at least the academic level of Master's degree, within the four subroles can have a major impact on outcomes when they are based in practice. What is not so explicit are the processes that such practitioners use. It is this area that subsequently became the focus of the action research project, as reflected by the research question: How does the advanced practitioner/consultant nurse facilitate the development of nurses and nursing to provide a quality nursing service?

METHODOLOGY

In light of the values held by staff and myself, as well as the objectives aspired to and the processes used to date, i.e. values clarification and reflection, it was important to choose a methodology that would be congruent, valuing staff as co-researchers and recognizing the messiness and complexity of both practice and the context in which practice takes place (Greenwood, 1984) (11), so well described by Schon (1983) (36) as "the swampy lowlands." Action research was therefore selected, specifically the approach underpinned by critical science (McCutcheon & Jung, 1990) (30) and associated with staff participation, collaboration and emancipation. To differentiate this approach to action research from other perspectives, Grundy (1982) (12) named it "emancipatory action research" in education. In nursing it has been called the "enhancement approach" (Holter & Schwartz-Barcott, 1993) (20) and in health and social care the "empowering type" (Hart & Bond, 1995) (14).

With hindsight the 3-year action project can be considered as falling within three broad but interconnected areas, each associated with innumerable action research cycles. The first area was at the macro/strategic level, where my role was linked inextricably to the stated purpose of the unit and to the facilitation of that

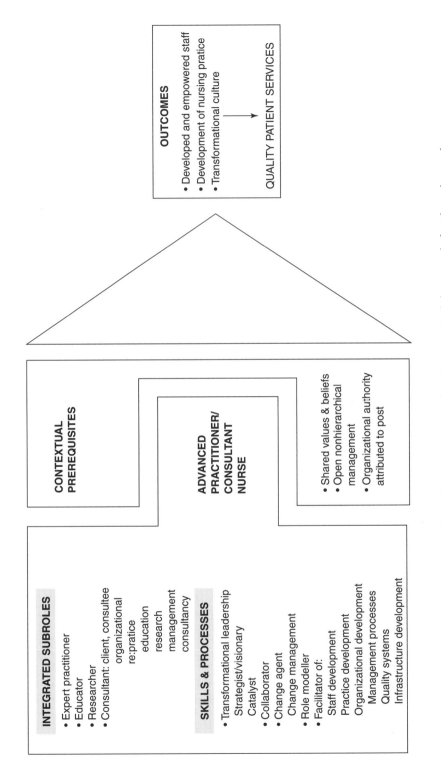

FIGURE A13-1. *Advancing nursing practice: A conceptual framework for the advanced practitioner/consultant nurse.*

purpose, namely developing a quality patient service. The second area was more concrete and middle in scope, as represented by action research cycles linked to each of the unit's eight objectives. Again my actions were inextricably linked to both the facilitation of and the collaboration with staff in achieving these objectives. The third area concerned my personal actions and reflections during the time the role was undertaken. This article draws mainly on work within the middle area, especially the staff's objective concerned with evaluating the post.

DATA ANALYSIS

A very crude analysis of my working diary was undertaken for the type of work activity performed during the first 2 years of the project (July 1992–June 1994). The work diary was and continued to be used to record all appointments, daily objectives and daily achievements in note form. More detailed field notes were also kept during the project.

Each member of staff was provided with a detailed itemized list of activities grouped under some loose thematic headings. Focused group discussions with each primary nursing team were used to explore how staff felt this advanced practitioner/ consultant nurse post was working, whether more or less of different aspects were desired and whether refinements were required. This also provided an opportunity for staff to participate in my performance review. Minor refinements were incorporated into the role, in relation to aspects such as clinical rounds, primary nurse reviews and the timing of such activities.

The conceptual framework presented here has resulted from re-analysing the 2 years' data in more depth, something that it was not possible to do at the time. One hundred and ninety-five different work items were identified, 77 from year 1 and 118 from year 2.

The analysis was undertaken in two stages: first, a thematic analysis of the work activities resulting in 22 categories and seven themes (Table 2); and second, a cross-analysis of the 22 categories for the types of processes used and the knowledge base drawn on. From this the following further nine themes were derived:

- role modeller;
- catalyst;
- facilitator;
- staff development;
- practice development;
- change agent;
- change manager;
- infrastructure development;
- strategist.

The combined 16 themes were then used to construct a conceptual framework which identifies the roles and skills necessary for operationalizing an advanced practitioner/consultant nurse role, linked to essential contextual prerequisites and outcomes (Figure 1).

THE CONCEPTUAL FRAMEWORK

The conceptual framework has three parts: the advanced practitioner/consultant nurse characterized by four integrated subroles and a set of skills and processes; the context in which the advanced practitioner/consultant nurse operates; and the

TABLE 2   CATEGORIES AND THEMES DERIVED FROM STAGE I OF DIARY ANALYSIS

Category	Theme
1. Developing teaching skills in others 2. Teaching 3. Establishing a staff development culture 4. Higher education 5. Obtaining information 6. Career guidance 7. Developing unit's resources	Educator
8. Practising nursing (direct) 9. Developing practice 10. Creating a reflective practice culture 11. Clinical supervision	Expert practitioner
12. Research 13. Collecting and rationalizing data	Researcher
14. Picking up issues for strategy/strategist 15. Initiating and facilitating practice projects/catalyst/strategist 16. Maintaining momentum through communication/catalyst 17. Facilitating effective teams	Transformational leadership
18. Consultancy	Consultant
19. Collaboration	Collaboration
20. Quality-related activities 21. Marketing, promotion and dissemination 22. Interviewing	Organizational development/management processes

outcomes in practice resulting when such roles, processes and contexts are combined.

Context

The context in which all practitioners operate will have an influence on their practice, a premise underpinning naturalistic inquiry: "realities are wholes which cannot be understood in isolation from their contexts. . ." (Lincoln & Guba, 1985, p. 39) (24). In this study three influences were identified as essential prerequisites for successful operationalization of the advanced practitioner/consultant nurse role:

- shared values and beliefs;
- open nonhierarchical unit management;
- organizational authority attributed to the post.

The first two influences particularly characterized the NDU culture in which the post was established. These are also factors identified by the King's Fund (Salvage, 1989) (32) as conducive to establishing a NDU. From the study, the third prerequisite emerged as important, particularly if (as in this study) the post-holder does not possess the positional power of a traditional management post. The post therefore requires senior status recognition, and hence legitimate authority from the senior management board, with the post-holder being recognized as an important contributor to trust strategy and a partner in the senior management nursing team.

Subroles

The four subroles previously identified by Hamric (1989) (13) clearly emerged from the data, but have been further expanded. Presented as separate entities within the conceptual framework, in practice the subroles demonstrate considerable overlap, each informing the other in terms of their respective knowledge bases and processes. The emphasis given to any one subrole varied according to the issues and needs being addressed, the changing needs of the service and the unit's purpose.

The expert practitioner role encompassed both direct and indirect practice. Direct practice involved caring for patients and their families, whereas indirect practice involved, amongst other activities, working with staff in planning care for their patients and developing practice protocols which were evidence based, supervising staff in guided structured reflection, facilitating reflective primary reviews and exploring practice issues. The role also involved creating a culture for staff to reflect on their own practice and nursing generally. This was achieved by being based in practice, through practising nursing and using strategies that facilitate practice development.

Although I was working within the specific field of intensive care nursing, the knowledge base, skills and values central to nursing generally were drawn on to inform both direct and indirect practice as much as those of intensive care nursing. Both knowledge bases complemented each other, and were manifested in both the "know-how" and "know-that" (Polanyi, 1958) (31) of nursing practice. It was through expertise in nursing practice and the practice of nursing that credibility was accorded to the post. This credibility made it easier to introduce and manage change. Direct practice also provided opportunities to be exposed to (and reminded of) the realities of practice, and the daily issues and struggles that exist for staff, patients and their families. This acted as a motivator for action.

The educator role clearly emerged as involving a broad view of education, encompassing development of others including their teaching skills, providing opportunities for others to learn, establishing a staff development culture and developing and facilitating the maintenance of the unit as a learning environment. Besides the skills and knowledge necessary to provide a positive learning environment in practice, knowledge and skills related to higher education and career development were also used. My experience in higher education was repeatedly drawn on by staff to help them to gain access to and to progress within the higher education system, to optimize their higher education experience to benefit practice, and to gain credit and recognition for their practice from higher education.

Other aspects of this subrole included providing opportunities for staff to develop new knowledge and skills, and developing and maintaining the unit's educational resources. Both staff development and practice development were therefore interlinked with the educator subrole.

The researcher role emerged clearly as described by Hodgman (1983) (18),

TABLE 3   THE THREE LEVELS OF RESEARCHER ACTIVITY
(HODGMAN, 1983)

Level 1	Utilizing, interpreting, evaluating, communicating research and deriving implications
Level 2	Testing and applying; translating into protocols; acting as a research co-ordinator and research generator
Level 3	Replicating; generating original ideas; supervising research projects; undertaking collaborative research

who identified the three levels outlined in Table 3. From the data, examples of level 1 working included: establishing a research culture and journal review group; critiquing and helping others critique research; exploring the implications for practice of research; updating practice protocols in light of resarch; and facilitating the rationalization of data collection and its implications. As the unit was a critical care unit, many data were routinely collected. With the development of audit tools and ongoing research projects, this potentially placed increasing demand on staff.

At level 2, examples of activity included developing research-based and evidence-based protocols for both quality assurance and educational purposes. Other activities included co-ordinating research, highlighting research questions, providing consultancy and teaching on research methodology and methods.

At level 3 collaborative research was undertaken so as to help others with no previous reseach experience to participate in and experience the research process.

To undertake such a role in practice requires a knowledge base which has a firm foundation in all ways of knowing in nursing, related and appropriate methodologies and the assumptions underpinning all three research paradigms—positivist, interpretive and critical science (Lucock, 1996) (25).

The data supporting the consultant role demonstrated that the content of the consultancy was drawn from all subroles, nursing practice, practice development, education in practice, educational theory, higher education, research methodology and methods, data collection, the nature of knowledge and theory development in nursing, and consultancy skills.

Caplan's model (1970) (2) based on mental health consultation provides an appropriate framework for illustrating the types of consultancy undertaken in this study—client-centred, consultee-centred, programme-centred and organization-centred. Appendix 1 illustrates the main characteristics of each and provides examples from the work activities highlighted in the diary analysis.

In practice, several types of consultancy may be used simultaneously and this point is further supported by Hendrix & LaGonda (1982) (15) who consider that consultants would use all four types at various times for maximal effectiveness.

In addition to levels of consultancy, the study data also demonstrated specific consultancy approaches. Schein (1988) (35) labelled three models representing these approaches as the purchase of expertise model, the doctor–patient model and the process model. Each is underpinned by different assumptions. The study data demonstrated that two of these approaches were used extensively: the expert model and the process model. The expert model encompasses giving advice and guidance, while the process model is more concerned with developing the skills and problem-solving activities of others. Process consultancy is underpinned by values about collaboration and how others develop.

Caplan's model therefore offers a way of understanding the potential for different levels of consultancy within nursing. The ability to operate within all four types would be a fundamental function of advanced practitioners/consultant nurses if the potential of nursing practice was to be realized at a strategic as well as a clinical level (Manely, 1996b) (29). The specialist–practitioner, in contrast, would predominantly be involved in client-centred consultancy and occasionally consultee-centred consultancy. To operate within the other two types of consultancy requires an understanding of organizational behaviour as well as culture and the other skills and knowledge alluded to by Caplan.

Thus it is when the skills and knowledge base of consultancy, underpinned by a strong nursing foundation and augmented by strong leadership, are combined with the educator and researcher functions that the attributes of the advanced practitioner/consultant nurse begin to become evident. This demonstrates the reason for linking the title of advanced practitioner to that of consultant nurse. To fulfil the function of consultant, however, requires more than expertise in one's area of nursing and the ability to give advice:

> *Many professionals, in fact, assume that experience in a particular field—for example, social work or communications—is adequate preparation for consultation. But helping others with their work is a far more intricate process than working directly on one's own task. Moreover the organizational milieu is fraught with conflicts that may ensnare consultants and leave them impotent. (Gallessich, 1982, p. x) (9)*

Skills and Processes

Some of the skills possessed and the processes used by the advanced practitioner/ consultant nurse have been implied by the subroles described. Again the skills and processes are inextricably linked with each other.

The processes I used focused on facilitating a culture in which staff could become leaders themselves. These processes reflected both my own values and those of the unit staff. It is only with hindsight and on reading the literature that the processes can be recognized as being of a transformational leadership nature (Sashkin & Rosenbach, 1993) (34). From the study data the following processes emerged which have also been identified by a number of writers and researchers on transformational leadership:

1. Developing a shared vision. Providing a sense of mission, vision, excitement and pride (Bass, 1985) (1); inspiring a shared vision (Kouzes & Posner, 1987) (23).
2. Inspiring and communicating. Inspiring, setting high expectations, expressing important purposes simply, communicating a vision (Bass, 1985) (1); clarity, focusing the attention of others on key ideas, active listening and providing feedback (Sashkin & Burke, 1990) (33); communication (Sashkin & Burke, 1990) (33).

3. Valuing others. Valuing the individual, focusing on the individual's needs, encouraging personal responsibility (Bass, 1985) (1); caring about others, unconditional positive regard (Sashkin & Burke, 1990) (33); encouraging, recognizing other's contributions and celebrating them (Kouzes & Posner, 1987) (23).

4. Challenging and stimulating. Providing intellectual stimulation and a flow of new ideas which challenge others to rethink old ways of doing things; stimulating others to develop own structures and problem-solving (Bass, 1985) (1); challenging the process—searching for opportunities and experimenting (Kouzes & Posner, 1987) (23).

5. Developing trust. By acting consistently over time, between words and actions (Sashkin & Burke, 1990) (33); developing respect and trust (Bass, 1985) (1).

6. Enabling. Creating opportunities, supporting others in taking on challenges and by minimizing the risks (Sashkin & Burke, 1990) (33); enabling others to act through collaboration, supporting the development of others (Kouzes & Posner, 1987) (23); fostering collaboration, modelling the ways (Kouzes & Posner, 1987) (23).

Linked to the processes of transformational leadership were those of being a strategist and a catalyst. Being a strategist included activities which involved actively looking for and raising awareness of potential future issues, developments and opportunities which nurses needed to explore and develop. Acting as a catalyst encapsulates those activities necessary to "get things going." Through facilitating and initiating developments, through supporting them and participating in them, it was possible for those with potential interest to become involved, to get started, to feel supported and to maintain momentum. Being a catalyst involved a great deal of communication, from getting people together, organizing somewhere for them to meet, co-ordinating diaries and off-duties, and helping groups clarify and formulate their purpose and frames of reference.

In operationalizing the advanced practitioner/consultant nurse role and working towards a common purpose and vision, collaboration was the predominant way of working with staff. Collaboration is pivotal to process consultancy, transformational leadership, being an educator, being a partner with patients, families and the multidisciplinary team, and facilitating change. The concept analysis by Henneman et al. (1995) (16) conveys the attributes which represent what is meant by collaboration.

The management of change and helping others with change permeated almost every activity undertaken. Again the values underpinning change management were congruent with the values underpinning collaborative ways of working, transformational leadership, process consultancy and reflected a normative re-educative change strategy (Chin & Benne, 1969) (4).

All activities provided opportunities for role modelling. Individual interviews with staff indicated that some began to aspire to similar roles for themselves within clinical practice—a clinical career ladder that they valued, and one they had not thought possible before.

All the subroles and processes facilitated staff development, practice development and organizational development. The organization and its infrastructure provided the context for practice and staff development. Knowledge of management processes was therefore essential not just in nurturing and fostering a transformational culture but also in supporting staff in their own management development. Activities in this area related to developing the organization and the infrastructure. This was reflected in activities concerned with facilitating staff in their:

- development of policies and practices regarding (i) skillmix, staff establishment, (ii) individual performance review, (iii) staff development and orientation;
- protocols and guidelines concerning (i) role definitions, (ii) interviewing, (iii) staff study leave and funding;
- reports and proposals for expanding and improving the service.

Many activities involved introducing quality systems. Such systems linked management processes to the development of practice, quality patient services, educational strategies and research evidence to support effective practice. Simultaneously this involved working with staff to develop their own skils in the area of quality.

Many of the management processes were therefore about establishing a sound infrastructure, where staff were able to optimize their practice for patients, enhanced by working in a culture that supported them.

Outcomes

The final part of the conceptual framework identifies the outcomes strived for. However, evidence from the study data also suggests these were achieved. The ultimate purpose of advanced practice/consultant nurse posts is to improve the quality of care experienced by patients and their families. Such posts and the processes used must therefore be linked to the effect they have on this purpose if they are to be supported and valued by stakeholders. Key to achieving this purpose is the role of the advanced practitioner/consultant nurse in developing a transformational culture. Such a culture will also facilitate staff empowerment and nursing practice development.

DISCUSSION AND IMPLICATIONS

The relationship of the conceptual framework presented here to Hamric's model (1989) (13) will first be discussed. Implications will be considered in relation to refining the framework and the future preparation and accreditation of advanced practitioner/consultant nurses.

This conceptual framework has resulted from experience of operationalizing an advanced practitioner/consultant nurse role within a British context. The original job description was initially guided by the model and four subroles identified by Hamric (1989) (13) in the absence of any other available framework of sufficient detail. This study identifies some similarities with Hamric's model, namely the four subroles themselves. However, there are a number of differences, e.g., the role of transformational leadership and its associated skills and processes.

Similarities relate to the existence of the four subroles in both models. The subroles in this study have, however, been derived from data obtained in the process of an action research project, in contrast to the policy and professional consensus informing Hamric's model (1989) (13). The subroles are by their nature broad, and reflect the need for both practical and theoretical expertise in areas of nursing practice, education, research and consultancy. This study particularly emphasizes the integration of the four subroles with one another and also further expands on the nature of the consultant and educator roles. It additionally highlights the benefits of having "one foot" in the higher education camp. Uniquely, all roles are linked to the skills and processes which facilitate the development of a transformational culture, staff development, practice development and organizational development. An understanding of and expertise in related management processes are therefore also emphasized.

Greater differences exist between the conceptual framework presented here and Hamric's model in relation to the skills and processes used. Several processes in this study are completely new, while some are made more explicit or expanded. The process of transformational leadership is one such example, and is central to the conceptual model presented. Transformational processes derived from the data are congruent with those in the literature. The importance of these processes has been linked to creating and sustaining a transformational culture. Transformational processes are also linked to being a strategist, a catalyst and using a number of other management processes—those concerned, for example, with quality systems and infrastructure development.

I feel a particular strength in this conceptual framework, which differentiates it from Hamric's model, is the explicit link between the advanced practitioner/ consultant nurse role, its context and its outcomes. This serves to acknowledge that, however much practical and theoretical expertise an advanced practitioner/ consultant nurse possesses, this on its own is of little value. The context has to be conducive and the basic ingredients need to exist, namely shared values and a nonhierarchical, open management style. Similarly, such posts always need to be linked to their ultimate purpose—that of facilitating quality services to patients and their families. The other strength of the conceptual framework is that it reflects more appropriately the culture in which it has developed—a British rather than an American one.

Future analysis will need to focus on explicating the links between the three components of the conceptual framework, developing further understanding of the processes used and developing their relationship to the outcomes. This is vital if both nursing and advanced practitioner/consultant nurse posts are to be valued by executive management, the government and the public.

The conceptual framework presented raises a number of implications for practice, particularly in relation to the preparation and accreditation of advanced practitioners/consultant nurses.

To operate successfully within all four subroles, and to develop the expertise, skills and processes required, will involve more than merely undertaking a theoretical course. All four subroles are practice based, requiring both practical and theoretical knowledge. It is likely therefore that practitioners en route to such posts will have followed diverse and individual pathways, where extensive and varied experience as well as formal study will be necessary components. The biggest challenge will be the identification of practice outcomes of the advanced practitioner/consultant nurse, as a basis for accreditation. From this study it is easy to argue that one needs preparation as an educator, consultant and researcher, built on a foundation of expertise in the practice of nursing, underpinned by a strong theoretical base and understanding of all the ways of knowing in nursing. Theoretical and academic outcomes are much easier to state and recognize but it is the "know-how" of expert practice within the four subroles that is much more difficult to explicate. Furthermore, a list of behaviourally stated competencies would be incongruent, as advanced practitioners/consultant nurses would autonomously decide which strategies and subroles they focus on at any one point in time, depending on the needs of practice, practitioners, the organization and the service—a complex process. However, from the processes and frameworks shared within this paper, some guiding principles for recognizing outcomes in practice could be developed.

With regard to the level of academic preparation, it is probably the researcher role that is the determinant, because to operate at all three levels as a researcher (Hodgman, 1983) (18) and to be able to work with the premises underpinning all three paradigms, requires preparation to at least Master's level. In the future this is likely to be to Doctoral level. This is because increasingly the role of interpreting and using research has been separated from that of doing research. Additionally the opportunities to carry out research are not now provided formally until studying at Master's level. Therefore, developing confidence in the three research paradigms, their underlying premises and their appropriateness for different ways of knowing within nursing, will probably only be possible at the post-Master's level.

In relation to accreditation, academic frameworks are well established but what does not exist (except in its infancy at the graduate level via the Higher Award [ENB, 1991]) (7) are mechanisms for accrediting expertise in practice. This, of course, begs the question of who will accredit such practitioners, even if outcomes can be made explicit? In relation to the conceptual framework presented here, it would seem that the best judges are those affected by the outcomes, namely practitioners, organizations and most importantly patients and families themselves. It is likely that any accreditation of practice would therefore involve multiple sources of evidence.

CONCLUSION

The conceptual framework presented has resulted from a study which attempted to operationalize the advanced practitioner/consultant nurse role. The post has developed from staff's own values and beliefs and aspirations for the future. The original job description was guided by the four subroles identified by Hamric (1989) (13). This model was chosen only in the absence of any other detailed guidance. Although some similarities with Hamric's model have resulted, namely the four subroles, there are several differences, particularly the skills and processes necessary for creating a transformational culture. The conceptual framework resulting has also highlighted implications to be considered regarding the preparation of advanced practitioners/consultant nurses. Those aspiring to advanced practice/consultant nurse posts will be guided in their career progression from this framework, in the sense that specific theoretical and practical expertise needs to be developed.

Future work on analysing data arising from the action research project is proposed to make the links between the three components within the conceptual framework more explicit and to expand on the processes used. In the mean-time it is hoped that the conceptual framework presented here will go some way to making explicit the multidimensional nature of advanced practice and the potential and powerful impact that such posts can have on the future advancement of nursing for the benefit of patients, clients and their loved ones.

ACKNOWLEDGMENTS

I would like to acknowledge the role and contribution of the coresearchers in this project, namely all the staff of the Chelsea & Westminster Intensive Care & Nursing Development Unit, and additionally the valuable support provided by Ricky Lucock and Carolyn Mills.

Appendix 1: Caplan's Model of Mental Health Consultation (1970) With Examples of Activities From the Work of Advanced Practitioners/Consultant Nurse (Adapted From Manley, 1996b) (29)

CLIENT-CENTRED CASE CONSULTATION (CASE-DIRECT)

The problem is case focused, i.e., client/patient focused, and involves the consultant making direct recommendations to the consultee on how the client should be treated or managed. A spin-off may be that the consultee may improve his/her knowledge and skills but this is secondary to the primary aim of focusing on the client. This is the traditional medical approach to consultation, referred to as the clinical approach (Gallessich, 1982) (9).

Examples of Activities From the Data

Responding to nurses' requests for help concerning:

- how to care for a patient who is experiencing hopelessness or powerlessness, or manifesting the signs of sleep deprivation;
- how to help a patient and their family make a difficult decision;
- clarifying the ethical issues within a particular patient situation.

CONSULTEE-CENTRED CASE CONSULTATION (CASE-INDIRECT)

The problem is again case focused but this time the consultant's primary focus is on the consultee's difficulty, which Caplan considers may be in the following four areas:

- lack of knowledge,
- lack of skill in making use of the knowledge,
- lack of self-confidence,
- lack of professional objectivity.

Examples of Activities From the Data

- Helping nurses to develop their family assessment skills or their psychological and physical assessment skills;
- Working through ethical frameworks to help nurses analyse and make sense of ethical dilemmas generally.

PROGRAM-CENTRED ADMINISTRATIVE CONSULTATION (ADMINISTRATION-DIRECT)

The problem focus is on the organization rather than the client or group of clients, otherwise it is similar to client-centred case consultation. A consultant may be invited by a group of administrators to help with a problem concerning perhaps some area of service provision or to help with planning and implementation of organizational policy. It would involve assessing the problem and then writing a report with the consultant's assessment and recommendations. The purpose is the improved understanding and operation of the consultees; it is therefore direct and usually short-term. Caplan makes parallels between this type of consultancy and management consultancy. He suggests that mental health consultancy is a competitor to the traditional management consultant because of the special expertise that mental health consultants have in relation to interpersonal skills and communication. He does recognize the need to have additional knowledge and experience in the areas of organizational theory, practice and planning, fiscal, personnel management and general administration to operate in this type of consultancy.

Examples of Activities From the Data

- Providing guidance on how to implement both a market strategy and a research strategy;
- Helping to develop, plan and evaluate programmes for the orientation of new staff or for developing essential competencies in inexperienced staff;
- Providing expertise in skillmix and establishment reviews.

CONSULTEE-CENTRED ADMINISTRATIVE CONSULTATION (ADMINISTRATION-INDIRECT)

Again the focus is on the organization but the methods are indirect in that the primary focus is on increasing the skills of the consultee(s) which will in return benefit the organization. In Caplan's words:

> Consultee-centred administrative consultation is probably the most complicated, interesting, and demanding type of mental health consultation. The consultant is called in by the administrative staff of an organization to help them deal with current problems in organizational planning, programme development, personnel management, and other aspects of the implementation of organizational policies. It is expected that he [sic] will help them to improve their capacity to handle such problems on their own in the future. The

*consultant centres his attention primarily on the work difficulties of the consul-
tees and attempts to help them improve their problem-solving skills and overcome their shortcomings. He is interested in collecting information about the
organization, its goals, programs, policies and administrative structure and
functioning, not in order to work out his own recommendations or a collaborative plan for improving these, but as an aid in assessing the problems that
impede the operations of the consultees and as a vehicle for assisting them
to improve their ways of overcoming their work difficulties. (p. 265)*

Examples of Activities From the Data

- Facilitating the development of a philosophy, mission statement, strategy;
- Working with team co-ordinators to develop their teambuilding and leadership
  skills or approaches to group clinical supervision;
- Helping staff develop skills in developing role definitions, quality assurance
  programmes, change management strategies.

REFERENCES

1. Bass B. M. (1985) Leadership and Performance Beyond Expectations. Free Press,
   New York. [Back to *The conceptual frame . . : SKILLS AND PROCESSES*]
2. Caplan G. (1970) The Theory and Practice of Mental Health Consultation. Tavistock
   Publications, London. [Back to *The conceptual frame . . : SUBROLES*]
3. Casey N. (1990) The specialist debate. Nursing Standard 4(31), 18–19. [*Medline
   Link*] [Back to *The post and its eva. .*]
4. Chin, R. & Benne K.D. (1969) General strategies for effecting change in human
   systems. In The Planning of Change (Bennis W.G. & Benne K.D., eds.), 2nd edn.
   Holt, Rinehart and Winston, New York. [Back to *The conceptual frame . . : SKILLS
   AND PROCESSES*]
5. Clayton J. & McCabe S. (1991) Continuing education in the NDU. Nursing Standard
   6(9), 43–31. [*Medline Link*] [*CINAHL Link*] [Back to *Background: the cont. .*]
6. Crabtree M. (1979). Effective utilization of clinical specialists within the organizational
   structure of hospital nursing services. Nursing Administration Quarterly 4, 1–10.
   [*Medline Link*] [Back to *Background: the cont. .*]
7. ENB (1991) Framework for Continuing Professional Education for Nurses, Midwives
   and Health Visitors. Guide to Implementation. English National Board, London. [Back
   to *Discussion and impli. .*]
8. Ford L. & Silver H. (1967) Expanded role of the nurse in child care. Nursing Outlook
   15, 43–45. [Back to *Background: the cont. .*]
9. Gallessich J. (1982) The Profession & Practice of Consultation. Jossey-Bass Publishers, San Francisco. [Back to *The conceptual frame . . : SUBROLES, Appendix 1:
   Caplan's . . : CLIENT-CENTRED CASE. .*]
10. Georgopoulos B. & Christman L. (1990) Effects of Clinical Nursing Specialization.
    Edwin Melson Press, New York. [Back to *The post and its eva. .*]
11. Greenwood J. (1984) Nursing research: a position paper. Journal of Advanced Nurs-
    ing 9, 77–82. [*Medline Link*] [*CINAHL Link*] [Back to *Methodology*]
12. Grundy S. (1982) Three modes of action research. Curriculum Perspectives 2(3),
    23–34. [Back to *Methodology*]
13. Hamric A. (1989) A model for CNS evaluation. In The Clinical Nurse Specialist in
    Theory and Practice (Hamric A. & Spross J., eds), 2nd edn. WB Saunders, Philadel-
    phia, pp. 83–104. [Back to *Background: the cont. ., The post and its eva. ., The
    conceptual frame. .: SUBROLES, Discussion and impli. ., Conclusion, GRAPHICS:
    Table 1*]
14. Hart E. & Bond M. (1995) Action Research for Health and Social Care. Open University
    Press, Buckingham. [Back to *Methodology*]
15. Hendrix M J. & LaGodna G.E. (1982) Consultation: a political process aimed at

change. In The Nurse as a Change Agent (Lancast J. & Lancaster W., eds). CV Mosby, St. Louis. [Back to *The conceptual frame. . . : SUBROLES*]

16. Henneman E. A., Lee, J. L. & Cohen J. I. (1995) Collaboration: a concept analysis. Journal of Advanced Nursing 21, 103–109. [*Medline Link*] [*CINAHL Link*] [Back to *The conceptual frame. . : SKILLS AND PROCESSES*]

17. Hickey J., Ouimette R. M. & Venegoni S. (1996) Advanced Practice Nursing: Changing Roles and Clinical Applications. Lippincott, Philadelphia. [Back to *Background: the cont.*]

18. Hodgman E. C. (1983) The CNS as researcher. In The Clinical Nurse Specialist in Theory and Practice (Hamric A., Spross, J., eds), 1st edn. Grune and Stratton, New York, pp. 73–82. [Back to *The conceptual frame. . : SUBROLES, Discussion and impli.., GRAPHICS: Table 3*]

19. Holt F. (1984) A theoretical model for clinical specialist practice. Nursing & Health Care 5, 445–449. [*Medline Link*] [*CINAHL Link*] [Back to *Background: the cont.*]

20. Holter M. & Schwartz-Barcott D. (1993) Action Research: what is it? How has it been used and, how can it be used in nursing? Journal of Advanced Nursing 18, 298–304. [Back to *Methodology*]

21. Jenkins D. (1991) Developing and NDU: the manager's role. Nursing Standard 6(8), 36–39. [*Medline Link*] [*CINAHL Link*] [Back to *Background: the cont.*]

22. Kitzman H. J. (1989) The CNS and the Nurse Practitioner. In The Clinical Nurse Specialist in Theory and Practice (Hamric A., Spross, J., eds), 2nd edn. WB Saunders, Philadelphia, pp. 379–394. [Back to *Background: the cont.*]

23. Kouzes J. M. & Posner B. Z. (1987) The Leadership Challenge. Jossey-Bass, San Francisco. [Back to *The conceptual frame . . : SKILLS AND PROCESSES*]

24. Lincoln YS, Guba EG (1985) Naturalistic Inquiry. Sage, London. [Back to *The conceptual frame. . : CONTEXT*]

25. Lucock R. (1996) Research Methodology. MSc in Nursing Distance Learning Module. RCN Institute, London. [Back to *The conceptual frame. . : SUBROLES*]

26. Manley K. (1990) The birth of a nursing developmental unit. Nursing Standard 4(26), 36–38. [*Medline Link*] [Back to *Background: the cont.*]

27. Manley K. (1993) The clinical nurse specialist. Surgical Nurse 6(3), 21–25. [Back to *Background: the cont.*]

28. Manley K. (1996a) Advanced practice is not about medicalising nursing roles. Editorial. Nursing in Critical Care 1(2), 56–57. [Back to *Introduction*]

29. Manley K. (1996b) Consultancy. MSc in Nursing Distance Learning Module. RCN Institute, London. [Back to *The conceptual frame. . : SUBROLES*]

30. McCutcheon Jung B. (1990) Alternative perspectives on action research. Theory Into Practice XXIX(3), 144–151. [Back to *Methodology*]

31. Polanyi M. (1958) Personal Knowledge. Routledge & Kegan Paul, London. [Back to *The conceptual frame. . : SUBROLES*]

32. Salvage J. (1989) Nursing development. Nursing Standard 3(22), 25–28. [*Medline Link*] [Back to *Background: the cont. . , The conceptual frame . . . : CONTEXT*]

33. Sashkin M. E. & Burke, W. W. (1990) Understanding and assessing organisational leadership. In Measures of Leadership (Clark K., Clark M. B., eds). Leadership Library of America/Centre for Creative Leadership, West Orange NJ. [Back to *The conceptual frame. . : SKILLS AND PROCESSES*]

34. Sashkin M. E. & Rosenbach W. E. (1993) A new leadership paradigm. In Contemporary Issues in Leadership (Rosenbach W. E. & Taylor R., eds). 3rd edn. Westview Press, Colorado, pp. 87–108. [Back to *The conceptual frame. . : SKILLS AND PROCESSES*]

35. Schein E. H. (1988) Process Consultation. Vol. I: Its role in Organizational Development, 2nd edn. Addison-Wesley, Reading, MA. [Back to *The conceptual frame. . : SUBROLES*]

36. Schon D. (1983) The Reflective Practitioner. Jossey-Bass Publishers, San Francisco. [Back to *Methodology*]

37. UKCC (1994) The Future of Professional Practice—the Council's Standards for Education and Practice following Registration. Position Statement on Policy and Implementation, March 1994. UKCC, London. [Back to *Background: the cont.*]

38. Vaughan B. (1987) Bridging the gap. Senior Nurse 6(5), 30–31. [*CINAHL Link*] [Back to *Background: the cont.*]

39. Vaughan B. (1989) Two roles—one job. Nursing Times 85(11), 52. [*Medline Link*] [*CINAHL Link*] [Back to *Background: the cont..*]
40. Wade B. & Moyer A. (1989) An evaluation of clinical nurse specialists: implications for education and, the organisation of care. Senior Nurse 9(9), 11–15. [*CINAHL Link*] [Back to *Background: the cont..*]
41. Warfield C. & Manley K. (1990) Developing a new philosophy in the NDU. Nursing Standard 4(41), 27–30. [*Medline Link*] [Back to *Background: the cont..*]
42. Wright S. (1991) The nurse as a consultant. Nursing Standard 5(20), 31–34. [*Medline Link*] [*CINAHL Link*] [Back to *Background: the cont..*]

Taken from: Manley, K. (1997). A conceptual framework for advanced practice: An action research project operationalizing an advanced practitioner/consultant nurse role. *Journal of Clinical Nursing*, 6, 179–190.

Triangulation as a Qualitative Research Strategy

Triangulation is an approach to research that uses a combination of more than one research strategy in a single investigation. Researchers describe four types of triangulation for qualitative research: (1) data, (2) investigator, (3) theory, and (4) methods (Denzin, 1970). Mitchell (1986) has suggested a fifth type, *multiple triangulation,* which uses a combination of two or more triangulation techniques in one study.

Navigators use the term *triangulation* to describe a technique of plotting a position using three separate reference points. Navigators must know the exact location of a ship or plane at any given time. However, navigation is not an exact science, particularly when the vessel is moving. Imagine the difficulty of describing the exact location of a ship when it is in the deep ocean far from shore. The ship navigator takes a compass reading between the boat and one reference point, often a star. This reading makes it possible for the navigator to draw a line on a map. The navigator knows the position of the ship is somewhere on the line drawn. That position on this line is far from accurate. To increase accuracy, the navigator then takes a compass reading between the boat and a second reference point, often a second star. This reading makes it possible for the navigator to draw a second line on a map that intersects with the first. The intersection of the two lines, still not an exact point, provides a more accurate location of the boat. This second location is inaccurate because both the first compass reading and the second compass reading have a margin of error. To decrease the margin of error, the navigator takes another compass reading from a third reference point. The line from this reading intersects the previous two lines at the location of the boat, providing a more exact location.

Campbell and Fiske (1959) were the first to apply the navigational term *triangulation* to research. The metaphor is a good one because a phenomenon under study in a qualitative research project is much like a ship at sea. The exact description of the phenomenon is unclear. To gain clarity about the phenomenon, researchers study the phenomenon from a particular vantage point, from which they learn additional information about the phenomenon. However, the information at this point is not precise. Like navigators, researchers then move to a different vantage point to study the phenomenon. Information from the second vantage point provides additional data about the phenomenon, hence making the description clearer. A third vantage point makes the description of the phenomenon far clearer than either of the first two vantage points. As in compass readings, techniques of qualitative research have their margins of error. The goal in choosing different strategies in the same study is to balance them so each counterbalances the margin of error in the other (Fielding & Fielding, 1989).

Choosing Triangulation as a Research Strategy

Qualitative investigators may choose triangulation as a research strategy to assure completeness of findings or to confirm findings (Campbell & Fiske, 1959; Miles & Huberman, 1989; Patton, 1980). Completeness provides breadth and depth to an investigation, offering researchers a more accurate picture of the phenomenon (Denzin & Lincoln, 1994). Triangulation reveals the varied dimensions of a phenomenon and helps create a more accurate description (Fielding & Fielding, 1989). The metaphor of a group of visually impaired people describing an elephant based on the area they touch provides a good description of completeness. The person touching the trunk describes the elephant based on what that person feels. The person touching the foot provides a different description because of what he or she feels. The person touching the tail provides a third description. The most accurate description of the elephant comes from a combination of all three individuals' descriptions. None of the three alone is complete or accurate. Combining data from the vantage point of all three people results in a more complete and holistic description of the elephant.

Researchers might also choose triangulation to confirm findings and conclusions. Any single qualitative research strategy has its limitations. By combining different strategies, researchers confirm findings by overcoming the limitations of a single strategy (Breitmayer et al., 1993). Confirmation occurs when investigators compare and contrast the information from different vantage points. Uncovering the same information from more than one vantage point helps researchers describe how the findings occurred under different circumstances and assists them to confirm the validity of the findings. In this case, researchers do not use validity to find an ultimate truth but, rather, to provide increased understanding and a more accurate picture.

Investigators have the option of using several different types of triangulation to confirm or assure completeness of findings. The choice of type depends on the research question asked and the complexity of the phenomenon under study. When planning a study, researchers carefully consider the research methodology necessary to adequately answer a research question. Qualitative researchers may choose to use triangulation as a strategy in any investigation when their goal is to provide understanding or to obtain completeness and confirmation. In designing their study, researchers may use data triangulation, methodological triangulation, investigator triangulation, and theory triangulation, or a combination. A discussion of each triangulation type follows.

DATA TRIANGULATION

Using data triangulation, researchers include more than one source of data in a single investigation. Denzin (1989) described three types of data triangulation: (1) time, (2) space, and (3) person. Researchers choose the type of data triangulation that is relevant to the phenomenon under study. Using *time triangulation,* researchers collect data about a phenomenon at different points in time. Time of day, day of week, or month of year are examples of times researchers would collect data for triangulation. Studies based on longitudinal designs are not considered examples of data triangulation for time because they are intended to document changes over time (Kimchi et al., 1991).

Space triangulation consists of collecting data at more than one site. For example, a researcher might collect data at multiple units within one hospital or in multiple hospitals. At the outset, the researcher must identify how time or space relate to the study and make an argument supporting the use of different time or space collection points in the study. For example, a researcher studying decision making on a nursing unit might collect data on six different nursing units to triangulate for space. The researcher might also collect data on each shift and on weekdays and weekends to triangulate for time. The rationale for using the various collection spaces and times is to compare and contrast decision making at each time and in each location. By collecting data at different points in time and in different spaces, the researcher gains a clearer and more complete description of decision making and is able to differentiate characteristics that span time periods and spaces from characteristics specific to certain times and spaces.

Using *person triangulation,* researchers collect data from more than one *level of person,* that is, a set of individuals, groups, or collectives (Denzin, 1989). *Groups* can be dyads, families, or circumscribed groups. *Collectives* are communities, organizations, or societies. Investigators choose the various levels of person relevant to the study. In the previous example of studying decision making on a nursing unit, the level of person might be individual nurses, the staff working on a given shift, or the staff assigned to a given unit. Researchers use data from one level of person to validate data from the second or third level of person. Researchers might also discover data that are incongruent among levels. In such a case, researchers would collect additional data to reconcile the incongruence.

When carried out responsibly, data triangulation contributes to the rigor of a qualitative study. When planning a study, investigators should consider their data carefully. They should decide if time, space, or level of person is relevant to the data. They should plan to collect data from all appropriate sources, at all appropriate points in time, and from all appropriate levels of person. The result will be a broader and more holistic description of the phenomenon under study.

METHODS TRIANGULATION

Qualitative researchers use methods triangulation when they incorporate two or more research methods into one investigation. Methods triangulation can occur at the level of design or data collection (Kimchi et al., 1991). Methods triangulation at the design level has also been called *between-method triangulation* and methods triangulation at the data collection level has been called *within-method triangulation* (Denzin, 1989). Design methods triangulation most often uses quantitative methods combined with qualitative methods in the study design. Sometimes triangulation design method might use two different qualitative research methods. For example, Wilson and Hutchinson (1991) described how researchers might use two qualitative research methodologies, Heideggerian hermeneutics and grounded theory, in qualitative nursing studies. They explained that using two unique methods in one study can explicate realities of the complex phenomena of concern to nursing that might remain illusive if researchers used either method alone. "Hermeneutics reveals the uniqueness of shared meanings and common practices that can inform the way we [nurses] think about our practice; grounded theory provides a conceptual framework useful for planning interventions and further quantitative research" (Wilson & Hutchinson, 1991, p. 263).

When researchers combine methods at the design level, they should consider the purpose of the research and make a cogent argument for using each method. Also, they should decide whether the question calls for simultaneous or sequential implementation of the two methods (Morse, 1991). If they choose *simultaneous implementation,* they will use the qualitative and quantitative method simultaneously. In *sequential implementation,* they will complete one method first, then, based on the findings of the first technique, plan and implement the second technique. Using simultaneous implementation, researchers must remember that they must limit interaction between the two data sets during data generation and analysis because the rules and assumptions of qualitative methods differ (Morse, 1991, 1994). For example, it is usually impossible to implement qualitative and quantitative methods on the same sample. Qualitative methods require a small, purposive sample for completeness, whereas quantitative methods require large, randomly selected samples. In simultaneous triangulation, the qualitative sample can be a subset of the larger quantitative sample, or researchers might choose to use different participants for each sample. An exception occurs if the quantitative measure is standardized. In this case, researchers would have the participants in the qualitative sample complete the quantitative measure and then would compare the findings with the standardized norms (Morse, 1994). If the measure is not standardized, then researchers must use a sequential triangulation technique as well as a much larger sample for the quantitative measure.

Morgan and Stewart (1997) used simultaneous methods triangulation at the design level in their study on the effects of the client care unit design on the care of elderly residents with dementia. The researchers designed a large study that compared the effects of a low-density special care unit with those of a high-density special care unit. They gathered quantitative data from staff and family care-givers in a quasi-experimental study. A smaller subset of the original sample participated in the qualitative portion of the study, which the researchers designed to provide complimentary data on questions raised by the quantitative data. The qualitative data, which provided detailed descriptions of clients' behavior the researchers did not obtain using the quantitative measures, was particularly valuable in providing information about the effects of the social environment on that behavior. The researchers found the combination of methods provided a more complete picture of the effects of the unit design than either method would have provided alone. Although the researchers did not provide the information necessary to determine if one researcher was a quantitative expert and the other was a qualitative expert, they did analyze the quantitative and qualitative data separately and provided for rigor in both methods.

In contrast, researchers using a sequential triangulation technique begin by collecting either the quantitative or qualitative data. If substantial theory has already been generated about the phenomenon, if the researchers can identify testable hypotheses, or if the nature of the phenomenon is amenable to objective study, the investigation would begin with a quantitative technique. If there is no theory, the theory is not well developed, or the phenomenon is not amenable to objective study, researchers would begin with a qualitative technique (Morse, 1991). Researchers who begin a study with a quantitative technique do so to further explore unexpected findings following the completion of a quantitative analysis. A study might begin with a qualitative technique to generate testable hypotheses that a researcher will then study quantitatively.

Morrison (1997) used sequential methods triangulation at the design level in an investigation intended to identify nursing management diagnoses. The study began with qualitative focus group interviews of 35 nurse–managers to determine the problems of managing nursing units and to ground the diagnoses in the nurse–managers' practice. The nurse–managers also described typical judgments they might make while managing a nursing unit. An initial listing of potential management diagnoses emerged from the managers' descriptions of problems and judgments. The researchers then used a quantitative Delphi technique to determine a final listing of nursing management diagnoses. The investigators completed the quantitative portion of the study with 400 randomly selected nurse–managers.

When combining research methods, it is essential that investigators meet standards of rigor for each method. Using qualitative methods, researchers should ensure sampling is purposive and should generate data until saturation occurs. Using quantitative methods, researchers should ensure sample sizes are adequate and randomly chosen. Theory should emerge from the qualitative findings and should not be forced by researchers into the theory they are using for the quantitative portion of the study (Morse, 1991). Likewise, investigators should appropriately use validity and reliability measures to assure rigor of quantitatively derived data. Analysis techniques should be separate and appropriate to each data set. The blending of qualitative and quantitative approaches does not occur during either data generation or analysis. Rather, researchers blend these approaches at the level of interpretation, merging findings from each technique to derive a cohesive outcome. The process of merging findings "is an informed thought process, involving judgment, wisdom, creativity, and insight and includes the privilege of creating or modifying theory" (Morse, 1991, p. 122). If contradictory findings emerge or researchers find negative cases, the investigators most likely will need to study the phenomenon further. If knowledge gained is incomplete and saturation has not occurred, additional data collection and analysis should reconcile the differences and result in a more complete understanding.

In another study, Dreher and Hayes (1993) used methods triangulation at the design level to study the effects of marijuana use during pregnancy and lactation on children from birth to school age. The researchers planned to study two groups of Jamaican women: marijuana users and nonmarijuana users. However, the tool they had expected to use had been developed in the United States and, thus, was culturally inappropriate to Jamaican society. Instead, the researchers used ethnographic interview and observation of Jamaican women to revise the tool for culture appropriateness. The ethnographic data helped the researchers refine the language and relevancy of the instruments and modify the manner in which the tool was administered. By administering the tool in a culturally appropriate manner, the researchers were able to elicit valid and reliable responses.

Using methods triangulation at the level of data collection, researchers use two different techniques of data collection, but each technique is within the same research tradition. In a qualitative study, researchers might combine interview with observation or diaries with videotaping. The purpose of combining the data collection methods is to provide a more holistic and better understanding of the phenomenon under study. When combining methods at this level, researchers must first carefully consider the advantages and disadvantages of each method. Then, they should combine methods so that each overcomes the weaknesses in the other. For example, observation is an excellent technique for qualitative data generation. However, using observation, researchers cannot determine the reasons behind actions observed. Interview is an excellent method for determining reasons behind behavior. However, researchers can never be sure that individuals' actions mirror what they say they would do in an interview. By combining the techniques, investigators can see behavior in action and hear the participants describe the reasons behind behavior.

Miles and Huberman (1989) described methods triangulation at the data collection level as a state of mind. They suggested that a rigorous qualitative researcher automatically checks and double checks findings and uses multiple data generation techniques to assure accuracy and completeness of findings. For this reason, many qualitative researchers do not specifically identify their use of triangulation when combining data collection techniques. However, designing qualitative research with multiple data collection methods triangulation requires careful planning. Researchers must carefully incorporate each data collection technique into the research design and state the rationale for the use of each technique. They also should delineate the strengths and limitations of each technique. Researchers may not always create the design a priori. A study may begin with two data generation techniques, each designed to overcome the weaknesses of the other. After collecting data, the researchers may realize an additional limitation in the data. At this point, the researchers may add a third data collection technique to the design. For example, an investigator studying a phenomenon using interview and observation might realize that participants have a sketchy memory of past experiences. To get a more accurate view of experiences that have occurred over time, the researcher might decide to add diaries to the research design.

Carr and Clarke (1997) reported using methods triangulation at the data collection level in their study on the phenomenon of vigilance in families who stay with hospitalized relatives. The researchers used informal, semistructured interviews and participant observation of the care-givers to confirm and complete the data. The interviews provided insight into the care-givers' perceptions of what it meant to have the day-to-day experience of staying with a hospitalized relative. The investigators also observed the family members as they interacted with their relative to gain insight into patterns of interaction. Participant observation allowed the investigators to observe the environmental aspects of the client unit, relationships, processes, and events. The observational data confirmed the interview data; that is, observations confirmed families' verbalized commitment to their hospitalized relative. In their report, the researchers indicated that the combination of interview and observation data resulted in a more complete and holistic picture of vigilance than either method would have provided alone.

It is not an easy task to use methods triangulation; it is often more time-consuming and expensive to complete a study using methods triangulation (Begley, 1996). The study design is more complicated, complex, and difficult to implement, and imprecise use may actually increase error and enhance the weaknesses of each method, rather than compensate for weaknesses (Fielding & Fielding, 1989; Morse, 1991). Often a single researcher is not expert in using more than one technique; consequently, investigator triangulation is required.

INVESTIGATOR TRIANGULATION

Investigator triangulation occurs when two or more researchers with divergent backgrounds and expertise work together on the same study. To achieve investigator triangulation, multiple investigators each must have prominent roles in the study and their areas of expertise must be complementary (Kimchi et al., 1991). Having a second research expert examine a data set is not considered investigator triangulation. Rather, all researchers need to be involved throughout the entire study so they may compare and neutralize each other's biases.

The choice of investigators depends on the nature of the phenomenon under study. Research method, data generation technique, data analysis, or theory may drive the choice. For example, the use of multiple theories in a study directs the choice of investigators when a researcher expert in parenting and a researcher expert in homelessness collaborate to study what parenting means to homeless women. In this example, each investigator brings theoretical expertise to the study. Or using methods triangulation, research method drives the choice of investigators—investigators expert in each method used in the study participate in the study. When each investigator participates fully in the investigation, his or her expertise contributes to every aspect of the study. Each investigator ensures that he or she has properly implemented the research method, data generation technique, or theory to formulate the ultimate study outcome. Then, all the investigators discuss their individual findings and reach a conclusion, which includes all findings.

Use of methods triangulation usually requires investigator triangulation because few investigators are expert in more than one research method (Oberst, 1993). Researchers experienced in each method need to collaborate to design and implement the study, particularly when combining qualitative and quantitative methods because the philosophic orientation and the requirements for rigor are so different between the two methods. An understanding of the phenomenon under study will increase as each researcher combines his or her differing perspectives and approaches. Through this collaboration, the researchers will synthesize new understandings and theories. It is vitally important that researchers representing each discipline approach the investigation with open minds. Ideally, each will come with his or her discipline-specific biases but, simultaneously, will be open to hearing other investigators' approaches. Open dialogue with articulation and acceptance of biases will result in unique understandings.

THEORY TRIANGULATION

Theory triangulation incorporates the use of more than one lens or theory in the analysis of the same data set (Duffy, 1987). In a quantitative study, researchers identify two theories a priori and articulate rival hypotheses. Through the investigation, the researchers test and compare the rival theories. The result might be accepting one theory over the other or merging the theories to form a new, more comprehensive theory. In qualitative research, more than one theoretical explanation emerges from the data. Researchers investigate the utility and power of these emerging theories by cycling between data generation and data analysis until they reach a conclusion. By considering rival explanations throughout analysis of qualitative data, researchers are more likely to gain a complete or holistic understanding.

Lev (1995) used theory triangulation to investigate efficacy in clients who were receiving chemotherapy. The theoretical framework for the study consisted of a combination of Orem's self-care theory (1991) and Bandura's self-efficacy theory (1986). The investigator triangulated the two theories because she believed neither theory completely explained efficacy in this client population. From the combined theories, the researcher designed an efficacy-enhancing intervention that she applied to clients who were receiving chemotherapy. The researcher implemented a combination of qualitative and quantitative methods to investigate the effectiveness of the intervention, using a form of methods triangulation at the level of data collection. Because the researcher used both theory triangulation and methods triangulation, the study is also an example of *multiple triangulation,* the use of more than one method of triangulation in a single study (Mitchell, 1986).

Summary

Triangulation can be a useful tool for qualitative as well as quantitative researchers. Used with care, it contributes to the completeness and confirmation of findings necessary in qualitative research investigations. As researchers plan and carry out investigations, they should strive to provide the most complete understanding possible, using triangulation freely in their search for understanding. They should complete gaps in data using methods and data triangulation. Analysis should include theory triangulation. If an investigator is not equally expert in the different methods used, he or she should use investigator triangulation. Multiple triangulation can sometimes provide the most complete understandings in a complex research study.

Nursing phenomena are complex and multifaceted. Rarely will one research method provide complete understandings. Qualitative researchers should approach investigations with an openness to philosophic approaches. If different philosophic and research traditions will help to answer a research question more completely, then researchers should use triangulation. Simultaneously, qualitative researchers must be honest about their limitations. If they are not an expert in multiple methods, they should call on the assistance of a second or third investigator. Investigator triangulation will help to ensure that the researchers implement each method according to its requirements for rigor.

REFERENCES

Begley, C. M. (1996). Using triangulation in nursing research. *Journal of Advanced Nursing, 24,* 122–128.

Beitmayer, B. J., Ayres, L., & Knafl, K. A. (1993). Triangulation in qualitative research: Evaluation of completeness and confirmation purposes. *Image, 25,* 237–243.

Campbell, D. T., & Fiske, D. W. (1959). Convergent and discriminant validation by the multitrait–multimethod matrix. *Psychological Bulletin, 56,* 81–105.

Carr, J. M., & Clarke, P. (1997). Development of the concept of family vigilance. *Western Journal of Nursing Research, 19,* 726–739.

Denzin, N. K. (1970). Strategies of multiple triangulation. In N. K. Denzin (Ed.), *The research act* (pp. 297–313). New York: McGraw-Hill.

Denzin, N. K., & Lincoln, Y. S. (1994). Entering the field of qualitative research. In N. K. Denzin & Y. S. Lincoln (Eds.), *Handbook of qualitative research* (pp. 1–17). Thousand Oaks, CA: Sage.

Dreher, M. C., & Hayes, J. S. (1993). Triangulation in cross-cultural research of child development in Jamaica. *Western Journal of Nursing Research, 15,* 216–229.

Duffy, M. E. (1987). Methodological triangulation: A vehicle for merging quantitative and qualitative research methods. *Image, 19,* 130–133.

Fielding, N. G., & Fielding, J. L. (1989). *Linking data.* Newbury Park, CA: Sage.

Kimchi, J., Polivka, B., & Stevenson, J. B. (1991). Triangulation: Operational definitions. *Nursing Research, 40,* 364–366.

Lev, E. L. (1995). Triangulation reveals theoretical linkages and outcomes in nursing intervention study. *Clinical Nurse Specialist, 9,* 300–305.

Miles, M. B., & Huberman, A. M. (1989). *Qualitative data analysis.* Newbury Park, CA: Sage.

Mitchell, E. S. (1986). Multiple triangulation: A methodology for nursing science. *Advances in Nursing Science, 8*(3), 18–26.

Morgan, D. G., & Stewart, N. J. (1997). The importance of social environment in dementia care. *Western Journal of Nursing Research, 19,* 740–761.

Morrison, R. S. (1997). Identification of nursing management diagnoses. *Journal of Advance Nursing, 25,* 324–330.

Morse, J. M. (1991). Approaches to qualitative–quantitative methodological triangulation. *Nursing Research, 40,* 120–123.

Morse, J. M. (1994). Designing funded qualitative research. In N. K. Denzin & Y. S. Lincoln (Eds.), *Handbook of qualitative research* (pp. 220–235). Thousand Oaks, CA: Sage.

Oberst, M. T. (1993). Possibilities and pitfalls in triangulation. *Research in Nursing & Health, 16,* 393–394.

Patton, M. Q. (1983). *Qualitative evaluation methods.* Beverly Hills, CA: Sage.

Wilson, H. S., & Hutchinson, S. A. (1991). Triangulation of qualitative methods: Heideggerian hermeneutics and grounded theory. *Qualitative Health Research, 1,* 263–276.

A Practical Guide for Sharing Qualitative Research Results

Developing a qualitative research study is a significant activity. Identifying a problem suitable for qualitative investigation, following through with data collection and analysis, and disseminating the findings can be a lengthy process. Researchers using qualitative designs will need a degree of tenacity to complete a qualitative project. However, the enthusiasm generated from completion of the first study will certainly support continuing work within the qualitative paradigm. Sharing the results of a qualitative investigation with other nurse–researchers becomes a reality at the completion of the study. This is an exciting opportunity to provide new insights, receive thoughtful critiques, and learn from others with similar interests.

Once qualitative researchers develop a degree of comfort with research activities involved in the conduct of a qualitative project, they may become interested in developing a grant proposal using qualitative approaches. Grant writing requires qualitative researchers to develop additional skills, an effort well worth the time, especially when researchers' ideas are validated through the receipt of grant funds.

This chapter informs qualitative researchers about the differences in presentation style when a researcher submits a qualitative manuscript for publication, offers suggestions on how to submit a qualitative proposal for grant funding, and shares creative strategies for presenting qualitative research findings. In addition, a funded qualitative research proposal and critique are included after the chapter.

Publication Preparation

All researchers are responsible for disseminating research findings. Sharing results with colleagues is an exciting event. Whether they share ideas in a journal article or in a public forum such as a conference, qualitative researchers need to be aware of the audience's expectations as well as the best way to offer their insights.

IDENTIFYING AN AUDIENCE

On completion of a study, when it is time to report results, researchers must identify for whom they are writing. If the audience comprises primarily qualitative researchers, the manuscript will read differently than if the audience is made up of nurse–educators interested in the research. Be clear from the start who the audience is, for example, by reviewing current journals to see which ones provide a format that supports qualitative approaches. Some nursing journals publish more qualitative research than others. Regular review of major research journals will alert investigators to these journals. Journals that publish qualitative studies on a regular basis include *Advances in Nursing Science, Image: The Journal of Nursing Scholarship, Nursing Science Quarterly, Qualitative Health Research, Research in Nursing and Health,* and *Western Journal of Nursing Research.* This list is not exhaustive, nor is it offered to suggest that other journals do not publish qualitative studies. The purpose is to share the names of journals that have demonstrated a sustained and ongoing commitment to the publication of qualitative research.

In addition to identifying a journal that will be receptive to qualitative research approaches, it is essential to identify a journal with a focus on the content area of the study. For instance, the purpose of *Qualitative Health Research* is to disseminate qualitative research; however, the journal focuses on practice issues in health care and does not usually publish nursing education research articles. Therefore, an education study that utilizes qualitative methods would best be reported in an education journal such as *The Journal of Nursing Education* or *Nurse Educator.*

Once researchers have identified the potential journal, it is essential they obtain a copy of the journal guidelines for authors. This document assists researchers to develop a manuscript that meets the editorial expectations of the chosen journal. Most guidelines for authors do not offer specific recommendations for the presentation of qualitative findings. Reading qualitative studies published in journals is the best way to develop an understanding of how to meet editorial guidelines when submitting results of a qualitative study for publication. Regardless of the journal in which the findings will be published, qualitative researchers should follow certain guidelines.

Each group of readers has a specific purpose in reading a particular journal. Therefore, researchers must speak to the important facets of the research as they relate to the audience. These facets should reflect the purpose of the journal. For example, if researchers are writing for a scientific journal such as *Nursing Research,* detailing methods and data analysis will be as important as sharing the findings. In contrast, if they plan to publish in *Home Health Care Nurse,* the findings and implications for practice will be more important to the readership than the actual methods for conducting the study.

Most novice scholars are educated to submit query letters. A query letter tells the editor about what the author wishes to write. Many journal editors now report that query letters are unnecessary and may prolong the editorial process because of the time from submission of the query letter to response by journal staff. Often a phone call will suffice to confirm whether the topic is of interest to the readership of a particular journal.

Remember that, when developing a manuscript, be certain to present the research well. Poorly prepared manuscripts can set the stage for a rejection letter even if the study has significant merit.

Once researchers have submitted a manuscript, editorial staff will review the new submission and decide whether the content reflects the journal's purpose and is well written. If not, they will return the manuscript. Researchers are then responsible for identifying a more suitable periodical. Authors should expect to receive a postcard or letter within a few weeks of submission reporting on the status of the manuscript. The time from submission to publication may take more than 1 year. However, if after 3 or 4 months, authors have not received a progress report on the disposition of the manuscript (ie, whether it has been accepted or rejected), they should follow up with a phone call or letter.

DEVELOPING THE MANUSCRIPT

The most difficult thing about writing is getting started. This observation is not intended to suggest that qualitative researchers have not been writing. However, documenting field notes and analyzing interviews are much different forms of writing than writing for publication. Those types of writing are personal and are not usually scrutinized by other readers. Researchers usually learn through the conduct of their projects that it is easy and even fun to write notes for themselves, but it is difficult to set personal ideas to paper for others to read. The very nature of data collection and analysis requires that researchers write. Documenting their feelings, perceptions, observations, theoretical directions, or insights is part of the implementation of the qualitative research experience. Transforming diaries, memos, or transcripts into a scientific manuscript requires a fair amount of rigor and determination, as well as keen synthesis and organizational abilities.

Qualitative research generates a large amount of raw data. In raw form, the data are interesting but unusable for research reporting. Qualitative researchers must condense and synthesize for readers the importance of the research while not losing the richness of the findings. This effort can be a real challenge because of the prolonged and intimate involvement of researchers with the participants.

One way to focus on research for publication in a journal is to break the study into parts. Researchers can develop more than one manuscript from a qualitative research study. If, for example, a researcher studies the culture of an open heart surgery unit over a 1-year period, he or she can develop a manuscript to examine the access and ethical considerations in this type of setting. The researcher may develop another manuscript that focuses on nurses and their activities and artifacts. Still another article might look at the interactions among clients, their families, and institutional structures. In addition, the researcher may develop a description of the process of conducting such an inquiry into yet another manuscript. Ideally, a book or several chapters of a book would provide researchers with the best opportunity for presenting an entire qualitative research study. As Morse and Field (1995) have pointed out, a book-length manuscript is best when researchers wish to share a description of the research process. However, time and opportunity may limit publication in this format.

If researchers are uninterested in publishing the study in parts, then they may certainly develop the study so that it will be of greatest interest to readers. For instance, using the open heart surgery unit example, the researcher can present findings in the context of practice implications in critical care journals. A manuscript for publication in a practice journal would not require a great deal of emphasis on method or analysis but would require significant attention to findings and implications.

The most difficult obstacle to overcome in developing a qualitative manuscript for publication is the need to report the study in 12–15 pages, as required by most journals. With this limitation, it is critically important to be concise, focused, and logical rather than to try to report the entire study.

Once researchers have identified the journal and determined the focus, the next step is to logically develop the ideas they wish to convey. "An outline provides guidance in writing" (Field & Morse, 1985, p. 130). The purpose of the outline is to keep the writer directed. It is easy to drift away from the focus of the manuscript without an outline. Depending on the preference of the author, the outline may be more or less detailed.

When writing begins, remember to organize ideas in a logical manner but also in a way that provides readers with an appreciation of the richness of the data. For example, in Beck's (1997) phenomenological study, she wanted to share a narrative that reflected the theme "contemplating the patient's life and death . . . as nursing students cared for their patients" (p. 411). The example she offered is as follows:

> He wasn't just a 96-year-old man who couldn't communicate very well. He waved at me and the nurses. The one thing I remember about him was his warm, caring blue eyes. He was on a pureed diet and didn't care for his meal except for orange sherbet. I was feeding him the sherbet and after a few spoonfuls he wanted to rest a little so I left the room. When I came back in a few minutes, he was feeding himself and he had drops of sherbert on his lap, chest, and face. He really enjoyed the sherbert and seemed proud of himself because he did a good job eating it by himself. Caring for this man gave me a lump in my throat because it made me think that there isn't just a dying body in the bed. It made me think of the life he led and his likes and dislikes and what kind of person he was. (p. 411–412)

This excerpt provides readers with an insider's (emic) view of what it is like for a nursing student to care for a dying client. It gives readers a "feel" for or depth of the experience. The excerpt demonstrates one way in which qualitative reporting differs from quantitative reporting. Qualitative reporting demands documentation of ideas or conclusions in words rather than numbers. Using words to justify the researcher's position takes a significant amount of skill because, unlike the presentation of statistics, the significance of the findings is found in the writer's syntax, not in the statistical manipulation of numerical values.

On completion of the manuscript, authors should ask colleagues to critique the ideas presented. Too often, neophyte qualitative researchers make the mistake of believing that, because they have spent much time immersed in the data, writing about the data is merely a technicality. Qualitative research manuscripts are subjected to rigorous review. It is essential that the ideas be clear and demonstrate important findings to the nursing community. Review by knowledgeable colleagues will assist in assuring the logic, consistency, and importance of the findings.

Once the manuscript is submitted, researchers should be ready to revise as requested by the reviewers. Few manuscripts, qualitative or quantitative, sustain juried review without requests for revision. Morse (1996b) has further suggested that, if researchers receive a request for revision in which reviewers' recommendations are contradictory, the researchers' responsibility is to attend to the most meaningful comments. Researchers should indicate why they did not use all of the reviewers' comments; however, when the comments do not reflect the truth of the study, researchers should not submit to revising based on those comments. Never be naive, though, to the point of not considering reviewers' comments. Researchers have a great deal to gain in positive and negative comments. They need to ask, Why did someone read this in a particular way? When asked to revise, researchers must work quickly. The sooner they return the revised manuscript, the sooner the acceptance, and the earlier the manuscript will be queued for publication (Morse, 1996b).

If the unfortunate circumstance occurs—receipt of a rejection letter—do not throw away the manuscript. Look carefully at the critique, use the comments to improve the manuscript, and try another journal. It is acceptable also to use the comments, revise the manuscript, and resubmit it to the same journal. Quality research should be published. At times, it takes a fair amount of tenacity to see ideas through to publication. But once published, researchers will enjoy the thrill of having the work available in print for readers interested in the topic and particular research approach.

Conference Presentation

Satisfaction results from the publication of a manuscript that shares the results of intensive study. Manuscript publication is just one of researchers' responsibilities in their dissemination of the findings. In addition to getting ideas in print, which may take between 10 and 18 months, researchers should present the findings to the scholarly community using other forums. One way to share results in an efficient and effective way is through a formal conference presentation as a paper or poster presentation. Whether presenting findings in a paper or poster, qualitative researchers need to address important considerations.

Most formal presentations result from a *call for abstracts,* which requires investigators to submit a synopsis of the research in a few paragraphs, with a limit of between 150 and 500 words. Guidelines for abstract submissions generally are available from the group sponsoring the research conference or workshop. It is essential that responses to the call reflect the theme of the conference and meet the criteria for presentation. The guidelines for abstract submission usually include the study purpose, the method the researcher used to conduct the inquiry, the sample, the findings, and the significance of the findings to nursing. Inclusion of the information requested will greatly improve the chances for abstract acceptance. However, because the results of a qualitative study are rich and dense, the question becomes, How do I demonstrate the richness of my work and the significance in 150–500 words when I have trouble writing it in 15 pages?

When submitting an abstract, it is essential to convince reviewers that the work has been done well, will be interesting, and is of significance to the profession. It is impossible to share the richness of the research in an abstract. What researchers should be striving for is to whet the reviewers' appetite so they say, We want to know more about this inquiry.

A call for abstracts generally asks researchers to indicate the format in which they prefer to present: poster or paper. Neophyte researchers would be wise to indicate both. Podium presenters of a paper often have demonstrated their ability to successfully engage a group in their work through their ability to clearly articulate their ideas in the abstract. For individuals who have their abstracts rejected for podium presentation, poster presentations offer the opportunity to discuss the findings in a comfortable, relaxed atmosphere. A poster presentation provides neophyte researchers with the chance to develop skill and confidence in presenting research findings.

PREPARING FOR AN ORAL PRESENTATION

If accepted for an oral presentation, researchers must keep in mind important aspects of sharing the results. They should present the qualitative research so that they engage the conference participants in the work. Presentation of a portion of the work will allow researchers to share the richness of the findings. Because the average length of podium presentation is between 20 and 30 minutes, be careful not to spend too much time discussing the method used to conduct the inquiry. Although the method is essential information, the audience will be most interested in the findings. Inform the audience about the method to give them the context and direction of the study, but do not share so much information that presentation of the findings is rushed. It is essential that presenters not hurry the presentation of quotations from informants or the analysis of a situation, because those elements *are* the study findings. Share the quotations and analysis thoughtfully, giving the audience time to absorb the words. Slides or overheads provide a visual representation of the quotes, giving the audience additional time to assimilate the meaning of the words. Photographs and illustrations add to the presentation as well. Be sure to leave adequate time for questions. If the research has been presented well, the audience will want to know more because their interest has been aroused. During the question-and-answer period, a unique opportunity is available to share additional findings and anecdotal information.

Be aware that not all questions will be easy or fun to answer. At times, the audience will demonstrate an interest in the trustworthiness or ethical considerations in the study. If you have executed a well-designed study, you can handle these questions. If you have not been insightful enough to predict questions and do not have ready answers, be honest. Use the critique questions shared in this text as a developmental learning experience. In this way you, too, will have learned from sharing your results.

PREPARING FOR A POSTER PRESENTATION

Presenting qualitative research in poster format is a unique challenge, but certainly one researchers may meet successfully. Many good articles are available on the mechanics of preparing and presenting a poster. Display poster presentations so that, in a glance, interested individuals can determine whether they want to know more or whether they prefer to move to the next poster. Anyone who has ever attended a poster session knows that the sheer volume of posters available limits interested parties from spending time with each poster presenter. Therefore, the poster must immediately capture the audience's attention. The title, color of the poster, size of print, and content should catch the passerby's interest first. However, the most important part of the poster is the title. It is essential to present a title that immediately informs readers of the topic and research approach. For instance, the title "The Near Death Experience" would attract individuals interested in the topic. Because the title is brief, passersby can decide in a moment whether they want to know more. Similarly, a title such as "Male Nursing Students' Perceptions of Clinical Experience: A Phenomenological Inquiry" quickly informs people about the subject matter and research approach.

In addition, researchers should present the content in an appealing way. Pictures and illustrations capture the passerby's attention and give presenters an opportunity to verbally share results. Specifically, for qualitative researchers, there is benefit in providing interested individuals with a handout of the abstract or handouts highlighting the important research findings or offering an exhaustive description, if appropriate. On the printed handouts, researchers should include their name and address so that nurses interested in the findings or the method may contact them for additional information. Russell, Gregory, and Gates (1996) also have suggested researchers place on a table with the poster a notebook in which they have inserted additional information, including narrative, pictures, and illustrations that would take up too much space on the poster. The notebook provides people interested in additional information about the study an opportunity to get it "on the spot."

In addition to using a matted poster format, some qualitative researchers have used audiovisual materials such as a slide projector with tape player to give an added dimension to their presentations. The inclusion of sound and changing visuals connects consumers to the work. Presenting a poster using audiovisual equipment, however, requires access to electricity and additional space. Researchers interested in presenting a poster in this format need to contact the conference planners to see whether there is accessible electricity and adequate space.

Creativity is the key to the successful presentation of ideas. Presenting qualitative research lends itself to creativity because of the nature of the data, the data collection strategies, and the dense data that result. Researchers presenting a poster demonstrating a qualitative research approach should take advantage of the possibilities open to sharing their findings and exploit those possibilities to share the interesting and exciting data revealed in the conduct of the inquiry.

Grant Writing

Having had one or more qualitative research studies published, researchers should seriously consider developing a grant proposal, the next logical step in their research career. The development of a competitive research proposal requires researchers to construct the project so they convince a panel of reviewers that they have the necessary knowledge, experience, and commitment to complete the proposed project. Reviewers will be looking at a researcher's credentials, the scientific merit of the project, and the potential contribution of the project to the profession.

IDENTIFYING FUNDING SOURCES

One of the first steps in developing a competitive proposal is to identify potential funding sources, a number of which are available to nurses interested in conducting a qualitative inquiry. Each organization offers materials on the types of projects they fund and their submission guidelines. For researchers seeking their first funding dollars, small grants are the most useful and are generally easier to access. Examples of small grant programs include college or university funds, which are accessible through small grant proposals available on a competitive basis within institutions. The monies generally come from allocations to faculty development budgets or foundations or alumni gifts.

In addition to college or university funding, several nursing organizations offer small grants. These organizations, among others, include Sigma Theta Tau International, National League for Nursing Council for Research in Nursing Education, American Nurses Foundation, American Association of Critical Care Nurses, and Association of Rehabilitation Nurses. Many businesses also offer small grants, including product organizations such as infant formula or durable medical equipment companies. Health care organizations, such as hospitals and community health organizations, frequently fund research as well.

Nurses interested in receiving funding need to identify the available resources. This effort will require a moderate amount of time to first determine the available funding sources and then to select the source that will most likely be interested in funding the project. Nurses might use resource libraries found in universities that have established nursing research centers to identity potential funding sources. These institutions, where available and accessible, generally have a plethora of diverse materials and experienced staff to assist in locating the appropriate resources and developing the proposal. However, it is no longer necessary for potential grant writers to spend hours in the library: the Internet is a wellspring of funding sources. If university-based nursing research centers are unavailable, researchers may log on to the websites of organizations such as the American Association of Colleges of Nursing, National League for Nursing, Sigma Theta Tau International, and American Nurses Association, which have resource materials on their websites as well as links to other sites to help focus the search.

Individuals interested in developing larger projects should have completed and had published results of small, funded projects before seeking monies from organizations that offer larger funding support. Such organizations include the National Institute of Nursing Research, National Institutes of Health (NIH), American Education Association, Kellogg Foundation, Robert Wood Johnson Foundation, and National Science Foundation. In addition, many nonprofit organizations such as the American Heart Association, National Arthritis Foundation, and American Cancer Society provide moderate-to-large funding for projects. Critical to receiving larger sums of money and submitting a well-developed project is experience. Organizations that make large awards do not do so unless single researchers or research teams demonstrate significant, documented experience.

DEVELOPING THE PROPOSAL

Because several good books focus on proposal development and grant writing, this section does not address the specific mechanics of developing a research proposal for funding. Instead, the section gives qualitative researchers ideas about the challenges and potential pitfalls in developing qualitative grant proposals. As Morse (1991) commented, "In comparison to the WYSIWYG (what you see is what you get) presentation of the quantitative application, the qualitative proposal is vague, obscure, and may even be viewed as a blatant request for a blank check" (p. 148). The idea of developing a proposal for funding knowing beforehand that the ambiguities cannot be written out of the grant presents a unique but not insurmountable challenge. Researchers interested in receiving funding for a qualitative study must convince reviewers not only of the merits of the project, which may seem obscure and undirected, but also of the researchers' experience.

In a qualitative proposal, pilot work serves very little purpose (Dialogue: The Granting Game, 1991), whereas in a quantitative study, pilot work demonstrates the potential design strengths and weaknesses. In qualitative proposals, the number of participants is determined by data saturation, which can include as few as 2 or more than 50 people. In a quantitative study, the number of participants is determined by the design, projected outcome, and number of variables under study. Based on these parameters, researchers can establish a precise number of participants for inclusion in a study. In qualitative studies, data collection and analysis require flexibility. In quantitative studies, data collection and analysis are largely objective. The preceding comparisons focus on the precise and often predictable nature of a quantitative research proposal versus the often imprecise and unpredictable nature of a qualitative proposal.

Morse (1994a) has recommended that "the first principle of grantsmanship is to recognize that a good proposal is an argument—a fair and balanced one" (p. 226). Therefore, qualitative researchers must clearly and persuasively present evidence that will convince grant reviewers the proposal is worth funding. To facilitate a clear understanding of the research ideas, proposal authors "should assume nothing and explain everything" (p. 227).

The second principle of grant writing offered by Morse (1994a) "is that one should think and plan before starting to write" (p. 227). Planning before writing will give proposal authors an opportunity to clearly delineate the research plan, beginning with development of the research question and ending with the distribution of research results. In addition to assisting with writing the actual proposal document, planning conclusively before beginning to write allows authors time to draft a complete budget. Because the budget is the part of the proposal that provides researchers with the resources to fully operationalize a project, it is essential that researchers develop the budget well and detail all expenses. Items to include in the budget are personnel, such as research assistants, transcription services, secretaries, and consultants; equipment, such as a tape recorder, computer, and data analysis program; supplies, such as paper, audiotapes or videotapes, and photocopies; and travel, including mileage between research sites, conference travel, presentation fees, and consultant travel. Carefully laying out the project will assist greatly in developing a proposal that is clear, succinct, and can be funded.

IDENTIFYING INVESTIGATOR QUALIFICATIONS

The challenge in obtaining larger funds for qualitative research is for prospective grant recipients to demonstrate their abilities to convince reviewers they are a risk worth taking. Proposal authors need to illustrate to reviewers a track record in scholarly publication, presentation, consultation, and success in acquiring small awards. "Granting bodies must [be made to] recognize the process nature of the research and that they are funding the *investigator* rather than the *proposal* per se" (Morse, 1991, p. 149). Morse added that "for major grant applications, evaluation of the *investigator* is critical and should be most heavily weighted" (p. 149). This is not to say that the research project does not need to have scientific merit and be described as fully as possible; rather, it illuminates the nature of the process that is decidedly imprecise when compared with a quantitative proposal.

In recent years, NIH and other funding agencies have begun requiring that research proposals include a qualitative component (Morse, 1994a). This situation is confusing: Does this requirement support the value of qualitative research and reflect the belief that qualitative research will be driven into the system, or is this a strongly misguided request that reflects a definite misunderstanding of research and the qualitative research process in general (Morse, 1994a)? In either case, it is up to grant developers to clearly provide the reasons why they have selected one paradigm over another and indicate how the paradigm and, more specifically, the method will provide the answers to the questions asked.

Furthermore, Morse (1996a) has pointed out that funding agencies have given the distinct impression that qualitative research is not an end but rather a means to an end. Based on the literature, qualitative researchers are led to believe that qualitative inquiry is a prelude to "good" quantitative design. This, too, may be a misguided belief. Researchers must make clear to funding agencies the project goal and clearly describe how the method selected is appropriate.

More than one researcher with expertise in quantitative methodology may be able to bring a dimension to an entire project that a qualitative researcher alone would be unable to do. It is up to the principal investigator to determine whether the study will be enhanced by the addition of a strong team with varied interests. Based on this author's experience with recently funded projects, grant reviewers are frequently viewing research teams more favorably, particularly if the teams are multidisciplinary.

IDENTIFYING MECHANISMS FOR ASSURING PARTICIPANT PROTECTION

Not only must qualitative researchers clearly demonstrate their expertise and qualifications, it is essential that their qualitative research proposals conclusively identify the mechanisms for assuring the protection of participants. One of the strengths of qualitative approaches is the unique opportunity to get to know individuals, groups, or communities over a long period. This strength creates its own potential hazards for participants' protection because the nature of the data—personal descriptions—precludes qualitative researchers from maintaining confidentiality, particularly when they publish quotes or use them as references in publications (Munhall, 1989). Nevertheless, qualitative researchers can assure anonymity. It is essential that they demonstrate how they will protect informants' identities. They may protect participants by way of methods such as ethnography, in which participant identification may actually contribute significantly to the position of groups or their ability to access resources. In such cases, qualitative researchers must document that participants have agreed that researchers may make the informants' identities public. Audiotaping interviews and taking photographs are additional examples of potential violations of participants' rights. Researchers must document informants' permission for such activities.

Although developing mechanisms for assuring confidentiality and anonymity contributes significantly to a grant proposal, it is also important to clarify for institutional review boards and funding agencies that mechanisms are in place to deal with potentially sensitive outcomes. For example, if a researcher is living with a community and discovers that one of the group rituals involves physically isolating and abusing children who do not excel in academics, the researcher must be able to clearly define steps he or she will take to protect the vulnerable group (ie, the children). It is essential to try to identify all the potentially sensitive situations and develop mechanisms to intervene or to have intervention available.

Sample Grant

Following this chapter, a funded research grant proposal completed by Margarete Lieb Zalon is presented to illustrate the processes discussed in this chapter. The grant was funded by Sigma Theta Tau International. Also following is a critique of the funded grant that shares reviewers' comments to further illustrate issues that are important in the development of a qualitative research proposal. To get an idea of the full cycle of the grant-writing process, readers may wish to refer to Zalon's (1997) published article—which resulted from the grant proposal—at the end of Chapter 5.

Summary

Qualitative research is an exciting opportunity to create meaningful nursing knowledge from individuals' lives and experiences. To make the knowledge accessible, researchers must share the findings in a significant way. Presenting a qualitative project in an article, poster, speech, or grant proposal requires imagination and refined presentation skills. Qualitative researchers have a responsibility to their consumers and to developing qualitative scholars to present their ideas in a clear and acceptable manner. They should share their research in a way that illustrates the richness and value of conducting research using the approaches described in this text.

The development of qualitative research projects and the refinement of social sciences approaches to human inquiry that are appropriate to nursing science establish a major research focus for the profession. Nurses interested in these projects have a unique opportunity to be on the cutting edge of the developments. It is an exciting time for nurses and for research. There is a vast and expansive qualitative research landscape waiting for interested nurse–researchers. This is a landscape of imagination that is colored by the lives and experiences of the individuals with whom nurses interact: clients, students, and other nurses. It is essential to document these unique experiences and share them to fully explore and describe the human experience. The challenge awaits those nurses who are willing to participate.

REFERENCES

Beck, C. T. (1997). Nursing students' experiences caring for dying patients. *Journal of Nursing Education, 36*(9), 408–415.

Dialogue: The granting game. (1991) In J. M. Morse (Ed.), *Qualitative nursing research: A contemporary dialogue* (rev. ed., pp. 240–244). Newbury Park, CA: Sage.

Field, P. A., & Morse, J. M. (1985). *Nursing research: The application of qualitative approaches.* Rockville, MD: Aspen.

Morse, J. (1991). On the evaluation of qualitative proposals [Editorial]. *Qualitative Health Research, 1*(2), 147–151.

Morse, J. M. (1994a). Designing funded qualitative research. In N. K. Denzin & Y. S. Lincoln. (Eds.), *Handbook of qualitative research* (pp. 220–235). Thousand Oaks, CA: Sage.

Morse, J. M. (1994b). On the crest of a wave [Editorial]. *Qualitative Health Research, 4*(2), 139–141.

Morse, J. M. (1996a). Is qualitative research complete? [Editorial]. *Qualitative Health Research, 6*(1), 3–5.

Morse, J. (1996b). "Revise and resubmit": Responding to reviewers' reports [Editorial]. *Qualitative Health Research, 6*(2), 149–151.

Morse, J. M., & Field, P. A. (1995). *Qualitative research methods for health professionals* (2nd ed.). Thousand Oaks, CA: Sage.

Munhall, P. L. (1991). Institutional review of qualitative research proposals: A task of no small consequence. In J. M. Morse (Ed.), *Qualitative nursing research: A contemporary dialogue* (rev. ed., pp. 258–272). Newbury Park, CA: Sage.

Russell, C. K., Gregory, D. M., & Gates, M. F. (1996). Aesthetics and substance in qualitative research posters. *Qualitative Health Research, 6*(4), 542-552.

Zalon, M. L. (1997). Pain in the frail, elderly women after surgery. *Image, 29*(1), 21–26.

FUNDED GRANT
PROPOSAL

ABSTRACT

This study proposes to use a phenomenological method to describe the lived experience of post-operative pain in frail, elderly women. Pain is one of the most common reasons for nurse–patient interaction. The proportion of the frail elderly in the population is increasing. Therefore, the overall goal is to understand the pain experience of frail, elderly women, which will enable nurses to improve pain relief measures and enhance recovery, while taking into consideration the special needs of this population. The purposive convenience sample will consist of 7 to 12 women aged 75 or over who have had abdominal surgery at a 376-bed community hospital. An unstructured, open-ended interview will be conducted on at least the fourth post-operative day with the question, "What comes to mind when you think about your experience of pain after your surgery?" Interviews will be tape-recorded and transcribed. Participants will be given the opportunity to review an interview summary for clarification. Data will be analyzed according to a constant comparative method using Colaizzi's (1978) methodology. Clusters of themes will be organized and referred back to each original description in order to develop a detailed description of the lived experience of pain in frail, elderly women after surgery. Procedures recommended by Lincoln and Guba (1985) will be used to establish data trustworthiness. Consultation will be used to provide guidance in data analysis. Finally, participants will have the opportunity to review the descriptions to determine if they validate their original pain experience.

GRANT PROPOSAL

Studies focusing on experimental pain or using chart retrieval do not provide information about the elderly person's perception of pain. Post-operative pain of the elderly is managed with less analgesic medication but this factor has not been clearly linked to age differences in pain perception or tolerance. Because pain is an intensely personal experience, chart retrieval or quantitative studies do not provide the necessary information about the multidimensional nature of the pain experience.

The multidimensional nature of pain has been explored by researchers, but not with a focus on an elderly population. Jacox (1979), interviewing patients, began by asking them if they were currently in pain. Ten to fifteen minutes later they were given a pain scale to complete, and 25% of the patients who indicated no pain at the beginning of the interview then indicated the presence of pain. Similarly, Donovan et al., (1987) found that 46 patients (N = 353), who indicated no pain in the beginning of the interview, later reported the presence of pain. Neither study reported whether age was a factor. These findings suggest patients may be initially hesitant to communicate the presence of pain. The findings are consistent with Fagerhaugh and Strauss's (1977) study of patients on 20 units in 9 hospitals that reflected hospital environment influences pain expression.

McCaffery and Beebe (1989, p. 311) noted that the elderly may be afraid to admit pain because they grew up in an era when hospitals were for dying. Some elderly may be fearful of becoming confused and addicted. According to Gioiella and Bevil (1985, p. 293), elders may stop talking about pain because they were told nothing could be done. These hypotheses have not been tested in research studies. Foreman (1986) and Williams et al. (1985) noted that narcotic administration is a factor related to confusion and that lack of pain relief is related to confusion as well. Platzer (1989) concluded that the relationship between pain, use of analgesics, and confusion is unclear. The elderly may be unwilling to take analgesic medication for pain relief, which may then contribute to confusion. The paucity of research in this area makes it difficult to draw conclusions that provide direction for nursing practice. Understanding the experience of post-operative pain in the elderly may potentially provide information about this problem.

Underassessment of pain and undermedication for pain is a significant problem in hospitalized patients (Cohen, 1980; Marks & Sachar, 1973; Weis et al., 1983; Zalon, 1989/1990). Donovan et al., (1987) reported that only 45% of the patients who experienced pain ever remembered a nurse discussing their pain with them. Perhaps this lack of discussion results in underassessment and hence, undermedication. Zalon (1989/1990) noted that nurses assessed their patients as having more pain if they spent more than five minutes with them. However, it is not known whether nurses chose to spend more time with patients once they assessed them as having more pain. Exploring patients' pain experience would provide insight from the patient's perspective.

Understanding the lived experience of pain in frail, elderly women who have had surgery will fill the gaps in our knowledge about the responses of frail, elderly women to pain and pain relief measures. Research focused on the actions of caregivers (ie, medication administration), rather than the patient, makes it difficult to draw conclusions about the needs of this particular population. Hamilton (1989, p. 281) noted that most gerontologic research examines the needs of the elderly from the perspective of the care-giver or expert. Although the gate control theory (Melzack & Wall, 1965) provides a theoretical model about the physiologic basis for pain, and McCaffery (1979) advocates a definition of pain as "whatever the patient says it is" (p. 11), there is no adequate theoretical model that describes the experience of pain in the elderly. According to Paterson and Zderad (1976, p. 83), phenomenological description is a basic and essential step in theory building.

A detailed pain experience description would provide the foundation for a theoretical model that would give needed direction for nursing practice. Specifically, this phenomenological study will serve to provide a detailed description of the experience of pain in frail, elderly women who have had surgery. According to Munhall (1982), "Nursing philosophy almost universally includes a belief about holistic man" (p. 176). Examining pain from a phenomenological perspective will facilitate a holistic description of the experience. A holistic description of the pain experience in this population will enable nurses to address their patients' concerns. It will also improve their decision making regarding measures selected for pain relief.

Although there is no specific preliminary study, the questions raised by the investigator's doctoral research (Zalon, 1989/1990) do provide a foundation for this study. While obtaining consents, a number of patients indicated a desire to talk at length about their pain experience, both present and past. Lengthy discussion was inappropriate for the purpose of the doctoral study, but the conversations did provide information that was rich in complexity. Patient comments were not necessarily congruent with their interactions with nursing staff. Comments by elderly patients indicated concerns about analgesics, fear of confusion, and addiction. These comments led the researcher to conclude a quantitative methodology cannot provide complete information about patients' pain experience.

As stated earlier, this study will use a phenomenological approach to examine the lived experience of post-operative pain in frail, elderly women. According to Merleau-Ponty (1962, p. 71), an existential phenomenologist, one's perceptual history is a result of relationships with the objective world. The phenomenological method attempts to describe human experience in the complexity of its context (Munhall & Oiler, 1986). According to Valle and King (1978, pp. 15–17), phenomenologically oriented research answers the questions, What is the phenomenon that is experienced and lived? and What is its structure or commonalities in the many diverse appearances of the phenomenon? The phenomenon of pain must be understood before explanations for patterns of behavior and interactions are offered. In this study, frail, elderly women will be interviewed after they have had surgery and asked to describe their pain experience. The open-ended unstructured interview, which is used for this study, is consistent with the phenomenological method.

This purposive convenience sample will include hospitalized, frail, elderly women (75 years of age or over) who have had abdominal surgery. Women are selected for this study because of the high proportion of elderly women in the population and men are excluded as there may be gender differences in pain experiences. Women with a diagnosis of cancer are excluded because the meaning that they may attribute to pain may cause a difference in their pain experience (Spross, 1985). Those with a history of psychiatric illness or substance abuse are also excluded (Black, 1980; Davis et al., 1980). The sample size is expected to range between 7 to 12 patients or until saturation of the data has been achieved. This size is consistent with samples used in phenomenological research (Riemen, 1986; Rose, 1990). Prospective participants will be included in the study if they acknowledge that they have experienced pain post-operatively (Coliazzi, 1978) and can talk about the experience.

An open-ended unstructured interview will be conducted to elicit a description of the participants' pain experience. The specific question will be, What comes to mind when you think about your experience of pain after your surgery? An additional probe to induce a response will be, What was the pain like for you? Additional questions will be asked only when it is necessary to clarify what is being said. When the participants have described their experiences, and no further clarification is necessary, then the interview will be considered complete. The initial interview will be conducted on at least the fourth post-operative day because the patient will still be recovering from the surgery, yet not so acutely ill that the interview will be too tiring. It is also close enough to the acute phase of the patients' illness that their pain experience recollections will be fairly recent. Patients must be alert and oriented at the time of the interview. Interviews are expected to last from 20 to 50 minutes. The nursing staff will be consulted so that the time of the interview will not interfere with any planned nursing care activities.

After each interview is transcribed, participants will be given the opportunity to discuss a summary of the interview. They will be asked if there is anything else that should be added or clarified. This may involve a home visit, depending on the length of the participant's hospitalization. At the conclusion of the data analysis, participants will be given the opportunity to read the pain experience descriptions (or have them read) to determine if they validate their original experience of pain. This will involve a home visit. Home visits are selected instead of phone interviews because the potential for hearing loss in this population may make clarification difficult.

The raw data (interviews) will be transcribed verbatim. The transcriptions will be compared with the tapes for accuracy. Analyses of the data will be conducted in accordance with Colaizzi's (1978) phenomenological methodology. The transcripts will first be read in their entirety so the investigator can acquire a feeling for them. Significant statements will then be extracted from each description. The meaning of each significant statement will be explained. Clusters of themes from the aggregate formulated meanings will be organized and referred back to each original description for validation. A constant comparative method will be used, whereby each participant will be compared and contrasted with the previous and following descriptions. The results will be integrated to yield an exhaustive description of the phenomenon in the sample. Finally, participants will be interviewed to determine whether the description validates their original experience.

Potential limitations are threats to reliability and validity. Since this is a qualitative study, these will be addressed by procedures operationalized by Lincoln and Guba (1985, pp. 289–331) to enhance the trustworthiness of the data. Credibility will be enhanced by the use of member checks that will allow the participants to review the interview summary and final descriptions. Persistent observation will be facilitated by keeping detailed notes about how the data are analyzed. Consultation will be obtained to explore aspects that may not have been considered by the investigator. Negative case analysis will be repeated until the description accounts for all known cases. Dependability and confirmability will be established by keeping detailed records of the study including raw data, field notes, summaries, formulated meanings and themes, and process notes.

This study may be limited in its generalizability because of the purposive sampling. The third interview may be difficult to complete because of the time elapsed between the first interview and completion of data analysis. The investigator's assumptions, derived from experience, the literature, and previous research, are a threat to validity and need to be bracketed or laid aside (Cohen, 1987). Therefore, a detailed list of assumptions will be written immediately before beginning interviews, a journal will be kept while conducting this study, and further literature review will be suspended until data analysis is complete.

The study will begin in October, 1991 and be completed in August, 1992:

10/1/91–10/21/91: Administrative preparation for the conduct of the study; distribution of study information to nursing staff and surgeons of prospective patients.

10/21/91–1/15/92: Interviews with study participants, transcription of interviews, and second interviews to review summaries. Beginning of data analysis.

1/15/92–6/1/92: Analysis of data and interviews with participants to review final descriptions.

6/1/92–8/1/92: Completion of final narrative report.

This study will be submitted to the University of Scranton Institutional Review Board and subsequently to the Institutional Review Board of Mercy Hospital, Scranton. The human subjects review should be completed by July 1, 1991. Prospective participants who meet the study criteria will be approached after hospital admission when they are resting quietly, and be given a standard explanation of the study. Those agreeing to participate will be asked to sign an informed consent form, and be advised of their right to confidentiality, their right to stop the interview(s) and recording process at any time, and their right to withdraw from the study. Names will be changed on transcription and tapes will be coded with numbers.

Dr. Carla Mariano, RN (Appendix C), has agreed to serve as a consultant. In the beginning of the study, she will listen to a portion of a tape to monitor the investigator's interview style. Dr. Mariano's expertise will also be used for assistance with data analysis, in particular, the evaluating of samples of extracted meanings and clusters of themes from the data as well as guidance in establishing trustworthiness.

This study will be conducted with patients having surgery in Mercy Hospital, a 376-bed community facility in Scranton (Appendix B). Over 600 surgical procedures are performed at this hospital on a monthly basis. Therefore, the facility is more than adequate for the sample.

REFERENCES

Belleville, J. W., Forrest, W. H., Miller, E., & Brown, B. W. (1971). Influence of age on pain relief from analgesics. *Journal of the American Medical Association, 217,* 1835–1841.
Black, R. G. (1980). The clinical syndrome of chronic pain. In L. K. Y. Ng & J. J. Bonica (Eds.), *Pain, discomfort and humanitarian care* (pp. 207–219). New York: Elsevier/North Holland.
Cohen, F. (1980). Post-surgical pain relief: patient's status and nurses' medication choices. *Pain, 9,* 265–274.
Cohen, M. Z. (1987). An historical overview of the phenomenological movement. *Image: Journal of Nursing Scholarship 19*(1), 31–34.
Colaizzi, P. (1978). Psychological research as the phenomenologist views it. In R. S. Valle & M. King (Eds.), *Existential–phenomenological alternatives for psychology research* (pp. 48–71). New York: Oxford University Press.
Davis, G. C., Buchsbaum, M. S., & Bunney, W. E. (1980). Pain and psychiatric illness. In L. K. Y. Ng & J. J. Bonica (Eds.), *Pain, discomfort and humanitarian care* (pp. 221–231). New York: Elsevier/North Holland.
Donovan, M., Dillon, P., & McGuire, L. (1987). Incidence and characteristics of pain in a sample of medical–surgical inpatients. *Pain, 30,* 69–78.
Fagerhaugh, S., & Strauss, A. (1977). *The politics of pain management.* Menlo Park, CA: Addison-Wesley.
Faherty, B., & Grier, M. (1984). Analgesic medication for elderly people post-surgery. *Nursing Research, 33,* 369–372.
Foreman, M. D. (1986). Acute confusional states in hospitalized elderly: A research dilemma. *Nursing Research, 35,* 34–38.
Gardner, J. (1984). Post-operative confusion in elderly hip surgical patients. *Australian Journal of Advanced Nursing, 1,* 6–10.
Gioiella, E. C., & Bevil, C. W. (1985). *Nursing care of the aging client.* Norwalk, CT: Appleton-Century-Crofts.
Giuffre, M., & Asci, J. (1988). Pain management for aging patients. *Research Review: Studies for Nursing Practice, 5*(2), 2.
Hamilton, J. (1989). Perceptions of comfort by the chronically ill hospitalized elderly. In S. G. Funk, E. M. Tornquist, M. T. Champagne, L. A. Copp, & R. A. Wiese (Eds.), *Key aspects of comfort: Management of pain, fatigue, and nausea* (pp. 281–289). New York: Springer.
Harkins, S. W., Kwentus, J., & Price, D. D. (1984). Pain and the elderly. In C. Benedetti, C. R. Chapman, & G. Morrica (Eds.), *Advances in pain research and therapy* (Vol. 7, pp. 103–121). New York: Raven Press.
Jacox, A. K. (1979). Pain assessment. *American Journal of Nursing, 79,* 895–900.
Jacox, A. K. (1989). Key aspects of comfort. In S. G. Funk, E. M. Tornquist, M. T. Champagne, L. A. Copp, & R. A. Wiese (Eds.), *Key aspects of comfort: Management of pain, fatigue, and nausea* (pp. 8–22). New York: Springer.
Kaiko, R. F. (1980). Age and morphine analgesia in cancer patients with post-operative pain. *Clinical Pharmacology Therapeutics, 23*(6), 823–826.
Kaiko, R. F., Wallenstein, S. L., Rogers, A., Grabinski, P., & Houde, R. W. (1986). Clinical analgesic studies and sources of variation in analgesic response to morphine. In K. M. Foley & C. E. Inturrisi (Eds.), *Advances in pain research and therapy* (pp. 13–23). New York: Raven Press.
Lincoln, Y. S., & Guba, E. G. (1985). *Naturalistic inquiry.* Beverly Hills, CA: Sage.
Marks, R. M., & Sachar, E. (1973). Undertreatment of medical inpatients with narcotic analgesics. *Annals of Internal Medicine, 78,* 173–181.

McCaffery, M. (1979). *Nursing management of the patient with pain* (2nd ed.). Philadelphia: J.B. Lippincott.

McCaffery, M., & Beebe, A. (1989). *Pain: Clinical manual for nursing practice.* St. Louis, MO: C. V. Mosby.

Melzack, R., Abbott, F. V., Zackon, W., & Mulder, D. S., (1987). Pain on a surgical ward: A survey of the duration and intensity of pain and the effectiveness of medication. *Pain, 29,* 67–72.

Melzack, R., & Wall, P. (1965). Pain mechanisms: A new theory. *Science, 150,* 971–979.

Merleau-Ponty, M. (1962). *Phenomenology of perception.* (C. Smith, trans.) New York: The Humanities Press.

Munhall, P. L. (1982). Nursing philosophy and nursing research: In apposition or opposition? *Nursing Research, 31,* 176–177, 181.

Munhall, P. L., & Olier, C. J. (1986). Philosophical foundations of qualitative research. In P. L. Munhall & C. J. Oiler (Eds.), *Nursing research: A qualitative perspective* (pp. 47–63). Norwalk, CT: Appleton-Century-Crofts.

Paterson, J. G., & Zderad, L. T. (1976). *Humanistic nursing.* New York: Wiley.

Platzer, H. (1989). Post-operative confusion in the elderly—A literature review. *International Journal of Nursing Studies, 26*(4), 369–379.

Portenoy, R. K., & Kanner, R. M. (1985). Patterns of analgesic prescription and consumption in a university-affiliated community hospital. *Archives of Internal Medicine, 145,* 439–441.

Riemen, D. J. (1986). The essential structure of a caring interaction: Doing phenomenology. In P. L. Munhall & C. J. Oiler (Eds.), *Nursing research: A qualitative perspective* (pp. 85–108). Norwalk, CT: Appleton-Century-Crofts.

Rose, J. F. (1990). Psychologic health of women: A phenomenologic study of women's inner strength. *Advances in Nursing Science, 12*(2), 56–70.

Short, L. M., Burnett, M. L., Egbert, A. M., & Parks, L. H. (1990). Medicating the postoperative elderly: How do nurses make their decisions? *Journal of Gerontological Nursing, 16*(7), 12–17.

Spross, J. A. (1985). Cancer pain and suffering: Clinical lessons from life, literature and legend. *Oncology Nursing Forum, 12*(4), 23–31.

Taylor, A. (1987). Pain. In J. J. Fitzpatrick & R. L. Taunton (Eds.), *Annual review of nursing research* (Vol. 5, pp. 23–43). New York: Springer.

Valle, R. S., & King, M. (1978). An introduction to existential–phenomenological thought in psychology. In R. S. Valle & M. King (Eds.), *Existential–phenomenological alternatives for psychology* (pp. 6–17). New York: Oxford University Press.

Weis, O. F., Sriwatanakul, K. A., Alloza, J. L., Weintraub, M., & Lasagna, L. (1983). Attitudes of patients, housestaff and nurses toward post-operative analgesic care. *Anesthesia Analgesics, 62,* 70–74.

Williams, M. A., Campbell, E. B., Raynor, W. J., Musholt, M. A., Mlynarczyk, S. M., & Crane, L. F. (1985). Predictors of acute confusional states in hospitalized elderly patients. *Research in Nursing and Health, 8,* 31–40.

Woodrow, K. M., Friedman, G. D., Siegelaub, M. S., & Collen, M. F. (1972). Pain tolerance: Differences according to age, sex and race. *Psychosomatic Medicine, 34,* 548–555.

Zalon, M. L. (1990). Nurses' empathy for patients' experience of post-operative pain as a function of the degree of humanism in the nursing environment, the patient's age and length of time since surgery (Doctoral dissertation, New York University, 1989). *Dissertation Abstracts International, 50*(7), 2825B.

CRITIQUE OF

FUNDED GRANT

The purpose of this phenomenological study is to describe the lived experience of post-operative pain in frail, elderly women. The theoretical background is based on a review of the literature that suggests conflicting information about how frail older individuals experience and are treated for pain. The justification for using the phenomenological approach based on the literature review is clear. The investigator plans to interview between 7 to 12 women over the age of 75 who have had abdominal surgery. Women were chosen based on the anticipation of an interaction between gender and pain perceptions. The open-ended interviews will be conducted approximately 4 days post-operatively. They will be tape recorded and transcribed verbatim. The investigator plans to analyze data using the Colaizzi phenomenological methodology. Attention has been paid to trustworthiness using the work of Guba and Lincoln. This method is new to the investigator and appropriate consultation is being sought.

This is an excellent proposal. The investigator clearly develops the need for the investigation as well as the need to use this type of approach to study the question. There is a good fit between the aims of the study, the design and sample, and the analysis techniques. The interview procedures and methods described are feasible and appropriate to the Coliazzi approach. The investigator does not include a discussion of the descriptive information that will be collected about the women who will be sampled. I would recommend that she carefully consider collecting among the descriptive information some data about analgesic use, pain perception of the nurse, and nursing interventions for the relief of pain. Although I know the focus is on the elderly women's perception of the experience, this type of descriptive information may prove very useful in the development of the conceptualization and interpretation at the end. I am impressed with the investigator's grasp of the analysis technique, given her admitted lack of experience with the method. She has carefully considered trustworthiness and is, as a result, likely to produce a very credible outcome for this research. IRB [Institutional Review Board] approval for this proposal is pending. I am very enthusiastic in my endorsement of this proposal.

GLOSSARY

Archives   Contain unpublished materials that often are used as primary source materials.

A Priori   Form of deductive thinking in which theoretical formulations and propositions precede and guide systematic observation.

Action Research   A research method characterized by the systematic study of the implementation of a planned change to a system.

Actors   Individuals within a particular cultural group who are studied by ethnographic researchers.

Analytic Induction   A method of qualitative data analysis wherein the researcher seeks to refine a theory through the identification of negative cases.

Auditability   The ability of another researcher to follow the methods and conclusion of the original researcher.

Authenticity   Term used to describe the mechanism by which the qualitative researcher ensures that the findings of the study are real, true, or authentic. In historical research refers to assuring that a primary source document provides the truthful reporting of a subject.

Biographical History   Studies the life of a person within the context of the period in which that person lives.

Bracketing   A methodological device of phenomenological inquiry that requires deliberate identification and suspension of all judgments or ideas about the phenomenon under investigation or what one already knows about the subject prior to and throughout the phenomenological investigation.

Category   Classification of concepts into broader categories following comparison of one category to another. Broader categories serve as an umbrella under which related concepts are grouped.

Chat Rooms   A computer-mediated method of communication and data collection whereby individuals log on to the world wide web and can communicate back and forth in a synchronous manner.

Coding   The process of data analysis in grounded theory whereby statements are grouped and given a code for ease of identification later in the study.

Conceptual Density   Data generation that is exhaustive and comprehensive and provides the researcher with evidence that all possible data to support a conceptual framework has been generated.

Confirmability   This is considered a neutral criterion for measuring the trustworthiness of qualitative research. If a study demonstrates credibility, auditability, and fittingness, the study is also said to possess confirmability.

Constant Comparative Method of Data Analysis   A form of qualitative data analysis wherein the researcher makes sense of textual data by categorizing units of measuring through a process of comparing new units with previously identified units.

Core Variable   The central phenomenon in grounded theory around which all the other categories are integrated.

Covert Participant Observation   A method of data collection that involves observing participants however, the individuals are unaware that they are being observed.

329

Credibility   A term that relates to the trustworthiness of findings in a qualitative research study. Credibility is demonstrated when participants recognize the reported research findings as their own experiences.

Critical Theory   A philosophy of science based on a belief that revealing the unrecognized forces that control human behavior will liberate and empower individuals.

Cultural Scene   An anthropological term for culture. It includes the actors, the artifacts, and the actions of the actors in social situations.

Deductive   The process of moving from generalizations to specific conclusions.

Dependability   This is a criterion used to measure trustworthiness in qualitative research. Dependability is met through securing credibility of the findings.

Dialectic   A form of logic based on the belief that reality is represented by contradiction and the reconciliation of contradiction.

Dialectical Critique   A form of qualitative data analysis wherein the researcher engages in dialogue with research participants to reveal the internal contradictions within a particular phenomenon.

Discipline of History   Both a science and an art that studies the interrelationship of social, economic, political, and psychological factors that influence ideas, events, institutions, and people.

Dwelling   A term used to demonstrate the degree of dedication a researcher commits to reading, intuiting, analyzing, synthesizing, and coming to a description or conclusion(s) about the data collected during a qualitative study. Also called immersion.

Eidetic Intuiting   Accurate interpretations of what is meant in the description.

Embodiment (or Being in the World)   The belief that all arts are constructed on foundation of perception, or original awareness of some phenomenon (Merleau-Ponty, 1956).

Epistemology   The branch of philosophy concerned with how individuals determine what is true.

Essences   Elements related to the ideal or true meaning of something that gives common understanding to the phenomenon under investigation.

External Criticism   Questions the genuineness of primary sources and assures that the document is what it claims to be.

Field Notes   Notes recorded about the people, places, and things that are part of the ethnographer's study of a culture.

Fittingness   A term used in qualitative research to demonstrate the probability that the research findings have meaning to others in similar situations. Fittingness is also called transferability.

Free Imaginative Variation   A technique used to apprehend essential relations between essences and involves careful study of concrete examples supplied by the participant's experience and systematic variation of these examples in the imagination.

Genuine   When a primary source is what it purports to be and is not a forgery.

Grand Tour Question(s)   General opening question(s) that offer(s) overview insights of a particular person, place, object, or situation.

History   Webster's New International Dictionary defines history as "a narrative of events connected with a real or imaginary object, person, or career. . . devoted to the exposition of the natural unfolding and interdependence of the events treated." History is a branch of knowledge that "records and explains past events as steps in human progress. . ." [it is] "the study of the character and significance of events." Barzen and Graff (1985) describe history as an "invention" and as an "art."

Historiography   Historiography requires that historiographers study and critique sources and develop history by systematically presenting their findings in a narrative. Historiography provides a way of knowing the past.

Historian/Historiographer   Balances the rigors of scientific inquiry and the understanding of human behavior; develops the skill of speculation and interpretation to narrate the story.

Historical Method   Application of method or steps to study history systematically.

Holism   A belief that wholes are more than the mere sum of their parts.

Immersion   A term used to demonstrate the degree of dedication a researcher commits to reading, intuiting, analyzing, synthesizing, and coming to a description or conclusion(s) about the data collected during a qualitative study. Also called dwelling.

Inductive Theory Building   Theory derived from observation of phenomena.

Induction   The process of moving from specific observations to generalizations.

Informed Consent   When engaging participants in a research study, ensuring that they have complete information, that they understand the information, and that they have freely chosen to either accept or decline participation in the investigation.

Intentionality   Consciousness is always consciousness of something. One does not hear without hearing something or believe without believing something.

Interpretive Phenomenology/Hermeneutics   The interpretation of phenomena appearing in text or written word.

Intuiting   A process of thinking through the data so that a true comprehension or accurate interpretation of what is meant in a particular description is achieved.

Internal Criticism   Concerns itself with the authenticity or truthfulness of the content.

Intellectual History   Studies ideas and thoughts over time of a person believed to be an intellectual thinker, or the ideas of a period, or the attitudes of people.

Life History   A research method wherein the researcher listens to the telling of life story for the purpose of understanding a particular aspect of the individual's life.

Local Theory   A theory that describes a particular group or sample that cannot be generalized to a larger population.

Narrative Picturing   A data collection method whereby participants are asked to imagine or picture an event or sequence of events as a method of describing an experience.

Naturalistic Inquiry   A research methodology based on a belief in investigating phenomena in their natural setting free of manipulation.

Participant Observation   The direct observation and recording of data that require the researcher to become a part of the culture being studied.

Phenomenological Reduction   A term meaning recovery of original awareness.

Present-Mindedness   Use of a contemporary perspective when analyzing data collected from an earlier period of time.

Primary Sources   Firsthand account of a person's experience, an institution, or of an event and may lack critical analysis; examples include private journals, letters, records.

Process Informed Consent   Requires the same criteria as informed consent, however is differentiated by the fact that this type of consent requires the researcher to re-evaluate the participants consent to be involved in the study at varying points throughout the investigation.

Reflexive   This term refers to being both researcher and participant and capitalizing on the duality as a source of insight.

Reflexive Critique   A form of qualitative data analysis wherein the researcher engages in dialogue with research participants to reveal each individual's interpretation for the meanings influencing behavior.

Reliability   The consistency of an instrument to measure an attribute or concept that it was designed to measure.

Saturation   Repetition of data obtained during the course of a qualitative study. Signifies completion of data collection on a particular culture or phenomenon.

Secondary Sources   Materials that cite opinions and present interpretations from the period being studied such as newspaper accounts, journal articles, and textbooks.

Social History   Explores a particular period of time and attempts to understand the prevailing values and beliefs through the everyday events of that period.

Selective Sampling   In a grounded theory investigation, selecting from the generated data those critical pieces of information relevant to the current investigation, and avoiding incorporation of material that is not connected to the current investigation.

Situated   A term that reflects the position of the researcher within the context of the group under study.

Social Situation   The activities carried out by actors (members of a cultural group) in a specific place.

Symbolic Interactionism   A philosophic belief system based on the assumption that humans learn about and define their world through interaction with others.

Tacit Knowledge   Information known by members of a culture but not verbalized or openly discussed.

Theme   Used to describe a structural meaning unit of data that is essential in presenting qualitative findings.

Theoretical Sampling   Sampling on the basis of concepts that have proven theoretical relevance to the evolving theory (Strauss & Corbin, 1990).

Theoretical Sensitivity   Personal quality of the researcher that is reflected in an awareness of the subtleties of meaning of data (Strauss & Corbin, 1990).

Transferability   A term used in qualitative research to demonstrate the probability that the research findings have meaning to others in similar situations. Transferability is also called fittingness.

Triangulation   Method of using multiple research approaches in the same study to answer research questions.

Triangulation of Data Generation Techniques   The use of three different methods of data generation in a single research study for the purpose of generating meaningful data.

Trustworthiness   Establishing validity and reliability of qualitative research. Qualitative research is trustworthy when it accurately represents the experience of the study participants.

Validity   The degree to which an instrument measures what it was designed to measure.

Page numbers followed by *f* indicate figures;
t following a page number indicates tabular material